JIMMY SCHMIDT studied French cooking under Madeleine Kamman in France and Boston. He is the proprietor of five restaurants, and chairman of Chefs Collaborative: 2000, an international group that promotes good nutrition and environmentally sound agricultural techniques. His passion for food and freshness is rooted in childhood memories of picking corn, raspberries, strawberries, and wild asparagus with his family in Champa

D1316369

JIMMY SCHMIDT'S COOKING CLASS

Seasonal Recipes from a Chef's Kitchen

By Jimmy Schmidt

Illustrated by Claire Innes

Ten Speed Press
Berkeley, California

Ten Speed Press
Post Office Box 7123
Berkeley, California 94707

Distributed in Australia by E. J. Dwyer Pty. Ltd., in Canada by Publishers Group West, in New Zealand by
Tandem Press, in South Africa by Real Books, and in the United Kingdom and Europe by Airlift Books.

Cover design by Catherine Jacobes
Book design, and illustrations by Claire Innes

Library of Congress Cataloging-in-Publication Data:
    Schmidt, Jimmy
        [Cooking Class]
        Jimmy Schmidt's cooking class / by Jimmy Schmidt
            p.   cm
        includes index
        ISBN 0-89815-804-4
        1. Cookery, American—Southwestern Style. I. Title.
    TX715.2.S69S35 1996
    641.5979—dc20   95-42180
                                                     CIP

Originally published in 1994 by the Detroit Free Press.
First Ten Speed Press printing, 1996
Printed in Canada

1   2   3   4   5   —   00   99   98   97   96

It would be difficult to find a chef who looks, talks and cooks as American as Jimmy Schmidt. Despite his sporting a beard, Jimmy's face still strikes me as coming straight off a cereal box, or out of a 1950s family sitcom where everyone always sat down to dinner together and dad always wore a tie and mom's hair was perfect…and there would be Jimmy feeding something he didn't like to a dog under the table.

He was born smack in the 1950s, grew up in Champaign, Illinois, and speaks with the oblique, Midwestern flatness that makes you believe he's always telling the truth. Why a kid like this went into cooking is beyond me. He looks as if he should have grown up to be a social-studies teacher at Champaign Junior High.

But thank God he didn't. Somehow Jimmy went off on a path that became a culinary crusade towards restoring the reputation of American food and drink. Back in the 1980s, his cooking at the London Chop House, and later at the Rattlesnake Club, was one of the most persuasive arguments that seasonal American ingredients, prepared with simple good taste, constituted some of the most delicious food on earth. His advocacy of American food culture and his dedication to charities that feed the hungry has been unstinting.

That he has come to dominate Detroit's culinary arena—a city never known for its excellence in this regard—probably embarrasses Jimmy, or makes him wonder why there aren't more American cooks creating fare similar to his own. The answer is that Jimmy has a natural talent buoyed by enormous innate intelligence, and, in his work with colleagues and in his cooking columns for the *Detroit Free Press*, he has tried to spread his American gospel in recipes that show how he has refined traditional dishes and come up with an array of brand new ideas that are entirely his.

Schmidt is no dogmatist, however. He has long realized that American gastronomy is made up of hundreds of immigrant cuisines, and is based on European and Asian techniques. Through careful investigation into these food cultures, and an inquiry into the history and nature of regional ingredients, he has been amazingly deft at creating French bistro fare, Italian trattoria dishes, and some of the most original Southwestern food in the country. Over the years, he has become convinced of the basic, wholesome goodness of these cuisines, and he has spoken and written often about the importance of good taste wed to a healthfulness that must underlie all good cooking.

All of these threads are woven into his recipes. As always, Jimmy pays attention to the seasons, believing that the best cooks use the best ingredients when they are at their peak. Thus, you'll find autumn recipes utilizing pumpkins and Hubbard squash, bright springtime dishes featuring asparagus and dandelions, winter warmers like root soups, and hot weather refreshments made with eggplant, corn and ripe tomatoes.

Perhaps the principal virtue of this highly accessible cookbook is Jimmy's tips on how to select and store ingredients and then best treat them to bring out their essential flavors. The price of this book would be worth every penny if it only contained his "tricks of the trade" notes. His evoking an old French technique for poaching fish in the oven is characteristic of Jimmy's openness to new ideas, no matter how old they might be.

If you want to know the direction American cooking is heading in the next century, *Jimmy Schmidt's Cooking Class* would be a good starting point. Savory, full of flavor, healthful, and respecting the great traditions of great cooks, these are recipes that are as expressive of Jimmy's love of food as they are his desire to make people happy.

—JOHN MARIANI

Eating is such a regular daily ritual that we usually take it for granted. For those of us lucky enough to live in an agriculturally rich country and never feel the pains of hunger, the value of food gets lost in the bustle of daily life. For many, nutrition has become what we should not eat or eat less of, rather than what our bodies rely on for growth and existence.

Food should make two important contributions to our life. The first is obvious: to provide basic nutritional needs. A lack of good nutrition results in poorer health, less energy and a shorter life. Proper nutrition is essential to prenatal and infant development, including brain development.

The second contribution, equally important, is the nourishment of spirit and soul, the satisfying feeling that accompanies a pleasant meal. This ability of food to calm and enrich our lives may contribute more to our overall well-being than we will ever understand. Enjoying a meal with family and friends can be sublime. If you think I'm exaggerating, answer this question: When was the last time you had a great meal with someone you despise?

My basic philosophy of food is straightforward: Food should taste terrific *and* be good for you. For me, the best diet is one that includes a balance of ingredients, prepared to enhance taste and nutrition without excessive fats. And, of course, enjoyed with good friends.

For taste, select ingredients that are at their seasonal peak, fresh and full of flavor. When ingredients are flavorful and of top quality, it is very easy to make a terrific meal. Seasonal ingredients are also more readily available and less expensive than those that are out of season.

Nutritional value is directly related to seasonal freshness. For example, a tomato harvested green in winter and shipped to its destination for ripening has about half the nutritional value of an in-season field-ripened tomato from your local farmer's market. Not only does the vine-ripened tomato taste great, it's better for you! This approach sounds great for spring, summer and

autumn, when a wide variety of foods are available, but what about winter? Though nothing seems to be alive in the country's northern regions, cool maturing winter greens, hearty root vegetables and rich legumes and grains provide earthy flavors that fortify nutritionally and fend off the cold. Traditional root cellars extend the longevity of winter squashes, apples and pears. Winter also brings citrus from warmer regions. For each season, there is a natural nutritional balance of foods if you look.

To balance your overall diet, the Mediterranean diet is a good model. This diet focuses on fresh vegetables, fruits, grains and legumes. Meats and fish are served in smaller portions as a condiment to a meal. I have found the diet easy to follow on a weekly rather than daily basis. Enjoy some meatless meals such as Quinoa & Roast Vegetable Risotto, leaving room for a juicy grilled steak as a weekly treat. Once you become accustomed to eating mostly vegetables and grains, you will find that they have deep, rich favors that are as satisfying as meat.

A plant-based diet of vegetables, fruits, grains and legumes will provide all of your dietary needs — as it does for two-thirds of the world's population. Employing sustainable agricultural techniques that respect and preserve the land along with adopting a diet that perpetuates our natural resources will enhance life not only for ourselves but for our children, grandchildren and future generations.

If our children understand the relation of food to short- and long-term health, if they understand the importance of sustainable agriculture, they may be able to choose the course of civilization in the next century. Informed and educated, they will have a rich future.

While I know these points may sound a bit heavy, I do not mean to underestimate the importance of having fun with food. Food is meant to be enjoyed, to sustain life both nutritionally and emotionally. Sometimes a good meal is the only good part of a day. Food is a gift of nature, the spice in a sometimes difficult existence. So enjoy the techniques and recipes in this book, and, above all, add the most important seasoning – your own personality – to each and every dish. Your life will be enriched beyond measure.

– JIMMY SCHMIDT

I started writing a column for the Detroit Free Press shortly before the release of my first book, "Cooking for All Seasons." That was more than four years ago. I never thought the column would survive this long.

Some of the columns were cranked out as effortlessly as pasta from a machine, but others still haven't come together. Cooking is a passion, but when I try to convert it to words, the passion sometimes dissipates, especially at 2 a.m. when nothing I write makes sense.

I commend my many editors at the Free Press over the years for their support and guidance in making the columns easy to read and understand. They helped clean things up when I lost drive and focus and kept their minds open to new and different ideas, even when — I could tell — they thought I was nuts.

The question I am most often asked about the column is how I find time to write it. A couple of days before deadline, I attack the article very late at night when the world is quiet and the day's pressures are over. I drove my family crazy before settling into this schedule. I would like to thank my wife, Darlene, and my children, Stephen and Taylor Rene, for putting up with the chaos.

The staff of the Rattlesnake Club also has borne the brunt of my weekly insanity. Jan Keller edits the columns into English, acts as a liaison to the Free Press and helps with research. Mike Schram and Keith Josefiak test the recipes each week. Without their support, I would have quit writing the column a long time ago.

Free Press staffers Pat Chargot, Helene Lorber and Claire Innes convinced me that we could convert the columns, which have changed in style over the years, into a coherent book. Their talent, creativity, determination and encouragement have been greatly appreciated. I hope you, too, will enjoy their efforts.

Finally, there are many others too numerous to name who inspired columns — readers, guests at my restaurants and associates. Purveyors, farmers and other food professionals also have planted seeds. So keep them coming, and thanks.

— JIMMY SCHMIDT

C O N T E N T S

CONTENTS

AUTUMN

WINTER

SPRING

**AMAZING
FOOD FACTS**

■

Asparagus is a
member of the
lily family and is
related to
onions and
leeks. It's
believed it was
first cultivated
in Greece about
2,500 years
ago.

GO WILD
WITH ASPARAGUS

■ *Why it tastes so good:* Unlike the classic tastes of hollandaise and butter, which are rich but somewhat plain, the strong flavors of garlic, chilies and seasoned oils bring out the robust characteristics of asparagus. The higher-heat methods concentrate the natural mineral flavors of asparagus while keeping the inner vegetable crisp. You get the best of both worlds — robust flavor and resilient texture.

■ *Health advantages:* This new direction provides full flavor without all the fat of the traditional butter-based sauce. There are just 40 calories in 1 cup of chopped asparagus, 20 calories in a six-spear serving. Asparagus is high in vitamins C and B6, folic acid, potassium, fiber, folacin, thiamine and glutathione, believed to be an anticarcinogen.

■ *Tricks of the trade:* Many flavors, such as those of garlic, chilies, ginger, lemongrass and

TODAY'S LESSON: Nothing says spring like the arrival of fresh asparagus in the market. Let's explore asparagus' wild side with flavors like sesame, chilies, garlic and lemongrass.

other herbs, are best infused into the oil before stir-frying or sauteing the asparagus. Certain oils, such as sesame oil, may be simply drizzled over the cooked asparagus to release its flavor. Spice-infused oils may be made in quantity and refrigerated to use on a moment's notice for a delicious asparagus-based dish.

■ *Selecting your asparagus:* Asparagus is best when picked and eaten as soon as possible. Select crisp stalks with moist, unshriveled stems of the same diameter to ensure even cooking. Once asparagus has been picked, the sugar converts to tough, indigestible fibers in the skin. You can peel the asparagus to remove these fibers, or

cut on the bias into 1-inch segments. The size of the stalk is a point of personal preference.

■ *Preparing asparagus:* The old rule is to grab the asparagus, with one hand at the base and the other hand on the tip, and bend. The spear will snap at the base of the tender part. I try to use all of the wonderful asparagus and trim away only the woody part. This lower stem is great for making soup or asparagus puree for vegetable pastas, so don't just throw it away.

■ *Choose your condiment:* There are infinite flavor combinations: Try garlic, or garlic with chilies, for a little spice; garlic with ginger for an Asian twist;

garlic with lemongrass, green onions or other members of the onion family; lemongrass or other complementary herbs solo, or straight sesame oil with or without a lace of chilies and toasted sesame seeds. A slight acid such as wine, citrus juice, rice wine vinegar or another flavor of vinegar will brighten and intensify the spice flavors. Add a tablespoon or so at the last second.

■ *The cooking begins:* Start by heating a neutral oil, preferably canola, until hot. Then add the garlic, ginger or other spice combination, cooking until just golden, about 3 minutes. Strain the oil through a fine sieve to remove the seasoning ingredients if you prefer (that's really only necessary for the tougher and bigger pieces that would add a coarse texture when eaten). Return the seasoned oil to the

wok or saute pan over high heat, and add the asparagus pieces. Cook until tender but still crunchy, about 2-3 minutes. Remove from the heat, add any seasonings such as salt, soy sauce, pepper, wine, citrus or vinegar, along with

any fresh herb or toasted seed garnish, and serve. If the fast method leaves the asparagus too crunchy for your taste, try blanching the asparagus in boiling water for 30-60 seconds before cooking with the spices.

■ *Serving suggestions:* Serve immediately. Fresh herbs or toasted sesame seeds on top make for a delightful presentation.

■ *Mix and match:* This basic technique also works as a complete meal with other vegetables, such as chunks of onion, broccoli or the Italian broccoli rabe, chunks of sweet red bell peppers, and meaty wild mushrooms. Start with the spices, then add the vegetables that take the longest to cook, and finish with those that take only a few seconds.

■ *Try your technique:* Try Asparagus Scented with Garlic, Ginger & Sesame, a wonderful introduction to this world of flavors.

Wild asparagus is considered to have a fuller, richer flavor than domesticated varieties.

Green asparagus is the common variety in the United States, although some specimens of this variety have slight purple tips.

White
asparagus is a
large European
variety with
a very
mild flavor.

ASPARAGUS WITH GARLIC, GINGER & SESAME

Makes 4 servings

1   pound fresh asparagus
4   tablespoons canola oil
2   cloves garlic, peeled,
    ends removed, minced
1   tablespoon fresh ginger
    root, peeled, finely
    diced
    Pinch crushed dried
    chili flakes, optional
2   teaspoons low-sodium
    soy sauce
2   tablespoons fresh lemon
    juice
2   tablespoons snipped
    fresh chives
    Salt and pepper to taste
1   tablespoon white sesame
    seeds

Trim away the woody base
from the asparagus stalks. Cut
the stalks on the bias into 1½-
inch segments and reserve.

In a large nonstick skillet or
wok, heat the oil over high
heat. Add the garlic, ginger,
and chili flakes if desired.
Cook until golden, about 2
minutes. Add the asparagus,
occasionally stirring until tender yet still crunchy, about 2-3
minutes. Add the soy sauce
and the lemon juice, tossing to
just combine. Remove from
heat and add the chives.
Season with salt and pepper.
Transfer to a warm serving
dish in a mound. Sprinkle
with sesame seeds and serve
immediately.

Nutrition details per serving
Calories .163
Percent of calories from fat 83%
Fat: .15 gm
Protein: . . . . .4 gm
Carbohydrate: . . . . .6 gm
Cholesterol: . . . . .0 mg
Sodium: . . . . .83 mg
Diabetic exchange: 1 vegetable, 3 fat.

ASPARAGUS IN CHARDONNAY SAUCE

Makes 4 servings

2   tablespoons unsalted
    butter, divided
½   cup sliced shallots
1   cup chardonnay wine
    (preferably without high
    oak flavors)
½   cup heavy cream
34 large asparagus spears,
    lower third peeled and
    stems trimmed to an
    even length
    Salt to taste
    Freshly ground black
    pepper to taste
¼   cup snipped fresh chives

Preheat oven to warm. Place
ovenproof serving plates into
the oven to warm.

In a medium-size saucepan,
melt 1 tablespoon butter over
high heat. Add shallots and
saute until tender, about 3
minutes. Add white wine and
cook until reduced by half,
about 8 minutes. Add the
cream and cook until thickened to coat the back of a
spoon, about 8 more minutes.

Strain through a fine sieve into another saucepan.

Fill a third saucepan with water and bring to a boil over high heat. Add asparagus, cooking until al dente, about 4-5 minutes. Taste to be sure. (There are two extra spears for you to try.) Drain. Carefully remove the warmed plates from the oven and begin placing the asparagus on the plates, with stems even and tips together.

Meanwhile, whisk the remaining butter into the sauce and cook until thickened to coat the back of a spoon, about 2 minutes. Add salt and pepper to taste. Transfer to a steel bowl, add most of the chives, and whisk until thick and silky. Spoon sauce over the asparagus, top with remaining chives and serve as an appetizer or with fish.

Nutrition details per serving
Calories 231
Percent of calories from fat 65%
Fat: . . . . .17 gm
Protein: . . . . .4 gm
Carbohydrate: . . . . .8 gm
Cholesterol: . . . . .48 mg
Sodium: . . . . .339 mg
Diabetic exchange: 1½ vegetable, 3½ fat.

■

RAGOUT OF SCALLIONS & ASPARAGUS

Makes 4 servings

Water

Salt to taste

24 spears of medium asparagus, trimmed, peeled as necessary and tied in a bunch for cooking

1 tablespoon butter

2 bunches of scallions, roots removed, washed, white and green parts separated, diced

½ cup whipping cream

3 tablespoons freshly squeezed lemon juice

Coarsely ground black pepper to taste

4 tablespoons grated Parmesan cheese

Fill a medium saucepan with enough water to cover asparagus and bring to a boil. Add salt to taste. Add asparagus, cooking until al dente, about 3 minutes. Drain in a colander and cool under running cold water. Remove the string and discard. Set asparagus aside.

In a large skillet over medium heat, add the butter, heating until just beginning to brown. Add white part of the scallions, cooking until tender, about 5 minutes.

Add the whipping cream, cooking until thickened to coat the back of a spoon, about 5 minutes.

Add lemon juice and asparagus. Salt and pepper to taste. If the sauce seems too thick, lighten with an additional few tablespoons of cream or asparagus cooking liquid.

Lay the asparagus across the plate with the tips in the same direction.

Using a slotted spoon, remove the cooked white scallions from the sauce and spoon over the asparagus.

Spoon the remaining sauce over both, and top with the diced green part of the scallions and Parmesan cheese. Serve immediately.

Nutrition details per serving
Calories 167
Percent of calories from fat 76%
Fat: . . . . .15 gm
Protein: . . . . .6 gm
Carbohydrate: . . . . .4 gm
Cholesterol: . . . . .46 mg
Sodium: . . . . .168 mg
Diabetic exchange: 1 vegetable, ½ meat, 2½ fat.

■

The asparagus plant is a perennial that begins producing sprouts in the third year and continues into its prime of about 6-8 years. The sprouts grow at irregular rates, necessitating hand harvesting.

ARTICHOKE HEARTS ARE WORTH THE TROUBLE

**AMAZING
FOOD FACTS**

■

The artichoke,
a member of the
daisy family, is
a giant thistle.
The plant grows
as high as
5 feet and
produces flower
buds in two to
three years.
Artichokes
produce for only
three or four
years before the
yield declines
sign²ficantly.

■ *What is an artichoke?* The artichoke (*Cynara scolymus*) is an immature flower bud that belongs to the thistle family. The prickly leaves surround the fibrous choke atop the prized edible fleshy base. The choke, if allowed to develop, would become a large, deep-violet flower. Artichokes range from small to softball-size, all growing on the same plant.

■ *Why they taste so good:* Artichokes contain cynarin, an organic acid that stimulates the sweetness receptors in the taste buds of cynarin-susceptible people. After eating an artichoke, these people have the sensation that foods, wines and even water taste sweeter.

■ *Health advantages:* Artichokes are rich in potassium, iron and vitamins A, B and C. They are low in sodium with only .2 percent fat. They also have few calories — about 63 in a 3½-ounce serving.

TODAY'S LESSON: Artichokes are forbidding vegetables with sharp stickers to keep the novice cook at bay. I'll show you how to unlock the wonderful eating treasure locked inside.

■ *How do you eat them?* The largest artichokes can be served by themselves, either steamed or boiled. Enjoy them with butter or olive oil. Mixed with a squeeze of lemon, a sprinkle of parsley or a blast of garlic, the artichoke rises to the sublime.

Medium artichokes are best used for salads, ragouts and risottos.

Small artichokes can be cooked, pureed and strained to remove the tougher vegetable fibers and make a terrific simple soup. This purèe can also be used as a sauce for pasta or poultry and in the liquids used to prepare grain and rice dishes..

■ *How to select and store:* Regardless of size, always select firm artichokes with tightly closed leaves. Check the stem end; it should be freshly cut and stiff, not soft and shriveled. Avoid soft artichokes with loose, rubbery leaves and any with black coloring. Lower temperatures during the final growing days may bronze the leaf tips but do not hurt the artichoke — the best actually are found in the coolest parts of the fields. The flavor of the artichoke declines as it matures.

■ *How to prepare:* To clean artichokes, soak them in salted water for 30 minutes to drive out any insects. Rub all cut surfaces with lemon juice or vinegar to slow discoloring. Clean artichokes by trimming the stem from the base. Cut about 1 inch from the top of the artichoke. To serve the whole vegetable, trim the spiky tops off the outer leaves with a pair of kitchen scissors. Pry the leaves open and scoop the inedible choke from the center. For just the heart, trim away all the leaves, then pare the heart into a regular shape with a small knife.

■ *The cooking begins:* The easiest way to cook any size artichoke is to boil it in salted water with a little lemon juice or vinegar. Simmer until tender; check by inserting a skewer into the center of the heart from the base. Heat will also kill enzymes, so make sure artichokes are thoroughly cooked to prevent them from blackening after partial cooking. Drain the artichokes upside down to remove all the

water. Artichokes also can be steamed; flavor can be enhanced by adding wine and aromatics to the liquid.

■ *Serving suggestions:* Acidic sauces and vinaigrettes bring

out the rich flavor of artichokes. Lemon, a little garlic, chopped parsley and melted butter make a perfect dip for whole, cooked artichokes.

■ *Artichokes are wonderful when eaten raw.* Remove the

leaves until you reach the heart, cut the choke from the heart and rub all surfaces with lemon juice. Slice the raw artichoke paper-thin, toss with more lemon juice and season with salt and pepper. Combine with ingredients such as fennel, sweet peppers or watercress and cloak in olive oil for a triumphant salad. The nutty flavor and crunchy texture are terrific, a perfect accompaniment for gravlax or smoked salmon.

■ *Mix and match:* Artichokes will complement both the taste and the texture of just about any full-flavored dish. Try the different artichoke sizes to enjoy all their unique flavor characteristics.

■

There are two principal varieties of artichoke: the globe or round bud, grown in both the United States and Europe; and the conical bud, found only in parts of Europe. Some of the conical varieties have an edible choke, as found in canned or pickled artichokes from Spain and Italy.

The artichoke originated in the Mediterranean basin, possibly Sicily. It was known to the Egyptians by 600 B.C. and was popular with the Greeks and Romans, but it wasn't until the 16th Century that it spread through Europe.

ARTICHOKE SOUP WITH HAZELNUT BUTTER

Makes 8 servings

2   pounds baby artichokes, no more than 2 inches in diameter
12   cups poultry stock
2   lemons, juiced
1   cup heavy cream
½   cup sour cream
¾   teaspoon ground cumin
     Salt to taste
     Freshly ground white pepper to taste
¾   cup Hazelnut Butter (see accompanying recipe)

Discard the tough outer leaves and stems from the artichokes. Place the artichokes in a large acid-resistant pot with the stock and lemon juice (avoid using an aluminum pot, as the artichokes will pick up an aluminum flavor). Bring to a simmer over medium-high heat, cooking until the artichokes are tender, testing for doneness by inserting a skewer, about 15 minutes. Puree the artichokes with the stock in a blender in batches. Strain through a medium sieve into a saucepan, pressing to extract as much pulp as possible. Whisk in the cream, sour cream and cumin, then adjust the salt and pepper. Ladle into warm bowls, garnish with hazelnut butter and serve.

Cook's note: You can substitute larger artichokes; just quarter them and remove the choke after cooking them in the stock.

Nutrition details per serving
Calories .196
Percent of calories from fat 61%
Fat: . . . . .14 gm
Protein: .5 gm
Carbohydrate: . . . . .16 gm
Cholesterol: . . . . .47 mg
Sodium: . . . . .290 mg
Diabetic exchange: 2¾ vegetables, ⅓ bread, ⅓ meat, 3 fat.

HAZELNUT BUTTER

Makes ¾ cup

½   cup hazelnuts, shelled
¼   pound (1 stick) unsalted butter, at room temperature
2   tablespoons chopped fresh parsley

Preheat the oven to 300 degrees. Place hazelnuts on an ungreased baking sheet. Toast in oven for 20 minutes or until light tan. Stir to avoid scorching. Remove from oven. Roll hot hazelnuts in a clean terry towel, rubbing off skins. Discard skins. Let cool. When completely cooled, chop hazelnuts.

Blanched hazelnuts can save time, worth the difference in price for the effort saved in rubbing off the skins one by one.

Using a mixer, combine the butter, hazelnuts and parsley. Refrigerate until ready to serve, or up to a week.

Nutrition details per serving
Calories .371
Percent of calories from fat 91%
Fat: . . . . .41 gm
Protein: .4 gm
Carbohydrate: . . . . .5 gm
Cholesterol: . . . . .62 mg
Sodium: . . . . .4,437 mg
Diabetic exchange: ⅛ meat, 7⅓ fat.

STEAMED ARTICHOKE WITH HAZELNUT VINAIGRETTE

Makes 4 servings

2   cups dry white wine

1   quart water, or more if
    necessary (if your tap
    water is hard or heavily
    chlorinated, use bottled
    water for best results)

1   bunch parsley stems
    (reserve leaves)

2   tablespoons whole black
    peppercorns

2   tablespoons toasted
    whole coriander seed,
    optional

4   large artichokes, top 1½
    inches of the leaves
    removed and flower
    stem at heart discarded

¼   cup fresh lemon juice

½   teaspoon salt

1   teaspoon coarsely
    ground black pepper

½   cup extra virgin olive
    oil (or substitute
    melted, unsalted butter)

1   cup coarsely chopped
    parsley

½   cup chopped toasted
    hazelnuts

In a medium saucepan, combine the wine, water, parsley stems, peppercorns and coriander seed. Position a steamer containing artichokes over the liquid mixture and bring to a simmer over high heat. Cover, allowing the artichokes to steam until tender, as tested by inserting a skewer through the center of the heart from the base. Remove from heat. Invert the artichoke to drain. Peel away a few coarse outer leaves. Place in the center of the serving plate.

To make the vinaigrette: In medium bowl, combine the lemon juice, salt, pepper and olive oil. Add half the parsley and hazelnuts and divide the vinaigrette to broad individual ramekins for dipping. Place a ramekin on each serving plate. Sprinkle the remaining parsley and hazelnuts over the artichokes. Serve with a large bowl in the center of the table for the discarded leaves and chokes.

To eat: Remove the outer leaves with your fingers, dipping the base in the vinaigrette and gently biting the inner base of each leaf to remove the edible section. This section is small but becomes larger as you near the heart. After the leaves are completely removed, take a spoon and carefully scoop the fibrous choke from the heart and discard. Cut the heart into bite-size pieces and enjoy.

Nutrition details per serving
Calories .474
Percent of calories from fat 71%
Fat: . . . . .40 gm
Protein: . . . . .7 gm
Carbohydrate: . . . . .22 gm
Cholesterol: . . . . .0 mg
Sodium: . . . . .543 mg
Diabetic exchange: 2⅓ vegetable, 7⅞ fat.

Wine enthusiasts usually avoid eating artichokes with fine wines because of the flavor change caused by cynarin. The Italian aperitif Cynar, which is made from the artichoke, is said to stimulate the appetite and enhance the flavor of food.

AMAZING FOOD FACTS

■

Maui onions are the same Yellow Granex variety as the Vidalia. They can be flat, round or like a teardrop. They are common on the West Coast and are the earliest sweet onion to market. This onion, usually hot-spirited, is mellowed by Hawaii's volcanic soil.

SWEET VIDALIAS MAKE SUBLIME ONION RINGS

■ *What is a Vidalia onion?* The Vidalia onion, commonly found at your local grocery each spring, is so extremely mild and sweet that it can be eaten like an apple. Vidalias contain an average sugar content of 12.5 percent —that's sweeter than Coca-Cola's 12 percent! The onions are the same Yellow Granex as most other yellow onions, but they do not develop the familiar onion bite because of the loamy soil and mild climate in which they grow in Vidalia, Ga.; Maui, Hawaii, and parts of Texas.

■ Vidalia and most other sweet onions are planted around Thanksgiving and are allowed to grow and mature during the cool winter climate for slow and even growth. They mature and are harvested in May and June.

■ *Why these onion rings taste so good:* Commercial onion rings are heavily coated in breading or batter, which

TODAY'S LESSON: The super-sweet, tearless Vidalia onion is perfect to eat straight, but when sliced, lightly coated and fried, it becomes sublime and produces probably the world's best onion rings. I'll show you all the tricks to make these or any other onion into the best onion rings around.

helps hide the onion bite. Our sweet Vidalia onions are so special, they need only a thin crust to capture the natural, mild flavor while adding just a light crunch for texture. The thin crust allows the onion to cook to al dente faster and with less oil saturating the breading.

■ *Keeping that special flavor:* Vidalia's wonderful sweet character will shine through on all cooked dishes as long as they are not overcooked until soft. Overcooking will diminish the already low acid content of the

sweets, resulting in bland onions with little distinguishable character. Reserve the sweets for raw and lightly cooked applications.

■ *Pick your sweet onions:* Select dry-skinned and firm-fleshed onions. Sweet onions are high in moisture, so they should feel heavy but never moist or soft, a sign of bruising. Store in clean hosiery with a knot separating them; onions tend to turn soft where they touch each other. Keep in a cool place with good ventilation. Refrigeration will extend their-shelf life, but ventilate to prevent mold.

■ *Cut your rings:* Peel the onions and cut parallel with the ends into ¼- to ¾-inch slices. Separate into rings. The smallest, inner rings may be eaten as a snack or diced to spunk up a salsa.

■ *Tricks of the trade:* Try soaking the rings in milk, buttermilk or even a little beer with a few spicy chili peppers to prevent the onions from drying out. The Vidalias are very delicate but can be enhanced by a little infused seasoning. Try a broader-flavored dark beer for an even fuller taste.

■ *Choose your frying oil:* Select oils such as canola or olive oil, which have little saturated fat but will stand up to high temperatures.

■ *Serving suggestions:* Although most people enjoy onion rings solo, try them with salsa or a little bit of malt vinegar and a dusting of spices and herbs. They are great as a snack for parties, sides for your barbecue dinner or even the perfect vegetable for an elegant meal.

■ *Grilling and roasting:* Grilling is a perfect way to produce the cooked, smoky flavor while maintaining an al dente crunch; roasting or baking is the easiest way to unlock the delicate flavor. Serve hot or at room temperature for an al fresco spring treat. Vidalias are also great baked into muffins, tarts and quiche. Remember to balance with bright, high-acid flavors.

■ *Try your technique:* The recipe below will produce the most delicate and sublime onion rings you'll ever taste.

■

VIDALIA ONION RINGS

Makes 4 side dish servings

Canola or olive oil for frying

2 cups all-purpose flour

1 tablespoon paprika

½ teaspoon granulated salt

½ teaspoon freshly ground black pepper

2 large eggs, lightly beaten

1 cup milk

2 large Vidalia or other sweet onions, sliced in ¼- to ¾-inch thick slices and separated into rings

¼ cup snipped fresh chives, optional

¼ cup malt vinegar, optional

Fill a deep, large skillet with oil to a depth of 3-4 inches. Heat over medium heat to 350-375 degrees as indicated by a deep-fat frying thermometer.

In a large bowl, sift together the flour, paprika, salt and pepper. In another bowl, combine the egg and the milk.

Dredge the onion rings through the flour, shaking to remove excess, and dip into the egg batter. Using a slotted spoon, lift the rings from the egg batter and allow the excess liquid to drain off. Transfer the moistened rings back to the seasoned flour and coat well. Shake off excess flour. Dry for about 15 minutes at room temperature.

Carefully slip the rings into the hot oil and cook until golden, about 3-5 minutes depending on the thickness of the rings and the volume of onions cooking at a time. Remove the rings from the oil and allow to drain on paper towels. Keep warm in a 200-degree oven while finishing the remaining onion rings. Mound the rings in the center of a serving platter. Dust with salt and pepper to your taste. Sprinkle with chives if desired, and drizzle with malt vinegar to your taste. Serve immediately.

Nutrition details per serving
Calories .472
Percent of calories from fat 37%
Fat: .19 gm
Protein: . . . . .13 gm
Carbohydrate: . . . . .62 gm
Cholesterol: . . . . .115 mg
Sodium: . . . . .363 mg
Diabetic exchange: ¼ milk, ½ medium fat meat, 2 vegetables, 3 bread, 2¾ fat.

A newcomer to the sweet onion clan is the Texas 1015 Supersweet, a very large, round onion with weight up to 1 pound and a tan or beige skin. It is a Yellow Granex variety developed for large size and sweet flavor. The name 1015 stands for the recommended planting date, Oct. 15.

ROAST VIDALIA ONIONS & ROSEMARY

Makes 4 servings

4   jumbo Vidalia onions, peeled, ends removed

2   tablespoons extra-virgin olive oil

¼   cup fresh rosemary leaves, chopped

Freshly ground black pepper and salt, to taste

¾   cup Mustard Vinaigrette (see accompanying recipe)

4   sprigs fresh rosemary for garnish, or substitute chives

Preheat oven to 400 degrees.

With a sharp knife, trim the core end of each onion flat. Place the onions core side down on cutting board. Slice down partially through the onion with the knife to just about ½ inch from the board. Repeat this cut with parallel cuts until you have worked your way across the onion. Rotate the onion 90 degrees and repeat, taking care to keep the onion intact. Repeat with the remaining onions. Place the finished onions in a baking dish.

In a small bowl, combine olive oil and rosemary. Drizzle the mixture across and into the onions. Sprinkle generously with pepper. Season with salt to taste.

Place on the lower rack of the oven, cooking until tender, about 1½-2 hours, depending on the size of your onions.

Remove from oven and allow to cool for about 15 minutes.

Transfer to the center of serving plates. Spoon vinaigrette over the onions, garnish with sprigs of rosemary or chives and serve.

Nutrition details per serving
Calories .127
Percent of calories from fat 49%
Fat: . . . . .7 gm
Protein: . . . . .2 gm
Carbohydrate: . . . . .15 gm
Cholesterol: . . . . .0 mg
Sodium: . . . . .272 mg
Diabetic exchange: 2 vegetables, 1⅓ fat.

MUSTARD VINAIGRETTE

Makes ¾ cup

2   tablespoons grained mustard

2   tablespoons aged red wine vinegar, or substitute aged sherry vinegar

½   cup extra-virgin olive oil

2   tablespoons freshly snipped chives

Salt and freshly ground pepper to taste

In a small bowl, combine mustard and vinegar. Slowly add olive oil while continuously whisking. Stir in the chives. Add salt and pepper to taste.

Nutrition details per serving
Calories .258
Percent of calories from fat 95%
Fat: . . . . .27 gm
Protein: . . . . .trace
Carbohydrate: . . . . .3 gm
Cholesterol: . . . . .0 mg
Sodium: . . . . .159 mg
Diabetic exchange: 5¾ fat.

GRILLED SWEET ONION, AVOCADO & TOMATO SALAD

Makes 4 servings

1 large Vidalia onion, or other sweet onion, cut into 8 thick slices

½ cup virgin olive oil, divided

   Salt to taste

   Coarsely ground black pepper to taste

2 avocados, cut into quarters, pit removed, peeled and cut into fan shape

3 tablespoons red wine vinegar

1 bunch arugula, cleaned and stems trimmed

2 large tomatoes, cut into a total of 8 slices

1 cup paper-thin slices of Parmesan cheese (or substitute coarsely grated Parmesan cheese)

Preheat grill. Rub the onion slices with a little olive oil. Season with salt and pepper. Place on the grill, allowing to sear well, about 4 minutes. Turn over and cook until just beginning to soften, about 3 additional minutes. Remove to plate and reserve at room temperature.

Place the avocados on the grill, cooking until slightly brown on the edges and tender, about 3 minutes. Remove to plate with the onions.

In a small bowl, whisk together the vinegar and the remaining olive oil. Season with salt and pepper to taste.

Position the arugula at the top of the serving plates. Alternate tomato slices with onion slices and avocado fans below the arugula on each serving plate. Spoon the vinaigrette over the salads, top with Parmesan cheese and serve.

Nutrition details per serving
Calories 528
Percent of calories from fat 81%
Fat: .50 gm
Protein: . . . . .13 gm
Carbohydrate: . . . . .12 gm
Cholesterol: . . . . .20 mg
Sodium: . . . . .747 mg
Diabetic exchange: ¾ vegetable, 1½ meat, 9 fat.

Walla Walla sweets, named after the city, are very large and round, with a gold or beige tint. They are an Italian hybrid originally introduced from Corsica around the turn of the century. They are planted in volcanic soil in the fall; harvesting begins in late June and goes through July and early August.

BRING OUT THE BEST IN YOUR MORELS

AMAZING FOOD FACTS

■

The morchella species (morel) has a hollow body with a conical or round honeycomb-like surface. There are eight principal species, ranging in color from white to gray to red-brown to black and even gold. Morels fruit only in the spring.

■ *Why they taste so good:* Mushrooms are mostly water, which contains almost all of the distinctive flavor. Cooking techniques that concentrate these juices will intensify the flavor. Besides the direct mushroom taste, high heat during cooking will caramelize the natural sugars to produce a wonderful, deep-toasted flavor. The overall combination of these two flavors produces that incredibly rich morel mushroom flavor.

■ *Advantages:* Cooking with low or no fat obviously has its health advantages, but it also allows the subtle flavor of the mushrooms to come forward. Morels are low in calories and have lots of fiber, some vitamins, minerals and, most importantly, great taste.

■ *How to select perfect morels:* Wild morels can be a number of different species, which will result in slight variations of flavor and texture. Select the best by freshness as indicated by

TODAY'S LESSON: Nothing is as delicious as fresh morel mushrooms sauteed in sweet butter, but how can you enjoy the flavor without all the fat? The trick is in the technique. I'll show you a couple of methods to bring out that special morel taste.

full, unshriveled stems. The texture should be supple, never dry or soggy. Avoid crumbly, paper-like mushrooms, which will disintegrate when cooked. Store in a paper bag with a few holes poked in it for ventilation, in the coldest part of the refrigerator. Use within a few days to enjoy them at their peak.

■ *Tricks of the trade:* Mushrooms are like sponges. Clean by trimming the stems, then brushing away the dirt with a stiff, small brush, such as a toothbrush. If they are dirty, rinse well under slowly running cold water, one by

one, and immediately drain in a colander.

Never soak or submerge morels in water. Dry well in a lettuce spinner or on paper towels. The trick to concentrated mushroom flavor and cooking without steaming is to keep the mushrooms dry.

■ There are three approaches to cooking morels with low or no fat:

1. *Dry-saute.* Start with a non-stick or well-seasoned skillet, such as a crepe pan. Preheat over medium-high heat and brush with a folded paper towel with a few drops of olive

oil to just lubricate the surface. Add the mushrooms, cut in half to allow the best surface exposure, and cook until browned and tender. Season with salt and pepper. As the mushrooms finish cooking, deglaze the pan with a splash of wine or light vegetable stock to loosen the pan drippings. This will quickly recoat the cooked mushrooms, letting no flavor escape.

Dry-sauteing gives the closest flavor to that of morels cooked in fat, although the texture may be softer than a high-fat sauce.

2. *Oven-roast in foil.* Select equal-size mushrooms, or cut to size to ensure even cooking. Lay out a large piece of foil, dull side down, on the counter. In a bowl, combine the mushrooms with salt, pepper, herbs or such condiments as garlic. Transfer to the center of half of the foil and fold over the remaining half. Crimp the edges to seal. Place on a baking sheet and bake at 450 degrees until tender, about

20-30 minutes, depending on size. Remove and allow to cool until warm to the touch. Open and serve, or use in your favorite dishes. Oven-roasting produces the silkiest texture in the mushrooms, while allowing the delicate flavor to come through.

3. *Grill.* This technique requires a little olive or canola oil to enhance the transfer of the dry heat to the mushrooms.

Although grilling without fat will work, it produces inferior results because it dries the surface of the mushrooms rather than concentrating the natural flavors.

Start by combining the mushrooms with seasonings, condiments and olive oil. Place on the grill and cook until well seared. With a metal spatula or tongs, turn the mushrooms over to facilitate even cooking. When done, remove from the fire and add any remaining seasonings, such as balsamic vinegar or fresh herbs. Grilling produces the rich-

est-flavored and smokiest mushrooms around, with a crunchy exterior.

■ *Serving suggestions:* The morels are perfect solo, but try a splash of simple balsamic vinegar to spark up the rich, woodsy flavor. Fresh herbs, such as chives, parsley, chervil, roasted rosemary and tarragon, bring out more flavors. Freshly ground black pepper and toasted spices such as coriander reinforce that special nutty flavor.

■ *Mix and match:* Morels mix well with other mushrooms, such as portobellos, field (the kind in the supermarkets), shiitakes and oysters, most of which are now farmed. The blend of the different mushroom flavors and textures is a wonderful combination.

■ *Try your technique:* Have fun with these three methods.

■

GRILLED MORELS WITH GARLIC, CHIVES & BALSAMIC VINEGAR

Makes 4 appetizer servings

1 pound morel mushrooms, cleaned, stems removed if woody

2 tablespoons extra-virgin olive oil

2 garlic cloves, peeled, ends removed, finely minced

Salt and freshly ground black pepper

¼ cup flat parsley leaves, washed and dried

¼ cup snipped fresh chives

¼ cup balsamic vinegar

4 sprigs chives or parsley, for garnish

Preheat grill or broiler.
In a medium bowl, combine the morels, olive oil and garlic. Season with salt and a generous dose of black pepper, mixing well to combine.

Transfer the morels onto the grill and spread evenly. Cook until well seared, about 3 minutes. Turn the mushrooms over with a metal spatula or tongs and cook until tender, about 3 minutes. Use a spatula to transfer the mushrooms back to the bowl.

Add parsley, chives and balsamic vinegar to mushrooms and toss to combine. Adjust seasonings as needed.

Divide the mushrooms among four serving plates. Place mushrooms in center of plate. Garnish with a sprig of chives or parsley. Serve additional vinegar and olive oil on the side.

Nutrition details per serving
Calories .71
Percent of calories from fat 60%
Fat: .5 gm
Protein: . . . . .2 gm
Carbohydrate: . . . . .7 gm
Cholesterol: . . . . .0 mg
Sodium: . . . . .6 mg
Diabetic exchange: 1 vegetable, 1 fat.

■

CHICKEN LINGUINE WITH MORELS & TARRAGON

Makes 4 servings

1 2½- to 3-pound chicken

1 tablespoon unsalted butter

2 tablespoons chopped shallots

3 cups morel mushrooms, stems trimmed

½ cup dry white wine

1 cup heavy cream
   Salt to taste
   Coarsely ground black pepper to taste

2 tablespoons fresh tarragon leaves

2 tablespoons snipped fresh chives

1 pound linguine

¼ cup grated Pecorino Romano cheese

¼ cup grated Parmesan cheese

Preheat oven to 400 degrees. Roast the chicken on a rack in a roasting pan set on the lower rack of the oven, about 1¼ hours, until golden brown. Remove from oven, let cool and pull off all the meat. Dice into ½-inch pieces.

In a large skillet over high heat, combine the butter, shallots and mushrooms and cook until browned, about 5 minutes. Add the white wine and cook until reduced by half, about 3 minutes. Add the cream, cooking until thickened to coat the back of a spoon, about 10 minutes. Stir in the chicken and heat thoroughly. Adjust salt and pepper to taste, and add the tarragon and chives. Keep warm over low heat. In a large pot of boiling water, cook the pasta until al dente. Transfer to a strainer, rinse with warm water and drain well. Add pasta to skillet and toss until evenly coated. Distribute to serving plates and top with cheeses. Serve immediately.

Nutrition details per serving
Calories 1,799
Percent of calories from fat 74%
Fat: . . . . .147 gm
Protein: . . . . .73 gm
Carbohydrate: . . . . .38 gm
Cholesterol: . . . . .338 mg
Sodium: . . . . .789 mg
Diabetic exchange: ⅓ vegetable, 2 bread, 8¼ meat, 23½ fat.

■

MORELS STUFFED WITH HERBS

Makes 4 servings

6 large cloves garlic with skin on

¼ cup extra-virgin olive oil, divided

½ cup chopped fresh arugula

½ cup chopped fresh parsley

2 tablespoons chopped fresh rosemary

2 tablespoons finely grated Parmesan cheese
   Salt and freshly ground black pepper to taste

1 pound large morel mushrooms, cleaned, stems removed

1 tablespoon aged sherry vinegar (or substitute balsamic or good red wine vinegar)

¼ cup snipped fresh chives

Preheat oven to 375 degrees. Rub the garlic cloves with a little olive oil and place in an ovenproof pan. Cook on the lower rack of the oven until tender, about 30 minutes. Remove and allow to cool. Gently squeeze the cloves, squeezing the garlic from the skin. Mince the roasted garlic and transfer to a small bowl. Add the arugula, parsley, rosemary, cheese and 1 tablespoon of the olive oil. Season with salt and pepper to your taste.

Invert each morel and spoon the stuffing mix through the base into the cap. Pack firmly with the back of the spoon to hold in place.

In a small bowl, combine the sherry vinegar and 2 tablespoons of the olive oil. Season with salt and pepper to taste.

In a large nonstick pan over high heat, add the remaining 1 tablespoon of olive oil. Carefully add the morels, cooking until well seared and crisp. Using tongs, carefully turn the morels over, not allowing the filling to fall out. Finish cooking until golden, about 2 minutes. Using a slotted spoon, remove and drain on paper towels. Repeat with the remaining morels, adding more olive oil if necessary.

Arrange the morels in a circle on serving plate.

Spoon on a little vinaigrette and top with chives. Serve immediately.

Nutrition details per serving
Calories .184
Percent of calories from fat 74%
Fat: .17 gm
Protein: . . . . .6 gm
Carbohydrate: . . . . .7 gm
Cholesterol: . . . . .2 mg
Sodium: . . . . .335 mg
Diabetic exchange: ⅓ vegetable, ¼ meat, 2¼ fat.

■

MORELS & ASPARAGUS WITH ANGEL HAIR PASTA

Makes 4 servings

24 spears medium asparagus, trimmed, peeled as necessary, tied in a bunch

Salt

2 tablespoons unsalted butter

¾ pound morel mushrooms, cleaned, stems trimmed

1¼ cups heavy cream

3 tablespoons freshly squeezed lemon juice

1 tablespoon finely grated lemon rind

Coarsely ground black pepper

½ pound angel hair pasta

¼ cup snipped fresh chives

3 tablespoons grated Pecorino Romano cheese (or substitute grated Parmesan cheese)

Fill a medium saucepan with enough water to cover asparagus and bring to a boil. Add salt to taste. Add asparagus, cooking until al dente, about 3 minutes. Remove to a colander and cool under running cold water. Remove the string and cut asparagus on an angle into 1-inch pieces.

In a large skillet over high heat, add butter, heating until it just begins to brown. Add morels; cook until tender, about 5 minutes. Add cream, cooking until thickened to coat the back of a spoon, about 10 minutes. Add lemon juice and rind. Adjust salt and pepper to taste. Keep warm over low heat.

In a large amount of boiling water, cook the pasta until al dente. Transfer to a strainer, rinse with warm water and drain well. Add asparagus and pasta to skillet and toss until evenly coated. If sauce seems too thick, lighten with an additional few tablespoons of cream or liquid. Distribute to serving plates and top with chives and cheese. Serve immediately.

Nutrition details per serving
Calories .458
Percent of calories from fat 71%
Fat: .37 gm
Protein: . . . . .11 gm
Carbohydrate: . . . . .24 gm
Cholesterol: . . . . .113 mg
Sodium: . . . . .450 mg
Diabetic exchange: ⅓ vegetable, 1 bread, ¼ meat, 6½ fat.

TASTE THE WOODS
IN FIDDLEHEAD FERNS

AMAZING
FOOD FACTS

■

**Vermont and
Maine are the
prime U.S.
terrain for
fiddleheads.
They typically
are found along
rivers and
streams as far
north as
Newfoundland,
as far south as
Virginia and as
far west as the
Mississippi
River.**

■ *What exactly is a fiddlehead fern?* Fiddlehead ferns are not a species but a stage of growth. The fern collected in this stage is the ostrich fern, selected for its delicate woodsy flavor and its healthfulness. Other species of ferns may be edible, but the bracken family especially has cancer-causing properties and should be avoided.

■ *Where they come from:* Fiddlehead ferns grow wild from the northeastern United States into Newfoundland and west through Michigan and into Wisconsin. Maine and Vermont have some of the largest crops because of their cool weather and undeveloped land. Maine ships fresh fiddleheads to market for about three or four weeks each year, starting in early to mid-May. Those not shipped fresh are canned, but, like many fragile vegetables, they lose a lot of character.

■ *Why they taste so good:* Fiddlehead ferns are gathered

TODAY'S LESSON: The first blast of spring warmth brings the delicate, wild fiddlehead ferns popping their heads out from the cool soil. Although they may look strange, they are worth taming.

exclusively from the wild. Their flavor is similar to asparagus, artichokes and green beans, but they have a woodsy scent. The tight heads are crisp and resilient to the bite and are best enjoyed in simple dishes.

■ *Health advantages:* Fiddleheads are high in vitamins A and C and are a good source of fiber.

■ *How to select and store:* Select fresh fiddleheads that are bright green, with firm and tight heads about 1½-2 inches in diameter. The best heads have the smallest tails. The tail also should be moist and full,

not shriveled. Avoid pliable, soft and mushy fiddleheads that are off-color; it indicates the delicate flavor has been lost. Some heads may have a brown paper-like coating, which is the crown material the ferns are breaking out of. Although the brown membrane may reflect that they were picked just as they emerged, check to be sure that it is easy to remove. Sometimes it is sticky and will drive you nuts trying to clean it. Fiddleheads are best soon after picking. If you must, store them in tightly sealed plastic bags in the vegetable crisper of your refrigerator. Try to eat them within a couple of days.

They will look good longer, but the flavor will change.

■ *Preparing your fiddlehead ferns:* Trim the excess tail from the head. Remove any brown membrane and rinse well under running cold water. Use a gentle scrub brush to loosen membrane.

■ *The cooking begins:* I prefer to blanch in boiling salted water until al dente, about 3 minutes, then finish in butter or olive oil with seasonings. But fiddleheads may also be steamed, sauteed and fried with a very light batter such as tempura.

■ *Serving suggestions:* They are ready to finish with a pat of butter, a squeeze of lemon juice, a little vinaigrette or any other light sauce.

■ *Mix and match:* Fiddleheads are great by themselves but are terrific when substituted for asparagus, green beans or even artichokes in many of your favorite dishes. Their rich flavor will stand up to all the spices you want to throw at them.

■

FIDDLEHEAD FERNS WITH PARMESAN CHEESE

Makes 4 servings

1   pound fiddlehead ferns, trimmed and cleaned (may substitute asparagus)

2   tablespoons unsalted butter

½   cup diced shallots (or substitute white part of scallion)

1   tablespoon balsamic vinegar (or substitute red wine vinegar)

Salt to taste

Freshly grated black pepper

¼   cup snipped fresh chives

¼   cup finely grated Parmesan cheese

In a medium pot, bring water to a boil. Add approximately 1 tablespoon salt per 2 quarts of water. Add the fiddleheads, cooking until al dente, about 3 minutes. Remove to a strainer to drain.

Meanwhile, in a large skillet, melt the butter over medium-high heat. Add the shallots, cooking until tender, about 2 minutes. Add the vinegar and allow to reduce for 1 minute. Add the ferns and toss to combine. Season with salt and a generous dose of black pepper to taste. Add the chives and remove from the heat. Divide fiddleheads into a mound in the center of each serving plate. Sprinkle Parmesan cheese atop the fiddleheads and serve immediately.

Nutrition details per serving
Calories .123
Percent of calories from fat 56%
Fat: . . . . .8 gm
Protein: . . . . .6 gm
Carbohydrate: . . . . .8 gm
Cholesterol: . . . . .12 mg
Sodium: . . . . .440 mg
Diabetic exchange: 1⅓ vegetables, ¾ meat, 1½ fat.

■

Fiddleheads got their name because of their resemblance to the tuning end of a violin. They are also known as croziers because of their likeness to a shepherd's staff.

SPRING PERFECTS
DELICATE WATERCRESS

AMAZING FOOD FACTS

■

Watercress is a herbaceous perennial found in shallow, slow-moving water. It has bushy, rounded leaves and succulent stems. Watercress has a very pungent odor when bruised.

■ *Where it comes from:* In the wild, watercress prefers creeks, streams and springs with shallow and slow-moving currents. This watercress is delightful but will transfer any impurities from the water. The commercially grown watercress in Midwestern markets is grown on the ground, not in wetlands. The roots are kept moist and fed nutrients to produce a crop every six weeks during the winter, accelerating to a harvest of every three weeks in summer. Watercress also may be commercially grown through hydroponics, farming on water. The water carries the necessary nutrients without bacteria and other impurities.

■ *Why it tastes so good:* The delicate leaves are tender, while the slender stems offer a delicious crunch. Raw watercress will perk up any salad; heated, it will mellow into a soft green with bright herbaceous flavors.

■ *Health advantages:* Watercress leaves provide great flavor and

TODAY'S LESSON: Watercress is the best of all greens, with a peppery flavor that refreshes the palate. Watercress is easily identified by its compound round leaves about a slender stem with a large end leaflet. Watercress *(Nasturtium officinale)* is a member of the mustard family and is also known as pepper leaf, water nasturtium and scurvy grass.

are high in vitamin A, calcium and potassium.

■ *How to select and store:* Select your source carefully and treat raw wild watercress by soaking in Halazone tablets (available at drugstores) to kill bacteria before eating. Select deep green leaves on crisp slender stems. Watercress deteriorates quickly, so be picky. Avoid wilted, browning or yellowing leaves. Refrigerate watercress in a plastic bag, but use it immediately. If you plan to store it longer

than a day, cover it with damp paper towels and a few ice cubes before refrigerating. Drain the water daily and refresh with more ice. The watercress should last for three or four days with this technique.

■ *Preparing your watercress:* This is probably the easiest green to prepare after washing by simply twisting off the lower third of the stemmy ends. The stems are edible but a little coarse compared to the delicate leaves.

■ *Tricks of the trade:* For chopping or cutting down to size, use the stems that you usually discard as a handle. Hold the lower, coarser third of the stem and cut the remaining prime leaves and stems with your knife. Remember, when cooking, add the watercress at the last second so it just wilts, to capture that spicy flavor.

■ *The cooking begins:* Watercress is a taste treat when added at the last second to stir-fry and sauteed vegetables. It is great used whole in clear soups or pureed into creamy soups for color and delicate flavor. Add a bunch of watercress to your favorite wilted greens, such as spinach, for a terrific vegetable dish.

One of the best uses for watercress is as a seasoning. The fresh watercress leaves are a great flavor enhancer for fish and poultry. My favorite seasoning rub is chopped watercress, parsley, chives, roasted minced garlic and a little grated lemon rind. I combine them and chop until a paste is formed. Rub on fish or poultry after broiling or grilling, then top with a couple of drops of lemon, lime or very good vinegar. The simple broiled fish becomes sublime — and best of all, it's healthy.

■ *Serving suggestions:* Raw watercress can be a salad by itself, highlighted by a simple vinaigrette or a robust blue cheese dressing. When mixed with other greens, it will jazz up a salad and awaken other mild and sleepy lettuces. Watercress may also be used to spark up a salad by pureeing it raw with your salad dressing ingredients.

■

WATERCRESS, SPINACH & MUSHROOM SALAD

Makes 4 servings

2   tablespoons aged sherry wine vinegar

¼   cup virgin olive oil

¼   teaspoon salt

¼   teaspoon freshly ground black pepper

3   bunches watercress, lower third of stems removed

2   cups spinach, cleaned, spin-dried and cut into bite-size pieces

1   cup sliced white mushrooms

1   small red onion, cut into quarters, then sliced fine

4   whole large radicchio leaves

½   cup snipped fresh chives

In a small bowl, combine the vinegar, olive oil and salt and pepper.

In a metal bowl, toss the watercress, spinach, mushrooms and onion with the dressing.

Position one radicchio leaf on the top half of each of four serving plates. Distribute the salad onto each radicchio leaf, letting it flow out onto the serving plate. Sprinkle with the chives and serve.

Nutrition details per serving
Calories 156
Percent of calories from fat 75%
Fat: . . . . .14 gm
Protein: . . . . .4 gm
Carbohydrate: . . . . .6 gm
Cholesterol: . . . . .0 mg
Sodium: . . . . .206 mg
Diabetic exchange: 1 vegetable, 2¾ fat.

■

Watercress can be found in every state in the United States, Canada and throughout the world. Watercress is native to Europe, where it is cultivated, as it is in this country.

■

Most watercress is enjoyed raw. But briefly simmering the leaves, roots, flowers and young pods can produce wonderful boiled greens.

LAWN NUISANCE
DESERVES A NIBBLE

AMAZING FOOD FACTS

■

Dandelions are believed to be native to every continent. They are popular as an immature green in Europe and have been cultivated in the United States since at least the late 1800s, although only recently have they become popular again in this country.

■ *Why it tastes so good:* Dandelions are the premier edible green to emerge when the temperature begins to rise. Dandelions flourish in the cool, wet weather of April and May, producing large bunches of leaves with mild flavor. Higher temperatures and a little sun produce the golden flowers but bring sharper, bitter leaves. Collect wild dandelion greens with their roots only from areas that have not been exposed to pesticides and harsh fertilizers.

■ *Health advantages:* The leaves are low in calories, about 35 in a cooked cup. They are high in vitamins A and C, and a good source of calcium and iron.

■ *How to grow:* Dandelions are one of the easiest garden crops to grow. Although related to the wild variety, the domesticated dandelion is a different species, with broader leaves and a less pronounced flavor. Sow the seeds in a shaded area for slower growth, pick the

TODAY'S LESSON: For most people, the dandelion is only a weed, a yellow nuisance in an otherwise green lawn. But to the cook, the dandelion is sublime served fresh in salads and wonderful cooked as a substitute for spinach.

leaves often from the stems before flowering, and you should get three to five crops.

■ *How to select and store:* In the market, select bright green leaves — avoid limp and yellowed ones. Dark green leaves look great but are the most bitter, so steer away from these as well. Dandelion leaves store best with the root attached, so use the loose leaves quickly while still crisp.

■ *Preparing your dandelions:* Clean by removing the leaves from the root and soaking in cold water. Agitate the water to loosen the dirt, then remove the leaves to a colander to

drain. Repeat if necessary, especially after a recent rainfall. Spin to dry or lay the leaves out on heavy paper toweling.

■ *Tricks of the trade:* For the best, most intense dandelion flavor, choose small leaves before the plant flowers. Saute in a nonstick pan with a little extra-virgin olive oil, sea salt and freshly ground black pepper until wilted and with no moisture left.

■ *Cooking with dandelion greens:* The smaller leaves are best for salads. They are enhanced when cloaked in dressings with the vibrant flavors of lemon, wine vinegars, mustards, bacon, and olive and nut oils. The larger and bitter leaves are best cooked. Blanch them in boiling salted water until tender, about 3 minutes, which will reduce the bitterness. Drain into a colander and cool under running cold water. For robust spring flavors, substitute dandelion for cooked spinach in your favorite recipe. To prepare as a vegetable, saute in olive oil or butter with seasonings of garlic and lemon. Dandelion also makes a great soup with shallots and chives.

■

DANDELION & PANCETTA SALAD

Makes 4 servings

½ cup virgin olive oil, divided

¼ pound pancetta, diced (or substitute slab or regular bacon)

3 tablespoons red wine vinegar

2 tablespoons coarse-grain mustard

¼ teaspoon salt

½ teaspoon freshly ground black pepper

4 cups dandelion leaves, stems removed

1 red pepper, roasted, peeled, seeded and diced

½ cup snipped fresh chives

2 tablespoons mustard seeds, toasted

In a medium-size skillet, combine 1 tablespoon of the olive oil and the pancetta. Cook over medium heat until golden and crisp, about 10 minutes. Remove from heat, drain the pancetta on paper towels and pour off and reserve the fat.

In a small bowl, combine the vinegar, mustard and remaining olive oil. Add pancetta drippings to taste. Add salt and pepper to taste.

In a metal bowl, toss the pancetta, dandelion leaves, red pepper and chives with the dressing. Distribute the salad to the serving plates. Sprinkle the toasted mustard seeds across the top of the salads and serve.

Cook's note: Pancetta is Italian cured pork belly, often smoked, which tastes quite similar to bacon. Pancetta is

available at Italian markets and groceries.

Nutrition details per serving
Calories 475
Percent of calories from fat 80%
Fat: .43 gm
Protein: . . . . .12 gm
Carbohydrate: . . . . .11 gm
Cholesterol: . . . . .24 mg
Sodium: . . . . .733 mg
Diabetic exchange: ¼ vegetable, ⅓ bread, 1½ meat, 7¾ fat.

■

DANDELION RAVIOLI

Makes 4 servings

4 tablespoons extra-virgin olive oil, divided

1 cup shallots, peeled, ends removed, cut into ¼-inch dice

4 garlic cloves, peeled, ends removed, minced

½ pound cleaned dandelion leaves, coarsely chopped

Salt and coarsely ground black pepper to taste

1 cup mascarpone cheese

½ cup snipped fresh chives, washed, divided

½ cup Parmesan cheese, grated, divided

½ pound Egg Pasta Dough (see recipe on page 26)

■

Dandelion roots are dried, toasted, ground and brewed to make a chicory or coffee-like beverage.

Dandelion
flowers are
used to
color and
flavor
dandelion
wine.

1 egg yolk

¼ cup cream or milk

Filling: In a large nonstick skillet, heat 2 tablespoons of olive oil over medium-high heat. Add the shallots and garlic, cooking until tender and translucent, about 3 minutes. Add the dandelions and cook until wilted and tender. Season with salt and pepper. Continue cooking until all juices have evaporated, then transfer to a medium bowl. Allow to cool to room temperature. Add the mascarpone cheese, ¼ cup chives and ¼ cup Parmesan cheese, mixing well to combine.

Making the ravioli: Using a pasta machine, roll a quarter of the pasta to make a very thin 2½-by-24-inch sheet. Repeat process to yield four sheets. Lay a pasta sheet flat on the work surface. Place 1 tablespoon of filling mixture every 2½ inches down the center of the sheet of pasta. In a small bowl, mix the egg yolk with cream or milk; brush the egg wash on the pasta around the filling. Cover with another sheet of pasta, pressing together to seal in the filling. With a crinkle ravioli cutter, cut the filled pasta into ravioli.

Repeat with remaining two sheets of pasta. Refrigerate to firm for at least 1 hour.

Cook the ravioli in a large skillet in 3 inches of boiling salted water until al dente, about 9 minutes. With a slotted spoon, remove to a colander or paper towels to drain. Transfer to a bowl and add the remaining 2 tablespoons olive oil to coat. Position the ravioli in the center of warm serving plates. Top with the remaining ¼ cup chives and ¼ cup Parmesan cheese. Serve immediately.

Cook's note: Mascarpone cheese can be found in Italian groceries, gourmet shops and some supermarkets.

EGG PASTA DOUGH

Makes ½ pound

1½ cups all-purpose flour

2 large eggs, beaten

On a large flat surface, sift the flour into a mound and make a well in the center. Pour the eggs into the well. Start mixing the flour into the eggs with a fork until the eggs and flour are combined. Begin working with your hands to combine the remaining flour into a ball. Knead the ball with your palms, pushing it away from your body. Fold and turn the pasta after each away motion until the texture is smooth and supple, about 8 minutes. Form into a smooth ball, cover with plastic wrap and refrigerate until ready to use. Can be made up to three days ahead.

Nutrition details per serving
Calories 624
Percent of calories from fat 58%
Fat: . . . . .41 gm
Protein: . . . . .20 gm
Carbohydrate: . . . . .47 gm
Cholesterol: . . . . .169 mg
Sodium: . . . . .609 mg
Diabetic exchange: 1¾ vegetables, 2¼ bread, 1¾ meat, 7 fat.

Nutrition details per serving
Calories 208
Percent of calories from fat 13%
Fat: . . . . .3 gm
Protein: . . . . .8 gm
Carbohydrate: . . . . .36 gm
Cholesterol: . . . . .107 mg
Sodium: . . . . .32 mg
Diabetic exchange: 2⅓ bread, ½ meat, ¼ fat.

IT'S EASY EATING GREENS

■ *Why they taste so good:* Greens and lettuces love hot, sunny days and cool nights, a combination that yields intense rich flavor and a delicate and crisp texture. Cooler temperatures are necessary for endive, frisee and especially radicchio, all of which disappear when hot weather arrives.

■ *Advantages:* Greens and lettuces are full of vitamins and minerals. They are rich in the antioxidant nutrients vitamin C and beta-carotene.

■ *Selecting your favorite greens:* Although you may be less familiar with some varieties, be adventurous when you examine what's available at local markets. Give red romaine a try, even if you swear that the green is the only real romaine. I think the red's flavor is superior. The tender red leaf variety and the beautiful red oak are the best of the reds. French Batavian is one of the stars of recent years.

TODAY'S LESSON: The first crops of the new season have begun to emerge from the chill of winter and early spring. These special greens and lettuces are full of delicate flavor — perfect for a refreshing salad.

Whatever your choice, freshest is the best. Greens and lettuces quickly deteriorate after picking, so store them in a vented plastic bag under mild refrigeration. Select heads with moist, freshly cut bases. All of the leaves, even the exterior, should be crisp and moist.

■ *Preparing the greens:* Pick leaves from the core of the lettuce and wash under cool, running water, then drain in a colander. Tear the lettuce into bite-size pieces. Transfer to a greens spinner or to a clean linen towel to remove the excess moisture. Store under refrigeration and covered with a damp towel until ready to toss.

■ *Tricks of the trade:* I usually wash the lettuce and stack it upside down as soon as it comes in from the farm so it slowly drains while staying moist. Any tearing or cutting will bruise lettuces, so wait until the last second to cut into a salad. Toss immediately and serve.

Save the larger, pretty leaves from the outside to line the salad plate. The form gives the salad a definitive shape. You can also arrange little bunches of baby lettuce so that the plate looks bushy and full.

■ *Mix and match:* The best salad has depth of flavor achieved by mixing different greens or lettuces together. Mix greens and reds, as well as soft and firm-textured greens.

■ *All dressed up and no place to go:* Dress that salad just before you eat it — not before you serve it. A perfect delicate texture will quickly succumb to all that vinegar and oil. Heavy creamy dressings do not allow the true flavor of these greens to come through. Try thinning with a little wine, cider or even water.

Try lighter vinaigrette-style dressings. Balsamic and other richer vinegars are very satisfying but may overpower the flavor of these lettuces. Lemon, red or white wine or herb vinegars are more delicate. Mix only with extra-virgin olive oil, which has a richer taste and is better for you than other oils.

■

SPRING'S FIRST SALAD

Makes 4 servings

3 tablespoons red wine vinegar

1 tablespoon extra strong mustard
   Sea or granulated salt
   Freshly ground black pepper

¼ cup extra-virgin olive oil

3 tablespoons low- or nonfat yogurt

¼ cup snipped fresh chives

6 cups mixed baby greens, washed and torn into bite-size pieces

1 small Vidalia onion, cut very thin

1 cup toasted sourdough croutons, cut very thin

2 tablespoons toasted whole mustard seeds

In a medium bowl, whisk together the vinegar and mustard. Season with a pinch of salt and pepper. Slowly pour in the olive oil while continuously whisk-

ing. Add the yogurt and mix until homogeneous. Stir in the chives. Adjust the seasonings as necessary to balance.

In a larger bowl, combine the greens and the onion. Add the dressing and toss to combine. Add the croutons. Transfer the greens to the center of the serving plates. Top with a sprinkling of the toasted mustard seeds and serve immediately.

Nutrition details per serving
Calories 222
Percent of calories from fat 63%
Fat: . . . . .16 gm
Protein: . . . . .5 gm
Carbohydrate: . . . . .16 gm
Cholesterol: . . . . .0 mg
Sodium: . . . . .272 mg
Diabetic exchange: ¾ vegetable, ½ bread, 2⅞ fat.

■

MESCLUN SALAD WITH DRIED CHERRY VINAIGRETTE

Makes 4 servings

3 tablespoons red wine vinegar

2 tablespoons dried cherries

¼ cup virgin olive oil

½ teaspoon salt

Fresh coarsely ground black pepper to taste

4 cups mesclun salad mix or mixed seasonal greens of your choice, washed and dried

24 Black Pepper Croutons (see accompanying recipe)

¼ cup fresh snipped chives

About 2 hours in advance: In a small saucepan, warm the vinegar, then add the cherries. Remove from heat and allow to steep until softened, at least 2 hours. Add a little water if the cherries are still firm. Place the vinegar and cherries in a blender and puree until smooth. With the blender running, add the olive oil in a steady stream until thickened. Add salt and pepper to taste.

Select a few of the larger-pointed lettuce leaves and arrange artistically, pointing outward from the center of the plate. In a medium-size bowl, combine the lettuces, dressing and the croutons, tossing until combined. Position greens in the center of the plate. Sprinkle with chives and serve.

Nutrition details per serving
Calories .141
Percent of calories from fat 85%
Fat: .14 gm
Protein: . . . . .1 gm
Carbohydrate: . . . . .5 gm
Cholesterol: . . . . .0 mg
Sodium: . . . . .274 mg
Diabetic exchange: ⅜ vegetable, 2¾ fat.

■

BLACK PEPPER CROUTONS

1   loaf Ficelle French bread (the smallest in diameter), sliced ¼-inch thick
¼   cup extra-virgin olive oil
1   tablespoon freshly ground coarse black pepper
½   cup grated Parmesan cheese

Lay the pieces of bread flat on a cookie sheet. Brush the surfaces of the bread with olive oil. Sprinkle the pepper across the bread and repeat with the Parmesan cheese. Place in a preheated 350-degree oven until golden, about 4 minutes.

GROW YOUR OWN LETTUCE

Here are some interesting lettuces to grow:

CRESSON

(25 days to maturity)
Curly cress quickly germinates and is the first green to the table. The tangy flavor brightens salads and sandwiches and picks up the flavor of many warm dishes. Grows well in the shade.

MESCLUN SALAD

(35-45 days to maturity)
Various seed blends, including Bibb, Romaine, Oakleaf, Red Romaine, Frisee, Crispheads, Mizuni and Red Mustard. Harvested young, the salad is an exceptional blend of colors, shapes and flavors. Great with limited space and limited gardening time.

TAT-SOI

(45 days to maturity)
This spoon-shaped green is mild, with tender leaves and crunchy stems. It is great in salads or wilted like spinach as a vegetable. Grows best in the cool weather of spring and fall.

ARUGULA OR ROCKET

(45 days to maturity)
Arugula is an all-time favorite, with its delicate leaves and distinctive nutty flavor. It prefers the cool temperatures of spring or fall. Pinch the flowers and add them to your salad. This stops the leaves from maturing and becoming bitter. Arugula is best in simple salads and especially with tomatoes.

RED OAKLEAF

(50 days to maturity)
This is the red cousin of the Green Oakleaf. Both are great, with their delicate texture, bright colors and oakleaf shape. It is a dependable producer in cool and hot weather, with a mild sweet flavor.

BABY ROMAINE

(55 days to maturity)
This small romaine produces exceptional heads of crisp leaves, about 6 inches long, with a very sweet flavor. It likes cooler temperatures.

PIQUANT SORREL DOUBLES AS HERB AND SALAD GREEN

AMAZING FOOD FACTS

■

Sorrel is a relative of the rhubarb family. Its Old French name is derived from *surele*, meaning "sour."

■ *What does sorrel taste like?* Sorrel has a tart, sour and piquant taste almost like lemon, which is best when blended in salads or used in sauce for fish. The smaller young leaves are less tart than older leaves.

■ *Health advantages:* Sorrel has about 25 calories in a 4-ounce serving and is high in vitamins A, B1 and C.

■ *How to select and store:* Select sorrel with bright, fresh-looking leaves and moist, crisp stems. The broad-based leaves with pointy tips are quite large when cultivated. The smaller, very sharp-tasting leaves occur in the wild. Avoid wilted, yellowed or fibrous-looking leaves. Sorrel can be stored in your vegetable crisper for just a couple of days; it quickly loses its kick.

■ *Enjoy sorrel in your salads:* To use raw in salads, tear up the leaves and toss with dressing. Choose dressings with less

TODAY'S LESSON: The sharp, acidic flavor of sorrel is more like an herb than a salad green, but this leafy green does duty as both. The trick is to capture its unique flavor raw or cooked.

sharp flavors to balance the taste of the sorrel. An extra splash of olive oil or a little pinch of salt will help reduce a sharp bite.

■ *The cooking begins:* When the leaves are heated, the tart taste diminishes. But don't cook sorrel for very long; blanch leaves for just a few seconds. Sorrel is traditionally prepared by blanching in boiling water, draining and processing into a puree. The puree is blended with other vegetables to be served alone or converted into soup. Pureeing is a great way to store fresh sorrel to avoid losing a good surplus, as well as providing an instant jolt of flavor for many less invigorating dishes. Try adding a dollop

of puree to finish off root and green vegetables, spark up a fish dish or bring life to a boring omelet.

■ *Sorrel as a seasoning:* If you use sorrel as a garnish, add it at the end to sauces and other warm preparations to capture the citrus-like flavor. The delicate flavor quickly dissipates with longer cooking.

■ *Mix and match:* I like adding chopped sorrel as both a visual and flavor garnish to a mustard sauce for serving with salmon or tuna, as in the accompanying recipe. Sorrel is also a good match for the delicate flavors of veal and poultry.

GRILLED SALMON WITH SORREL & MUSTARD SAUCE

Makes 4 servings

¼ cup finely diced shallots

½ cup dry white wine

1 cup whipping cream

8 escallops of salmon, 3 ounces each

Salt and freshly ground black pepper to taste

2 tablespoons grained mustard

½ cup chopped sorrel

8 small sorrel leaves for garnish

Preheat grill or broiler. In a medium saucepan, combine shallots and white wine. Bring to a boil over medium-high heat and cook until reduced to ¼ cup, about 5 minutes. Add cream and cook until lightly thickened, about 8 minutes. Remove from heat.

Season the salmon with salt and pepper. Place on grill or under broiler, allowing to sear, about 3 minutes. Turn the escallops over and cook until done, about 3 minutes, depending on thickness.

Return the sauce to a simmer. Remove from heat and stir in mustard and sorrel. Season with salt and pepper to taste. Spoon a little sauce in the center of the serving plates. Position 2 escallops in center of sauce, slightly overlapping each other. Spoon the remaining sauce over the salmon.

Garnish plates with a couple of the sorrel leaves and serve.

Nutrition details per serving
Calories 444
Percent of calories from fat 58%
Fat: . . . . .28 gm
Protein: . . . . .37 gm
Carbohydrate: . . . . .5 gm
Cholesterol: . . . . .170 mg
Sodium: . . . . .247 mg
Diabetic exchange: ⅜ vegetable, 4¾ meat, 4⅓ fat.

In Britain, sorrel has been revered as a medicinal herb, elixir and culinary ingredient for centuries. The English used it in a sweet-sour relish, called greensauce, which was served until the 19th Century.

THE TRICK TO LIGHT, CRISPY FRIED FISH

AMAZING FOOD FACTS

■

Smelt are a delicate fish, usually not longer than 7 or 8 inches, with a slender body and silvery skin. They are revered for their tender flesh and light but rich flavor. They are high in oil from their winter solitude.

■ *Why it tastes so good:* Delicate fish is fried at 375 degrees, almost twice as hot as poaching or baking. The second the little fish is plunged into the hot oil, the high temperature seals the exterior skin or flesh, trapping moisture and flavor. The fish is thoroughly cooked in just a couple of minutes.

■ *Health advantages:* The best advantage to frying is the crisp texture and flavor. Little fat will be absorbed during the cooking process, provided the oil is at the correct high temperature when starting and the fryer is not overloaded.

■ *Not all oils are equal:* Select one of the following oils for the healthiest and best-tasting fried food:

Canola oil will withstand the high temperatures without breaking down; it has no cholesterol and little, if any, distinguishable flavor.

Olive oil will stand up to frying temperatures for a few batches, which is sufficient for

TODAY'S LESSON: Although fried foods generally have a bad reputation for being heavy and greasy, crispy frying done right produces the most delicately crunchy fish while preserving the flavorful, moist inner flesh. I'll show you the trick to perfect fish frying.

the home cook. It is a good, healthy oil and has the best flavor for simple fried foods.

Corn oil also will handle the temperature, but it has some cholesterol and a richer, fuller flavor.

Vegetable oils can also be used, but check their individual heat ranges and health attributes.

■ *Select your fish:* Whole cleaned smelt or small perch fillets are my choice for spring. Select smelt that have a bright, shiny, almost wet-looking skin and smell almost of watermelon or cucumber. Smelt may be purchased whole, but gut

before eating. An old expression says, "You can eat all of the smelt except the wiggle," but most people prefer to remove the heads and sometimes the tail. Smelt also can be purchased gutted, without the head. Before cooking, rinse thoroughly under running cold water. Select small fillets of perch that are almost translucent and dense in texture, never white or mushy. Trim the belly flap and remove the skin if you prefer, or just fry as is. Neither fish should feel slimy or smell fishy.

■ *Flour or batter?* The simplest method is to dredge the fish through an egg-and-milk wash, drain and dust with seasoned flour. The wash helps the flour stick and ensures an even seal when cooked. The flour should be seasoned with salt and pepper, but you can include paprika and ground spices such as fennel seed, cumin or dill seed for a delicate accent. The seasoned flour allows more of the fish's flavor and texture to come through. For best results when frying a large amount of fish, add the salt and pepper to the egg wash; if it is added to the flour, the salt will accelerate the breakdown of the oil.

The batter is a mixture of egg, flour and milk, beer or water. The batter generally gives a little thicker coating to the fish, which fries up crispier. Batters can carry more seasonings, such as a fresh puree of ginger or horseradish. For the lightest batter, use club soda, sparkling wines or beer; the bubbles will keep the texture light and extra crisp.

■ *Preparing your dinner:* Since the cooking occurs so quickly, it is essential to have everything assembled. Lay out all

the ingredients, set the table, warm the serving plates in the oven, cut lemons and other garnishes and prepare any sauce or side dishes so they're ready as soon as the fish has finished cooking. With every second the fried fish waits to

be served, its texture and flavor decline.

When everything is ready, fill a large, deep skillet or pot to a depth of 3-4 inches with the selected oil. Make sure there is room for the bubbling oil to expand during cooking without overflowing onto the stove. Have a strainer or wire

ladle ready for removing fish from the oil, and a cookie sheet lined with paper towel for draining.

■ *Tricks of the trade:* The trick to frying is temperature. Make sure the oil is the proper temperature by setting the fryer gauge. If you are serving a large party, have a number of skillets or fryers on the fire, so all the fish can be cooked and presented quickly. Never overload the fryers, since adding too much cold fish to the oil will cause the temperature to drop, which will cause more oil to be absorbed and result in soggy food.

■ *The cooking begins:* Dredge the fish through the egg wash and allow to drain. Add each fillet to the seasoned flour while shaking to coat all the surfaces evenly. Shake fish in a coarse sieve to remove all excess flour. Carefully drop fillets into the hot oil and cook until they begin to hiss, about 2-2½ minutes for smelt and a little longer for perch. The hissing sound means they are releasing their juices and are done. Remove them to paper

■

Smelt mature in two to three years and die after spawning. One female may lay up to 25,000 eggs.

■

Nine species of smelt are native to North America. The two most popular for eating are the Rainbow smelt, of the Great Lakes and the Northeast; and the Eulachon or Hooligan, of the region from Oregon to Alaska.

towels. Garnish and serve immediately on a warm platter.

■ *Serving suggestions:* The standard green herbed tartar sauce is OK, or even just a squirt of lemon and some fried parsley.

■ *Mix and match:* Try different seasonings in the flour or batter to enhance the natural fish flavor. Experiment with your favorite herbs — fried just before the fish to add flavor to the fish after cooking.

■

CRISPY FRIED SMELT WITH LEMON, GARLIC & ROSEMARY

Makes 4 servings

Olive oil or canola oil for frying

6   cloves garlic, peeled, ends removed, cut in half lengthwise

2   large sprigs fresh rosemary, washed, dried

1   cup flat parsley leaves

2   cups all-purpose flour

2   teaspoons hot paprika

2   teaspoons ground fennel seed, optional

1   teaspoon fine sea salt

2   large eggs, lightly beaten

2   cups low-fat milk

2   pounds small smelt, cleaned

    Salt and pepper to taste

2   lemons, cut into ⅛-inch wedges

Fill a large, deep skillet with olive or canola oil to a depth of 4 inches. Heat over medium-high heat to 375 degrees. Add the garlic and cook until golden. Remove garlic with a slotted spoon to a paper towel to drain. Finely chop the garlic. Set aside.

Add the rosemary to skillet, cooking until crisp, about 3 minutes. Remove to a paper towel to drain. Remove the leaves from the stem. Add the parsley leaves to skillet and cook until crisp, about 1 minute. Drain on a paper towel. When drained, transfer to a large bowl and add the rosemary leaves and garlic, mixing to combine.

In another large bowl, sift together the flour, paprika,

ground fennel seed if desired and sea salt. In a medium bowl, combine the eggs and milk. Drench the smelt in the egg and milk wash, then shake off excess. Transfer smelt to the seasoned flour and shake to coat all surfaces of the smelt. Shake smelt in a coarse sieve to remove excess flour.

Increase the heat of the oil. Run a dry, fine, small sieve through the oil to remove any remaining herb particles. Slip the smelt into the hot oil, stirring occasionally, and fry until evenly golden, about 2-3 minutes depending on the fish size and the oil volume. Remove smelt to paper towel to drain. Transfer to the large bowl with the garlic, rosemary and parsley; toss. Season to taste with salt and pepper. Serve immediately on a warmed platter lined with lemon wedges.

Nutrition details per serving
Calories .638
Percent of calories from fat 29%
Fat: .21 gm
Protein: . . . . .55 gm
Carbohydrate: . . . . .59 gm
Cholesterol: . . . . .275 mg
Sodium: . . . . .832 mg
Diabetic exchange: ½ milk, 4½ lean meat, 3 bread, 2¼ fat.

GET THE BEST
OUT OF AN OYSTER

When to buy: Oysters are best in the winter months when their meat is dense and compact. As late spring and early summer arrive, the water temperatures rise and the oysters spawn, depleting much of their strength. They produce glycogen to restore themselves, which gradually is converted to the shell and body.

Selecting oysters: Select oysters that are crusty, dirty, heavy and tightly closed. I prefer the smaller, compact oysters for eating raw on the half shell, and reserve the large ones for cooking. Oysters will "gape" or open during extreme temperature changes. When gaping, they should close if gently tapped. They do not necessarily die when they open, but their juices will escape if the oyster is not upright, cupped shell on the bottom, and level.

Storing oysters: Store them cupped shell down, with a packing of seaweed or wet paper, at 39-44 degrees. Clean

TODAY'S LESSON: Deep in the recesses of history, one of our ancestors cracked open a crusted rocky mollusk, extracted the creature inside, mustered the courage and swallowed the first oyster. The oyster was taken to heart, and it's been a love affair ever since.

the mud from the oyster under running cold water only just before opening. After cleaning, try an old shucker's trick: Throw the oysters in the freezer for 30 minutes, then open. Oysters are easier to open when deeply chilled, but do not ice during storage or they will gape and quickly die.

Preparing your oysters: It is very important to open oysters at the last minute. The adductor muscle, which opens and closes the shell, hardens quickly after opening, causing a very chewy texture. For cooking, cut the muscle out and

discard it, but for serving raw, there is no way to hide it. After shucking, scrub the bottom cup shell, place it upright in a bed of rock salt and heat in a 300-degree oven for 30 minutes to an hour. Then place the shells on additional rock salt or seaweed at room temperature on the serving plates to keep them level. You can fill the shells with your cooked oysters, and they will maintain the heat from the oven. The rock salt base also evenly heats your favorite baked oyster dishes.

AMAZING
FOOD FACTS

■

The Italians are credited with the first true cultivation of oysters. They suspended branches from the water surface onto which the oysters attached themselves.

■

Oysters begin their lives as free-swimming larvae called spats and must attach themselves to smooth, clean and hard surfaces to survive. This will be their home for life.

■

Many look for pearls in eating oysters, but those pearls are caused by parasites.

■ *The cooking begins:* Most people overcook oysters. Oysters should be silky and tender — not chewy. They may be baked, poached or fried, but just until the edges begin to curl. A medium oyster will be cooked by poaching (212 degrees) or frying (350 degrees) in about 45 seconds — yes, 45 seconds. The oyster is mostly water, so the heat will quickly penetrate the whole meat. Cooking any longer will only drive out the moisture the oyster spent two or three years to build.

■ *Serving suggestions:* Serve oysters raw on the half shell while still attached to the lower shell. Properly served, they should not be loose in the shell — an old trick of unscrupulous dealers is to buy shucked oysters and place them in recycled shells. The usual accompaniments are fresh horseradish, lemon, Tabasco, cocktail or mignonette sauce.

■

FRIED OYSTERS WITH TARTAR SAUCE

Makes 4 servings

24 medium to large oysters, shucked (save lower half of shell)
Blanched seaweed or rock salt to cover serving plates
Corn oil for frying
1½ cups yellow corn meal
1 cup all-purpose flour
2 tablespoons paprika
1 teaspoon salt
¾ teaspoon white pepper
¼ cup snipped fresh chives (or substitute chopped fresh parsley)
1 cup Herbed Tartar Sauce (see accompanying recipe)
1 lemon cut into 8 wedges

Wash lower cup shells from oysters to remove mud and any loose shell. Place shells in ovenproof pan and heat in preheated 300-degree oven about 30 minutes. Prepare serving dishes with a bed of seaweed or rock salt.

Fill a large, heavy, deep skillet with corn oil to depth of 3

inches. Heat over medium-high heat to 350 degrees.

In a medium-size bowl, sift together the corn meal, flour, paprika, salt and pepper. Dredge the oysters in the seasoned flour, cook until evenly golden, about 45-60 seconds. Transfer to a bowl and toss with the chives.

Place the oysters on the warm shells. Top with a dab of tartar sauce or serve the tartar sauce on the side. Garnish the plates with the lemons and serve.

Nutrition details per serving
Calories 435
Percent of calories from fat 23%
Fat: . . . . .11 gm
Protein: . . . . .17 gm
Carbohydrate: . . . . .69 gm
Cholesterol: . . . . .42 mg
Sodium: . . . . .642 mg
Diabetic exchange: ¼ fruit, 4 bread, 1¼ meat, 1⅜ fat.

HERBED TARTAR SAUCE

Makes 2 cups

2 large egg yolks

1 tablespoon Dijon mustard

¼ cup fresh lemon juice

1 cup corn oil

1 hard-boiled egg, chopped, optional

2 tablespoons diced green bell pepper

2 tablespoons diced red onion

2 tablespoons sweet relish, drained

2 tablespoons diced dill pickle

¼ cup capers, drained and minced

2 anchovy fillets, minced

1 tablespoon minced scallion greens

1 tablespoon minced fresh parsley

½ teaspoon chopped thyme leaf

½ teaspoon salt

1 teaspoon freshly ground black pepper

Tabasco to taste

In the bowl of a mixer, combine the yolks, mustard and lemon juice. With mixer on high speed, gradually add the corn oil in a steady stream. On slow speed, mix in the remaining ingredients.

Adjust salt, pepper and Tabasco to taste.

Refrigerate until ready to use. Can be made up to four days ahead.

Nutrition details per serving
Calories 76
Percent of calories from fat 48%
Fat: . . . . .4 gm
Protein: . . . . .4 gm
Carbohydrate: . . . . .6 gm
Cholesterol: . . . . .160 mg
Sodium: . . . . .597 mg
Diabetic exchange: ¼ vegetable, ½ meat, ½ fat.

Preparing oysters

Hold the oyster with the hinge facing your palm with the deeper half of the shell on the bottom.

Insert the thick blade of an oyster knife between the shells near the hinge.

Run the knife around until you cut the muscle that holds the halves together. Discard the top of the shell.

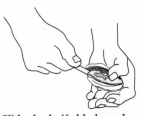

Slide the knife blade under the oyster to free it from the shell and serve.

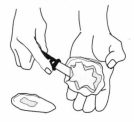

In the 4th Century B.C., Aristotle saw fishermen at Rhodes tossing broken pottery into the sea so the oyster larvae could affix themselves. After the oysters were developed, they were moved with their pottery bases to rich tidal pools for fattening and reproduction.

THIN, ICE-COLD BATTER MAKES THE BEST TEMPURA

AMAZING FOOD FACTS

■

Tempura was originally taken to Japan by early Portuguese traders. As Catholics, the Portuguese fasted from meat on Ember Day, which they called by the Latin name Quattuor Tempora, or "four times" a year.

■ *Advantages:* The crispy thin batter contains less fat than traditional heavy frying. The thin batter also allows the flavor of the vegetable, fish, shellfish or poultry as well as the spices and seasonings to shine through.

■ *Tricks of the trade:* The secret to great tempura is to keep the batter thin and ice-cold. The batter should be made with ice water and is best if held in a bowl over ice.

■ *Preparing your tempura foods:* Use vegetables, fish, shellfish or poultry. Cut the foods into small portions — even bite-size — that will cook fast.

■ *Preparing the tempura batter:* The easiest way is to buy packaged tempura mix, which usually is mixed with egg white and ice-cold water. The mix is available at most specialty grocers and some supermarkets. Without the premix batter, follow my recipe.

TODAY'S LESSON: Modern-style crispy tempura frying.

■ *The cooking begins:* Dip chilled prepared foods in batter one piece at a time, allowing excess batter to run off. Carefully ease foods into the hot oil, making sure they don't touch in the pan. Cook until golden, turning as necessary to ensure all surfaces are evenly crisp. Drain on paper towels. Serve immediately or keep hot in a warm oven. Foods will soften while waiting. Skim any food particles from the oil between batches.

■ *Serving suggestions:* Tempura crunch is complemented by bright, high-acid cole slaws and spicy side vegetables. Whether hot or cold, the crunch is best with crunchy sides or silky sides such as grains. Try a refreshing green salad composed of more exotic lettuces that will cool and cleanse the palate while enjoying the super crispy tempura.

■

SOFT-SHELL CRABS WITH LEMON TEMPURA

Makes 4 servings

Canola or olive oil, or equal parts of both, for frying

2 cups Tempura Mix (see accompanying recipe)

3 tablespoons finely grated fresh lemon rind

1 tablespoon finely grated fresh lime rind

Salt to taste

1 teaspoon hot red pepper flakes, or to taste

12 soft-shell crabs, cleaned (see cook's note)

2 lemons, cut in half

½ cup parsley, washed, dried, chopped

1 cup Scallion Aioli Sauce (see accompanying recipe)

38

Fill a large, heavy, deep skillet with oil to a depth of 3 inches. Heat over medium-high heat to 375 degrees. In a medium-size bowl, combine tempura mix and lemon and lime rinds. Season with salt and red pepper flakes.

Dip crabs in the batter, then remove to a rack set over a cookie sheet to allow excess batter to drip off. Lower crabs into the hot oil and cook until golden, about 4 minutes. Drain on paper toweling, then transfer to a large bowl. Squeeze lemons over the crabs, add parsley leaves and toss. Divide onto serving plates. Drizzle with aioli sauce and serve.

Cook's note: Clean crabs by pulling the key (lower belly flaps) and opening the body shell. Remove the lungs and guts, then replace the body shell. Snip the face, if you choose. Keep refrigerated until ready to cook.

Nutrition details per serving
Calories 343
Percent of calories from fat 12%
Fat: . . . . .4.5 gm
Protein: . . . . .34 gm
Carbohydrate: . . . . .40 gm
Cholesterol: . . . . .188 mg
Sodium: . . . . .478 mg
Diabetic exchange: 2⅔ bread, 3 meat, trace fat.

■ TEMPURA MIX

Makes 2 cups

1 large egg yolk
2 cups ice-cold water
¼ teaspoon baking soda
1⅓ cups sifted all-purpose flour

In a medium bowl, combine egg yolk with ice water and baking soda. Whisk in the flour very slowly to avoid lumps. The batter should be just thick enough to coat the food.

Cook's note: 1 large whipped egg white may be substituted for the egg yolk.

■ SCALLION AIOLI SAUCE

Makes 2 cups

¼ cup fresh lime juice
¼ cup fresh lemon juice
2 large egg yolks
1 tablespoon water
1 tablespoon Dijon mustard
1 bunch of scallions, green part included, chopped fine
1 cup virgin olive oil
Salt to taste
Tabasco sauce to taste

In a microwave-safe dish, combine lime and lemon juices and egg yolks with 1 tablespoon of water. Heat the egg yolk mixture at high (100-percent power) for 15 seconds or so until it begins to expand. Remove from the microwave and mix well with a clean fork. Return to the microwave for 15 seconds and mix well, repeating until the mixture reaches 170 degrees as read on a small instant thermometer. This should take about five or so heating processes.

In a blender, combine yolk mixture, mustard and scallions. On high speed, gradually add olive oil in a steady stream until thick. Season with salt and Tabasco. Refrigerate until ready to use. Can be made two days ahead.

Nutrition details per serving
Calories 520
Percent of calories from fat 96%
Fat: . . . . .57 gm
Protein: .2 gm
Carbohydrate: . . . . .3 gm
Cholesterol: . . . . .106 mg
Sodium: . . . . .188 mg
Diabetic exchange: ⅛ vegetable, ¼ fruit, ¼ meat, 11½ fat.

INDULGE A SOFT SPOT
FOR SOFT-SHELL CRAB

■ *Where they come from:* In my mind, the best soft-shells come from Maryland. Their season begins as the waters warm in May and usually runs through October. Soft-shells from points south are available earlier, but the longer cold season in Maryland seems to develop the perfect match of texture and sweetness. The blue crab actually sheds its shell about 20 times in three years, with the peak time in late spring and early summer.

■ *How to select and store:* Soft-shells are sold in a number of sizes: whales, 5½ inches; jumbos, 5-5½ inches; primes, 4½-5 inches; hotels (my preference), 4-4½ inches, and mediums, 3½-4 inches. They are priced per piece. Select soft-shell crabs that smell sweet and salty, just like the ocean, never fishy or strong. Have your market clean the crabs by removing the lungs, face and, if you prefer, the tomalley (liver) and brains. They're best eaten the day you pick them up from the fish

TODAY'S LESSON: The garden may be sprouting green, but the highlight of spring comes from the water — soft-shell crabs. Soft-shell crabs are really plain old blue crabs just after they've shed one shell in order to grow a larger one. Caught at this stage, the crab is a simple, but wonderful, masterpiece.

market, but they can be refrigerated a day or two.

■ *The cooking begins:* I prefer dredging them in a well-seasoned tempura-style batter rather than the traditional frying batters that are heavy and tend to cloud the flavor with the scent of grease.

For the best crab flavor, sauteing with just a dusting of seasoned flour lets all the crab character come through.

Try both methods, and you can decide which is your favorite.

■

SOFT-SHELL CRABS
WITH LEMON &
CAPERS

Makes 4 servings

2 quarts low-fat milk
2 tablespoons grated fresh
   lemon zest (yellow part
   of skin)
   Salt to taste
12 soft-shell crabs, cleaned
   (see cook's note)
8 cups all-purpose flour

1 teaspoon freshly ground
black pepper

2 tablespoons ground
paprika

½ cup (1 stick) unsalted
butter, divided

½ cup drained nonpareil
capers

¼ cup fresh lemon juice

¼ cup fresh chives

In a medium bowl, combine the milk, lemon zest and salt to taste. Add the crabs and reserve while preparing the rest of the ingredients.

In a large shallow baking pan or dish, combine the flour, pepper and paprika.

In a small saucepan, melt half of the butter. Add the capers and lemon juice. Remove from heat and keep warm.

In a large skillet over medium-high heat, melt the remaining butter. Working very quickly, remove the crabs from the milk mixture and allow excess liquids to drain off. Dredge the crab through the seasoned flour, one at a time, and shake off excess. Lower the crabs into the hot butter and cook until golden, about 3 minutes. Cover with a lid as necessary to prevent hot

butter from splashing out. Turn crabs over and cook until done, about 2 minutes. Drain on paper toweling.

Divide crabs onto four serving plates. Drizzle caper butter over crabs and sprinkle with chives.

Cook's note: Clean crabs by pulling the key (lower belly flap) and opening the body shell. Remove the lungs and guts, then replace the body shell. Snip the face, if you choose. Or have the market clean the crabs when you buy them.

Nutrition details per serving
Calories 1,426
Percent of calories from fat 23%
Fat: . . . . .36 gm
Protein: . . . . .54 gm
Carbohydrate: . . . . .219 gm
Cholesterol: . . . . .146 mg
Sodium: . . . . .440 mg
Diabetic exchange: 2 milk, ⅛ fruit, 13 bread, 1½ meat, 6⅓ fat.

Fishermen recognize when blue crabs are about to molt. The molting process takes about two hours. The soft-shell crab must be removed from the water within an hour or two of shedding its shell, or the new shell will begin hardening.

WOOD GIVES A SPECIAL TOUCH TO BAKED FISH

AMAZING FOOD FACTS

■

Whitefish is found in lakes and streams throughout North America. It is a member of the salmon family.

■ *How do you cook on a plank of wood?* The wood is first heated in an oven, then the fish is placed on top and returned to the oven.

■ *Will any wood do?* The best wood on which to cook is oak, about 1 inch thick and a little larger than the fillet. Avoid resinous woods such as pine, which will release a very strong flavor to the fish, as well as any wood that has been treated with chemicals.

■ *Why it tastes so good:* Heated wood releases its own natural aroma, which delicately seasons the fish. This flavor, along with a dusting of herbs or spices, complements the fish.

■ *Tricks of the trade:* Just as a good pan gets better when seasoned, so does the wood. I heat the plank the first time, then rub the cooking side with a little olive oil.

■ *Preparing your fish:* Planking works best for medium to thick

TODAY'S LESSON: Spring lake fish, with firm, rich flesh from cold winter waters, are terrific. We'll cook fish fillets on a plank of aromatic wood, which adds flavor without fat.

fillets. Whitefish, salmon, pickerel, sauger, walleye and pike are terrific planked.

Remove all the bones and any fatty belly tissue. Do not remove the skin — it helps retain the moisture. Season the exposed flesh side with sea salt, freshly ground pepper, spices and herbs to your taste. These seasonings also seal the surface of the fish to retain more of its delicate moisture.

For spices, I prefer a little paprika, cayenne, ground fennel or dill seed. Fresh herbs such as chives, scallions, tarragon and parsley are great. Greens such as sorrel, mustard and arugula will complement the fish. Sprinkle the spices across the exposed fish surfaces before baking.

■ *The cooking begins:* Heat the plank in a preheated 400-degree oven until hot. Place the fish with its skin side on the board. Return the plank to the oven and cook until done, about 10-15 minutes depending on fillet size.

■ *For 1 or 2 servings:* Try using oak shakes or shingles — the nontreated variety, of course. Start by broiling the fish on the plank then turning the oven from broil to bake (or transfer to a preheated 400-degree oven), and cook until done. The thinner wood shake will release its wood flavor quickly under the broiler and is perfect for smaller gatherings.

How to clean the board: The plank should be quickly washed with a stiff brush in hot, soapy water and thoroughly rinsed, without allowing it to sit and soak up excess water.

It should be dried with clean paper towels, then allowed to air-dry or returned to the oven until the moisture is gone.

■ *Serving suggestions:* The flavor is sublime just as is but may be enhanced with a squirt of lemon or lime. Of course, the planked fish will stand up to more serious sauces that are complemented by the slightly smoky flavor.

■

PLANKED SPICED WHITEFISH

Makes 4 servings

2 planks of wood large enough to accommodate a jumbo fillet of whitefish

2 jumbo whitefish fillets, about 16 ounces each, cleaned of all bones and fatty tissue

Sea salt to taste

Freshly ground black or white pepper to taste

1 teaspoon paprika

2 teaspoons ground fennel seed

2 tablespoons snipped fresh chives

2 tablespoons chopped fennel green or dill weed

2 tablespoons chopped flat leaf parsley

2 large sprigs of flat leaf parsley for garnish

2 lemons cut into crowns or in half for garnish

Preheat oven to 400 degrees.

Place the boards on the lower rack of the oven until hot, about 15 minutes. Remove the boards to a cake rack. Place one fillet of whitefish on each board, skin side on the wood. Season the fish with salt and pepper to taste. Sprinkle the paprika and fennel seed evenly across the fillets. In a small bowl, combine chives, fennel or dill greens, and chopped parsley. Sprinkle the herbs over the fish. Return the oak planks to the oven and cook until the fish is done, about 15 minutes, depending on the thickness of the fillets. Remove the planks and gar-

nish with the sprigs of parsley and lemon crowns.

To serve, squeeze the lemons over the fillets.

To serve on plates, slide a metal spatula between the skin and the flesh, separating the flesh from the skin, and transfer to warm serving plates. Garnish the fish with the sprigs of parsley.

Cook's notes: The plank should be grooved to retain the natural juices.

Fish can be planked for cooking on the grill, too. The plank must be placed at an angle toward the fire and should be turned once so the fish is cooked evenly. Brush with basting sauce or oil during cooking. Whole fillets can be tied with twine or stainless steel wire to the plank, then suspended over the fire by piles of bricks or a rod.

Nutrition details per serving
Calories 323
Percent of calories from fat 38%
Fat: .14 gm
Protein: . . . . .44 gm
Carbohydrate: . . . . .7 gm
Cholesterol: . . . . .136 mg
Sodium: . . . . .121 mg
Diabetic exchange: 5¾ lean meat.

■

Whitefish produces the only golden caviar or roe. It is a delicacy, but not of the same quality as sturgeon caviar.

**AMAZING
FOOD FACTS**

■

Fresh Atlantic
halibut is more
readily available
in the spring,
when there is
an active
rookery off
Nova Scotia,
and in early fall,
when some
swordfish boats
hunt for halibut.

THE BEST BROILED FISH

TODAY'S LESSON: Broiling fish is one of the cleanest and easiest methods to prepare fish in your home. Here are the tricks for broiling to perfection.

■ *Health advantages:* The high top heat of broiling allows the fish to cook without additional fat, while slightly searing the surface to capture all the delicate, moist flavor.

■ *Selecting your fish:* Broiling will bring out the best of just about any fish, but it is best with less dense fillets of fish. These thinner fillets or slices will cook quickly under the intense heat with the right amount of surface searing. Thicker, denser fillets will cook longer and may become dry.

■ *Prepare your fish:* Trim all the connective tissue from the fillet, including the darker fat tissue. The skin may be removed before or after broiling. Remove any remaining bones from the fillet with needle-nose pliers or hemostats. Keep refrigerated until time to cook.

■ *Put some spice in your life:* The simple fish fillet may be dusted with ground spices. Everything from Cajun blackening powder to a couple of grinds of black pepper will pick up the flavor. Dry spices work best under the intense heat and won't burn unless the heat source is too close to the fish.

Liquid seasonings such as Tabasco and barbecue sauces are best added in the last couple of minutes to prevent burning.

■ *Broiling technique:* To broil, place your fish on an oven-proof pan. Rub the surface of the fish with olive oil and spices to taste. Cook for about 8 minutes. Look for moisture beads to determine doneness. Most fish will retain its natural color when cooked, with little or no browning. If you prefer the brown surface color, dust with paprika before broiling, or bread the fish.

■ *Tricks of the trade:* The skin may be left on the fish fillet, which will stick to the broiling pan when cooked and is simply removed by inserting a metal spatula between skin and fish after cooking.

■ *Mix and match:* Broiled fish is best accentuated by bright, citrus-flavored sauces and mild herbs. Cream sauces are wonderful, but keep them light.

WHITEFISH WITH CITRUS AIOLI

Makes 4 servings

½ cup lemon juice

1 cup orange juice

1 large egg yolk

1 tablespoon Dijon mustard

½ cup virgin olive oil

Salt to taste

Tabasco sauce to taste

Freshly ground white pepper

¾ cup chopped fresh parsley

¼ cup snipped fresh chives (optional)

4 whitefish fillets, about 8 ounces each, boned and trimmed

Mild paprika to dust the fish (optional)

Sprigs of parsley for garnish

Preheat the broiler. In a small saucepan, combine the lemon and orange juices and bring to a simmer over high heat. Cook until reduced to ¼ cup, about 7 minutes. Cool. In the bowl of a mixer, combine the reduced citrus, egg yolk and mustard. With mixer on high speed, gradually add olive oil in a steady stream. Season with salt and Tabasco or white pepper. Add the parsley and chives. Refrigerate aioli until ready to use.

Season the whitefish with salt, pepper and a generous dusting of paprika. Place on an ovenproof broiler pan. Cook in the broiler until done, about 8 minutes, depending on thickness. Insert a thin spatula between the fish and the skin and discard the skin. Invert fish and remove the dark fatty tissue. Position the whitefish on serving plates. Spoon a little aioli over the fish, garnish with parsley sprigs and serve.

Nutrition details per serving
Calories .503
Percent of calories from fat 57%
Fat: . . . . .32 gm
Protein: . . . . .43 gm
Carbohydrate: . . . . .10 gm
Cholesterol: . . . . .205 mg
Sodium: . . . . .487 mg
Diabetic exchange: ⅓ fruit, 6 meat, 6 fat.

HALIBUT WITH CITRUS, CAPERS & CHIVE SALSA

Makes 4 servings

½ cup nonpareil capers, drained

¼ cup snipped fresh chives

1 red bell pepper, roasted, peeled, seeded and diced

3 tablespoons fresh lemon juice

1 clove garlic, minced

½ cup virgin olive oil, divided

Salt to taste

Tabasco sauce to taste

4 halibut fillets or steaks, about 8 ounces each

Pepper to taste

Sprigs of chives for garnish

Preheat broiler. To make salsa, combine the capers, chives, pepper, lemon juice, garlic and ½ cup of the olive oil in a medium-size bowl. Season to taste with salt and Tabasco. Refrigerate until ready to use.

Lightly rub the surfaces of the halibut with the remaining olive oil and lightly season with salt and pepper. Place on an ovenproof broiler pan. Place in the broiler and cook until done, about 8 minutes, depending on thickness of fillet.

Position halibut on serving plates. Spoon a little salsa over the fish; garnish with the chive sprigs and serve.

Nutrition details per serving
Calories .496
Percent of calories from fat 59%
Fat: . . . . .32 gm
Protein: . . . . .48 gm
Carbohydrate: . . . . .3 gm
Cholesterol: . . . . .72 mg
Sodium: . . . . .390 mg
Diabetic exchange: ⅓ vegetable, 6¾ meat, 5¾ fat.

AMAZING FOOD FACTS

■

The European perch is somewhat larger but otherwise similar to our yellow perch. Other members of the perch family include walleye and sauger.

■

The white perch family includes striped bass and giant sea bass.

■ *Why does it taste so good?* The high heat of the skillet sears and crisps the light dusting of flour. This toasted flavor on the exterior of the fish creates a wonderful aroma as well as a crisp coating perfect for the tender sweet fish fillet inside.

PERCH: ANOTHER REASON TO SAVOR SPRING

■ *The best of the season:* The famous yellow perch is at its peak in the spring along with its cousins the walleye, pickerel and sauger. They have incredibly sweet flesh that is absolutely perfect for sauteing.

■ *Health advantages:* If you cook in canola or olive oil in a nonstick skillet, a crisp exterior can be produced without all the fat of traditional sauteing. Canola has a more neutral flavor, but the olive oil tastes pretty good to me. Or forget the health angle, go for the fla-

TODAY'S LESSON: A fresh-caught fish in a skillet is the perfect method for capturing that fresh flavor. I'll show you the tricks for perfect sauteing of fish.

vor and use clarified butter. Clarified butter will stand up to the high heat and accentuate the nutty flavor of the flour coating.

■ *How to select:* Yellow perch may be found at fish markets in single or butterfly fillets. The butterfly fillets are two fillets connected by the belly skin. They have a slightly larger proportion of skin to meat than the single fillets, which means they will cost more than single fillets.

Select perch with flesh that is translucent, not white or cloudy. The perch should smell sweet, never fishy. Buy about 8-10 ounces per person, which yields about 6-8 ounces when cleaned. True yellow perch has an olive-colored back, blending

into golden-yellow sides and white bellies. Ocean perch have reddish skin.

■ *How to prepare:* Removing the skin improves the fish's delicate texture. Place the fillets skin side down on a cleanable cutting board. Select a thin, flexible, very sharp knife. Secure the tail skin with your fingers and insert the knife blade away from your fingers, perpendicular to the fillet and parallel to the skin. Quickly move the knife away from your hand, thus removing the fillet from the skin. Check the belly section for bones and remove as necessary.

Remove any large bones from the center of the fillets. Keep the fish well chilled in the refrigerator, but not in contact with water or ice, until ready to serve.

■ *The cooking begins:* Start by heating the skillet over medium-high heat with a small amount of mild fat, such as clarified butter, canola oil or pure olive oil (extra-virgin isn't necessary for sauteing). Take the fish fillets, lightly dip in an egg wash just to moisten, drain well, then dust with your seasoned flour. Carefully lay the fillets in the pan, placing the side that had the skin up. Cook until golden, about 2 minutes. Turn over and cook until crisp, about 1-2 minutes depending on the thickness of the fillets. Transfer to paper toweling to drain. Season with a sprinkle of salt and freshly ground pepper to taste. Serve immediately.

■ *For that fresh sauteed flavor:* Pour off any remaining cooking fat, carefully wipe the pan clean with a wad of paper toweling before cooking the next batch. Otherwise, the flavor of the fish will be overcome by the slight off-taste of the used oil.

■ *Serving suggestions:* Sauces and condiments high in acid provide bright flavor that contrasts perfectly with the sweet flesh. Delicate new potatoes are a perfect traditional garnish when boiled and tossed in fresh chopped parsley.

■ *Mix and match:* Select a crispy vegetable such as asparagus or snow peas to contrast the delicate perch texture.

■
Yellow perch are readily caught by the uncounted millions throughout the year, especially in the spring and winter.

Sauteing is the cooking method that relies on the conductive transfer of heat, the direct movement of energy from the pan to the meat. Enough fat or oil is added to the pan to prevent sticking.

LAKE PERCH WITH RED TARTAR SAUCE

Makes 4 servings

2 cups all-purpose flour

2 tablespoons paprika

1 teaspoon salt

¾ teaspoon freshly ground white pepper

2 large eggs, lightly beaten

1 cup milk

2 pounds lake perch fillets, skinned

¼ cup clarified butter or corn oil

2 lemons cut into wedges for garnish

Parsley for garnish

1 cup Red Tartar Sauce (see accompanying recipe)

In a medium-size bowl, sift together the flour, paprika, salt and pepper.

In another medium-size bowl, combine the eggs and milk. Drench the fillets in the egg-and-milk mixture, then shake off any excess and dredge them in seasoned flour.

Coat evenly, then shake to remove excess flour.

In a large skillet over high heat, warm the butter or corn oil until just about smoking. Lay in the perch, one by one, cooking them until golden, about 2 minutes. Turn the fillets over, cooking until done, about 1 minute. Remove to a rack or paper towels to drain. Repeat with the remaining pieces.

Mound the fillets on serving plates, garnish with the lemons and parsley, and serve with the Red Tartar Sauce.

Nutrition details per serving
Calories 670
Percent of calories from fat 31%
Fat: . . . . .23 gm
Protein: . . . . .58 gm
Carbohydrate: . . . . .59 gm
Cholesterol: . . . . .517 mg
Sodium: . . . . .757 mg
Diabetic exchange: ¼ milk, ⅜ fruit, 3⅛ bread, 6¼ meat, 3½ fat.

RED TARTAR SAUCE

Makes 2 cups

2 large egg yolks

1 tablespoon Dijon-style mustard

¼ cup fresh lemon juice

1 cup corn oil

2 red peppers, roasted, peeled, seeded and diced

1 poblano pepper, roasted, peeled, seeded and diced (or substitute green bell pepper for a milder flavor)

2 tablespoons diced red onion

¼ cup capers, drained and minced, optional

1 tablespoon minced scallion greens

1 tablespoon minced fresh parsley

¼ teaspoon salt

Tabasco to taste

In a food processor, combine the yolks, mustard and lemon juice. While the food processor is still running, gradually add the corn oil in a steady stream, until thickened. Add half the red peppers, pureeing until smooth. Stop the processor, add the remaining ingredients and pulse to combine. Adjust salt and Tabasco to taste. Refrigerate until ready to use. Can be made up to four days ahead.

Nutrition details per serving
Calories 529
Percent of calories from fat 95%
Fat: . . . . .57 gm
Protein: . . . . .2 gm
Carbohydrate: . . . . .4 gm
Cholesterol: . . . . .107 mg
Sodium: . . . . .322 mg
Diabetic exchange: ½ vegetable, ¼ meat, 11⅓ fat.

DELICATE SAUGER PROVIDES A MEAL OF TEXTURAL CONTRAST

■ *What is it?* The sauger, well known to some anglers, often masquerades under such aliases as sauger pike, river pike and spotfin pike. It is a close cousin of the walleye, also known as pickerel.

■ *How to prepare:* Skin sauger to prepare for cooking. With a sharp knife, carefully trim away with the bones, the darker, fattier tissues and the belly portion. Run your finger across fillets from tail to head to locate and raise the remaining bones. Remove the bones with pliers.

■ *The cooking begins:* I prefer to egg-wash and lightly dust the fillets with seasoned flour, then saute. Sauteing creates a crunchy crust that is a perfect contrast to the delicate-textured fish.

■

SAUGER WITH LEMON & CAPERS

Makes 4 servings

2   cups all-purpose flour
2   tablespoons paprika
1   teaspoon salt
¾   teaspoon freshly ground white pepper
2   large eggs, lightly beaten
1   cup milk
2   pounds sauger fillets, skinned
½   stick unsalted butter
¼   cup lemon juice
½   cup nonpareil capers
2   lemons, cut into wedges or crowns, for garnish
4   parsley sprigs, for garnish

In a medium-size bowl, sift together the flour, paprika, salt and pepper. In another medium-size bowl, combine the eggs and milk. Drench fillets in the egg-milk mixture, then shake off any excess and dredge in the seasoned flour. Coat evenly, then shake to remove excess flour.

In a large skillet over high heat, warm the butter until bubbling. Put in the fillets one by one to fill the pan. Cook until golden, about 2 minutes. Turn the fillets over, cooking until done, about 2 minutes. Remove to a rack or paper toweling to drain. Keep the fillets warm in an oven. Repeat with the remaining fillets. Keep the pan with the remaining cooking butter on the heat. Add the lemon juice and capers and cook for 1 minute. Remove from the heat.

Place the fillets on serving plates and spoon a little of the caper butter atop each. Garnish the plates with lemon crowns and parsley. Serve with Crispy Cole Slaw (see recipe on page 53).

Nutrition details per serving
Calories .606
Percent of calories from fat 27%
Fat: .18 gm
Protein: . . . . .52 gm
Carbohydrate: . . . . .60 gm
Cholesterol: . . . . .271 mg
Sodium: . . . . .799 mg
Diabetic exchange: ¼ milk, ½ fruit, 3⅛ bread, 6 meat, 2½ fat.

■
Sauger is a smaller version of the walleye. It has excellent flesh — sweet, finely flaked, very white and lean.

CRAYFISH: LOBSTER'S AFFORDABLE STAND-IN

■ *What they are:* These lobster-like freshwater crustaceans, with their rich flavor and resilient texture, are a great delicacy. I even like them better than lobster in some dishes.

■ *How to select and store:* The best bet is to buy fresh, cleaned crayfish tails. They come with and without "fat," the Southern name for the crayfish tomalley, or liver. The "fat" is highly revered for the distinct flavor it adds to the sauce. Store crayfish meat at 35 degrees, if possible buried in ice over a drain pan to ensure freshness. Tail meat with the fat has a shorter shelf life, so use within 48 hours. Crayfish meat freezes well.

■ *How to use it:* You can substitute crayfish in any recipe that calls for lobster. Because the crayfish already have been cooked, they just need a thorough heating to finish.

■ *Tricks of the trade:* Buy the tail meat with fat. Once your

TODAY'S LESSON: The annual crayfish harvest starts with farm-raised crayfish and continues through the wild harvest in May.

sauce and garnishes are perfect, stir the fat in to enrich and return to a boil. Add the tail meat for one short boil and remove from the heat. The stored heat energy will finish the reheating or cooking of the crayfish and maintain its silky texture.

■ *The cooking begins:* To cook crayfish, add them as your dish is finishing to allow the crayfish to warm and exchange some flavors. This technique ensures the delicate texture will be preserved.

Longer cooking tends to dry them out and make them a little chewy. Dry heat methods such as grilling or broiling also dry out the meat. Crayfish work well in fricassees, gumbos, stews or other dishes with sauces. They also are perfect for ravioli, wontons and seafood cakes in which the meat is enclosed during cooking. The flavor really comes through, and the resilient texture is maintained.

■ *Mix and match:* Crayfish have a terrific rich flavor that can stand up to spices. They take the heat of hot peppers with ease, while lobster's flavor is killed. Crayfish are great with saffron, coriander, cumin, garlic, tomato and just about every fresh herb. Use your imagination and enjoy.

CRAYFISH WITH ANGEL HAIR PASTA

Makes 4 servings

1 tablespoon roasted garlic, peeled, ends removed, minced

   Oil for roasting

1 cup clam juice

1 cup dry white wine

2 cups whipping cream

1 tablespoon tomato paste

   Salt to taste

   Freshly ground white pepper to taste

3 tablespoons fresh chopped basil or 1 teaspoon dried

3 tablespoons snipped fresh chives, or 1 teaspoon dried

1 tablespoon grated lemon rind (yellow part only, no white)

¾ pound angel hair pasta

1½ pounds cooked crayfish tail meat

1 red bell pepper, roasted, peeled, seeded and diced

½ cup grated Parmesan cheese

To roast garlic: Preheat oven to 400. In a large ovenproof skillet, combine a whole head of garlic with enough oil to coat. Place on the lower rack of the oven and cook until the skin is brown and the head is tender, about 30-60 minutes, depending on size. Let cool. With a little pressure from your hand, the cloves will come easily out of their skin. You may cover tightly and refrigerate leftover roasted garlic with or without the skin for up to three days.

To make sauce: In a medium saucepan, combine the clam juice and white wine over medium-high heat. Bring to a simmer and cook until reduced by half to 1½ cups, about 6 minutes. Add the cream and cook until thickened to coat the back of a spoon, about 10 minutes. Whisk in the tomato paste. Adjust the salt and pepper to taste. Remove from the heat. In a small bowl, combine the roasted minced garlic, basil, chives and lemon rind until well mixed. Reserve.

Cook the pasta according to package directions. Transfer to a strainer to drain.

Meanwhile, return the sauce to a simmer over high heat. Add the crayfish, cooking until hot, about 3 minutes. Transfer to a larger bowl. Add the herb mixture, pasta and red pepper. Toss to combine. Arrange the pasta onto warm serving plates. Sprinkle with the cheese.

Nutrition details per serving
Calories .819
Percent of calories from fat 55%
Fat: .50 gm
Protein: . . . . .44 gm
Carbohydrate: . . . . .38 gm
Cholesterol: . . . . .406 mg
Sodium: . . . . .880 mg
Diabetic exchange: 1¼ vegetable, 1½ bread, 5½ meat, 9 fat.

Louisiana is the leading crayfish farming state, harvesting more than 20 million tons per year. Alabama, Arkansas, Mississippi and Texas are also significant producers of farmed crayfish.

Crayfish are also plentiful in streams, rivers and lake shallows from Wisconsin to Maine.

■

Many crayfish are shipped alive, packed in onion bags that weigh between 30 and 50 pounds. If the bags are kept chilled, the crayfish can survive up to four days. Sometimes the crayfish are kept in tanks before shipping long enough to excrete the food in their stomachs.

■

CRAYFISH CAKES WITH TOMATO-MINT SALSA

Makes 4 servings

½ pound sea scallops, foot removed

1 large egg white

½ pound (2 sticks) plus 1 tablespoon unsalted butter, divided

½ teaspoon salt

¼ teaspoon fresh ground white pepper

1 tablespoon tomato paste

4 cloves garlic, roasted and minced

1 cup heavy cream

½ pound crayfish, evenly sized

¼ cup chopped cilantro
   Bread crumbs
   Tomato-Mint Salsa (see accompanying recipe)
   Mint leaves for garnish

In a food processor, puree the scallops. Add the egg and continue to puree until smooth. Refrigerate. With a mixer, cream 1 stick of the butter, salt and pepper. Gradually add the scallop puree, mixing until homogeneous. Add the tomato paste and the garlic. With the mixer on slow speed, gradually add the cream until just incorporated. (Do not overwork the mousse, or it will become grainy.) Fold in the crayfish and cilantro. Form into 8 cakes and coat with bread crumbs. Place on a cookie sheet lined with parchment paper and refrigerate for at least 2 hours. In a heavy skillet, heat the remaining butter over medium-high heat. Add the cakes (breading again if necessary) and cook until golden, about 3 minutes. Turn over and cover the skillet. Cook until done, about 5 minutes. Remove and drain on paper towels. Spoon the salsa onto the center of the serving plate. Position 2 crayfish cakes atop the salsa. Garnish the plate with mint leaves and serve.

Nutrition details per serving
Calories .849
Percent of calories from fat 77%
Fat: .73 gm
Protein: . . . . .26 gm
Carbohydrate: . . . . .24 gm
Cholesterol: . . . . .306 mg
Sodium: . . . . .673 mg
Diabetic exchange: ⅜ vegetable, 1¼ bread, 3 meat, 14 fat.

■

TOMATO-MINT SALSA

4 large, vine-ripened tomatoes

1 tablespoon chili powder, mixed with a little water, just enough to make a paste

3 tablespoons fresh lime juice

¼ cup virgin olive oil

2 tablespoons chopped mint
   Salt to taste
   Freshly ground black pepper to taste
   Puree of Chipotle chilis

Blanch the tomatoes in a small pan of boiling water for 10 seconds to loosen the skins. Remove the skins with a paring knife. Cut the tomato in half horizontally and squeeze out the seeds. Dice the tomatoes into ¼-inch pieces.
In a small bowl, combine the tomatoes, rehydrated chili powder, lime juice, olive oil and mint. Add salt, pepper and Chipotle puree to taste. Refrigerate until ready to serve.

Cook's note: Puree of Chipotle chilis is available at most specialty stores.

Nutrition details per serving
Calories 43
Percent of calories from fat 50%
Fat: . . . . .3 gm
Protein: . . . . .1 gm
Carbohydrate: . . . . .5 gm
Cholesterol: . . . . .0 mg
Sodium: . . . . .20 mg
Diabetic exchange: ⅓ vegetable, ⅜ fat.

■

CRISPY COLE SLAW

Makes 10 servings

1   cup sugar
2   teaspoons salt
1   tablespoon ground caraway
1   tablespoon freshly ground black pepper
1   head red or green cabbage
½   cup cider vinegar
½   cup red wine vinegar
½   cup virgin olive oil

In a small bowl, combine the sugar, salt, caraway and pepper. Shred the cabbage about 1/16 inch thick. Spread a thin layer of the cabbage over a large colander. Sprinkle with some of the spice mix. Repeat with layers of cabbage and spice mix until both are used up. Allow to weep for 4 hours. Transfer to a large bowl and add the vinegars and olive oil. Mix well. Refrigerate overnight. Mix again, then adjust the salt and pepper to your taste. Serve.

Nutrition details per serving
Calories 201
Percent of calories from fat 47%
Fat: .11 gm
Protein: . . . . .0.8 gm
Carbohydrate: . . . . .27 gm
Cholesterol: . . . . .0 mg
Sodium: . . . . .439 mg
Diabetic exchange: ½ vegetable, 1⅜ bread, 2 fat.

Preparing crayfish

Wash thoroughly in salted water and let soak for 5 - 8 minutes. Stir gently to get rid of grit.

Lift the crayfish out of the pan, pour off water, rinse any grit and return them to the pan.

Pour boiling water over crayfish and let stand 10 minutes.

When cool enough to handle, separate the heads from the tails.

Remove the bright orange fat from the head with a small knife and reserve if desired.

Remove the tail meat from the shell and carefully pull out the veins.

■

The Pacific crayfish is abundant in the slow-moving rivers of Oregon, Washington and northern California.

■

Crayfish must be handled quickly and kept cold to avoid melanosis, or darkening of the meat. The flavor and texture are not affected; only the appearance is altered.

GUMBO IS A MEAL IN ITSELF

■ *Why it tastes so good:* There are as many gumbos as there are cooks, so each recipe has its own intricacies. The secret to great gumbo is the marriage of flavors from the wide range of ingredients, especially the seafood and the sausage.

■ *Gumbo basics:* There are two principal types of gumbo — those thickened with okra and those thickened with file powder (dried sassafras leaves). Both versions are initially thickened with a roux, a combination of cooked flour and oil, at the beginning of the preparation. In okra versions, the vegetable releases a juice when cooked that thickens the gumbo. Okra once was used only in spring and summer, when the vegetable was available, but now it can be used year-round with frozen okra.

In file versions, the powder is added at the last second to thicken the gumbo. File powder turns stringy if boiled.

TODAY'S LESSON: Gumbos, perhaps the most famous use for crayfish, are terrific, full-bodied stews from southern Louisiana. In spring down there, fresh seafood, tender poultry and spicy sausage join in harmony to revitalize the spirit after winter. Today's lesson shows the secrets of making good gumbo at home.

■ *Preparing your roux:* The traditional roux calls for equal parts flour to oil, but you can get by with about one-third of the oil. Start with a heavy, small, oven-proof saucepan, heating the oil over medium-high heat. Add the flour slowly, while whisking until the flour and oil are combined. Transfer the entire pan to a preheated 375-degree oven, stirring occasionally, and bake until golden, about 20-30 minutes. Remove from the heat and transfer to a large heavy pot.

■ *The cooking begins:* Add your vegetables to the roux over medium-high heat and cook until tender. Add the stock of your choice, such as seafood or chicken or both, and then add the sausage. Bring to a simmer. Add seared poultry, ham and spices, and cook until tender and thickened, about 1½-2 hours.

■ *Tricks of the trade:* Although the poultry, sausage and shellfish need time to cook, keep an eye on them to ensure they don't overcook. I remove these ingredients when they are just about done, keep them covered on the side so they don't dry out, then add them back to the gumbo just at the finish. Tender seafood such as oysters, scallops, crab meat and cooked fish or cooked shellfish are added just at the end so their delicate textures are preserved.

■ *The finish:* As the gumbo finishes cooking, start adding the final ingredients according to the time they need to cook, such as shrimp, then scallops and oysters last. This will ensure great flavor and optimal texture for all of the ingredients. Remove from the heat, and add the file powder just before ladling into serving bowls.

■ *Mix and match:* Pairing seafood and poultry can be a little tricky, so go by your own tastes. Chicken goes with shrimp, crayfish, lobster, crab and most firmer shellfish. Duck and squirrel go well with delicate shellfish such as oysters and scallops. If you aren't a fan of seafood, try the poultry and sausage combinations.

■

CRAYFISH, CHICKEN & SAUSAGE GUMBO

Serves 6 as a main course

2 tablespoons olive oil
½ pound chicken breast or thigh meat, skin, fat and any bones removed, cut into ½-inch dice
¾ cup all-purpose flour
1 medium onion, peeled, ends removed, chopped
4 cloves garlic, peeled, ends removed, minced
1 red pepper, washed, cored, seeded, chopped
1 green pepper, washed, cored, seeded, chopped
½ cup celery, washed, ends removed, chopped
6 cups fish stock or light poultry stock, heated
½ pound Italian fennel sausage, cut into ¼-inch dice
2 bay leaves
½ teaspoon dried thyme

½ teaspoon dried oregano
1 pound crayfish tails with head butter
   Salt, freshly ground black pepper to taste
   Ground cayenne pepper to taste
2 teaspoons file powder
6 cups freshly cooked long-grain white rice or basmati rice

Preheat oven to 375 degrees.

In a nonstick skillet, heat the olive oil over high heat until hot. Add the diced chicken just to sear, about 2 minutes. Remove to a colander over a bowl to drain and collect the olive oil. Transfer the olive oil back to the skillet and add the flour, whisking to combine. Heat until the mixture begins to bubble, then transfer to the lower rack of the oven. Cook until golden brown, about 20-30 minutes. Transfer to a large pot that will hold all the ingredients that will follow.

Place the pot with the cooked flour and oil, called a roux, over high heat. Add the onion and garlic and

cook until golden, about 8 minutes. Add the red and green peppers and the celery, cooking until tender, about 5 minutes. Stir the hot stock of your choice into the roux and vegetable mixture. Add the sausage, bay leaves, thyme and oregano. Return mixture to a boil. Reduce heat to a simmer and cook until thickened and the flavor develops, about 1½-2 hours. When thickened to sauce-like consistency, add the crayfish and the seared chicken meat, cooking just until thoroughly heated through to maintain their delicate texture, about 2-3 minutes. Remove the pot from the heat. Adjust the seasoning with salt, freshly ground black pepper and cayenne pepper to your taste and spice level. Stir in the file powder. Transfer to your soup tureen. Serve over steaming rice.

Nutrition details per serving
Calories .767
Percent of calories from fat 27%
Fat: . . . . .22 gm
Protein: . . . . .37 gm
Carbohydrate: . . . . .103 gm
Cholesterol: . . . . .152 mg
Sodium: . . . . .1,397 mg
Diabetic exchange: 6⅓ vegetables, 4½ bread, 4 meat, 3 fat.

SAVOR THE FLAVORS OF CORNED BEEF

AMAZING FOOD FACTS

■

Salt naturally inhibits the growth of microbes by drawing the moisture out of the bacteria and mold cells. The cells are killed or slowed down to limit their reproduction, minimizing spoiling.

■ *What is corned beef?* The term "corned" may seem odd, but it originated in the times of the Anglo-Saxon tribes of Britain, where beef was cured in rock salt crushed to the size of wheat kernels, commonly called "corns."

People have used salt to cure and preserve fish and meats for centuries. Refrigeration eliminated that need, but our lust for the cured flavors has continued. Today's curing is a major improvement from the original processes, which were 20-50 times saltier.

■ *How to "cure" corned beef:* The technique for corning is quite simple. Puncture the meat to draw off the blood and enhance the cure. The meat is then immersed in a saltwater brine with pickling spices and sometimes sodium nitrite under cool conditions for about 5-10 days, depending on size and thickness of the meat. After curing, the meats are rinsed and stored in a lighter holding brine, or cooked.

TODAY'S LESSON: Corned beef, cabbage and green beer are the classic trio of St. Patrick's Day. The combination of these piquant flavors framed by a heady dose of sharp mustard sauce satisfies the soul. Good friends in revelry match the spirit and the food of this celebration.

■ *The cooking begins:* Traditionally, the meat is cooked until almost falling apart, with cabbage, potatoes, onions and more pickling spices. This method is easy and sure, but the results tend to be ordinary and a little bland. The longer the cabbage cooks, the stronger the flavor and smell become, often overpowering the delicacies of the corned beef and accompaniments. I prefer to braise corned beef, which allows the tougher tissues to gently break down, resulting in very tender corned beef. The cabbage and other complementary vegetables are cooked separately, then combined just before serving. This allows the vegetable's individual characteristics to show through.

■ *Seasoning your corned beef:* The mustard sauce is the key to sublime corned beef. Mustard flavors diminish when cooked, so the condiment should be added to the sauce only at the last second, right before serving, to capture the aroma and fiery bite.

■ *Recycle the leftovers:* Corned beef hash, also called Red Flannel Hash for the comfort and warmth it imparts, is guaranteed to wake up the taste buds the day after St. Patrick's Day.

■

CORNED BEEF BRISKET WITH RAGOUT OF CABBAGE & MUSTARD

Makes 4 servings

4 pounds corned beef brisket, raw

1 cup pickling spice or to taste

1 large onion, cut into large pieces

2 pounds new potatoes, washed

6 tablespoons unsalted butter, divided

¼ cup chopped parsley

1 bottle beer

¾ cup heavy cream

Salt to taste

Freshly ground black pepper to taste

½ head young cabbage, cut into ¼-inch julienne

3 tablespoons grained mustard

2 tablespoons extra-strong Dijon mustard

¼ cup snipped fresh chives

4 sprigs of parsley for garnish

Preheat the oven to 375. In a large, ovenproof skillet, combine the corned beef, pickling spice and onion, and cover with water. Bring to a boil over high heat. Float a sheet of aluminum foil, dull side down, on the surface of the liquid.

Cover the skillet with a lid, place on the lower rack of the oven and cook until tender, about 1 hour and 45 minutes. The brisket is done when a skewer inserted into the thickest section of the meat is removed without resistance. Reserve liquid for making Red Flannel Corned Beef Hash.

In a large pot, combine the new potatoes and cold water. Bring to a simmer over high heat, cooking until tender, about 40 minutes. Drain. Peel the potatoes if you prefer. Just before serving, add 2 table-

spoons of the butter and the chopped parsley.

Meanwhile, in a large saucepan, bring the beer to a simmer, cooking until reduced to ½ cup. Add the cream and simmer until reduced to ¾ cup, about 10 minutes. Add salt and pepper to taste. Remove from heat.

In a large skillet, melt the remaining butter over high heat. Add the cabbage, cooking just until tender, about 5 minutes. Add the beer-cream mixture, cooking until it thickens to coat the cabbage, about 3 minutes. Remove from the heat. Stir in the mustards and chives.

Slice the corned beef. Spoon the cabbage and sauce onto the plate. Lay the corned beef slices across the cabbage. Garnish with parsley sprigs and serve with the parsleyed new potatoes.

Nutrition details per serving
Calories 1,593
Percent of calories from fat 62%
Fat: .110 gm
Protein: . . . . .91 gm
Carbohydrate: . . . . .55 gm
Cholesterol: . . . . .520 mg
Sodium: . . . . .5,358 mg
Diabetic exchange: 1⅓ vegetables,
2¾ bread, 11¼ meat, 14 fat.

■

Saltpeter, or potassium nitrate, was used to cure corned beef and other meats from the 16th Century until it was replaced by sodium nitrite in 1923. Nitrites may combine with amino acids and related compounds to form nitrosamines, known to cause cancer in animals.

Vitamin C has been found to improve the antibacterial characteristics of nitrites and reduce the formation of nitrosamines. Tomatoes, citrus and other sources could provide more than just flavor to your corned beef sandwich.

RED FLANNEL CORNED BEEF HASH

Makes 4 servings

2   tablespoons olive or canola oil, divided

1   green pepper, washed, stem removed, seeded and cut into ⅓-inch dice

1   large red onion, peeled, ends removed, cut into ⅓-inch dice

1¾ pounds cooked corned beef, trimmed of all fat and cut into ½-inch dice

1   cup cooking liquid from the corned beef

1   cup potatoes, boiled until tender, cut into ⅓-inch dice

2   tablespoons dry English mustard, preferably Coleman's

¼   cup Worcestershire sauce

    Tabasco to taste

¼   cup fine dried bread crumbs

4   poached eggs, optional

¼   cup chopped parsley for garnish

1   cup spicy tomato salsa, optional

In a large nonstick skillet, heat 1 tablespoon of the olive or canola oil over medium-high heat. Add the green pepper, cooking until the edges are slightly brown but still crisp, about 3 minutes. Remove to a strainer to drain.

Return the same skillet to the heat and add the remaining oil. Add the onion, cooking until the edges are caramelized, or browned and tender, about 5 minutes. Add the diced corned beef and the cooking liquid and return to a simmer. Cook until all the liquid is reduced to coat the corned beef, about 4 minutes.

Add the green peppers and potatoes, cooking for about 2 minutes. Remove to a strainer to drain. Transfer to a bowl. Sift the mustard across the mixture, add the Worcestershire, Tabasco and bread crumbs, delicately mixing to combine. (Add a few additional bread crumbs if the mixture seems wet.) Form the hash into 4 balls and refrigerate for about 30 minutes.

To serve, heat a 6- to 7-inch diameter nonstick pan over medium heat. Put the hash into the pan and flatten into a pancake shape with the back of a cooking spoon. Cook until browned on the bottom, about 7 minutes. Turn the hash over with a spatula, or place the entire pan in a preheated 400-degree oven to finish cooking, about 4 minutes. Turn the hash onto a cookie sheet and keep warm. Repeat with the remaining patties.

Position the finished hot hash in the center of the serving dish. Position the poached egg in the center of the hash and dust with a sprinkling of parsley. Serve spicy tomato salsa in a sauce boat.

Nutrition details per serving
Calories 762
Percent of calories from fat 60%
Fat: . . . . .50 gm
Protein: . . . . .46 gm
Carbohydrate: . . . . .29 gm
Cholesterol: . . . . .407 mg
Sodium: . . . . .3,155 mg
Diabetic exchange: 1 vegetable, 1 bread, 5¼ meat, 6¼ fat.

THE BEST LAMB COMES WITH THE SPRING

AMAZING FOOD FACTS

■

There are five grades of lamb, based on the proportion of fat to lean meat. Beginning with the best, they are prime, choice, good, utility and cull.

TODAY'S LESSON: Spring lamb is the most delicate and flavorful lamb of the year. The name is given to sheep born from February through May that arrive to market at the tender age of 1-3 months. These lambs have a diet of milk and fresh grasses, which provide a fuller flavor to the lamb than the hay of winter. This combination of fresh feed and young age produces an incredible fork-tender meat with light, sweet flavor.

■ *Why it is better:* Spring lambs produce small and delicate cuts. They're too young for significant fat development, allowing for a much leaner cut with more compact connective tissues. Throughout its growth, lamb produces none of the fat marbling that is common in prime beef. The fat occurs around the meaty muscles and, in mature animals, between the muscles. The fat may be trimmed away easily before cooking.

■ *Mix and match:* All of the cuts, from chops to roasts, are very tender at this age. But the leg is perfect because it is easy to prepare and a good size for Easter gatherings of 6-8 people. A roasted leg of lamb offers something for everyone — rare cuts close to the bone and more well-done cuts on the exterior.

■ *How to select spring lamb:* Select light red meat from flexible pink bones. Avoid mature lamb with dark red meat and yellowish fat from whitish bones. Searing the meat with high heat is essential to develop the rich robust flavor. High heat caramelizes the meat's natural amino acids and sugars to create the typical browning effect and intensify the wonderful taste and aroma.

■ *Preparing the leg:* Before cooking a leg of lamb, trim away all but the final layer of fat and connective tissue that covers the leg. The bone may be left intact, or removed and the meat tied into a roast.

■ *Season with care:* Lamb may be marinated in olive oil, spices, vegetables and herbs. Acid-based marinades such as wine or citrus will flavor lamb but also will break down the surface, resulting in a drier cut.

No meat animals have had as long and profound an association with civilized people as sheep and their offspring. Curly-horned wild sheep called mouflons, whose descendants still exist on Sardinia and Corsica, were domesticated tens of thousands of years ago in what is now Kurdistan.

■ *The cooking begins:* Be gentle when cooking young lamb. It is best cooked rare to medium-rare to preserve the moist and tender texture. Further cooking only makes it tough and dry.

■ *Cooking chops:* Thick chops are best when grilled over moderate to high temperatures to develop wonderful caramelized flavors. Thinner chops should be sauteed over high heat to sear in flavor. Large cuts are best roasted or braised. After your lamb is cooked, allow it to rest before serving — 2-4 minutes for smaller cuts such as chops and about 8 minutes for large roasts, to allow the juices to stabilize.

■ *Serving suggestions:* The juices from seasoned lamb and potatoes make a wonderful sauce. But if you prefer a more complex sauce, reduce the stock, add a splash of red wine and a few of the herbs used in seasoning the exterior of the lamb. Roasted cloves of garlic and shallots are perfect to flavor the sauce and act as garnish. Roast them on top of the potatoes for a gustatory punch

if you prefer more sauce strength.

Lamb is best served with the natural bitter greens of spring, such as dandelion, spinach, mache and watercress. Round out a spring menu with asparagus, served plain or with a gloss of butter.

Carve the lamb perpendicular to the bone in large, thin slices. Spoon any juices from the baking dish over lamb slices. Garnish each serving plate with a sprig of fresh herbs.

■

ROAST SPRING LEG OF LAMB

Makes 6-8 servings

1   leg of spring lamb, about 6-8 pounds, bone-in and trimmed of the fattier tissues

1   head fresh garlic, peeled, ends removed, thinly sliced

1   bunch fresh rosemary, washed, dried

2   tablespoons extra-virgin olive oil

4   large baking potatoes, peeled, eyes removed, sliced paper-thin

    Salt and freshly ground black pepper to taste

2   cups vegetable or light poultry stock

    Sprigs of fresh rosemary, parsley or mint for garnish

Preheat oven to 425. Place trimmed leg of lamb on a cutting board. Insert the tip of a paring knife at a 30-degree angle into the lamb to create a small incision, repeating every inch or so across the surface. Insert garlic and twigs of rosemary alternately in the pockets.

Put olive oil in large baking dish and turn the leg so that all sides are oiled. Place a layer of potatoes across the bottom. Season lightly with salt and pepper. Repeat until all potatoes have been used. Pour the stock across the potatoes just to moisten, not submerge.

Place lamb on top of potatoes. Season the lamb with a generous dusting of black pepper. Place baking dish on the lower rack of the oven and cook 15 minutes to sear. Turn oven temperature down to 375 if you prefer rarer lamb, or 325 degrees for well-done. Use a meat thermometer to determine when it's done. Remove from oven, and place pan on a cake rack to rest about 10 minutes before serving.

■

LAMB LOIN CHOPS WITH MINT PESTO & ARTICHOKES

Makes 4 servings

Salt

16 baby artichokes, trimmed

6 cloves garlic, roasted and minced, divided

¾ cup olive oil, divided

8 lamb loin chops, about 4 ounces each

1 cup fresh mint, chopped

½ cup parsley, chopped

¼ teaspoon black pepper

1 tablespoon balsamic vinegar

¼ cup whole mint leaves

In a large pot, bring at least 1 gallon of water to a boil. Add 2 tablespoons salt. Add the artichokes, cooking until just tender; test by inserting a skewer through the base. Drain the artichokes and allow to cool slightly. With a sharp knife, cut the artichoke into quarters lengthwise. Hold the artichoke quarter by the heart with the outer leaves down on the cutting board. Starting 1 inch from the top of the leaves, cut down through the artichoke, from the inside to the outside, until the knife encounters resistance by the outer leaves. Hold the knife stationary while peeling the heart and tender inner leaves from the outer leaves. Repeat with the remaining artichokes.

In a small bowl, combine 2 cloves of garlic and 2 tablespoons of the olive oil. Rub mixture on surfaces of lamb chops. Preheat grill or broiler.

In a blender, combine the remaining garlic and olive oil, mint, parsley and pepper. Puree until finely chopped. Add vinegar. Adjust salt to taste. Reserve at room temperature.

Place chops on the grill, cooking until well seared, about 5 minutes. Turn over and cook until desired temperature, about 4 minutes for medium-rare, depending on thickness.

Spoon pesto over chops. Garnish with mint leaves and serve.

Nutrition details per serving
Calories 976
Percent of calories from fat 38%
Fat: . . . . .40 gm
Protein: . . . . .130 gm
Carbohydrate: . . . . .16 gm
Cholesterol: . . . . .404 mg
Sodium: . . . . .602 mg
Diabetic exchange: ¼ vegetable, 5⅔ bread, 21½ meat, 4⅜ fat.

Nutrition details per serving
Calories 1,349
Percent of calories from fat 61%
Fat: . . . . .94 gm
Protein: . . . . .76 gm
Carbohydrate: . . . . .59 gm
Cholesterol: . . . . .227 mg
Sodium: . . . . .907 mg
Diabetic exchange: 11 vegetables, 8⅓ meat, 13⅔ fat.

FRUITS ARE PERFECT
IN COBBLERS

AMAZING FOOD FACTS

■

The peach tree originated in China, where it has been grown since the 5th Century B.C. It was introduced to Japan, then to Persia, where it was discovered by Alexander the Great. He in turn introduced the peach to the Greeks.

■ *Why cobblers taste so good:* The fresh, sweet fruit releases its juices into an intense, fragrant sauce, some of which is absorbed into the light and tender biscuit-like batter.

■ *Advantages:* Cobblers taste best when made with really ripe, mature fruit and berries, which are often not the most beautiful or perfect. Cobblers are great with bruised or irregular fruit. They are terrific to handle the surplus of berries and fruits from your yard, garden or local farmer's market.

■ *Tricks of the trade:* The first trick is to select the sweetest fruit by tasting it. You can usually get a great deal on blemished or surplus berries and fruits, especially close to closing time at a farmer's market. The second trick is to bake the fruit with sugar and spices without the crust, to allow even heat penetration. That will really get the fruit juices flowing and result in a silky,

TODAY'S LESSON: Fruit cobblers are among the best desserts to take advantage of the bounty of berries and stone fruits in season.

moist texture. The third trick is to make sure the pastry or batter does not touch the sides of the baking dish, which allows the steam to escape for thorough cooking of the fruit and also allows the sauce to develop. If you seal the baking dish with the pastry, your fruit will not cook, the sauce will be watery and the simple cobbler will become a complicated disaster.

■ *Fruits that work best:* Berries and fruits that are high in moisture content produce the best sauce. Use tart cherries and other small, moist fruits. Larger stone fruits such as nectarines, peaches and plums are perfect. Apricots, apples and firmer pears are less sweet and moist and thus produce less sauce, so you'll need to add

juice and more sugar for the best results.

■ *Preparing your fruit:* Berries and small fruits require just a quick rinse under cold water before being mixed with sugar and spices. Stone fruits may be peeled to remove coarse skins. Slice or dice your fruit, remove the pit and toss in lemon juice to retard browning before mixing.

■ *Season the cobbler:* The real concentration of flavor in a cobbler comes from the fruit, so add your spices and seasonings here. Try citrus rind such as lemon, orange and lime to pick up your fruit flavors. Spices such as ginger, cinnamon, nutmeg and vanilla are a perfect match. Be adventurous with unusual combinations such as green peppercorns, cassia and even herbs.

■ *The cooking begins:* Place the seasoned fruit in the baking dish and place on the lower rack of the oven. Cook the fruit until it begins to soften and the juices begin to weep. Gently mix to ensure even heat penetration. After a while, top with the pastry or batter, making sure it does *not* touch the sides of the baking dish. Bake until golden brown and the juices become thickened. Remove to a cake rack to cool to room temperature.

■ *Serving suggestions:* The intense fruit flavor of the slightly warm or room-temperature cobbler is hard to beat just by itself. Serve this delicacy with ice cream or a little whipped cream, and you have a masterpiece.

■ *Mix and match:* Fruits can be mixed for some outrageous combinations. Combine peaches with a sprinkling of raspberries, apricots with candied fresh ginger root or, for a taste of the exotic, papaya

with a dusting of whole green peppercorns and mint.

■ *Try your technique:* One of my all-time favorites is peaches and raspberries, which is easy and sure to thrill your guests this summer. But cobblers aren't just for summer. Keep this technique handy into the fall for cranberries, quince, persimmons and even the more tropical flavors of papaya, mango and pineapple.

■

PEACH & RASPBERRY COBBLER

Makes 6-8 servings

6 cups sliced fresh peaches
1¼ cups granulated sugar, divided
1 tablespoon orange peel
¼ teaspoon vanilla extract
1 tablespoon butter for pan
1 pint raspberries, cleaned
¼ cup mint leaves, picked whole, 6-8 reserved for garnish

1½ cups all-purpose flour
2 teaspoons baking powder
¼ teaspoon salt
6 tablespoons unsalted butter
1 egg, beaten
¼ cup buttermilk
4 scoops vanilla ice cream
Confectioners' sugar

Preheat oven to 400 degrees.
In a medium bowl, combine peaches, 1 cup sugar, orange peel and vanilla, tossing to combine. Butter a 9-by-9-inch baking dish. Place peach mixture in baking dish. Sprinkle the raspberries and mint through the peaches. Place baking dish in oven for 15 minutes.
Meanwhile, in a large bowl, combine flour, remaining ¼ cup sugar, baking powder and salt. Cut in the unsalted butter until well mixed. In a small bowl, combine beaten egg and buttermilk. Slowly add to the flour mixture by hand until mixed.
Remove the peaches from the oven. Spread the batter across the peaches to cover evenly, making sure it does not touch the edges of the baking

Peaches and nectarines are so closely related that seeds from either one can produce trees that bear either fruit (and occasionally both). Nectarines tend to be smaller and sweeter than peaches. The differences are growing slighter as agriculturists breed peaches with less fuzz.

dish. Return the cobbler to the oven and cook until golden, about 30 minutes.

Remove from the oven and place on a cake rack to cool.

Serve the cobbler by cutting into squares and scooping onto the center of the serving plates. Scoop the ice cream and position beside the cobbler. Dust with confectioners' sugar. Garnish with mint sprigs and serve.

Nutrition details per serving
Calories .447
Percent of calories from fat 30%
Fat: . . . . .15 gm
Protein: . . . . .6 gm
Carbohydrate: . . . . .75 gm
Cholesterol: . . . . .57 mg
Sodium: . . . . .279 mg
Diabetic exchange: 1⅛ fruit, 1¾ bread, ⅛ meat, 3 fat.

NECTARINE COBBLER

Makes 4 servings

1   tablespoon butter for pan

6   cups sliced fresh nectarines

1¼ cups granulated sugar, divided

1   teaspoon orange peel

¼   teaspoon vanilla extract

1½ cups all-purpose flour

2   teaspoons baking powder

¼   teaspoon salt

6   tablespoons unsalted butter

1   egg, beaten

½   cup buttermilk

4   scoops of vanilla ice cream

    Confectioners' sugar

    Sprigs of fresh mint for garnish

Preheat oven to 400. Place the nectarines in a buttered 9-by-9-inch baking dish. In a small bowl, combine 1 cup of the sugar, the orange rind and vanilla. Sprinkle over the nectarines. Place the dish in the oven for 15 minutes while making the dough.

In a large bowl, combine the flour, the remaining ¼ cup of sugar, baking powder and salt. Using a pastry blender or two knives, cut in the butter until well mixed. Combine the egg and the buttermilk, then slowly add to the dry ingredients by hand until mixed. Remove the nectarines from the oven. Spread the batter across the nectarines to cover. Make sure the batter doesn't touch the edges of the baking dish.

Return the cobbler to the oven and cook until golden, about 30 minutes. Remove to a cake rack to cool. Serve the cobbler by cutting into squares and scooping onto the center of the serving plates. Scoop the ice cream and position beside the cobbler. Dust with confectioners' sugar. Garnish with sprigs of mint and serve.

Nutrition details per serving
Calories .944
Percent of calories from fat 24%
Fat: . . . . .27 gm
Protein: . . . . .15 gm
Carbohydrate: . . . . .170 gm
Cholesterol: . . . . .129 mg
Sodium: . . . . .510 mg
Diabetic exchange: ⅛ milk, 2¾ fruit, 4⅜ bread, ¼ meat, 5 fat.

SPRING RHUBARB IS BEST IN DESSERTS

The leaves of rhubarb contain large amounts of oxalic acid and are poisonous.

■ *What is it?* Rhubarb, a perennial, requires winter frost to produce tender stalks in the spring. The plant loves the cool spring weather which slowly brings the stalks to tender maturity. Rhubarb grown from seed will take three springs to reach full foliage and has a hearty production for about 10 years. The stalks emerge from root bases called crowns or corms and are best when harvested at about 12-18 inches. Only half of the stalks should be harvested, allowing the remainder to regenerate the roots for the next year's production.

■ *How to select:* Choose crisp, firm, cherry-red stalks when field-grown or light pink stalks if hothouse-raised. The stalks should be free of blemishes, with the leaves still attached. Avoid pale, limp stalks.

■ *How to store*: The stalks can be stored wrapped in moistened paper toweling and enclosed by a plastic bag for

TODAY'S LESSON: The crimson stalks of the leafy rhubarb plant paint a red relief to the green early spring foliage. Although the crimson color may remind you of strawberries, you won't be confused by rhubarb's acidic flavor, so sharp that it must be sprinkled with sugar to be made palatable. Rhubarb is best cooked in pies, tarts and preserves as a spring substitute for the sweeter tree fruit of summer. After winter, rhubarb is a welcome break for the palate.

up to about a week. Remove the leaves just before using for the best results.

■ *When to use:* The first rhubarb of the season is best for making pies, tarts and other desserts. As the field temperatures begin to rise, the rhubarb will become more coarse. Use the warm-weather rhubarb for preserves and

other longer-cooking-time preparations that will give the fibrous texture time to break down further.

■ *How to cook:* The traditional method of cooking rhubarb is to coat it with sugar and spices and bake in a pie or flan. The oven cooking tenderizes the rhubarb while developing the natural gelatinous texture of

The name "rhubarb" comes from the Greeks, who called this plant the vegetable of barbarians beyond the Volga River. Rhubarb is native to the southeast part of Russia and is known to have been cultivated in Italy since the 17th Century. It was introduced to America just after the Revolutionary War.

the pulp for the pie filling.

Stewing with sugar and spices is the typical method for preserves. Strawberry is a natural flavor combination. Other sweet fruits that need acidity to round out their flavor are good combinations as well.

Saute rhubarb in butter to soften, then add sugar and a splash of brandy for crepes, waffles and even ice cream sundaes.

■ *Try your technique:* Rhubarb will reach new culinary heights in creme brulee and dessert fruit gratins. It is actually very versatile if you cook it slightly to tenderize, then add sugar and spices to balance the acidic qualities. You will be amazed at how well this lowly vegetable will perform!

GRATIN OF RASPBERRIES & RHUBARB

Makes 4 servings

½	cup superfine sugar, divided
10	large egg yolks
2	teaspoons vanilla
2	cups heavy cream, scalded
½	cup Grand Marnier
2	tablespoons unsalted butter
2	cups rhubarb, cut into 1-inch pieces
2	pints raspberries, rinsed, drained

Preheat broiler.

To make custard: In a bowl, combine ¼ cup of the sugar, the egg yolks and vanilla. Stir in the hot cream, then add the Grand Marnier. Strain through a fine sieve. Keep warm.

In a large skillet over high heat, melt the butter. Add the rhubarb and the remaining sugar. Cook until warm and all juices are reduced, about 5 minutes. Spoon the rhubarb into hot, broiler-proof soup plates, and distribute the rasp-

berries over it. Pour the custard over to fill, then broil until the custard sets and the tops are golden, about 8 minutes. Serve.

Cook's note: The gratin works best when the soup plates are hot, the fruit is warm or at room temperature and the custard is warm. That way, the top of the gratin will brown quickly, and the custard thickens almost immediately when put under the broiler. Cold ingredients in cold soup plates will take forever to heat and then cook with poor results. When using fresh berries and tender fruit, do not cook before covering with the custard. Use the saute technique, as with the rhubarb in this recipe, for firm and sour fruit only.

Nutrition details per serving
Calories .717
Percent of calories from fat 64%
Fat: . . . . .52 gm
Protein: . . . . .10 gm
Carbohydrate: . . . . .38 gm
Cholesterol: . . . . .662 mg
Sodium: . . . . .106 mg
Diabetic exchange: ⅓ fruit, 1 meat, 9⅓ fat.

STRAWBERRIES ARE SWEETNESS AND LIGHT

AMAZING FOOD FACTS

■

There are about 75 different species of wild strawberries in the United States alone. The largest of the wild varieties is the famous Virginia strawberry.

■ *How many kinds are there?* There are three main varieties of strawberries:
June or early bearing. These produce one large crop over a few weeks' time in June, or at the beginning of the season.
Everbearing. These produce a sparse crop throughout the season.
Alpine (fraise de bois). These are about ½ inch in size and concentrated in flavor.

■ *Health advantages:* Strawberries are high in vitamin C and low in sodium. They have only 26 calories per 100 grams or 3½-ounce serving.

■ *How to select:* Select bright red, shiny berries that are firm yet supple, without bruises. Size is less important than taste; the smallest berries are usually the sweetest. Pick strawberries by pinching the stem about 2 inches above the fruit and gently twisting to break off, allowing the berry to roll into your cupped hand.

Strawberries are a false fruit. The red fruit we love is produced from the base of the flower rather than the ovary. The true fruit of the ovaries is the tiny seeds on the surface of the strawberry. Although it isn't a true fruit or berry, the strawberry is still considered the king of the berry family.

Do not pull on the fruit. Keep the berries out of direct sunlight and take them home in an air-conditioned car, not in the oven-like trunk.

■ *How to store:* To store, lay the unwashed berries on a cookie sheet lined with paper toweling, making sure the berries are not touching each other. Refrigerate immediately. When the berries are cool, loosely tent them with plastic wrap but do not seal. The berries will hold for only 3 or 4 days, depending on ripeness.

■ *How to clean:* Clean the strawberries just before serving. Wash them with their caps still on under gently running cold water. Pat dry with paper towels. Remove the hulls and serve. If the stems and hulls are fresh and green, the berries may be served with them on for an attractive presentation.

■ *Sweet enough?* If the strawberries are tart, add sugar just before serving. The sugar will soften and discolor them. Another method for sweetening is to hull the berries and

invert them, hulled side down, onto light brown sugar. Cover with paper towels at room temperature for about 2 hours.

■ *Tricks to making the best strawberry shortcake:* First, for absolute best results, buy new flour and baking powder. Flour and baking powder that have been opened and left sitting around tend to absorb smells and moisture. Use unsalted sweet butter and heavy or whipping cream for the shortcakes as well as the topping. Substitutes are shallower in flavor.

As usual, the dry ingredients are combined with butter. The trick is to cut cold butter into small pieces and blend it in a mixer with the paddle attachment until a very fine meal is achieved, about 5 minutes. This is essential to producing shortcake's delicate texture.

Next, add the cream. (Yes, milk, buttermilk and half-and-half work, but there is a significant flavor difference.) Mix as little as possible, but enough to get the dough to come together. I turn the mixer on and off while set at the slowest speed. Once the dough begins

to come together, I transfer it to the countertop and give it a couple of kneads to finish pulling it together. That's it; don't touch it anymore.

Bake so it still will be warm when it reaches the table.

■ *How to cook:* For pies and cooking, strawberries should be washed, dried, hulled, sliced if needed and allowed to drain on paper toweling. Pies and tarts will be more concentrated in flavor and will weep less. The berries also will hold their shape better. Select overripe or imperfect berries for preserves, jams, sorbets and ice creams. The flavor and sweetness of such berries are usually at their peak, ideal for these applications.

■ *A frozen treat:* To freeze strawberries, wash and pat dry. Lay out the individual berries on a cookie sheet and place in the freezer until firm. Remove the cookie sheet from the freezer, mist the berries with cold water from a spray bottle and return to the freezer until the water has become solid. Transfer the berries to a heavy freezer bag, seal and return to

the freezer. To use frozen berries, thaw in the refrigerator overnight. The frozen berries will have a softer texture and a slightly flatter taste. The best way to capture the strawberry flavor by freezing is to puree the fresh berries with sugar and lemon juice to taste. Strain through a fine sieve to remove the seeds. Transfer to an airtight freezer container and freeze. The puree may be defrosted for drinks and desserts.

■

STRAWBERRY SHORTCAKE

Makes 4 servings

1 quart fresh strawberries, sliced

¼ cup maple sugar (or substitute white granulated), divided

1 cup whipping cream

2 teaspoons vanilla extract

¼ cup Grand Marnier (optional)

4 Deluxe Shortcakes (see accompanying recipe)

4 giant sprigs fresh-picked mint

In a medium bowl, combine the strawberries and 2 tablespoons of the sugar. Allow to marinate while whipping cream. In a mixing bowl, combine the cream and the remaining sugar. Whip until soft peaks begin to form. While continuing to whip, add the vanilla and the Grand Marnier. Continue whipping until soft peaks are formed.

Split shortcakes in half. Spoon the excess juice onto the center of the serving dishes. Place the shortcake bottom in the middle of the strawberry juice. Divide the strawberries over the shortcakes. Spoon the whipped cream over the berries. Place the shortcake tops on the whipped cream. Garnish each plate with a sprig of mint.

Nutrition details per serving
Calories 307
Percent of calories from fat 65%
Fat: . . . . .23 gm
Protein: . . . . .2 gm
Carbohydrate: . . . . .26 gm
Cholesterol: . . . . .82 mg
Sodium: . . . . .26 mg
Diabetic exchange: ¾ fruit, 4⅓ fat.

■

DELUXE SHORTCAKES

Makes 4 servings

Butter for cookie sheet
1½ cups all-purpose flour
¼ cup maple sugar (or substitute white granulated), divided
Pinch of salt
¾ tablespoon baking powder
4 tablespoons unsalted butter
½ cup plus 1 tablespoon whipping cream

Preheat the oven to 400 degrees. Butter a cookie sheet.

In a medium-sized mixer bowl, sift together the flour, 2 tablespoons of the sugar, salt and baking powder. Add the 4 tablespoons butter. Mix on slow to medium speed with the paddle attachment until the dough texture resembles fine meal. Add the cream. Mix as slowly as possible just until the pastry sticks together. Transfer to a cool countertop and knead two or three times just to form a smooth ball. Dust the dough with flour and roll it out to ¾ inch thick. Cut into cake, 3 inches in diameter. Transfer to the prepared cookie sheet and refrigerate until ready to bake. Brush the tops of the shortcakes with a little whipping cream. Sprinkle the remaining maple sugar over the shortcakes. Bake on the middle rack of the oven until golden, about 20-25 minutes. Remove to a cake rack to cool.

Nutrition details per serving
Calories 443
Percent of calories from fat 50%
Fat: . . . . .25 gm
Protein: . . . . .6 gm
Carbohydrate: . . . . .50 gm
Cholesterol: . . . . .61 mg
Sodium: . . . . .266 mg
Diabetic exchange: 2⅓ bread, 4¼ fat.

■

STRAWBERRIES MACERATED IN RED WINE

Makes 4 servings

2 quarts ripe strawberries
½ bottle fruity, light pinot noir red wine
4 tablespoons balsamic vinegar, optional
½ cup granulated sugar, or to taste
4 sprigs of mint for garnish

Wash the strawberries under trickling cold water. Pat dry with paper towels. Remove the hulls and stems. Invert on paper toweling to drain for ½ hour at room temperature. Cut the berries in half or quarters depending on size. Transfer to a glass bowl. Pour the wine and balsamic vinegar over the strawberries. Add sugar to balance the flavor of the strawberries. Refrigerate for 2 hours, stirring about every ½ hour. Spoon the strawberries with a little bit of the juice into a soup plate or bowl. Garnish with mint. Serve with a fork and dessert spoon. This classic marriage of fruit and wine is the perfect dessert for a glowing sundown.

Nutrition details per serving
Calories 213
Percent of calories from fat 4%
Fat: . . . . .1 gm
Protein: . . . . .2 gm
Carbohydrate: . . . . .37 gm
Cholesterol: . . . . .0 mg
Sodium: . . . . .14 mg
Diabetic exchange: 1⅜ fruit.

SUMMER

FOR TOMATO LOVERS

■ *What is a tomato?* The tomato, actually a fruit, is a member of the nightshade family, which includes peppers and eggplant. It originated in the Andes Mountains of South America and was first cultivated by the Aztecs in Mexico.

■ *Why it tastes so good:* Vine-ripened and right to the table is hard to beat. Try tasting the tomato with the seedy pulp, then just the meat. Often the meat will seem soft and bland, with most of the flavor in the pulp. All parts of the best tomatoes taste terrific.

■ *We love them even when they are bad!* Summer tomatoes are a distant relative to those winter cardboard creatures. Because they must stand up to the rigors of shipping and handling, commercial tomatoes are bred to have less of the tissue that makes garden tomatoes so flavorful. The vine-ripened tomatoes from your backyard taste so wonderful because the

TODAY'S LESSON: Tomato-loving Americans consume an average of 18 pounds of commercially grown fresh tomatoes and 22 pounds of tomato products each year. And that's not counting the even tastier tomatoes and tomato products from local farmers and backyard vegetable gardens. The flavor of those vine-ripened, never-chilled tomatoes truly is summer's masterpiece. Once you've enjoyed them, every other tomato you eat will pale — in both flavor and nutritional content.

additional time spent ripening on the vine develops their flavor, texture and nutrients.

■ *Health advantages:* The tomato is high in beta-carotene and loaded with vitamin C. It's low in fat and calories, about 38 in a medium-sized tomato. The vine-ripened tomato contains 2½ times the beta-carotene and twice the vitamin C of the winter tomato.

■ *Seductive varieties:* Cherry or miniature tomatoes are the first to ripen. Cherry tomato varieties range in color from red to bright pink to golden yellow. They are best in salads. Cherry tomatoes also can be added at the last second to savory salads made with chicken, shrimp and other delicate seafoods, and cold pastas or grains. The standard, medium-size garden tomato is the summer staple. They are common in red and yellow varieties at many farmer's markets. The red seems richer, but the yellow usually is lower in acid and a little lighter in flavor. The red finds its way into cooked as well as fresh dishes. Yellow tomatoes are best fresh in simple preparations where stronger flavors will not overshadow them. Beefsteak tomatoes are best for sandwiches, burgers and recipes that need good solid tomato meat. Plum tomatoes are perfect for sauces because of their density and intense red color.

■ *How to select:* Tomatoes mature from the bottom of the plant upward, so always pick from the bottom. Leave top ones to ripen fully. Select deep red tomatoes with a supple texture when lightly squeezed. The smaller to medium-size

tomatoes generally have more flavor. Avoid bruised, soft or cracked fruits. Even vine-ripened tomatoes can use a couple of days to further mature. To ripen, place tomatoes stem side up in a brown paper bag pierced with a few holes and store at room temperature for one to two days. Put an apple in the bag if you want to hasten the ripening. Do not ripen in direct sunlight. Judge the ripeness not just by color but by smell and a gentle squeeze. Your nose will know.

■ *Tricks of the trade:* Never refrigerate tomatoes. The temperature will cause the metabolic rate to slow, all ripening to stop and the delicate flavors composed of natural sugars and acids to decline.

■ *How to prepare:* Many recipes ask you to remove the skin, because it's the toughest part of the tomato and probably has been sprayed with pesticides.

Blister technique: Hold the tomato with tongs or a large cooking fork over an open flame to separate the skin from the meat. Allow the tomato to cool to room temperature before sliding the skin free. This method is preferred for concentrating the flavor of the tomato.

Blanching: Add the tomato to boiling water for 15-30 seconds, then plunge it into ice water to cool. The peel will come away easily with a paring knife. This is fast and easy but may dilute the tomato flavor.

■ *Get rid of those seeds:* Although the jelly-like substance surrounding the seeds contains sugars and acids, it is generally removed along with the seeds. The seeds have a bitter flavor that can strongly scent a sauce, as well as contribute an unappealing texture. To remove seeds, slice the peeled tomato in half across the middle (not stem to end),

■

In the late 19th Century, scientists in England and the United States thought tomatoes caused cancer. This was later proved false.

■

Botanists tell us the tomato is a fruit. But the U.S. Supreme Court legally declared it a vegetable in 1893.

then hold the tomato with one hand and squeeze like an orange.

■ *How to cook:* For stuffed tomatoes, peel, seed with a small spoon, then invert on a paper towel for about 15 minutes to drain excess liquid. Turn the cut side up and fill. For grilling, slice tomatoes about 1 inch thick, rub with a little olive oil, season with salt and pepper and grill over a high fire just to sear and heat, about 2 minutes. Turn over with a flat metal spatula until they begin to soften, about 1 minute.

■ *On to the sauce:* The most important rule to concentrating the natural tomato flavor is to keep the sauce simple. Don't overwhelm it with tons of garlic, onions, meats, sauces, fats, vegetables and herbs.

1. Start with extra-virgin olive oil. Gently heat to about 300 degrees. Saute fresh minced garlic, cooking until golden to develop that unique nutty flavor. Browning the garlic will also

prevent a strong garlic breath, pungent aftertaste and occasional burp. The garlic may be strained from the oil to remove pieces. Be ready for the next step, because the garlic can burn and become bitter if allowed to cook too long.

2. Add the herbs. Basil and Italian parsley are the most common and complementary to the tomato flavor. Let the herbs cook in the hot oil until they wither, about one minute.

3. Add the peeled, seeded and diced tomatoes, cooking until the sauce forms, about 10 minutes. Add sea salt and fresh ground black pepper to taste. Continue cooking as necessary to reach sauce consistency, depending on the type and water content of the tomatoes.

4. Cook the pasta al dente, or firm to the bite, drain and add to the sauce. Adjust the seasonings again to balance the more bland pasta flavor.

■ *No time to cook:* Try a room-temperature sauce of diced tomatoes, extra-virgin olive oil and seasonings of

sea salt, fresh ground black pepper, a few chili pepper flakes and, of course, fresh chopped basil or parsley, all tossed together. Add to hot pasta and serve. The pasta will gently warm the sauce to bring the rich flavors forward.

■

CHILLED PASTA, ROAST GARLIC & TOMATOES

Makes 4 servings

1 head garlic
¾ pound pasta, any shape
¼ cup virgin olive oil, divided
8 medium tomatoes, peeled, seeded and diced
¼ cup chopped fresh basil
Salt to taste
Freshly ground black pepper to taste
¾ cup grated Parmesan cheese
4 sprigs fresh basil

Preheat oven to 400. In an ovenproof dish or skillet, coat the head of garlic with olive or other oil. Place in lower rack of oven and cook until just tender, about 30 minutes, depending on size. Set aside to cool. Cook the pasta according to package directions. Transfer to a strainer, drain and rinse with tepid water. Transfer to a medium-size bowl. Add 2 tablespoons of olive oil and toss to coat the pasta. Chill in refrigerator.

Peel and mince garlic. In a medium-size bowl, combine the remaining 2 tablespoons of olive oil with the garlic, tomatoes and chopped basil. Season with salt and pepper. Add pasta, toss and mix well. Distribute the pasta to the serving plates. Top with grated Parmesan cheese. Garnish with basil sprigs.

Nutrition details per serving
Calories 394
Percent of calories from fat 48%
Fat: . . . . .22 gm
Protein: . . . . .16 gm
Carbohydrate: . . . . .38 gm
Cholesterol: . . . . .49 mg
Sodium: . . . . .717 mg
Diabetic exchange: 3½ vegetables, 1¼ bread, 1¼ meat, 3½ fat.

SLICED TOMATO & AVOCADO SALAD

Makes 4 servings

¼ cup balsamic vinegar

½ cup virgin olive oil

Salt to taste

Coarsely ground black pepper to taste

¼ cup red onions, finely diced

¼ cup fresh basil, washed, dried, snipped

2 ripe avocados, quartered, pit and skin removed

3 large, ripe tomatoes, peeled and cut into 4 slices each

¼ cup finely grated Parmesan cheese, optional

4 large sprigs fresh basil

In a small bowl, whisk together the balsamic vinegar and olive oil. Season with salt and a generous dose of pepper to taste. Wrap the diced onions in the corner of a lint-free or linen towel. Twist the towel tight to squeeze out the juices into the sink and rinse under running cold water. Squeeze again to remove excess water. Add to the dressing with the snipped basil.

Place an avocado quarter on your cutting board. Insert a paring knife through the avocado about 1 inch from one end and slice lengthwise through the remaining avocado. Repeat this partial slicing to make three or four attached slices of avocado per quarter. With light pressure of your hand, spread the slices out to form a fan. Repeat with the remaining avocado quarters.

On the serving plate, alternate tomato slices with two avocado fans to create an arched presentation. Spoon the vinaigrette over the salads, sprinkle with Parmesan, top with sprigs of basil and serve.

Nutrition details per serving
Calories .474
Percent of calories from fat 80%
Fat: .44 gm
Protein: . . . . .6 gm
Carbohydrate: . . . . .18 gm
Cholesterol: . . . . .5 mg
Sodium: . . . . .411 mg
Diabetic exchange: 1⅓ vegetables, ⅓ meat, 8½ fat.

THE SIMPLEST TOMATO SAUCE

Makes 4 servings

2 tablespoons extra-virgin olive oil

1 tablespoon minced fresh garlic, or to your taste

1 cup fresh basil leaves, chopped coarse

6 cups fresh perfectly ripe tomatoes, peeled, seeded, and diced (from about 3 pounds of tomatoes or about 6 large, 10-12 medium round tomatoes or 18 large plum tomatoes)

Sea salt

Freshly ground black pepper

1 pound dried pasta of your choice

¼ cup finely grated Parmesan cheese

4 sprigs herbs for garnish

In a large acid-resistant skillet, heat the olive oil over medium heat. Add the garlic and cook until golden, about 2-3 minutes. Add the basil and allow to wilt into the oil, about 1 minute. Add the tomatoes and cook until thickened, stirring frequently, about 10 minutes. Season with salt and pepper to taste. Continue cooking until you reach sauce consistency, thickened to coat the back of a spoon, about 5 minutes more depending on tomato variety.

Meanwhile, bring a large pot of water to a boil. Add salt and pasta. Cook until the pasta is al dente, then transfer to a colander to drain. Add the pasta into the tomato sauce and allow to cook for a couple of minutes to develop flavor. Adjust the seasonings. Divide the pasta among the serving plates. Top with the cheese and garnish with a sprig of fresh herbs. Serve immediately while the steam is still rising from the dish.

Nutrition details per serving
Calories 320
Percent of calories from fat 29%
Fat: .10 gm
Protein: . . . . .11 gm
Carbohydrate: . . . . .48 gm
Cholesterol: . . . . .5 mg
Sodium: . . . . .414 mg
Diabetic exchange: 3 vegetables, 2⅛ bread, ⅓ meat, 1½ fat.

SWEET WAYS TO PREPARE CORN

AMAZING FOOD FACTS

■

Corn has been cultivated in Central America since 3500 B.C. It was an important foodstuff of the Incas, Aztecs and Mayans of Mexico, as well as the cliff dwellers of the U.S. Southwest. Cortes took corn to Spain; from there it spread to France and Italy.

■ *What makes it sweet:* The fresher the corn, the sweeter the flavor. From the moment the corn is picked, natural sugar in the kernels begins converting to starch. At room temperature, corn loses up to 40 percent of its sugar to starch conversion in just 6 hours. Chilling corn slows this conversion, but the sweetest corn is enjoyed the day it is picked. So a supersweet variety that is picked and stored at room temperature could be less sweet than a standard sweet corn that has been properly chilled.

■ *Advantages:* Corn is high in fiber, potassium and vitamin A.

■ *Picking corn yourself:* The best time is at dusk after a hot day. The corn will be at its sweetest and can be prepared immediately. Or store it upright in the refrigerator with the cut ends in a little cool water.

■ *How to select:* If you can't pick it yourself, select ears

TODAY'S LESSON: When handled properly, sweet corn is one of nature's sweetest and most versatile vegetables. It's ready to eat after a simple bath of hot water or a roll on the grill. Or it can star in soups, chowders, salsa, relishes, breads, muffins, pancakes and souffles.

with moist, fresh-looking stems. The silk should be dark amber or golden, never black or dry-looking. The silk and the husks should be moist and pliable, not merely damp from a spray from the garden hose. Check ears for even plump kernels that are full of juice when punctured with a fingernail.

■ *How to store:* Corn should be stored in the coldest part of your refrigerator in its natural husks. Soak ears in cold water before refrigerating to help the chill penetrate the ears more quickly.

■ *A classic technique:* The classic technique for sweet corn comes from the Shakers. Place husked and de-silked corn in a large pot of cold water seasoned with a pinch of sugar. Bring to a boil over the largest burner on your stove set at high heat, and cook for exactly 1 minute after the boil is detected. Drain and serve.

■ *Tricks of the trade:* Whether you choose the Shaker method or your own technique, avoid adding salt to the water because it will harden the kernels. After cooking, however, salt, freshly ground pepper and butter are all important ingredients.

■ *The crimp:* With or without husks, add corn to boiling water and cover. Return to a boil, turn off the heat and allow to crimp (cook without direct heat) for about 8 minutes. Drain, clean and serve. Corn is extremely tender when cooked this way.

■ *To roast:* Remove only the silk and place the ears in an ovenproof pan, without touching each other. Place in a preheated 350-degree oven for about 45 minutes. Using rubber gloves, remove husks.

■ *To grill:* Carefully peel back the husks, but do not remove from the stem. Remove all the silk. Soak the ears of corn in cold water for 30 minutes, then drain. Rub the corn kernels with room-temperature butter and season with salt and freshly ground black pepper. Return the husks back over the corn kernels and tie the top end with a corn husk string to secure. Place on the grill and rotate frequently to ensure even cooking. If ears begin to

burn, move them toward the cooler, outer sections of the grill. Baste with water as necessary. Cook for about 15-20 minutes until the corn is tender. Serve with husks on to keep warm and moist.

■ *To grill in aluminum foil:* Husk the corn. Place in the center of a piece of aluminum foil, shiny side up. Add spices, seasonings, herbs and butter to taste. Roll up the foil tightly, making sure the ear is well sealed. Place on the grill as described above.

The dry heat techniques of roasting and grilling help concentrate the flavors and firm the corn's texture. These techniques are best for cooking corn to be added to salsas, salads, compotes and other condiments.

■ *Mix and match:* Some of my favorite condiments include butter made with chives, chervil and parsley. Roasted red peppers, tomatoes and even roasted garlic add another dimension to the flavor of the grilled corn.

■ *Corn off the cob:* Hold the cob upright and firmly planted on the cutting board surface.

■
Corn is second only to rice in world cultivation of grains. Its uses extend beyond food to chemical and oil production.

■
Corn is the New World's most important contribution to the human diet; it is second only to wheat in planted acreage.

With your French knife blade facing toward the board, cut downward to remove a strip of the corn kernels. Cut just deep enough to get the full kernel without the cob. A little practice, and you will clean an ear of corn in a few seconds. This corn can be used in relishes and salsas.

Relishes are wonderful when they marry fresh corn with caramelized onions, roasted shallots and garlic, sun-dried tomatoes and roasted celery or fennel. The ingredients usually are at least partially cooked separately, then finished cooking together.

My favorite salsas pair grilled corn that has been browned slightly with roasted peppers, tomatoes and grilled mushrooms. Try your hand at combinations of ingredients you like with corn, add a little splash of good vinegar, olive oil and herbs and enjoy.

For some dishes, you'll want more of the sweet corn pulp and juice known as corn milk. Draw the knife across the corn lengthwise, cutting about halfway into the kernels. Repeat across the rest of the ear. Holding the cob upright again, this time in a large bowl, scrape downward with the back of the knife to release part of the kernels and all of the corn milk. The mixture is perfect for adding the corn flavor to chowders, soups and baked dishes.

Creamed corn is best made from the gathered corn kernels and corn milk combination. Creamed corn is is the perfect use for 1- or 2-day-old fresh corn. A pinch of sugar will refresh that just-picked sweetness.

■ *Serving suggestions:* Corn breads, muffins, pancakes and fritters take on a summer-fresh flavor with the addition of fresh corn to the batters.

■

GRILLED CORN WITH PEPPER BUTTER

Makes 4 servings

1   red pepper, roasted, peeled, seeded and diced

½   cup unsalted butter, room temperature

½   cup chopped fresh cilantro

¼   cup snipped fresh chives

    Salt

    Freshly ground black pepper

    Tabasco

4   ears fresh sweet corn

In a food processor, combine the red pepper, butter, cilantro and chives. Adjust the seasonings with salt, black pepper and Tabasco to your taste. Husk and clean the corn. Place each ear individually in the center of a piece of aluminum foil, shiny side up. Coat the ear with a quarter of the butter mixture. Wrap the foil around the corn, making sure the ear is well sealed by the foil. Refrigerate until ready to cook. Preheat the grill. Place the corn on the grill near the edges or cooler areas. Cook until tender, turning frequently, about 10-15 minutes. Carefully unwrap the corn and serve.

Nutrition details per serving
Calories 333
Percent of calories from fat 63%
Fat: . . . . .25 gm
Protein: . . . . .4 gm
Carbohydrate: . . . . .29 gm
Cholesterol: . . . . .30 mg
Sodium: . . . . .350 mg
Diabetic exchange: ¼ vegetable, 1¼ bread, 4¾ fat.

■

GRILLED SHRIMP WITH SWEET CORN CAKES

Makes 4 servings

½   cup low-fat sour cream

¼   cup chopped cilantro leaves

    Generous shot of Tabasco (to your taste)

    Juice of 2 limes, divided

½   cup all-purpose flour

¼   cup yellow corn meal

½   teaspoon baking powder

    Pinch of salt

Freshly ground black pepper

¾ cup buttermilk

1 large egg, beaten

1 cup sweet corn, cut fresh off the cob, with the corn milk

¼ cup scallion greens, washed, dried, diced

¼ cup fresh chives, washed, dried, snipped

¼ cup (½ stick) unsalted butter, melted, divided

16 jumbo shrimp, shelled and deveined

½ cup of your favorite spicy barbecue sauce

Sprigs of cilantro for garnish

Preheat the grill for the shrimp. In a small bowl, combine the sour cream, cilantro, Tabasco and the juice of 1 lime. Reserve.

In a large bowl, combine the flour, corn meal, baking powder, salt and pepper. Stir in the buttermilk and the egg. Add the corn, scallions and chives. Fold in 2 tablespoons of the melted butter. Reserve.

In a nonstick pan, heat 1 tablespoon of butter until hot over medium-high heat. Spoon the corn cake batter into the pan to form a 4-inch diameter cake. Repeat until the pan is filled. Cook until the cakes begin to bubble on the top surface and they are light brown, about 2 minutes. Turn over until done, about 1 minute. Transfer to an ovenproof plate and keep warm until ready to serve. Repeat with the remainder of the butter and batter to make 8 cakes.

Place the shrimp on the hot grill, cooking until well seared, about 3 minutes. With a pair of tongs, turn over each shrimp and brush heavily with barbecue sauce. Cook until done, about 2 more minutes depending on size and the temperature of your fire.

Transfer shrimp to a clean platter and brush again with barbecue sauce. Squeeze the remaining lime over the shrimp. Arrange two corn cakes in the center of each plate. Position 4 shrimp per serving in the center of the corn cakes. Divide the reserved sour cream mixture onto the center of the shrimp. Drizzle the remaining barbecue sauce over the shrimp and corn cakes. Garnish with the cilantro sprigs and serve.

Nutrition details per serving

Calories	442
Percent of calories from fat	37%
Fat:	19 gm
Protein:	32 gm
Carbohydrate:	39 gm
Cholesterol:	255 mg
Sodium:	1,309 mg

Diabetic exchange: ⅛ milk, ¼ vegetables, ⅛ fruit, 4¾ bread, 1⅜ meat, 5⅜ fat.

■

CORN CHOWDER

Makes 8 servings

2 red bell peppers, roasted, peeled, seeded and chopped

1 cup dry white wine

3 tablespoons unsalted butter

2 cups chopped onions

4 cups poultry stock

1 cup yellow cornmeal

Salt to taste

Freshly ground white pepper to taste

½ cup fresh lemon juice

4 cups sweet corn cut from the cob

½ cup chopped fresh basil

In a small saucepan, combine the red peppers and wine. Bring to a simmer over medium heat and cook until tender, about 5 minutes. Transfer to a food processor and puree until smooth. Set aside. Melt the butter in a large saucepan over low heat. Add the onions and saute until they begin to soften, about 10 minutes. Add the stock and simmer until tender, about ½ hour. Slowly whisk in the cornmeal, and cook until thickened, about 5 minutes.

Puree the soup in the blender in batches and strain through a fine sieve. Return to the saucepan over medium-high heat, adjust the salt and pepper, then add the lemon juice and fresh corn and cook until the corn is tender, about 5 minutes. Ladle the soup into warm bowls. Spoon the reserved pepper puree onto the soup decoratively, garnish with the basil.

Nutrition details per serving

Calories	559
Percent of calories from fat	21%
Fat:	14 gm
Protein:	12 gm
Carbohydrate:	96 gm
Cholesterol:	11 mg
Sodium:	801 mg

Diabetic exchange: 1½ vegetables, ⅛ fruit, 24⅛ bread, 10 meat, 16⅞ fat.

THE EGGPLANT AND I

■ *What can you do with eggplant?* Because of its spongy
texture, it is seldom served less
than fully cooked. It complements tomatoes, peppers, garlic, onions and herbs. It mar-
ries well with fish, poultry and
any kind of meat.

■ *Health advantages:* Eggplant
adds bulk and texture to meatless dishes. It is low in calories,
only about 30 calories per cup.
Eggplant is a wonderful source
of folic acid and a pretty fair
source of potassium and fiber.

■ *How to select:* Eggplant is
available most of the year, but
summer is the peak season. It is
highly perishable and best
when prepared immediately
from the garden or farmer's
market. The true, sweet, nutty
flavor tends to disappear
quickly as the eggplant ages. A
fresh eggplant will keep in the
refrigerator for only three to
four days.

 Smaller is better, for a sweet,
rich flavor.

TODAY'S LESSON: Eggplant – an edible
member of the nightshade family — is a
sun lover that matures to its true beauty
when the days are long and hot and the
nights are warm. Eggplant is tender and
fleshy with a rich, subtle flavor perfect
for sauteing, frying, stewing, grilling,
broiling and baking.

 The cap should be green, a
little fuzzy and fresh-looking,
with about ½ inch of the stem
still attached. The stem left
intact during harvesting will
prevent moisture loss.

 Skin should be taut and
shiny. The skin will begin to
wrinkle and soften and turn
dull as the eggplant begins to
spoil. Dull skin is also a sign of
a more mature eggplant, which
will have browner seeds and a
bitter flavor.

 Heaviness and firmness
characterize the best and freshest eggplant.

 Seeds, when the eggplant is
cut open, should be pale, not
brown.

 Look at the end of the eggplant opposite the stem or cap.
If it's oval-shaped, the eggplant
will have fewer seeds and more
meat. If it's round, the eggplant will have more seeds and
less meat.

■ *How to prepare:* Remove the
skin by peeling. It's easier to
slice eggplant first, then trim
off the skin. Oriental and
softer-skin varieties usually are
prepared with the skin on

because it becomes quite tender during cooking. After cutting or peeling, an eggplant quickly will turn brown. Salting or rubbing the surface with lemon juice or vinegar will slow this. The heat from cooking will eliminate any discoloration.

Salting the eggplant also draws out excess moisture and bitterness — although most varieties, when properly selected, tend to be fairly sweet.

Generously salt all surfaces of the sliced eggplant and place in a strainer. Place a bowl atop the eggplant and add a few food cans for extra weight to help press the moisture out. Allow the eggplant to drain for 30-45 minutes. Rinse under cold water to remove the salt and dry on paper towels. Check seasonings carefully before adding more salt.

■ *How to cook:* Baking is probably the easiest way to prepare whole eggplant. Select a small eggplant, rub the skin lightly with olive oil, add aromatic herbs, onion and garlic, cover tightly with foil and put in an ovenproof baking dish. Place

in a 400-degree oven and cook for 45-60 minutes, depending on size and weight, until very tender. The more you cook eggplant, the creamier the flesh. Serve warm or at room

temperature with a good spicy vinaigrette.

Broiling is faster and less messy. Slice the eggplant, brush with olive oil, season with fresh pepper and lay flat on a baking sheet. Broil for about 8 minutes, turn the slices over and cook until golden. The eggplant is ready to complement your favorite dish or, seasoned with herbs and spices, can be a stand-alone vegetable.

Small eggplants stewed with a splash of white wine, tomatoes, roasted peppers, garlic, onions and herbs are great. Select small eggplants with thin skins, so the skins will almost melt away.

■ *Tricks of the trade:* The simplest way to prepare an eggplant is to roast it whole in its skin until completely tender. Place in a heavy baking dish and bake on the lower rack of

■

The greatest devotees of eggplant are probably people from Italy and the Middle East. It is said that the Syrians and Turks know a thousand ways to prepare eggplant!

Eggplant
blossoms
pollinate
themselves.
Each blossom
has both male
and female
elements.

a preheated 400-degree oven for about 1 hour, depending on size. Check doneness by inserting a skewer, which should meet no resistance and be very hot when removed. Cool enough to handle, then peel and cut into your desired shape. Season well and give a good splash of olive oil.

GRILLED EGGPLANT, ONION & TOMATO SALAD

Makes 4 servings

2   medium eggplants

¼   cup kosher salt

8   tablespoons extra-virgin olive oil, divided

    Black pepper

2   medium-sized sweet or mild onions, peeled and sliced ½ inch thick

¼   teaspoon salt

¼   cup red wine vinegar

½   cup sweet basil leaves

2   large red tomatoes, cut into 4 slices each

4   sprigs basil or other fresh herbs for garnish

Peel the eggplant and slice ½ inch thick. Sprinkle all surfaces with the kosher salt and place in a colander. Cover with a bowl containing a couple of cans of food for extra weight. Allow the salt to draw out the moisture for about 35-40 minutes. Rinse the eggplant under cold running water. Pat dry with paper towels. Rub the eggplant slices with 1 tablespoon of the olive oil.

Preheat grill. Place the eggplant on the grill, searing well, about 4 minutes. Turn over and cook under tender, another 4 minutes. Transfer to a dish and season with black pepper to your taste. Add 3 tablespoons of the olive oil.

Rub the surfaces of the onions with 1 tablespoon of the olive oil. Place the onions on the grill, cooking until well seared, about 3 minutes. Turn over and grill for 2 minutes. Remove to a plate and season with salt and pepper to your taste.

Combine the vinegar, basil, ¼ teaspoon salt and black pepper in a blender. While the blender is running, slowly add the remaining 3 tablespoons

olive oil. Add a little white wine or water, if necessary, to maintain a sauce-like consistency. Adjust the seasonings to taste. On the serving plate, alternate slices of eggplant, onion and tomatoes. Spoon the sauce across, garnish with herbs and serve.

Nutrition details per serving
Calories 326
Percent of calories from fat 73%
Fat: .28 gm
Protein: . . . . .2 gm
Carbohydrate: . . . . .20 gm
Cholesterol: . . . . .0 mg
Sodium: . . . . .150 mg
Diabetic exchange: 1¾ vegetables, ⅓
bread, 5¾ fat.

EGGPLANT LASAGNA

Makes 8-10 servings

2   large purple eggplants
    Salt to taste
½   cup extra-virgin olive
    oil, divided
    Freshly ground black
    pepper to taste
4   cloves minced garlic
    (or more)
3   pounds seeded, diced
    and drained fresh ripe
    tomatoes (substitute
    28 ounces canned
    Italian plum toma-
    toes, drained, seeded
    and diced)
½   cup white wine,
    optional
½   cup chopped fresh
    basil leaves
1   pound lasagna
    noodles
½   pound grated
    mozzarella cheese
2   cups finely grated
    Parmesan cheese
    Sprigs of fresh basil or
    other herb for garnish

Preheat broiler.

Slice the eggplant length-wise into ⅓-inch slices. Salt both surfaces of the slices, place in a colander and allow to drain for about 30 minutes. Rinse under running cold water to remove the salt. Pat dry. Lay on a baking sheet and brush with olive oil. Season with black pepper. Place on the upper rack of the broiler and cook for about 8 minutes.

Turn the slices over, brush with olive oil and continue cooking until golden and tender, about 8 minutes. Remove the baking sheet to a cake rack to cool.

In a large saucepan, heat ¼ cup of the olive oil over medium heat. Add the garlic and cook until translucent and tender, about 3 minutes. Add the tomatoes and wine, cooking until thickened to coat the back of a spoon, about 15 minutes. Add basil, then salt and pepper to taste. Remove from heat.

Meanwhile, bring a large pot of water to a boil. Add salt. Add the lasagna noo-dles, cooking until al dente, about 6 minutes, depending on the type and thickness of your brand. Drain in a

colander and cool under running warm water to stop the cooking. Drain well and transfer to a bowl. Add ⅛ cup of olive oil just to coat the noodles and prevent them from sticking.

Rub the surfaces of an 8-by-12-inch baking dish with the remaining olive oil. Lay in a third of the lasagna noo-dles just to cover the bot-tom, slightly overlapping one another. Spoon about a cup of the sauce across the noodles. Lay half of the egg-plant slices across the noo-dles, slightly overlapping one another. Spoon about a cup of the sauce over the eggplant. Distribute half of the cheeses over the sauce. Repeat the assembly, ending with a layer of pasta and a layer of sauce.

Cover with aluminum foil. Place in a preheated 375-degree oven for about 45 minutes until the cheese is melted. Remove the foil and allow to brown slightly, about 15 additional minutes. Remove from the oven and allow to cool for about 15 minutes before serving.

Serve as a whole dish or cut into individual servings. Garnish the plate with the

basil sprig.

Cook's note: If you prefer, cooked, drained and sea-soned ground meats and sausages also may be layered in when assembling this egg-plant lasagna.

Nutrition details per serving
Calories .856
Percent of calories from fat 50%
Fat: .49 gm
Protein: . . . . .51 gm
Carbohydrate: . . . . .54 gm
Cholesterol: . . . . .102 mg
Sodium: . . . . .1,734 mg
Diabetic exchange: 3½ vegetables, 2⅛ bread, 5¾ meat, 6⅛ fat.

SUMMER YIELDS TASTY TOMATILLOS

■ *What is a tomatillo?* The tomatillo is a native of Mexico, and it also goes by the names of tomate verde, Mexican green tomato, husk tomato and ground cherry. It is an important ingredient of such classic dishes of Mexico as salsa verde, or green salsa, which is frequently served with enchiladas, empanadas and tacos.

■ *Where do they come from?* Commercial farming of the tomatillo has increased in California and other Southwestern states with fresh distribution throughout the United States. I have recently seen them offered at local fruit markets and supermarkets. They are reasonably priced and a wonderful taste treat.

■ *Health advantages:* Tomatillos are rich in vitamin A and also contain niacin and vitamin C. They contain about 100 calories per cup.

TODAY'S LESSON: One of the treasures of late summer is the arrival of the tomatillo. These small green to yellow tomato-like fruits are enclosed in a tan papery husk. They have a firmer texture than a tomato, with a lemony flavor that's perfect for late-summer salsas, salads and sauces.

■ *How to select:* Tomatillos grow to sizes from 1 inch in diameter to that of a plum. On average, the yield is about 22 per pound. They are commonly found with a green or green-yellow color or with a purple tinge.

Select tomatillos with dry papery husks that show no signs of mold or rot. Peel the husks back slightly to see the flesh, which should be umblemished and smooth. The tomatillo should be firm (not soft like a tomato) but not rock-hard when mature.

Smaller tomatillos tend to have fewer seeds and more flesh. Although tomatillos are green, they should not be eaten when immature, while the flesh is quite hard, fibrous and dry. They will continue to ripen off the plant as long as they are in the papery husks.

■ *How to store:* Store tomatillos at room temperature in an open basket until the flesh softens from hard to just firm and the inside becomes moist. Once ripe, they may be stored uncovered in a parchment-

tomatillos are a fresh addition to your favorite salad.

■ *The cooking begins:* Tomatillos are more commonly served cooked, to soften the firm texture and skin while developing the lemony flavor. Cooked tomatillos are diced for salsas and garnishes, pureed for sauces and quartered in stews and other preparations.

■ *To roast:* Rinse with the husks on and place in an oven-proof dish without overlapping. Cook in an oven preheated to 450 until tender, about 10-15 minutes. Remove from the oven and allow to cool. Peel away the husks. Cut or puree.

■ *To saute:* Preheat skillet with a little olive oil. Add cleaned whole tomatillos to the pan and cook over medium heat until tender and the skins are lightly browned, about 5-10 minutes. Allow to cool and use in your favorite dishes.

■ *To boil:* Fill a medium-sized pot with cleaned whole tomatillos and cover with cold

■
The tomatillo is also known as the cape gooseberry. In its wild state, it's found chiefly in Mexico, Guatemala and South America below the equator.

lined bowl or dish in your refrigerator for up to 30 days. Check occasionally to ensure the husks are dry and the tomatillos are not molding.

■ *How to prepare:* Peel away the husks and remove the stems. Wash under running cold water to remove most of the sticky film.

■ *As they are:* Tomatillos are eaten raw in salads and salsas. They have a bright citrus flavor. They may be peeled to remove the coarse skin but are usually consumed in their entirety. Dice them and combine with peppers, red tomatoes and herbs with a splash of citrus juice and olive oil for a terrific salsa. Thinly sliced water. Bring to a simmer over high heat. Turn down the heat to just below a boil (to prevent splitting) and cook until tender, about 10-15 minutes from the simmer. Drain and allow to cool before using.

■

GRILLED CHICKEN WITH TOMATILLO & PEPPER SALSA

Makes 4 servings

¼ cup sesame seeds, toasted

½ chipotle pepper (smoked jalapeno), rehydrated or canned (or substitute a hot pepper sauce to taste; the weak of heart can substitute a little barbecue sauce)

½ red pepper, roasted, peeled and seeded

2 tablespoons fresh lime juice

Salt to taste

4 chicken halves, boned except wing and drumstick (your butcher can do this)

2 tablespoons virgin olive oil

Roast Tomatillo & Pepper Salsa (see accompanying recipe)

4 sprigs herbs of your choice for garnish

To make the spice compound for the chicken: In a food processor, combine sesame seeds, chipotle pepper and red pepper and process until a smooth paste is formed. Add the lime juice, then salt to taste. Transfer to a small bowl. Refrigerate until ready to use. Preheat the grill or broiler to 450. Lift the chicken skin and rub 2 tablespoons of the spice compound underneath. Rub chicken all over very lightly with olive oil. Place skin side to the heat on the grill until seared and golden, about 7 minutes. Turn over and cook until desired doneness is reached, about 8 minutes. Place the chicken in the center of the serving plate. Spoon the salsa over the chicken, garnish with herbs and serve.

Cooks note: Chipotle peppers are usually found canned. They are very hot with a great smoky flavor.

Nutrition details per serving
Calories 532
Percent of calories from fat 49%
Fat: .21 gm
Protein: . . . . .69 gm
Carbohydrate: . . . . .5 gm
Cholesterol: . . . . .166 mg
Sodium: . . . . .273 mg
Diabetic exchange: ¼ vegetable, 8⅓ meat, 2⅓ fat.

■

ROAST TOMATILLO & RED PEPPER SALSA

Makes 2 cups

10 medium tomatillos

2 red bell peppers, roasted, peeled, seeded and diced

2 tablespoons fresh lime juice

3 tablespoons virgin olive oil

½ cup snipped fresh chives

Salt to taste

1 jalapeno pepper, roasted, peeled and diced, optional

Preheat oven to 450. Wash tomatillos with the husks on. Transfer to an ovenproof pan or dish large enough that they do not overlap. Place on the lower rack of the oven and cook until tender, stirring often, about 10-15 minutes. Remove from oven and cool. Peel the husks and rinse the tomatillos if sticky. Cut all the tomatillos into fine dice.

To prepare the salsa: In a medium bowl, combine the peppers, tomatillos, lime juice, olive oil and chives. Season with salt and jalapeno pepper to your taste. Refrigerate until ready to serve.

Nutrition details per serving
Calories 198
Percent of calories from fat 48%
Fat: .12 gm
Protein: . . . . .4 gm
Carbohydrate: . . . . .24 gm
Cholesterol: . . . . .0 mg
Sodium: . . . . .411 mg
Diabetic exchange: 4½ vegetables, 2 fat.

TINY SQUASH HAS BIG FLAVOR

■ *Why it tastes better:* As members of the squash family mature, the vegetables grow to enormous size. But the flesh is mushy, filled with large seeds and covered by tough skin, which is not the least bit appetizing. The summer squash family is best enjoyed young and immature. The best are 2-3 inches in length. These sweet-tasting tiny squashes have crisp, delicate flesh and skin and virtually no seeds.

■ *What is summer squash?* Summer squash are the soft-skinned part of the family. They tend to spoil rather quickly compared to their winter squash cousins. Their names "summer" and "winter" refer not to their growing season but to the time of year they are best to eat. Winter squash grow right alongside their summer kin but need additional growing time into the fall to mature.

The summer squash family in the United States is com-

TODAY'S LESSON: Some gardeners and shoppers think bigger is better, but that's not so when it comes to summer squash.

posed of crookneck, patty pan (also called scallop or scallopini), straightneck, summer yellow and zucchini. There are many hybrids and variations of each of these species that emphasize the better characteristics of the vegetables.

■ *How to harvest:* To make sure you harvest squash soon enough, watch their development very carefully. In the heat of summer, they may grow up to a couple of inches in just one day!

■ *How to select:* Cut the squash from the plant, leaving about an inch of the stem attached to the vegetable. You can store them in the refrigerator for up to a week, but they are best if eaten immediately after picking. If you are harvesting at

your local market, select tiny, crisp, bright-colored vegetables without blemishes.

■ *How to cook:* A simple but wonderful preparation is to lightly saute or quick-steam, then splash with olive oil and a touch of great vinegar. Slice the squash into long pieces and add to your favorite pasta and herbs of the season. Whole miniature squashes are great sauteed in a splash of olive oil to concentrate the flavors, then added to your favorite baked pasta. Reserve the larger mature squash for breads, baked vegetable dishes and sauteed soft vegetable preparations.

■ *Great taste and tasty blossoms, too:* Summer squash also produce terrific blossoms that are

fantastic as a summer vegetable as well. The brightly colored blossoms are most prolific early in the season. The blossoms are very popular in Mediterranean ethnic recipes but are so delicate that they are not widely distributed.

■ *Harvesting blossoms:* If you have summer squash plants, harvest the male flowers, reserving a few for pollinating the female flowers. Save the females to produce the squash crop. The male blossoms have a narrow, stem-like base, while the females are easily identified by a swollen base that resembles the squash under development. It is common to get the blossom still attached to the miniature squashes, which is a double prize.

From the market, select tight squash blossoms with a freshly cut stem. The petals are usually quite delicate and limp. Refrigerate and keep moist until ready to use. The petals quickly deteriorate to a tissue-paper consistency, so use immediately.

■ *How to prepare:* Clean the squash blossoms by carefully peeling back a couple of petals and removing the stamens (the upright filaments of the flowers). Some people prefer not to clean the blossoms, but I suggest that you inspect each blossom for the large and slimy stamens that are often found. Gently dip or rinse the blossom in cool water to remove dirt or insects. Allow to dry on paper toweling. Squash blossoms are terrific dredged through milk or an egg wash, dusted with seasoned flour, then fried or sauteed until crisp. Their delicate flavor and texture are reinforced by the crispy texture of the light batter. Tempura-style batters, which are very thin yet crunchy crisp, are also terrific.

■ *How to cook:* Try stuffing the squash blossoms with fillings that complement zucchini-type flavors, such as olives, artichokes, fresh and sun-dried tomatoes, roasted sweet and hot peppers and, of course, garlic. I could eat a platter or two of squash blossom fritters with capers and olives any day of the week. Whether your preference is for the vegetable or the blossom, the delicate flavor and texture of summer squash will paint wonderful food memories for years to come.

■

FRIED SQUASH BLOSSOMS WITH ROAST PEPPER VINAIGRETTE

Makes 4 servings

16-20 squash blossoms, about 3 inches long
  Corn oil or virgin olive oil for frying
2 cups all-purpose flour
2 tablespoons paprika
1 teaspoon salt
¾ teaspoon freshly ground white pepper
2 large eggs, beaten
1 cup milk
1 cup Roast Pepper Vinaigrette (see accompanying recipe)
  Sprigs of fresh herbs to garnish

Working with one squash blossom at a time, carefully peel back one petal and remove the stamens. Fill a large, heavy, deep skillet with corn oil or olive oil to a depth of 3 inches. Heat over medium-high heat to 350. In a medium-size bowl, sift together the flour, paprika, salt and pepper.

In another medium-size bowl, combine the eggs and milk. Carefully drench the blossoms, one at a time, in the egg mixture. Shake the excess from the blossoms and transfer to the seasoned flour. Coat evenly, then shake to remove excess flour. Place the blossoms in the hot oil and cook until golden, about 4 minutes. Transfer to paper towel to drain. Arrange the blossoms in the center of the serving · plates, spoon the Roast Pepper Vinaigrette over the top, garnish with herbs and serve.

Cook's note: Select squash blossoms that are closed and bright in color. They deteriorate quickly after being cut from the plant, so use them immediately. The blossoms can also be sauteed instead of fried.

■

ROAST PEPPER VINAIGRETTE

Makes 1½ cups

1 red bell pepper, deeply roasted, peeled and seeded

½ cup balsamic vinegar

¼ teaspoon salt

½ cup virgin olive oil
   Freshly ground black pepper to taste

In a blender, combine the bell pepper, vinegar and salt; puree until smooth. Still processing, gradually add the olive oil. Adjust the salt and pepper to taste.

Nutrition details per serving
Calories .183
Percent of calories from fat 88%
Fat: .18 gm
Protein: . . . . .0 gm
Carbohydrate: . . . . .6 gm
Cholesterol: . . . . .0 mg
Sodium: . . . . .92 mg
Diabetic exchange: ⅛ vegetable, 3½ fat.

Summer and winter squashes

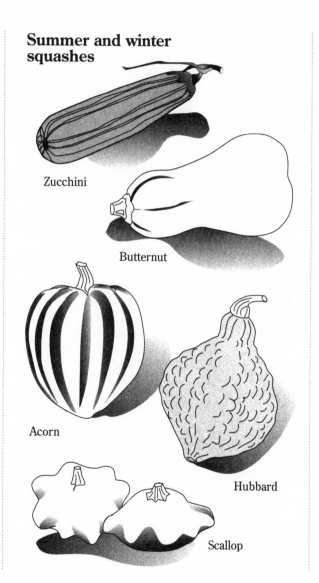

Zucchini

Butternut

Acorn

Hubbard

Scallop

GIANT POD HOLDS TASTY FAVA BEANS

■ *What they are:* Fava beans are popular throughout the world, but especially in the Mediterranean and Middle East, where they are enjoyed fresh while immature, or dried and prepared, or fried and salted as a snack. In Italy, favas are elevated to the sublime in many regional and specialty dishes. So what has prevented this terrific bean from reaching popularity on our tables? Maybe the giant pod, which insulates and cradles this delicacy, is imposing to the novice cook. Whatever the reason, the serious food lover should look again. Beauty is not always on the surface; it may be hidden for the adventurous to discover.

■ *What it tastes like:* The young fava, especially, is very delicate, with a wonderful deep earthy flavor. The silky texture almost melts in the mouth, without the thick and starchy characteristics of dried favas.

TODAY'S LESSON: With summer, produce markets are chock full of the most popular members of the bean family, such as green and wax beans. But pity their poor cousin, the fava bean. In America, it's often ignored.

■ *Health advantages:* Fava beans are low in calories — 80 per cup of cooked beans. These beans are high in protein, fiber and iron. They are high in vitamins A and C and potassium. They also contain some vitamin B.

■ *How to select:* Farmer's markets and ethnic Mediterranean markets are good sources for favas. Select smaller pods, preferably with even green color. The pod should be crisp and the stem end moist — the sign of a recent harvest. Store the beans loosely wrapped in plastic in the coldest part of your refrigerator for up to a week.

■ *How to prepare:* Shell the pods by tearing or cutting the ends off, then squeezing to open the pod and release the beans. Blanch beans in boiling salted water for just 30 seconds, then cool under running cold water or in an ice bath. Place each bean between your thumb and index fingers and squeeze firmly to pop and release from its coarse outer skin. The beans will need an additional few minutes of cooking depending on their maturity.

■ *Tricks of the trade:* You do the final cooking in the dish you're making. Avoid long cooking that will turn the delicate texture to mush; fresh fava beans require but a fraction of the time their dried counterparts do.

■ *Serving suggestions:* This recipe for Fava & Roast Shallot Linguine is a perfect side dish for salmon, chicken or lamb or served alone as a hearty vegetarian pasta.

■

FAVA & ROAST SHALLOT LINGUINE

Makes 4 side dish servings

2   cups peeled whole shallots

4   cloves peeled garlic

¼   cup extra-virgin olive oil, divided

Salt to taste

Freshly ground black pepper

2   cups cleaned fava beans, shelled, blanched and inner skin removed

½   cup dry white wine (or substitute water and juice of 1 lemon)

½   pound linguine noodles

¼   cup freshly snipped chives

¼   cup chopped Italian parsley

½   cup finely grated Parmesan or Romano cheese

Preheat oven to 400. In a baking dish or pan, combine the shallots, garlic and 1 tablespoon of the olive oil. Season with salt and generous sprinkling of pepper. Tightly cover the dish with aluminum foil, dull side out,

making sure the steam will not escape while cooking. Place on the lower rack of the oven and cook until tender, about 30 minutes. Remove from oven and cool on a cake rack to room temperature, about 1 hour. Do not open the foil until cool.

Meanwhile, remove the shells from the fava beans. Blanch the beans in boiling salted water for 30 seconds, then immediately drain and cool under running cold water. Place fava beans between your thumb and index finger and firmly squeeze to pop and release

the coarse outer skin.

Bring a large pot of water to a boil for the pasta. Add salt.

In a large skillet, heat the remaining olive oil over medium-high heat. Add the fava beans, cooking until crisped, about 2 minutes. Add the shallots, garlic, any juice from their cooking pan and the white wine. Cook until the wine is reduced to coat the back of the spoon, about 3 minutes. Adjust the salt and pepper to your taste.

Meanwhile, add the linguine to the boiling water, cooking until al dente, about 5-6 minutes. Drain and add to the skillet, tossing to combine all the ingredients. Adjust the seasonings with salt and pepper to your taste. Add the chives and the parsley, tossing to combine. Divide the pasta to your serving dishes. Top the pasta with the cheese and serve.

Nutrition details per serving
Calories .465
Percent of calories from fat 34%
Fat: .18 gm
Protein: . . . . .16 gm
Carbohydrate: . . . . .52 gm
Cholesterol: . . . . .9 mg
Sodium: . . . . .262 mg
Diabetic exchange: 1¾ vegetables, 2⅝ bread, ¾ meat, 3 fat.

STEAMED VEGGIES KEEP THEIR FLAVOR

■ *Why steaming makes them taste so good:* Steaming over water preserves more of the true, natural flavors than boiling, which causes vegetables to lose more of their water-soluble nutrients, essential oils and flavors. Using a seasoned liquid will impart the seasoning flavors to the vegetables, often with interesting results.

Steaming in foil uses little additional moisture; the vegetables steam in their own or another vegetable's juices. The technique concentrates the natural juices to a new high of pure, clean, rich vegetable flavor.

■ *Other advantages:* Steaming is probably the fastest and most healthful way to cook vegetables. It does not add fat, and preparing vegetables al dente — firm to the bite — yields the highest possible nutritional value.

■ *Tricks of the trade:* Because they are so simply prepared,

TODAY'S LESSON: Steaming fresh vegetables, on the stove or in foil packets on the grill.

the vegetables must be of superior quality. Choose absolutely fresh vegetables at the peak of their season.

Add salt to the water after it comes to a boil in a steamer pot; because salt raises the water's boiling point, the steam will be hotter and will result in faster cooking. The salt in the water does not enter the vegetables.

Do not cover the steamer pot. Although the cover will hold the steam in, the vegetable's acids being released during cooking will collect on the lid and drip back, discoloring the vegetables.

■ *Preparing the vegetables:* Steaming works best on small to medium-sized vegetables such as asparagus, baby artichokes and snow peas. Cut

large vegetables into uniform, medium sizes before steaming. Large vegetables can be steamed, but they take a long time and may get too soft outside before the inside is cooked. Vegetables may be peeled, especially if they have a coarse outer skin, to ensure even cooking.

■ *The cooking begins:* Bring water to a boil over high heat in an acid-resistant pan. Add salt to raise the boiling point. Insert the steamer screen or basket containing vegetables. Do not cover. Cook until al dente and enjoy.

■ *Steaming on the grill:* Lay out a big piece of aluminum foil with the shiny side up. Place prepared vegetables in a single layer in the center of the foil.

Moisten with a little water or wine, and add your choice of herbs and spices. Fold the foil over, and firmly crimp the edges to seal. Carefully transfer the foil package to the grill on a cookie sheet to keep the vegetables from mounding up inside.

Cook the packet directly on the grill if the heat is moderate, or cook on the cookie sheet if the heat is high. Turn the foil over if you can about halfway through cooking — after about 5 minutes for small vegetables or 10 minutes for large or dense vegetables. Allow to cool slightly in the foil before serving.

Another method that works extremely well is to enclose the vegetables in lettuce leaves inside the foil; the lettuce provides additional moisture as the packet steams and protects the vegetables from excessive heat.

■ *Serving suggestions:* The purity of steamed vegetables is hard to beat. Add a little butter or extra-virgin olive oil for richness if you choose. I prefer a splash of citrus vinaigrette with a few fresh herbs to let those best-of-summer flavors come through.

■ *Try your technique* in my recipe for Sweet Corn & Chives steamed with the lettuce-and-foil method.

■

GRILL-STEAMED SWEET CORN & CHIVES

Makes 4 servings

8   large lettuce leaves, preferably the coarse outer leaves from a big head of romaine lettuce, washed, dried

4   ears fresh sweet corn, husk and silk removed

Salt to taste

Freshly ground black pepper to taste

¼   cup snipped fresh chives, divided

Preheat grill.

Lay out two lettuce leaves slightly overlapping each other. Place one ear of corn in the center of the lettuce leaves. Season with salt, pepper and 1 tablespoon of the chives. Roll the lettuce leaves around the corn to enclose. Transfer to the center of a piece of aluminum foil, shiny side up, and wrap tightly. Repeat this procedure with the remaining three ears of corn, salt, pepper and remaining 3 tablespoons chives.

Place corn wrapped in foil on a medium-hot area of the grill. Cook for about 5-10 minutes, depending on size of corn. Turn the corn over to ensure even cooking and continue to cook another 5 minutes. Check ears to see if they are cooked. Continue cooking for another few minutes if necessary.

Remove from grill, carefully open the foil and remove the corn from the lettuce leaves. Discard leaves. Serve with sweet butter or olive oil if desired.

Nutrition details per serving
Calories 118
Percent of calories from fat 6%
Fat: . . . . .1 gm
Protein: . . . . .4 gm
Carbohydrate: . . . . .28 gm
Cholesterol: . . . . .0 mg
Sodium: . . . . .276 mg
Diabetic exchange: ¼ vegetable, 1¾ bread.

THE THRILL OF GRILLED VEGGIES

■ *Why grilled vegetables taste so good:* The distinct grilled flavor comes from the caramelization of natural sugars with amino acids. This combination of fire, sugars and acids creates hundreds of soul-satisfying flavor compounds.

■ *Health advantages:* Grilling is one of the most healthful ways to prepare vegetables. A light brushing of olive or canola oil to help sear and cook the food is the only fat necessary. The caramelized flavor eliminates the need for salt; with a few herbs or spices, it will never be missed.

■ *Tricks of the trade:* The secret is to sear the outside of the vegetable by cooking quickly over high heat. This way, you retain the moisture and flavor inside. Don't grill vegetables slowly over low heat.

■ *Preparing the veggies:* Different vegetables require different handling.

TODAY'S LESSON: Grilling vegetables is a way to celebrate the outdoor season without missing meats.

Divide the vegetables into two categories: firm and light.

Firm vegetables such as carrots, large asparagus, artichokes and leeks are best if first blanched until tender in boiling water. Firm vegetables should be sliced as thin as ¼ inch to be cooked through.

Light vegetables will cook easily in a few minutes on the grill and do not need blanching. Peppers, onions and mushrooms will cook quickly without burning and can be put on the grill in larger pieces. Large vegetables such as eggplant and zucchini must be cut to ¼- to 1½-inch thickness before grilling to ensure even, thorough cooking.

■ *The cooking begins:* Brush or toss the vegetables in a very little bit of good olive oil with fresh ground black pepper and a few herbs of your choice. Start with too little olive oil, and add 1 tablespoon at a time. Do not soak the vegetables. The oil should just glaze the veggies so the dry heat of the fire is quickly transferred to the vegetables for a good sear. Too much oil will drip from the vegetables onto the fire and cause flare-ups.

■ *Season the grill:* Before you start, rub the grill with a tightly rolled paper or cloth towel lightly dabbed in oil. The grill should be about 3 inches from the coals.

■ *Cooking:* Make sure to keep the firm and light vegetables separate. Place vegetables on the grill starting with those that take longest to cook. Place vegetables skin side up for searing. Position the largest vegetables over the hottest part of the fire with the most tender ones on the cooler edges.

Once the vegetables are seared on one side, usually in 3-5 minutes, carefully turn them over to finish cooking. Season with a light sprinkle of sea salt, if desired. They should have some grill marks on them, but don't burn the vegetables just trying to get the marks. The vegetables are best al dente.

■ *Serving suggestions:* Grilled vegetables can be served simply or enhanced with fresh herbs, a few drops of good vinegar or fresh citrus, and a drizzle of extra-virgin olive oil. Top them with shaved or finely grated cheese.

■ *Mix and match:* Sweet peppers, garlic, onions and zucchini are a perfect summer combination. Wild and cultivated mushrooms seasoned with garlic, olive oil, salt and black pepper are incredible when grilled. Grilled vegetables are great mixed into green salads and warm and chilled pasta dishes.

■

GRILLED MUSHROOMS, SCALLIONS & SWEET ONION SALAD

Makes 4 servings

1½ pounds assorted wild and domestic mushrooms, brushed clean, cut if necessary into large pieces

2 garlic cloves, peeled, ends removed, minced

¼ cup extra-virgin olive oil
Generous dose of freshly ground black pepper

1 bunch green onions, cut into ½-inch slices

2 sweet onions, peeled, ends removed, cut into ½-inch slices

3 tablespoons balsamic vinegar

2 tablespoons snipped fresh chives, divided

¼ cup loose Italian flat parsley leaves

1 bunch arugula leaves

Preheat the grill. In a large bowl, combine mushrooms,

garlic, olive oil and pepper, mixing just to evenly coat. Add green onions and sweet onions, mixing to coat well.

Lay the onion slices in the center of the grill over the highest flame. Position the mushrooms around the onions, making sure not to crowd. Lay the scallions perpendicular to the cooking grates on the edge of the grill to prevent them from falling into the fire. Cook until the vegetables are seared, about 4 minutes, then turn to expose the uncooked surfaces. Season with salt as necessary to taste. Cook for about 3 more minutes until hot yet still slightly crunchy.

Transfer to a large bowl. Add the vinegar, 1 tablespoon of the chives and parsley; toss to mix.

Arrange the arugula greens on a serving plate. Distribute grilled vegetables atop the greens in a mound. Drizzle with a little additional olive oil if you prefer. Sprinkle remaining 1 tablespoon chives over the salad. Serve immediately.

Nutrition details per serving
Calories .212
Percent of calories from fat 64%
Fat: . . . . .17 gm
Protein: . . . . .7 gm
Carbohydrate: . . . . .15 gm
Cholesterol: . . . . .0 mg
Sodium: . . . . .17 mg
Diabetic exchange: 1¼ vegetables, 2¾ fat.

■

GRILLED ONION, FENNEL & PEPPER SALAD

Makes 4 servings

2   Vidalia onions, peeled and sliced ¼ inch thick

2   medium fennel bulbs, stalks trimmed, coarse outer leaves removed, sliced ¼ inch thick

   Salt to taste

   Freshly ground pepper to taste

2   red bell peppers, whole

2   yellow bell peppers, whole

2   ears corn, husk and silk intact

¼   cup lemon juice

¼   cup fresh basil leaves, chopped

2   tablespoons olive oil

4   springs basil for garnish

   Preheat grill or broiler. Lay the onion and fennel slices across the grill. Cook until seared, about 4 minutes. Using a metal spatula, turn over and continue cooking until tender, about 3 more minutes. Remove to a platter. Season with salt and pepper.

   Place the corn and peppers on the grill. Cover. Cook the peppers and corn until the outer skin and husks are blackened. Rotate to cook all exposed surfaces.

   When done, transfer to a bowl to cool. Clean the peppers under running cool water to remove the skin. Then core and remove seeds and stems from the peppers. Tear into 1-inch-long strips. Transfer to the platter with the onions and fennel.

   Remove the husks and silk from the corn. Using a sharp knife, cut the corn kernels from the cob and transfer to a medium-size stainless steel bowl. Add the lemon juice, basil and olive oil, mixing to combine. Season with salt and pepper to taste.

   To serve, arrange the vegetables artistically onto the serving plates. Spoon the corn vinaigrette over the vegetables. Garnish with a sprig of basil and serve.

Nutrition details per serving
Calories 185
Percent of calories from fat 34%
Fat: . . . . .8 gm
Protein: . . . . .4 gm
Carbohydrate: . . . . .29 gm
Cholesterol: . . . . .0 mg
Sodium: . . . . .167 mg
Diabetic exchange: 1½ vegetables, 1¼ bread, 1⅜ fat.

DRYING CAPTURES SUMMER'S BOUNTY

■ *Why they taste so good:* The best fruits and vegetables are harvested at their peak. The slow drying concentrates the fruit's already superior flavor, while compacting its bulk. The resulting flavor is more intense and far richer, perfect for using now or to save for more robust fall dishes.

■ *Advantages:* Concentrated flavors of dried produce can pick up the depth of just about any savory or sweet dish. This method is great for using up extra-ripe fruit and taking advantage of the summer season's inexpensive prices. And less salt will be needed in recipes because the flavor is so intense.

■ *What kinds of foods to dry:* Fruits and moist vegetables work best. Fruits such as peaches, apricots, cherries and apples are my favorites. Tomatoes — which are really fruits, by the way — and chili peppers are the most popular vegetables to dry.

TODAY'S LESSON: Drying fruits or vegetables under the sun or in the oven.

■ *Tricks of the trade:* For the best flavor, select the ripest fruits and vegetables, even nearing the point of overripeness. Make sure they are about the same size so they will all take about the same time to dry.

Many of these foods can be dried under the sun on a hot day to keep the heat out of the kitchen.

Prepare as directed and place on a screen in the sun, covering entirely with a layer of cheesecloth to protect against insects. Keep them in even heat all day until finished. If the sun doesn't do the trick, transfer to an oven to finish.

■ *Preparing your fruits and vegetables:* Thoroughly scrub the skins to remove any chemical sprays and bugs. Cut in half, usually lengthwise, retaining

as much of the juices as possible. Lay on a cake rack atop an ovenproof sheet or cookie pan. Season the vegetables with salt and fresh ground pepper and a few complementary herbs if you wish. Fruits may be seasoned with sugar and spices to taste.

■ *The drying begins:* Preheat the oven to 200 degrees. Place the pan with fruit or vegetables on the lower rack of the oven. Position a wooden spoon at the top of the oven door to keep it slightly ajar when closed. The spoon will create a small draft through the oven to facilitate drying.

Convection ovens work very well for drying because of the recirculating air flow inside. The drying process is enhanced by the air flow, which will reduce drying time by about half.

AMAZING FOOD FACTS

■

Drying fruits and vegetables is an old technique being rediscovered. It was practiced to preserve fruits and vegetables for use during harsh winter months. The drying technique preserved the vitamin content as well as the product itself.

■ *Drying is a slow, easy job:* Check the foods hourly to see that at least slight progress is being made. Small tomatoes will take 6-8 hours, depending on the relative humidity of the day and your oven. Check the foods about every half hour once they begin to shrivel, until they are about half their original size. They should still be supple and pliable, never dry and hard. Remove from the oven to cool.

■ *Storing the fruits of your labor:* Vegetables such as tomatoes and peppers are best stored tightly packed in a clean jar and submerged in good olive oil under refrigeration. The oil will prevent the foods from additional drying or becoming soggy.

Fruit tightly packed in heavy-duty, zip-closure bags and refrigerated maintain that fresh-picked flavor, but only for a month or two. For longer storage, they may be frozen or, better yet, packed tightly in a jar like the vegetables and covered with

wine or brandy. Covering the fruit with vinegar will also make a good vinegar over a short period. Refrigerate the bottles.

■ *What do you do with them?* Savory vegetables such as the tomatoes and chili peppers can be used anywhere you would use fresh ones. But use less because of the concentrated flavor.

Sun-dried tomatoes can be used on pizza, with pasta, on a rack of lamb, in a salad and even pureed for a boost to tomato flavors.

The sweeter fruits are perfect for a stand-alone souffle, great when added in pies, tarts and other fruit preparations and perfect for spicy chutney and salsa. I enjoy them best as a snack, or pureed with champagne and a few other condiments for eye-opening frozen cocktails.

■ *Mix and match:* To get started, try using the surplus fruit in your kitchen. Different fruit can be mixed on the tray and simply removed as each one gets done; no need to separate.

■ *Try your technique:* My favorite is tomatoes with seasoned oils.

■

OVEN-DRIED TOMATOES

Makes about 1 pound

2   pounds roma
    tomatoes
    Salt
    Freshly ground black
    pepper
    Chopped herbs of
    your choice, such as
    oregano or thyme
    Olive oil

Preheat the oven to 200 degrees.

Wash the tomatoes under running cold water and drain until dry. Cut the tomatoes in half lengthwise and place on a large cake rack atop a cookie sheet. Season the tomatoes with salt, pepper and herbs. Place the tomatoes on the upper rack of the oven and slide a wooden spoon between the oven and the door to create a small opening for ventila-

tion. Allow the tomatoes to dry until shrunken by about half but still pliable, about 8 hours. Remove from the oven and allow to cool. Store in a clean glass jar, tightly packed and covered with olive oil or in a zip-closure bag under refrigeration.

Nutrition details per serving
Calories 52
Percent of calories from fat 63%
Fat: .4 gm
Protein: . . . . .1 gm
Carbohydrate: . . . . .5 gm
Cholesterol: . . . . .0 mg
Sodium: . . . . .9 mg
Diabetic exchange: ¾ vegetable, ¾ fat.

OVEN-DRIED TOMATOES, CAPERS & BASIL PIZZA

Makes one 9-inch pizza

1 pizza crust (see accompanying recipe)

Cornmeal for dusting the pizza

½ cup chopped fresh basil, divided

1 tablespoon virgin olive oil

¼ cup grated fontinella cheese

¼ cup grated mozzarella cheese

¼ cup nonpareil capers, drained

½ cup diced oven-dried tomatoes

¼ cup finely grated Parmesan cheese

Place a pizza stone in the lower third of the oven and preheat to 550 degrees. Dust the bottom of the crust with cornmeal. Combine half of the chopped basil with the olive oil and spread across the dough. Cover with the fontinella and mozzarella cheeses. Distribute the capers and tomatoes over the cheeses.

Place on the stone. Bake 8-12 minutes, until the crust is golden.

Remove from the oven, sprinkle with the Parmesan cheese and the remaining basil.

Nutrition details per serving
Calories 294
Percent of calories from fat 55%
Fat: . . . . .17 gm
Protein: . . . . .12 gm
Carbohydrate: . . . . .22 gm
Cholesterol: . . . . .52 mg
Sodium: . . . . .278 mg
Diabetic exchange: 1¼ medium fat meat, ¼ vegetable, 1¼ bread, 2 fat.

PIZZA DOUGH

Makes five 9-inch circles

1 package yeast

2 tablespoons sugar

1 cup lukewarm water, about 110 degrees

4 cups all-purpose flour
Pinch of salt

2 large eggs, beaten

1 tablespoon virgin olive oil

In a small bowl, combine the yeast, sugar and warm water. Let set until it foams.

In a food processor with a plastic dough blade or regular blade, combine the flour and salt. Mix in the eggs, then the yeast mixture, until a ball forms. Work just until the dough pulls away from the side of the bowl, then add the olive oil. Remove the dough immediately to an oiled bowl, cover with a clean cloth and allow to rise to double in a dry, warm place, about 45 minutes. Punch down, then allow to double again, about 20 minutes. Form into 5 balls.

Lightly flour the dough and counter. Roll into very thin 9-inch circles.

Proceed with toppings and bake or grill according to individual recipes, or hold between wax paper in the refrigerator till needed, up to 3 days.

Cook's note: The pizza dough is quite fluffy when baked the same day. The following day, the dough produces a flatter, more cracker-like crust.

Nutrition details per serving
Calories 444
Percent of calories from fat 17%
Fat: .8 gm
Protein: . . . . .13 gm
Carbohydrate: . . . . .77 gm
Cholesterol: . . . . .85 mg
Sodium: . . . . .75 mg
Diabetic exchange: ¼ medium fat meat, 4¾ bread, 1 fat.

COOL PASTA FOR A HOT DAY

AMAZING FOOD FACTS

■

Traditional pasta is made from durum wheat, ground into flour called semolina. There is a resurgence of interest in two grains called spelt and kamut and in turning them into pasta and other products. Both grains are more nutritious than wheat.

■ *Why pasta salad tastes so good:* Pasta salad tastes great because it allows the flavor of the ingredients to come through. The slightly sweet and nutty pasta flavor works so well with raw and cooked garden-fresh vegetables – for instance, squeezed ripe tomatoes scented with just-picked basil. Pasta is also a terrific background for fish and poultry, scented with herbs and easily served as the main course. It adapts to most sauces, from a splash of vinegar to a rich aioli or mayonnaise.

■ *The best pasta for chilled salads:* The taste and texture of great pasta come from extra hard durum wheat, which when ground becomes semolina flour. Great pasta is made from 100 percent semolina flour, water and maybe a touch of olive oil. It is then carefully kneaded, formed into long noodles and short shapes, then dried to develop resilient texture when cooked.

TODAY'S LESSON: When the mercury rises on those sultry days of August, few things are as satisfying as a cool pasta salad.

Lesser pastas may use semolina, but usually it's blended with flour from winter wheat, then combined with eggs. This produces a softer, almost mushy texture, which becomes very apparent the second day in a soggy, chilled salad.

■ *Health advantages:* Pasta is almost all carbohydrate, a preferred energy source for the body. It is nutritious and provides fuel for summer sports and recreation. Selecting fresh fruits and herbs will keep fat levels low but keep the nutrition and taste levels high. Grilled fish and meat will also keep the recipe lean. Avoid richer mayonnaise-style sauces; instead, add a splash of extra-

virgin olive oil for a silky texture.

Chilled pastas are easy to make. They are also great served au naturel. Toss in fresh or grilled ingredients with the room-temperature pasta and garnishes. Chill leftovers thoroughly.

■ *Tricks of the trade:* Begin by seasoning the cooking water. Salt will prevent the pasta from tasting bland, and a few strong, dried hot chili peppers will enrich the flavor without burning your taste buds. If you are avoiding salt, add lemon juice with the chilis.

To serve chilled pasta, cook it slightly longer than you would to serve it hot. Drain in a colander and rinse under running lukewarm water. Lukewarm water washes away some of the starch gel outside the pasta; cool water sets the gel. Gradually change the water temperature to cool. Drain well, then coat with a splash of olive or canola oil to keep pasta from sticking.

■ *Choose your shape:* Any shape will work chilled, but the best are the short, broader cuts such as fusilli (twisted spaghetti), penne (quill), rotini or rotelle (twists, screws or spirals) and ruote (wagon wheels). These shapes stay more distinct in the salads; the long noodles tend to lump together.

■ *To cook or not to cook:* For a fast and simple method, fresh, raw ingredients make a wonderful pasta salad if their flavors are fully developed and quite strong, such as with chilis, herbs and onions. For my taste, grilling, sauteing or roasting vegetables concentrates their flavors and develops their natural sweetness, the best

to marry with the subtle flavors of pasta.

■ *The mixing begins:* Make sure the pasta is very strongly seasoned with salt, pepper, spices and any acids such as vinegar or citrus. Add the vegetables, poultry and herbs and mix. Fish is more delicate, so add at the last second and gently mix to prevent it from shredding beyond recognition. Adjust the seasoning again, because the new additions will drink their share from the mix. Refrigerate until cold.

■ *Serving suggestions:* Remove the salad from the refrigerator a short time before serving to allow the flavors to come alive. Check the seasoning one last time because the pasta will continue to absorb seasoning. Check the texture, especially if you have great olive oil, which tends to become thick and viscous when cold.

■

CHILLED ROCK SHRIMP & PENNE PASTA SALAD

Makes 4 servings

1 pound penne pasta
¾ cup virgin olive oil, divided
⅓ cup balsamic vinegar
    Salt to taste
    Freshly ground black pepper to taste
1 tablespoon minced garlic
½ cup diced red onion
1 pound rock or gulf shrimp, shelled
¼ cup chopped basil
¼ cup chives
2 red bell peppers, roasted peeled, seeded and diced
2 yellow bell peppers, roasted, peeled, seeded and diced
¼ cup grated Parmesan cheese
4 sprigs basil or fresh herbs for garnish

In a large amount of boiling water, cook the pasta until just beyond al dente.

Transfer to a strainer, rinse with warm water and then cold to chill. Drain well, then toss with ½ cup olive oil, vinegar, salt and pepper to taste. Refrigerate.

In a medium-size saucepan, over medium-high heat, heat remaining ¼ cup of olive oil. Add the garlic and onions, cooking until tender, about 3 minutes. Add the shrimp and cook until hot, about 3 minutes. Remove from heat and season with salt and pepper. Transfer to a large bowl and stir in the basil, chives and peppers. Refrigerate.

To serve, combine the shrimp mixture with the pasta. Adjust the salt and pepper to taste. Distribute onto four serving plates, top with Parmesan cheese, garnish each with a basil sprig and serve.

Nutrition details per serving
Calories 955
Percent of calories from fat 43%
Fat: . . . ./ . . . . .46 gm
Protein: . . . ./ . . . . .40 gm
Carbohydrate: . . . . .93 gm
Cholesterol: . . . . .176 mg
Sodium: . . . . .266 mg
Diabetic exchange: 1 vegetable, 2½ lean meat, 5¾ bread, 7½ fat.

ADD LIFE
WITH FINE HERBS

CHERVIL

CHIVES

PARSLEY

TARRAGON

■ *What are the fine herbs?* These fine herbs are best known as the pronounced flavors of sauce bearnaise: chervil, chives, parsley and tarragon. The blend may be used in many wonderful spring and summer dishes, or two or more may be mixed for many terrific combinations.

■ *Where do they come from?* Chervil and parsley come from the carrot family. Chervil, popular in France, has a delicate flavor similar to fennel. Tender chervil is best when harvested and eaten young. To preserve chervil, freeze it. Drying diminishes its true flavor.

Parsley is the kitchen's cornerstone, the universal herb for everything from stocks, salads and sauces to fish and meats. Curly parsley is most common and popular for its culinary and ornamental qualities, while flat parsley is superior for flavor and cooking. The turnip-rooted parsley variety produces the edible root, but

TODAY'S LESSON: Herbs embellish smell, taste and sight. They stimulate the appetite and aid digestion. Combined as bouquet garnis, sachets and potpourri, their most famous blend for seasoning is "fines herbes."

its coarse leaves are of little culinary significance.

The tender greens of chives, a member of the onion family, have a taste between onion and garlic and can go into any dish that calls for onion. Pinch the flowers to keep the chive plant from maturing and add them to your salad. The tiny bulbs are great pickled at the end of the season.

Tarragon is the only herbal member of the daisy family and is truly the king of herbs. The delicate licorice-like flavor brightens even the simplest dishes. Tarragon's pronounced flavor is the best herbal replacement for salt and pepper, the perfect match for sub-

tle poultry and fish and romaine salad, and a special spark in tart pickles, vinegars and mustards.

■ *How to save for a rainy day:* The bounty of the spring and summer herb crop may be captured in vinegars and oils to save for another day's preparation. These lightly scented ingredients will add a spark to your vinaigrettes, salad dressings and other dishes.

■ *Can you freeze?* To help the more delicate herbs such as chervil and tarragon retain that fresh flavor, place in a heavy freezer bag, expel all the air, seal and freeze. To use:

Remove only the amount of herbs necessary and add them directly to your recipe while still frozen. Reseal the bag and return the remaining herbs to the freezer without allowing them to thaw.

■ *Fresh is best:* Herbs are best when picked and served immediately. If you harvest herbs before preparation, refrigerate them immediately to prevent wilting and allow them to chill before using. Store in the vegetable crisper of your refrigerator in a plastic or paper bag pierced with holes to prevent condensation, which will discolor them.

■ *How to get the most of the flavor:* Add all fresh herbs to your recipe at the last second to capture the fresh flavor. There are two ways. The first method is to complete the sauce, then add the chopped herbs and allow to infuse for an hour or longer. Reheat and serve the sauce but avoid simmering. The second method uses the stems. Leaves are added to balance the infused and fresh flavors just before

serving. The stems may be added loose if the sauce is to be strained, or they can be wrapped in cheesecloth.

■

ROMAINE & PIMIENTO SALAD WITH FINE HERB DRESSING

Makes 4 servings

24 ¼-inch thick slices of ficelle, a long thin baguette of French bread, about the diameter of a silver dollar

4 ounces goat cheese
Freshly ground black pepper

1 head romaine lettuce, cut into 2-inch pieces

4 pimientos, cut into large julienne strips (or substitute red peppers, roasted, peeled, seeded and cut)

1 cup Fine Herb Dressing (see accompanying recipe)

Preheat oven to 375 degrees. Lay the ¼-inch thick

slices of bread across a cookie sheet. Toast in the oven until crisp, about 5 minutes. Turn over and toast, making sure the bottom is crisp. Allow the croutons to cool.

Spread the goat cheese across the croutons. Sprinkle with a liberal coating of black pepper and press into the cheese.

In a large bowl, combine the lettuce, pimientos and dressing. Toss. Add the croutons, tossing just to combine. Distribute to plates.

Nutrition details per serving
Calories 384
Percent of calories from fat 22%
Fat: . . . . .9 gm
Protein: . . . . .15 gm
Carbohydrate: . . . . .60 gm
Cholesterol: . . . . .25 mg
Sodium: . . . . .686 mg
Diabetic exchange: ⅓ vegetable, 4¼ bread, ⅞ meat, 1½ fat.

■

FINE HERB DRESSING

Makes 2 cups

2 tablespoons minced shallots

2 tablespoons red wine vinegar

¼ cup fresh lemon juice

¾ cup virgin olive oil

½ teaspoon salt (or to your taste)

1 teaspoon coarsely ground black pepper

¼ cup snipped fresh chives

¼ cup snipped fresh chervil

¼ cup chopped fresh tarragon

¼ cup chopped fresh parsley

In a medium-size bowl, combine the shallots, vinegar, lemon juice and olive oil. Season with the salt and pepper to taste. Stir in the herbs. Refrigerate until serving. Will hold for up to 2 weeks in refrigerator.

Nutrition details per serving
Calories 369
Percent of calories from fat 96%
Fat: .41 gm
Protein: . . . . .0 gm
Carbohydrate: . . . . .3 gm
Cholesterol: . . . . .0 gm
Sodium: . . . . .269 mg
Diabetic exchange: ⅛ vegetable, 8¼ fat.

PLEASE DO EAT THESE FLOWERS

■ *Why would you want to eat flowers?* For centuries, edible flowers have been added to dishes. They provide not only a touch of bright color but also a subtle, fresh flavor.

■ *Can you eat any flower?* Carefully identify and research all the flowers you intend to eat, because not all are edible. Some are poisonous. Pesticides, herbicides and fungicides have a residue that stays with flowers, so do not eat those that have been exposed to these agents. Flowers from a florist probably were treated with many agents, so don't eat them.

■ *Added bonus:* Harvesting flowers helps prevent herbs and certain lettuces from reaching maturity. Pinch the flowers from the plant and toss them into your favorite recipes. The herb or lettuce leaves will stay tender as the plant generates more flowers to reach its maturity.

TODAY'S LESSON: The most wonderful ingredients in your garden may be the very thing you're overlooking.

■ *How to harvest edible flowers:* Pinch the flower from the stem just below the blossom. Shake the flowers to remove any insects. Remove the flower's stem, base, stamen and sepal. The simplest way to enjoy edible flowers is to add them to a green salad. You can add smaller blossoms to the salad whole, but you probably will prefer to snip the larger petals into julienne-size pieces. Select light and simple vinaigrette dressings that will allow the flowers' flavors to come through. Flowers can be stored in an airtight plastic bag for a few days.

■ *How to select:* The best flowers for salads are nasturtiums, chives, rosemary, thyme and other herb flowers. The nasturtiums have a terrific peppery flavor, and the herb flowers have a soft floral hint that reflects their herb species. Some edible flowers, such as those from the squash family — zucchini, summer and pumpkin — are perfect for cooking. They can be stuffed and sauteed or fried, or added to frittatas, omelettes, pancakes and crepes.

■ *How to cook:* Both hot and chilled light clear soups come alive when garnished with a dusting of edible flower petals. Add the petals just before serving. The delicate petals also are great paired with grilled vegetables or sliced fresh cucumber in a tea sandwich. Some edible flowers, such as violets, roses, lemon blossoms and acacia, are perfect for candying. Their delicate flavors, captured in the candy, make them glorious garnishes for desserts.

EDIBLE FLOWERS

ANISE HYSSOP

Lilac-colored blossoms that bloom for several months. The flavor resembles root beer and is great in salads and sweet pastries and as a garnish. The leaves also produce a wonderful tea.

BORAGE

Large blue flowers with a cucumber-like flavor. Great in salads and fruit compotes and candied for desserts.

HERB FLOWERS

The most popular are chives, rosemary, thyme, lavender, oregano, marjoram, basil, onion and garlic blossoms, cilantro and sage.

JOHNNY JUMP-UPS

Small flowers of violet, mauve, yellow and white that resemble little pansies. Light wintergreen flavor is terrific in salads and garnishes for desserts and pastries.

MUSTARDS

Bright yellow flowers with a pungent mustard bite that will spark up any salad or other dish. The green usually becomes too strong for salads after the flowers have set.

NASTURTIUMS

One of the largest families of edible flowers, ranging from whirlybirds to traditional blossom shapes in a rainbow of colors. Nasturtiums are my favorite for salads, spicing up summer salsas, compound butters, vinaigrettes and grilled dishes. They bloom until frost if kept well picked and maintained.

ROSE PETALS

A delicate addition to salads and teas. The petals are used for jams, sugars, vinegars, syrups and jellies. Older varieties seem to have better flavor. Compared with the lighter-colored varieties, the red flowers have a mineral flavor. (The mature set flower produces the seed pods called rose hips, which have a very high vitamin C content and are terrific for teas.)

PANSIES

Mild flavor in blue, orange and purple colors, best for garnishes, salads and candying.

SAFFLOWER

This small orange blossom is slightly bitter. Good in salads and cooked in rice or added to pasta as a summer garnish.

SQUASH FAMILY

Zucchini, summer and pumpkin flowers are my favorite for stuffing and frying or sauteing. Check carefully for insects and remove the stamen and sepals. Cut the flowers into julienne for pancakes, omelettes, soups and salad.

VIOLETS

Easy-to-identify small purple flower, which has been captured in candy for centuries and is a natural for dessert garnishes. Also good in salads and on tea sandwiches.

GRILLED SALMON WITH NASTURTIUM VINAIGRETTE

Makes 4 servings

3   tablespoons red wine vinegar

¼   cup fined diced shallots, placed in a clean lined towel and rinsed under running cold water; squeeze out excess moisture (or substitute white of scallions)

5   tablespoons extra-virgin olive oil

    Salt to taste

    Freshly ground black pepper

¾   cup snipped nasturtium flowers

¼   cup snipped fresh chives

8   salmon escallops, 3 ounces each

4   sprigs chives or parsley for garnish

Preheat the grill or broiler. In a small bowl, combine the vinegar, the shallots and 4 tablespoons of the olive oil. Whisk until combined. Season with salt and pepper to taste. Add the nasturtiums and chives.

Rub the surfaces of the salmon with the remaining olive oil. Season the salmon with salt and pepper. Place on the grill, allowing to sear, about 3 minutes. Turn the escallops over and cook until done, testing by inserting a skewer for firmness and warmth, approximately 3 minutes, depending on thickness.

Place two escallops of salmon on each serving plate slightly overlapping each other. Whisk the vinaigrette and spoon over the salmon. Garnish the plate with the sprig of herbs and serve.

Nutrition details per serving
Calories 411
Percent of calories from fat 62%
Fat: . . . . .28 gm
Protein: . . . . .34 gm
Carbohydrate: . . . . .5 gm
Cholesterol: . . . . .94 mg
Sodium: . . . . .344 mg
Diabetic exchange: ¼ vegetable, 4⅓ meat, 3⅝ fat.

DRESSED-DOWN SALADS

■ *Dressing up:* The best way to produce clean-tasting new salads is to splash them with seasoned vinegars. For a mild fruit overtone that enhances many green vegetables and pastas, try vinegars flavored with raspberry or strawberry. Sherry and balsamic vinegars are also good choices with richer flavors. Season your salad with salt and spices to balance the sharper flavors of the vinegars. Salsas, both the traditional red and the newer, wilder flavors, can spunk up a basic salad. Yogurt works well just about any time sour cream is called for in dressed salad. Yogurt is more tart than sour cream, so balance the flavors with salt and a good shot of fresh herbs. If you prefer creamy-style salads, mayonnaise can also be made using mustard and lemon as the base, which will give your salad the texture of mayonnaise without the heaviness.

TODAY'S LESSON: Summer salads of yore, laden with mayonnaise and sour cream, have given way to lighter salads that use bright vinaigrettes, seasoned vinegars, citrus, salsa and, for the creamy dishes, low-fat yogurt.

■ *Don't forget your favorites:* Your favorite vinaigrette or light salad dressing will work well, too. Make sure that you mix them well to evenly distribute the oil and the vinegar. On heavier or duller-tasting vegetables — potatoes — you may need a flavor boost. Splash additional vinegar or citrus to raise the flavors over the oil content of the dressing.

■ *Marrying summer flavors:* Flavor boosters for summer salads come from easy-to-grow herbs. Some of the perfect matches are green beans or their tiny cousin, the haricot

vert (ah-ree-koh VAIR), with tarragon and chives.

Tomatoes, roasted sweet peppers and onions are naturals for the basil family. Dill seems created for cucumbers, and it's not bad for onions or summer squash, either. Corn is highlighted by the light flavor of chives and garlic.

Members of the hot pepper family definitely spark up any summer gathering. Try roasting hot fresh peppers over the grill or open flame until the outer skin is blackened. Cool in a bowl covered tightly with plastic wrap, then peel under running cold water. Remove

AMAZING FOOD FACTS
■

Unlike wine, which ages best in the cool dark cellar, balsamic vinegar is ideally stored in the hot, direct sunlight of an attic in summer and a cool atmosphere during winter.

■

The first reference to balsamic vinegar dates back to A.D. 1046, when the newly crowned Holy Roman Emperor, Enrico III of Germany, asked to taste it. Originally, balsamic vinegar was used as a balm and even today is recognized for its therapeutic properties.

the seeds and stem and add the peppers to your salad.

To decide how much to add, take a small bite of the roasted, cleaned pepper to get an idea of the heat level. Every pepper is different.

Dried spices such as paprika, curries, caraway and celery seeds are best added after the flavors are developed. Add the spices to a little olive oil in a small skillet and heat over medium heat until they begin to bubble. Cook gently for just a couple of minutes to build the flavor and soften the dry texture, before adding to your savory salad.

■ *How to cook your vegetables:* Overcooking will result in the loss of essential nutrients. Blanch vegetables in salted boiling water until al dente, firm to the bite. The salt water is essential to help preserve the natural salt levels in the vegetables. Stop the vegetables

from overcooking by draining into a colander and rinsing under running cold water. A bowl of ice water will shock the vegetables, but don't let them languish and become soggy in the chilling bath. Drain properly to avoid excess

water that will thin and water down your salad.

Whole potatoes are best added to cold water, then brought to a boil for cooking. Cool well before adding dress-

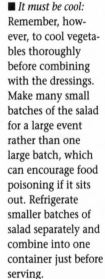

ing if you prefer distinct separation of the dressing from the potato flavor. Or cool the potatoes just slightly, cut into desired shapes and toss with the dressing while still warm to infuse the dressing flavors into the potatoes.

■ *It must be cool:* Remember, however, to cool vegetables thoroughly before combining with the dressings. Make many small batches of the salad for a large event rather than one large batch, which can encourage food poisoning if it sits out. Refrigerate smaller batches of salad separately and combine into one container just before serving.

Many salads will improve in flavor if allowed to mature overnight in the refrigerator. Check the seasonings the next day; the colder the salad, the more seasonings it will need to develop a full, well-seasoned flavor.

CUCUMBER SALAD

Makes 4 servings

2   English cucumbers, peeled, cut in half lengthwise, seeded and cut into ¼-inch slices

2   tablespoons salt

¼   cup freshly squeezed lemon juice

Freshly ground white pepper to taste

1¼ cups low-fat or plain yogurt

¼   cup chopped fresh dill

¼   cup chopped fresh mint

Sprigs of mint or dill for garnish

In a colander, combine the cucumbers and salt. Place a bowl on top of the cucumbers and weigh the bowl down with several unopened cans. Allow to drain until cucumbers are limp, about 1 hour. Rinse under cold running water, then submerge in ice water until recrisped, about 5 minutes. Drain well and pat dry with paper towels. Taste the cucumbers to verify they are not salty; if they are, repeat the rinsing steps. Transfer to a medium-size bowl. Add the lemon juice, mixing well. Add a generous dose of white pepper. Stir in yogurt, dill and mint. Adjust additional salt and pepper to taste. Refrigerate. Garnish with the herbs just before serving.

Nutrition details per serving
Calories 64
Percent of calories from fat 4%
Fat: . . . . .0.3 gm
Protein: . . . . .6 gm
Carbohydrate: . . . . .11 gm
Cholesterol: . . . . .1.5 mg
Sodium: . . . . .56 mg
Diabetic exchange: ½ milk.

DIJON MUSTARD POTATO SALAD

Makes 4 servings

½   cup good red wine vinegar

½   cup coarse grained Dijon mustard

½   cup virgin olive oil

Salt to taste

Freshly ground black pepper to taste

1   cup snipped fresh chives

2   pounds new potatoes, about 1 inch in diameter

In a medium-size bowl, combine the vinegar, mustard and olive oil, and season with salt and pepper to taste. Add the chives. In a large pot of cold water, bring the potatoes to a boil over medium-high heat and cook until tender, about 15 minutes. Drain. Cut into ¼-inch thick slices. Pour the vinaigrette over them while still warm. Refrigerate overnight, then serve.

Nutrition details per serving
Calories .467
Percent of calories from fat 55%
Fat: . . . . .29 gm
Protein: . . . . .7 gm
Carbohydrate: . . . . .47 gm
Cholesterol: . . . . .0 mg
Sodium: . . . . .690 mg
Diabetic exchange: 2⅗ bread, 5¾ fat.

Vinegar is known to stimulate the appetite, stop hiccups, aid digestion and soothe throat inflammation.

THE RICH PERFUME
OF FRESH GINGER

■ *What is it?* Ginger is one of the oldest spices, originating in tropical southeast Asia and cultivated for more than 3,000 years. The cuisines of Asia are perfumed with its essence, as are the sweet breads of northern Europe.

■ *What it tastes like:* Fresh ginger root is the most exciting, with the most pronounced ginger flavor. Raw ginger root also has à sharp bite, similar to horseradish, and is never eaten uncooked. Cooking diminishes its raw bite to a palatable level and enhances the rich flavor.

■ *How to select:* Select fat, firm, plump roots with pale tan skin. Snap off one of the tiny knobs on the side of the root and observe the strength of the fragrance, the fibrous texture and the moisture of the broken surface. The freshest will be crisp with a pronounced scent, few fibers and a moist surface. Avoid shriveled, wrinkled, limp roots, especially those with

TODAY'S LESSON: Folks who think of ginger as just the dried spice found on grocers' shelves are missing this fragrant spice at its very best.

mold. Break or cut off a piece of ginger root the size your recipe requires. Cover the remaining open surface with plastic wrap, place in a small paper bag and refrigerate in the coldest part of the refrigerator for up to two weeks.

■ *How to prepare:* Peel ginger root when making purees and serving in a dish as a garnish. When the purpose is solely to flavor a dish, cut the ginger across the grain of the root without peeling and remove the ginger before serving.

■ *How to cook:* For ginger garnishes, slice it very thin (mechanical slicer or mandolin slicer works best), with the grain or fibers. Cut it into julienne or other garnish shapes

across the grain. Blanch the ginger in 1 quart of simmering water with ¼ cup of granulated sugar until tender, about 6-8 minutes for the thinnest of cuts. Drain and rinse under cold running water. Dry on paper toweling. The garnish may be added to a vinaigrette or to a hot sauce at the last second just to heat.

Fine julienne of ginger is best when fried crisp. The bright fresh flavor will spark up just about any dish with an interesting crunch; it's especially good in salads and fish dishes. To fry, pour about 2 inches of canola or corn oil into a skillet and heat to 325. Add the blanched, drained ginger, cooking until tan and very crisp, about 5 minutes (the oil will just about stop bubbling).

Remove the ginger with a strainer to paper toweling. Store at room temperature to hold. The ginger may be refried to crisp if necessary.

■ *You can also infuse the ginger flavor into creams and liquids.* Here's how: Slice the ginger across the grain as thinly as possible. Add it to liquids around 180 degrees and allow to cool to room temperature. Reheat the liquids, then strain the ginger for the fullest flavor. Do not boil the liquids, because the ginger flavor will dissipate and become slightly bitter.

Ginger-infused oil is terrific for salad dressings and vinaigrettes. Follow the above instructions for infusing ginger into creams and liquids, but substitute corn or safflower oil, and refrigerate the oil for three days. The ginger will settle to the bottom of the jar along with any small particles. Pour the oil off the ginger and store in an airtight jar. Add the ginger oil to your own tastes or blend with other neutral oils for unusual dressings.

Infusing ginger flavor into oil is an old process derived

from Chinese cooking methods. The traditional technique calls for heating the oil in a wok, adding fresh ginger root and often hot peppers and garlic, then allowing the spices to cook for a few minutes to impart their flavors into the oil. The spices may be removed and the fish or meat added to the wok, resulting in a wonderfully seasoned dish. Fresh gin-

ger root is far superior to dried roots for this technique.

■

GRILLED ESCALLOP OF SALMON WITH GINGER

Makes 4 servings

½   cup granulated sugar
½   cup fine julienne of fresh ginger
     Corn oil for frying
¼   cup balsamic vinegar
1   cup extra-virgin olive oil, divided
     Salt
     Freshly ground white pepper
¼   cup chopped fresh basil
¼   cup chopped fresh parsley
8   escallops of salmon, about 3 ounces each, skin and bones removed
½   cup Ginger Puree (see recipe on page 112)
2   tablespoons ground coriander (optional)

In a small saucepan, combine the sugar with 4 cups of

■

Besides tropical Asia, ginger can be found growing in Australia, South America, west Africa, Jamaica and Puerto Rico. Jamaican ginger is pale in color and delicate in flavor.

Jamaica supplies most of the world's exports of peeled (white) ginger. India exports a particularly hot variety of unpeeled (gray) ginger.

water. Add the ginger and bring to a simmer over medium heat, cooking until tender, about 30 minutes. Drain well in a colander. In a medium skillet, add corn oil to depth of ½ inch. Heat to 325. Carefully add the ginger, cooking until golden and crispy, about 3 minutes. Using a slotted spoon, remove to paper toweling to drain. Reserve at room temperature.

In a small bowl, combine the vinegar and ¾ cup of the olive oil. Add salt and pepper to taste. Stir in the basil and the parsley; set aside. Lay the escallops of salmon on a cookie sheet. Rub the ginger puree evenly across the top of the escallops. Sprinkle the coriander over the ginger puree. (Note: The seasonings are applied only to one surface.) Preheat the broiler or a grill.

In a large nonstick skillet over high heat, add the remaining olive oil. Lay the escallops, spice side down, in the pan; avoid overlapping. Cook until seared and golden, about 2 minutes. Turn over for 30 seconds and transfer to a broiler pan. The salmon will not be completely cooked at this point. Repeat with the

remaining escallops, adding olive oil if necessary.

Place the broiler pan with the salmon in the oven broiler. Cook until done, about 5 minutes depending on thickness of the escallops. Position two escallops, slightly overlapping each other, on each serving plate. Repeat with the remaining escallops. Spoon the basil sauce across the salmon and top with the fried ginger. Serve immediately.

Nutrition details per serving
Calories .515
Percent of calories from fat 49%
Fat: . . . . .28 gm
Protein: . . . . .35 gm
Carbohydrate: . . . . .31 gm
Cholesterol: . . . . .94 mg
Sodium: . . . . .347 mg
Diabetic exchange: 4½ meat, 3½ fat.

GINGER PUREE

Makes 1 cup

1½ cups peeled and diced fresh ginger
½   cup fresh lemon juice
2   tablespoons sugar

In a small saucepan, combine all the ingredients, simmer over high heat and cook until tender, about 30 minutes. Transfer to a food processor and puree until smooth. Reserve in the refrigerator for up to one month.

Nutrition details per serving
Calories .55
Percent of calories from fat 4%
Fat: . . . . .0 gm
Protein: . . . . .1 gm
Carbohydrate: . . . . .14 gm
Cholesterol: . . . . .0 mg
Sodium: . . . . .5 mg
Diabetic exchange: ⅛ vegetable, ¼ fruit.

MODERN CHUTNEY'S BALANCING ACT

AMAZING FOOD FACTS

■

Chutneys

can be made

from just about

any mixture

of fruits

but usually

include a few

aromatic

vegetables.

■ *Why it tastes so good:* Lightly cooking vegetables and fruits in a chutney concentrates their natural sugars and flavors, resulting in an intensely condensed flavor. The flavors are kept in balance with the tartness of vinegar or citrus, and framed by a little honey or sugar.

■ *What makes the modern chutney different?* Modern chutneys are cooked quickly to preserve their natural bright fruit and vegetable flavors. Traditional chutneys are cooked for many hours, resulting in concentrated but somewhat muddled flavors. Modern chutneys may have a delicate or a strong spice tone, while traditional methods concentrate heavy spice levels for style and as a preservative.

■ *Advantages:* These new chutneys are easy and fast to make with no added fat. They are a great complement to grilled or steamed foods and add

TODAY'S LESSON: Traditional chutney is an English specialty served with mostly bland meats, but a modern approach combines the fresh flavors of salsa and transforms chutneys into exciting, warm, rich and vibrantly scented condiments that balance the fruit and vegetable flavors with sweet and sour chutney tones all spunked up with your favorite spices. They're perfect for vegetables, grains, fish, poultry and meats.

another dimension to even the simplest of foods.

■ *What are the common spices of a chutney?* The most common spice in traditional and modern chutney is probably ginger. Cumin, coriander and ground pepper and hot chilis are popular, too. Curry powder and the heavier flavors of cloves, nutmeg and cinnamon find their way in, but those spices are either too intense or too dessert-like for me.

■ *Tricks of the trade:* The best way to get the flavor of the spices into the chutney is either to cook them in a fat

■
Chutney originated in India. It can be eaten raw or cooked and ranges from exotic combinations of fruits, vegetables and spices to rather plain affairs of grated vegetables with a few other flavors.

such as olive oil or in the sugar syrup before adding to the primary ingredients, or to roast them with the vegetables. Adding dry ground spice into the chutney will create a gritty texture and an "off," floury flavor. Cooking the spices is necessary to develop them into a full flavor profile.

■ *Select your fruits and vegetables:* Here's a brief overview of the most complementary:

Fruits. The most solid, moist and dense-textured, such as pears, papayas, mangos, pineapples and apples, work best. Softer fruits, such as plums, peaches and cherries, are very delicate and should be added only at the last minute of preparation or reserved for desserts.

Vegetables. Focus on vegetables that are complementary to fruits. That eliminates green vegetables such as broccoli or peas. The onion family is the best for savory applications, along with chilis, tomatoes — green, red, yellow and tomatillo. Orange vegetables such as carrots, sweet potatoes and squash are good but tend not to contribute much flavor.

Pair the fruits and vegetables that will offer a broader flavor profile, such as roasted onions, sweet red peppers and papayas for a tropical flair.

■ *Preparing the vegetables:* The vegetables are the tougher of the combination, so they must be cooked to soften their texture as well as develop their natural sweet flavor. Roasting, baking in foil, sauteing or even grilling will work well. Cook until they are tender but still have a bite.

■ *Preparing the fruit:* Peel, seed and cut fruit into the desired shape. If necessary, rub the surface with lemon juice to prevent browning while awaiting the cooking phase.

■ *The cooking begins:* Combine the vegetables with the vinegar or citrus, the honey and the cooked spices. Bring to a simmer over medium-high heat and cook until the vegetables are softened and the flavors combine. Add the fruit, cooking until just softened and hot. Balance the flavors with vinegar for sour and honey for sweet. Salt, pepper or hot sauces will complete the spunky finish. Remove from the heat immediately and transfer to a serving dish or to food.

■ *Serving suggestions:* Spoon the chutney onto the plate surrounding the main food; even a dollop on top looks good. A light sprinkling of a complementary fresh herb such as chives, cilantro or parsley will liven up the presentation.

■ *Try your technique:* One of my favorite flavor combinations is roast sweet peppers and papaya, perfect over just about any grilled fish.

PAPAYA & ROAST PEPPER CHUTNEY

Makes 4 servings

2 large red peppers,
   washed, roasted (see
   directions)

1 tablespoon olive oil

1 teaspoon ground
   cumin

1 teaspoon ground
   coriander

1 tablespoon fresh
   ginger root, peeled
   and diced very fine, ⅛
   inch

1 cup red onions,
   peeled, ends removed,
   diced

½ cup lime juice

¼ cup honey

1 large papaya, peeled,
   cut in half, seeded
   and diced

   Salt and freshly
   ground black pepper
   to taste

   Cayenne pepper or
   hot sauce such as
   Tabasco or Habanero
   to taste

To roast red pepper: Place
the whole red pepper on
open gas flame or grill or
under broiler and cook until
the skin is black. Place the
pepper in a bowl and cover
the bowl with plastic wrap.
Allow the pepper to cool.
Using your hands, remove
the skin and discard. Seed,
core and dice the pepper.

In a large nonstick skillet,
heat olive oil over medium
heat. Add the cumin and
coriander, cooking for 1
minute. Add the ginger and
the onions, cooking until
just browning, about 8 minutes. Add the lime juice,
honey and peppers, cooking
until tender, about 5 minutes. Add the papaya and
cook until softened and hot,
about 2 minutes or longer, if
papayas are not fully ripe.
Balance the seasonings with
salt, pepper or cayenne pepper to taste. Remove from
heat and keep warm if serving immediately, or cool and
hold covered in refrigerator
for up to a week.

Nutrition details per serving
Calories 208
Percent of calories from fat 33%
Fat: .7 gm
Protein: . . . . .2 gm
Carbohydrate: . . . . .37 gm
Cholesterol: . . . . .0 mg
Sodium: . . . . .13 mg
Diabetic exchange: 1 vegetable, 2 fruit,
1¼ fat. Not recommended for diabetics.

GRILLED SALMON WITH PAPAYA CHUTNEY

Makes 4 servings

4 fillets of salmon,
   boneless and skinned

   Olive oil to moisten

   Salt

   Freshly ground black
   pepper

   Paprika

1 recipe for Papaya and
   Roast Pepper Chutney
   (see accompanying
   recipe)

¼ cup picked fresh
   cilantro leaves

Preheat the grill or broiler.
Lay the salmon on a
cookie sheet. Rub the surface
of the salmon with a drop or
two of olive oil to moisten.
Season the fish with salt,
pepper and a generous dusting of paprika.

Lay the fish on the grill
and cook until well seared,
about 4 minutes. Turn over
and cook to your desired
degree of doneness, about 3
minutes for medium. Transfer to the center of your serving plate.

Meanwhile, warm the
chutney in a small saute
pan. Spoon the chutney
artistically on the plate
around the salmon with a
dollop atop the fish. Sprinkle
the cilantro leaves around
the fish. Serve immediately.

Nutrition details per serving
Calories 574
Percent of calories from fat 41%
Fat: .26 gm
Protein: . . . . .48 gm
Carbohydrate: . . . . .37 gm
Cholesterol: . . . . .148 mg
Sodium: . . . . .126 mg
Diabetic exchange: 6¾ lean meat, 1
vegetable, 2 fruit, 1¼ fat.

GARLIC,
THE STINKING ROSE

■ *Where does garlic's bite come from?* Garlic, as well as its cousins — onions, shallots, leeks and chives — contains an odorless chemical that is stable under normal conditions. Once garlic is cut, this compound comes in contact with enzymes that convert it into the mild garlic flavor. The garlic flavor and scent intensify as the compound further breaks down to produce the pungent garlic odor.

In simple terms, the garlic scent is created only by cutting, mincing and mashing. It becomes strongest in flavor and scent when allowed to sit for a while after cutting.

■ *How to control flavor intensity:* Cooking will tame the garlic flavor. Some of the odor compounds are driven into the air during cooking, while the remaining ones may be converted to chemicals that have a sweet garlic flavor. The best methods are to saute the garlic until lightly browned to cap-

TODAY'S LESSON: Garlic is one of nature's most powerful seasonings. It will add spark to just about any dish, especially during the warm months. I'll show you how to harness its flavor without its mean bark and bite.

ture that special nutty flavor, or oven-roast the garlic encased in foil.

■ *Why it tastes so good:* Raw garlic has a certain zing that ignites the taste buds with its strong and pungent flavor. Raw garlic on the palate continues to break down, causing garlic breath and aftertaste. Cooked garlic, on the other hand, tames the preliminary taste of garlic to a sweeter, milder flavor with less aftertaste and less lingering scent on the breath.

■ *Health advantages:* Garlic has terrific medicinal benefits. For example, garlic preparations have been shown in laboratory

studies, and sometimes in patients, to suppress the formation and growth of cancer cells and to counter blood conditions that foster atherosclerosis, heart attacks and strokes.

■ *Picking a head of garlic:* Fresh garlic is best purchased by the head or bulb, which contains numerous cloves under its papery skin. Select fresh, recently harvested, firm, hard heads and store in a cool, dry place.

■ *Tricks of the trade:* The most bitter part of the garlic clove is the darker green central strip or shoot. Slice the garlic clove in half lengthwise and discard before preparing. This step is especially important in the spring, when the germ starts to sprout.

Garlic presses should be reserved for a little fresh garlic bite in a dish, if at all. The crushing effect maximizes the odor compound, and the juice is impossible to cook until it breaks down.

■ *Peeling the cloves:* There are a number of methods, but I prefer to cut off the root end of each clove. Then cut in half lengthwise or smash with a heavy knife or cleaver to free the flesh from the skin.

■ *How to cook:* Try these methods to extract the flavor:

Saute. Heat a little olive oil in a pan and cook the chopped garlic until lightly golden, which will properly develop that nutty, non-offensive garlic flavor. The garlic may be strained from the oil and the

flavored oil used for cooking your dish. Or leave the browned garlic in the pan, but add moisture to prevent burning, such as in the preparation of a marinara-style tomato sauce.

Oven-roast. Combine the garlic cloves, a touch of olive oil and a little salt and pepper. Lay out a large piece of aluminum foil, dull side down, and position the garlic mix in the center of one half. Fold the

foil over and crimp the edges to seal the garlic into a large envelope or pouch. Roast on a cookie sheet at 400 degrees until tender and sweet, about 30-45 minutes. Remove from the oven and keep the foil pouch sealed until cooled.

Bake. Lightly oil the entire bulb or head of garlic and bake at 375 degrees until tender, about 45 minutes. Allow to cool. Remove the garlic by squeezing the end to pop out the individual cloves.

Boil or cook in moisture. This method does not develop that toasty or nutty garlic flavor, but it will soften the garlic bite. Depending on the exact method, the odor compounds may be captured in the liquid or sauce and still produce the bite you are trying to eliminate in cooking.

■
The British government bought tons of garlic during World War I for use as an antiseptic, and Russian infantrymen in World War II are said to have packed garlic cloves to rub on wounds. The oil in garlic is known to wipe out many strains of fungus.

■ *Words of caution:* Storing whole cloves, peeled or even chopped, at room temperature may result in the growth of harmful bacteria that naturally occur in the garlic. To prepare a garlic-scented olive oil for the table or to store garlic for the kitchen, heat the oil with the garlic to at least 180 degrees for about 10 minutes to kill off any bacteria. Store in a clean, well-sealed jar *only* under refrigeration.

■ *Mix and match:* Garlic will stand up to the stronger flavors of chilis, ginger, mustards and vinegars. Cooked to develop its sweeter, milder characteristics, it will enrich just about any dish.

■ *Try your technique:* Start by sauteing the garlic until golden to taste the toasty, nutty flavor that is the true essence of garlic cooking. Once you realize the softer side of garlic, try the oven-roasted cloves whole. You'll be addicted for life.

■

40 THIEVES ROAST CHICKEN

Makes 4 servings

40 large garlic cloves, peeled, ends removed

1 tablespoon olive oil

  Salt and freshly ground black pepper

1 roasting chicken, about 3 pounds, washed, patted dry

2 whole lemons, divided

1 tablespoon finely minced garlic

½ cup dry white wine

1 tablespoon fresh thyme leaves, picked from the stem, washed, dried

2 tablespoons chopped fresh flat leaf parsley

4 sprigs thyme or parsley for garnish

  Preheat the oven to 400 degrees. Lay a large piece of aluminum foil, dull side down, on counter. In a small bowl, combine garlic cloves and olive oil. Season with salt and pepper to taste. Mix well and transfer to the center of one half of the foil. Fold the remaining half of the foil over

the garlic and seal the edges by crimping. Position on a baking sheet.

  Clean the chicken thoroughly inside and out under cold running water. Pat dry with paper toweling. Season the cavity and outside of the bird with salt and pepper. With an ice pick, poke numerous holes throughout one of the lemons. Put the lemon into the cavity of the chicken. Place the chicken in a roasting pan. Rub minced garlic over the skin of the chicken. Place roasting pan on the lower rack and the baking sheet with the garlic on the upper rack of the oven. Bake until the garlic is tender, about 45 minutes. Remove the garlic and allow to cool before puncturing the foil pouch.

  Continue cooking the chicken until an instant thermometer inserted into the thigh section registers 170 degrees, about a total cooking time of 1-1¼ hours (15-30 minutes after the garlic is done). Remove chicken from the oven and allow to rest while finishing the sauce. Pour the juices from the pan into a glass container and siphon off the chicken juices without the fat.

  In a medium nonstick skillet, combine the chicken juices

and the garlic and its juices from the foil pouch. Add the wine and the juice of the remaining lemon. Bring to a simmer over medium-high heat and cook until the liquids are reduced to coat the garlic, about 5 minutes. Remove from the heat. Add the thyme and parsley. Adjust the salt and pepper to taste.

Carve the chicken, with or without the skin, into four portions. Position each portion in the center of a serving plate. Spoon the sauce and the cloves of garlic over the chicken. Garnish with a sprig of herbs and serve.

■

RIB CHOPS OF LAMB WITH ROASTED GARLIC CLOVES

Makes 4 servings

36 cloves roasted garlic, divided

4 racks of lamb, four bones each

Salt to taste

Freshly ground black pepper to taste

2 large vine-ripened tomatoes

2 cups lamb or poultry stock

2 cups red wine

2 tablespoons sun-dried tomato puree

½ cup pitted nicoise olives

Olive oil as needed

¼ cup fresh oregano leaves (or substitute basil)

¼ cup fresh snipped chives

Preheat grill or broiler. Mince 12 of the roasted garlic cloves. Rub the minced garlic over the lamb racks on all surfaces. Season with salt and pepper. Place the lamb, meat side down on the grill, allowing to sear, about 5 minutes. Turn over and cook until rare, about 4 minutes. Remove from the grill and allow to cool to room temperature.

Place the tomatoes on the grill, cooking until charred and the skin begins to peel back. Remove from the grill and allow to cool enough to handle. Remove the skin. Cut in half on the equator and squeeze the seeds out. Dice the tomato and reserve.

In a large saucepan, combine the stock and red wine. Bring to a boil over high heat and cook until reduced to 1 cup, about 15 minutes. Add the sun-dried tomato puree and continue cooking until the sauce coats the back of a spoon, about 4 minutes. Add the remaining whole garlic cloves. Keep the sauce warm.

In a food processor, puree the olives until a smooth paste is formed, adding olive oil as necessary. Cut the lamb rack into chops with one chop per bone. Generously rub the surfaces of the meat with the olive spread. Season with additional black pepper to your taste.

Return the lamb chops to the grill. Cook until you reach your desired temperature. Transfer to the serving plates. Add the tomato dice to the sauce. Spoon the sauce over the lamb chops. Sprinkle the oregano and chives over the lamb and serve.

AMAZING FOOD FACTS

■

Tuna has a
rich-flavored
flesh that is
moderate to
high in fat, firm,
flaky and
tender.

IN THE SWIM WITH MIGRATORY FISH

■ *What fish are we talking about?* Although many fish species migrate, we'll talk about swordfish, tuna and shark.

■ *Why do they taste so good?* The migratory swim takes a little out of them, but their lean meat is at a taste peak after they fatten up on the bounty of the North Atlantic. The colder water also seems to firm up their flesh.

■ *Health advantages:* These fish are pretty lean yet still firm-textured for a lower fat content. Trim any remaining fatty tissue before preparing.

■ *Selecting your fish:* All of these species are best when fresh. They should look translucent, never opaque or milky. They should be moist but never slimy, wet or sticky. They should smell fresh, not fishy. Store well-wrapped in the coldest part of the refrigerator until ready to cook. Fish are best

TODAY'S LESSON: The most visible sign that summer has arrived is the flocks of ducks, geese and other birds that return from their winter in the South. A similar event occurs underwater, with the migration of large ocean fish from the waters off South America to the rich summer feeding grounds of the northern Atlantic. You can unlock their wonderful taste at the seasonal peak.

enjoyed the same day as purchased. Although individual varieties of each species vary slightly in color and texture, the same signs apply:

Swordfish. It cooks up white but looks slightly gray and translucent when raw. Most moist when cooked medium-rare to medium.

Tuna. It cooks up pale pink to white in color, depending on the species. Raw tuna looks like red beef to reddish gray. Tuna is extremely lean, thus moist and tender when cooked rare to medium-rare. From medium temperature on, it gets very dry.

Shark. Cooks white to gray, with a pretty wide range of colors raw. Shark has a less dense and delicate texture than swordfish and is best cooked more toward medium since it can be a little stringy on the rare side.

■ *What cut?* The best, and often most expensive, is the center cut. The portion of the fish closest to the head may be more coarse because of the tissue formations, while the tail tends to be smaller, fibrous and a little tougher because of all the work it has to do.

■ *Tricks of the trade:* Choose your cut and cooking temperature to match your preferred degree of doneness — thinner cuts work for medium to more well done; thicker cuts are best for rare. Both should be cooked at high heat. If you prefer a thicker cut, but cooked medium to more well done, use a medium temperature to enable the heat to penetrate. The fillets or steaks should be trimmed of all skin and darker fatty tissue and, of course, free of bones. they

should be of a consistent thickness to ensure even cooking.

■ *Seasoning your fish:* After the grill or pan has been preheated, dust the surface of the fish with salt, pepper and

other seasonings you enjoy. Seasoning the fish with dry spices too early draws the moisture from the surface of the fish, making the fish more difficult to sear and retain internal moisture.

■ *How about a wet marinade?* Seasoned marinades will enhance the flavor of the fish but may also dry out the surface during cooking and prevent the surface from searing properly. Herbs, garlic, onions and a few spices blended with olive oil will enhance the flavor without detracting from the texture. Acids such as lemon and lime juice will coagulate the surface of the fish, resulting in a dry texture when cooked. Squirt the acids over the fish after searing just before they are finished for best texture and flavor. Citrus rind carries lots of flavor and can be added to the marinade described above for best precooking seasoning technique. Barbecue and other sauces are best added toward the end to prevent burning or interfering with the cooking process.

■
Shark's flavorful, low-fat flesh is dense and meat-like. The shark's metabolism gives it a tendency to smell like ammonia. The offputting odor can be easily eliminated by soaking the fish in milk.

■
While Americans are just beginning to appreciate shark, other cultures have eaten shark for eons. Sharks marketed for food range from 15-120 pounds.

■
Tuna is a member of the mackerel family. The best-known varieties are albacore, bluefin, yellowfin and bonito.

■ *The cooking begins:* Preheat the grill or pan to ensure a good sear, which will enhance the retention of moisture. A cool pan or grill will cause the fish almost to steam or poach in its own juices, which will escape to the pan. If cooking the fish more toward done, sear the fish initially at high heat, then turn down the flame or move to a cooler part of the grill to allow the lower heat to penetrate the fish. Turn over the fish after it is well seared but not burnt. Cooking on the second side will occur faster because of all the stored heat energy.

■ *How can you tell it's done?* A fish steak or fillet feels about the same as a tenderloin of beef at a similar degree of doneness. At medium, the moisture will just start to escape and rise to glisten on the surface. As you continue cooking, you are driving out the moisture or juices, which

you will see sizzling in the pan or hear spitting onto the charcoal. The fish will continue to cook after removal from the heat source, so have all your

ingredients ready to serve immediately. Pull the fish from the heat at the very first sign that it is done so that it will not overcook on its way to the table.

■ *Serving suggestions:* Serve all fish on hot plates to maintain

a warm temperature while enjoying the fish. This is especially important if you prefer your fish on the rare to medium-rare side where the fish's internal temperature is not very hot.

■ *Mix and match:* These seasonal fish are so wonderful, that their natural flavor may be enhanced with a squirt of lemon, embraced by a spicy or exotic flavored salsa or enrobed in an elegant sauce. Their silky texture is complemented by crispy seasonal vegetables and cool pasta or grain salads for a nutritious summer feast.

■ *Try your technique:* Swordfish is one of the most noble fish, especially on the grill as in my favorite, Grilled Swordfish with Caper & Citrus Vinaigrette. The flavor of the swordfish with the simple but colorful vinaigrette is terrific!

GRILLED SWORDFISH WITH CAPER & CITRUS VINAIGRETTE

Makes 4 servings

4 tablespoons capers, drained and diced fine if large

2 tablespoons minced red bell pepper

2 tablespoons minced yellow bell pepper

1 tablespoon minced red or yellow onion

2 lemons, juiced and the rind of one grated fine

¼ cup extra-virgin olive oil

2 tablespoons snipped fresh chives

2 tablespoons chopped fresh basil

Salt

Freshly ground black pepper

4 swordfish steaks, trimmed of skin and fatty tissues, about 6-8 ounces each (cut thicker for less done, thinner for more well done)

Sprigs of fresh green herbs for garnish

Preheat the grill.

In a small bowl, combine the capers, red and yellow peppers, onion, lemon juice and rind, olive oil, chives and basil. Season with salt and pepper to taste. Reserve at room temperature.

Season the fish lightly with salt and pepper on both sides. Place the fish on a clean and oiled grate, cooking until well seared, about 3-4 minutes. Turn over with a metal spatula, taking care not to tear the fish. Cook to your desired degree of doneness, about 3 minutes for a thinner cut to medium. Your results may vary depending on the temperature of the grill and the thickness of your swordfish steak. Transfer the swordfish to the center of a warmed serving plate. Stir the vinaigrette well and spoon a little over the fish, or, if you prefer, serve on the side. Garnish the fish with a sprig of herbs and serve immediately.

Nutrition details per serving
Calories 408
Percent of calories from fat 50%
Fat: .23 gm
Protein: . . . . .46 gm
Carbohydrate: . . . . .7 gm
Cholesterol: . . . . .88 mg
Sodium: . . . . .471 mg
Diabetic exchange: ⅛ vegetable, ⅜ fruit, 6¼ meat, 2¾ fat.

Swordfish weigh 200-600 pounds, though some have been caught that weighed more than 1,000 pounds.

FISH, POACHED AND CRIMPED

■ *Why fish tastes so good this way:* Cooking fish by wet heat creates tender, succulent fish with a light, delicate flavor. When fish is heated in hot liquid, there is a gentle gelling of the fibers. The cooking liquids help hold juices in.

■ *Health advantages:* Poaching and crimping are done in a court bouillon or broth that seasons the fish without adding fats. Serve chilled for summer dining.

■ *Tricks of the trade:* Whether you prefer poaching or crimping, the secret is to turn the heat down very low or off after the fish has returned to a simmer.

■ *Choosing a cooking vessel:* The traditional fish poacher is a long rectangular pan about 6 inches deep. If you don't have one, use a stainless steel or other acid-resistant skillet about 3 inches deep that will hold the fish without crowding.

TODAY'S LESSON: There's a difference between the techniques. In poaching, the fish is added to simmering broth and cooked. In crimping, the heat is turned off once the broth has returned to a simmer. I prefer the more delicate crimping method.

■ *Prepare broth or court bouillon:* Fill the poacher or skillet about halfway with water. Season with wine (about a third of the water's volume) and a splash of vinegar; or skip the wine and add vinegar until the liquid has a pronounced acid taste. The acid helps congeal as well as season. Add a good shot of salt to balance the flavor and prevent the cooking liquids from depleting the fish's natural salt flavor. Add peppercorns, herbs, onions, shallots and carrots to your own taste. Bring the court bouillon to a boil and simmer about 1 hour.

■ *Choose the fish:* Any fish can be cooked by these methods, but best results come with denser and thicker-fleshed fish such as salmon, swordfish or tuna. Fillets or steaks are best. Poach whole softer-fleshed fish, such as trout, because the skin and frame help hold the fillets and flesh intact.

■ *Prepare the fish:* Cut fillets to produce an even thickness. Leave the skin intact, but remove pin bones with a pair of tweezers or needle-nose pliers. Steaks are best poached first, then easily cleaned with the same tools.

■ *The cooking begins:* With court bouillon at a simmer, gently add the fish, making sure not to overlap or crowd the pieces. Return to a short simmer, then turn down the heat just to maintain a bubble for poaching or turn off the heat for crimping.

Cook the fish until slightly opaque and firm. Use the general rule of 10 minutes of cooking time for every inch of fillet or steak thickness. Gently lift the fillet from the liquid with a spatula and check for doneness by cutting through the center with a paring knife. Remove the fish to a cooling rack when just about done. The fish will continue to cook even after being removed from the liquid because of stored heat.

Clean fish of any remaining skin and bones, brushing with a little of the court bouillon to clean up. Refrigerate to chill for later serving.

■ *Serving suggestions:* The finished fish fillet or steak is a work of art as the centerpiece of a plate. Lemon juice, a delicate herb sauce or a mild salsa are good complements. To contrast the silky texture of the fish, serve with crunchy, refreshing vegetables, such as cucumber salad. Robust, mustardy potato salad or a great pasta salad are also good matches.

■ *Try your technique:* My favorite for the summer is Atlantic salmon. Its rich flavor and lean flesh are a perfect match for many summer flavors, such as tarragon, dill, chives, cucumbers, tomatoes and peppers.

■

CHILLED CRIMPED SALMON FILLETS

Makes 4 servings

3   cups red wine vinegar or cider vinegar

3   cups dry white wine

1   large onion, cut into 1-inch pieces

2   bay leaves

1   tablespoon thyme, fresh or dried

¼   cup white peppercorns

2   tablespoons salt, plus more to taste, divided

4   fillets of salmon, boned, 6-8 ounces each

3   tablespoons fresh lime juice

½   cup diced cucumbers, peeled and seeded

¼   cup chopped fresh dill

¼   cup extra-virgin olive oil

Freshly ground black pepper

1   head red oakleaf lettuce

4   sprigs fresh dill for garnish

In a fish poacher or acid-resistant pot, combine red wine vinegar or cider vinegar, white wine, onion, bay leaves, thyme, peppercorns and 2 tablespoons salt. Bring to a simmer over medium heat and cook 1 hour.

Place the salmon in the simmering liquid and return to a boil. Turn off the heat and cook until fish is firm, about 8 minutes. Remove to a plate and peel any skin or dark fat tissues from the fillet with a sharp paring knife. Using a soft brush, dip into the poaching liquid and brush any herbs from the surface of the fish. Cover and refrigerate.

In a small bowl, combine the lime juice, cucumbers and dill. Stir in the olive oil. Season with salt and a generous pinch of black pepper. Arrange the lettuce leaves and dill sprigs on the serving plates. Position the fillets over the greens and top with the cucumber salsa.

Nutrition details per serving
Calories 686
Percent of calories from fat 47%
Fat: .38 gm
Protein: . . . . .47 gm
Carbohydrate: . . . . .20 gm
Cholesterol: . . . . .134 mg
Sodium: . . . . .684 mg
Diabetic exchange: ¾ vegetable, 6⅓ meat, 4⅓ fat.

AMAZING FOOD FACTS

■

Michigan is the largest producer of tart or sour cherries in the United States and the fourth largest grower of sweet cherries after Washington, Oregon and California.

SWEET CHERRIES

■ *Sweet and tart:* The climate of the Pacific Northwest is perfect for growing sweet cherries, while Michigan's is more suited to the tart cherries, which are due in early July and used primarily in processed foods.

■ *Where do the majority come from?* The nation's largest sweet cherry orchards are on the eastern slopes of the Cascade Mountains, where the trees flourish in volcanic soil. This region receives less than 10 inches of rainfall each year, so the orchards must be irrigated. The lack of rain has its benefits, though, because water on mature cherries can cause them to burst open.

■ *How many varieties are there?* The three largest cherry varieties in the Northwest are Bings, Lamberts and Rainiers. They account for 95 percent of production. Bings probably are the best known of the sweet cherries, with a deep

TODAY'S LESSON: With mountains of crimson sweet cherries arriving at supermarkets, it would be a shame to miss a single opportunity to savor them. Sure, cherries eaten fresh from the hand are wonderful, but if you are patient enough, they are terrific cooked or preserved. The cherry season begins each spring when the sweet varieties from Washington, Oregon and Idaho reach the market.

mahogany-red skin and firm, juicy flesh.

Topping them are Lamberts, which are very similar to Bings but have a more refined flavor. The Lambert generally is considered the connoisseur's cherry of the black sweet cherries.

Rainier cherries are the biggest and possibly the best sweet cherries produced in the Northwest. They are creamy yellow with a pink blush and

firm flesh. Rainiers are about twice as sweet as Bings, but they are more difficult to find, because the lighter color shows more shipping bruises.

■ *How to select:* At the market, you should select sweet cherries that are firm and bruise-free, with the stems still attached. Take your time and select the cherries with a deep color and natural shine.

■ *How to store:* Store them in a plastic bag in your vegetable crisper.

■ *How to prepare:* Rinse cherries under cool running water. Drain them in a colander, then pat dry if you're serving them fresh.

■ *How to cook:* For cooking, a cherry pitter is worth its weight in gold for the speed and convenience of dislodging the pits. They are available at better gourmet supply stores. One pound of cherries will yield about 1 cup of pitted and stemmed cherries.

■

SWEET CHERRY SUNDAE

Makes 4 servings

1 pound sweet cherries, stems and pits removed

1 cup red wine, preferably pinot noir, or substitute dry white wine

½ cup honey

4 scoops of your favorite vanilla ice cream or frozen yogurt

4 sprigs mint for garnish

Heat a large nonstick skillet over high heat until just about smoking, about 5 minutes. Add the cherries to the pan (without any butter or fat), cooking until tender, about 3 minutes, while constantly stirring to prevent excessive browning. Add the wine and the honey. Cook until the sauce is thickened to coat back of spoon, about 3 minutes. Remove from the heat, transfer to a bowl and reserve.

Place a scoop of ice cream in the center of each serving bowl. Divide the warm cherries and sauce over the ice cream. Garnish with mint and serve immediately.

Nutrition details per serving
Calories 520
Percent of calories from fat 25%
Fat: . . . . .15 gm
Protein: . . . . .6 gm
Carbohydrate: . . . . .86 gm
Cholesterol: . . . . .59 mg
Sodium: . . . . .156 mg
Diabetic exchange: 1½ fruit, 2 bread, 3 fat.

■

TURKEY SCALOPPINE WITH CHERRIES & CHIVES

Makes 4 servings

1 cup whole shallots

¼ cup balsamic vinegar

1 cup poultry stock

Salt to taste

Black pepper to taste

2 cups all-purpose flour

1 medium boneless turkey breast, about 1½ pounds, trimmed and skin removed, then cut into thin slices

2 tablespoons olive oil (or substitute canola or corn oil), divided

1 cup stemmed and pitted sweet cherries

½ cup fresh snipped chives

Preheat oven to 425. Place shallots in a small ovenproof pan. Place on lower oven rack and cook until tender, about 30 minutes. Allow to cool, then peel. In a medium-size saucepan, combine vinegar and stock, and simmer over medium-high heat. Cook until thickened to coat the back of a spoon, about 15 minutes. Adjust the seasonings with salt and pepper to taste. In a pie tin, spread flour across the bottom. Dredge the turkey slices through the flour and brush excess off to lightly coat the meat.

Meanwhile, in a large skillet, heat half of the olive oil over medium-high flame. Carefully add the turkey slices to the skillet, making sure they do not overlap. Cook until seared and slightly brown, about 2 minutes. Turn over and finish cooking, about 2 additional minutes. Remove to paper towel to drain. Keep warm while you finish cooking the remaining turkey with the remaining oil as necessary. Return the sauce to a boil over high heat. Add the cherries and shallots until just warm. Season with salt and pepper to taste. Position turkey on plates. Spoon sauce with the cherries and shallots over turkey. Sprinkle with chives.

Nutrition details per serving
Calories 684
Percent of calories from fat 27%
Fat: .20 gm
Protein: . . . . .57 gm
Carbohydrate: . . . . .66 gm
Cholesterol: . . . . .127 mg
Sodium: . . . . .384 mg
Diabetic exchange: ¾ vegetables, ½ fruit, 3 bread, 7 meat, 1⅓ fat.

■

MUSHROOM & DRIED CHERRY SALAD

Makes 4 servings

¼ cup pine nuts

1 large red pepper

3 tablespoons red wine vinegar

¼ cup dried sweet cherries

½ cup olive oil, divided

Salt to taste

Black pepper

½ pound morel or other wild mushrooms (or

substitute fresh regular mushrooms)

2 cups baby spinach leaves, stemmed and washed

2 cups mixed baby lettuces of your choice

2 bunches watercress, stems removed, washed, dried

1 small red onion, diced

½ cup finely grated Parmesan or Romano cheese

To toast pine nuts: Preheat oven to 300. Place pine nuts on an ungreased cookie sheet and place on lower rack of oven. Stir frequently until nuts are light tan in color, about 25 minutes. Set aside

To roast peppers: Preheat broiler. Place pepper on broiler pan lined with aluminum foil and broil. Rotate pepper until skin is black on all sides. Remove and place in a brown paper bag or bowl. Enclose bag or seal bowl with plastic wrap and allow pepper to cool 15 minutes. When cool, peel, seed and dice. Set aside.

To prepare dressing: In a small saucepan, combine vinegar and cherries. Bring to simmer over high heat and remove from the heat. Allow cherries to sit and soften, about 15 minutes.

Transfer the cherries and vinegar to a blender or food processor fitted with a metal blade. With the motor running, in a steady stream add 7 tablespoons of the olive oil and puree until smooth. Add a tablespoon or two of water as necessary if the dressing is too thick. Adjust the seasonings with salt and pepper.

To assemble and serve salad: In a large skillet, heat remaining olive oil over high heat. Add the morels or mushrooms, cooking until well seared, about 5 minutes. Season with salt and pepper to taste. Remove to a strainer to drain.

In a large bowl, combine the spinach, lettuces, watercress, mushrooms, onion and pepper. Add the dressing, tossing to combine. Divide the salad to the serving plates. Top with the cheese and the pine nuts and serve.

Nutrition details per serving
Calories 377
Percent of calories from fat 73%
Fat: .33 gm
Protein: . . . . .9 gm
Carbohydrate: . . . . .17 gm
Cholesterol: . . . . .10 mg
Sodium: . . . . .531 mg
Diabetic exchange: 1 vegetable, ¾ fruit, ¾ meat, 5¾ fat.

■

SWEET CHERRY & CHOCOLATE CAKE

Makes 10 servings

8 ounces extra-bittersweet chocolate (not baking chocolate)

8 tablespoons (1 stick) unsalted butter

5 large eggs, separated

¼ cup sugar

Pinch of salt

1 tablespoon vanilla

¼ cup all-purpose flour

3 cups pitted, stemmed and halved sweet cherries

Confectioners' sugar for decoration

Ice cream of your choice

Sprigs of mint for garnish

Preheat oven to 400. Grease a 10-inch springform pan.

In the top of a double boiler with water at a low simmer, combine chocolate and butter. Heat until melted and smooth. In a mixing bowl, combine the egg yolks, sugar, salt and vanilla. Whip until a thick ribbon forms and the yolks are pale and frothy. Using a spatula, fold in flour. Transfer to a large mixing bowl. Meanwhile, in a clean mixing bowl, whip egg whites until they form firm peaks. Do not overbeat.

Add chocolate into the yolk mixture and, using a large spatula, fold until combined. Add a third of the whites and fold until smooth. Add remaining egg whites and fold until homogeneous. Pour half of the batter into the prepared springform pan. Sprinkle cherries over the batter in the pan and cover with the remaining batter. Place on the lower rack in the oven and bake for 16 minutes. Remove from oven and place in a warm spot, preferably on top of the oven. Place a large plate over the cake pan and allow to finish

cooking and cool to room temperature, about 1 hour.

To serve, remove plate, loosen springform collar and place the cake on a serving platter. Dust the top of the cake with sifted confectioners' sugar. Garnish with mint. Serve ice cream on the top or side of the cake.

Nutrition details per serving
Calories 251
Percent of calories from fat 54%
Fat: . . . . .17 gm
Protein: . . . . .7 gm
Carbohydrate: . . . . .26 gm
Cholesterol: . . . . .112 mg
Sodium: . . . . .86 mg
Diabetic exchange: 1 fruit, ¼ bread, ½ meat, ⅓ fat.

■

CHERRY & PISTACHIO TART

Makes a 10-inch tart, serves 6-8

2 tablespoons unsalted butter

1 cup sugar

¼ cup fresh lemon juice

½ cup water

½ cup shelled and husked pistachios

2 pounds of sweet cherries, stemmed and pitted

½ pound puff pastry (homemade or frozen)

Vanilla ice cream

Mint sprigs to garnish

Preheat oven to 400. Rub a 10-inch nonstick, ovenproof saute pan with the butter. Set aside.

In a medium-size saucepan, combine sugar, lemon juice and water. Bring to a simmer over high heat and cook until it becomes light caramel, about 320 on a candy thermometer. Add pistachios and stir to coat. Pour into the buttered saute pan.

Spread cherries over the pistachio-caramel sauce. Roll out the pastry to ⅛ inch thick. Lay the pastry over the cherries in the pan. Trim the pastry ½ inch smaller than the inside edge of the pan.

Bake on the lower rack of the oven until pastry is golden, about 30 minutes. Remove from the oven and return to stove burner. Bring the liquids in the pan to a boil, cooking until thickened like a syrup, about 5 minutes. (Remember to be careful; the pan handle is still very hot from the oven.) Remove from heat and allow to cool to room temperature. Carefully invert onto a serving platter. To serve, cut into slices, top with a scoop of ice cream and garnish with mint.

Nutrition details per serving
Calories 373
Percent of calories from fat 40%
Fat: . . . . .17 gm
Protein: . . . . .5 gm
Carbohydrate: . . . . .53 gm
Cholesterol: . . . . .12 mg
Sodium: . . . . .248 mg
Diabetic exchange: 1 fruit, ¼ bread, 3½ fat.

THE TART SIDE OF THE CHERRY FAMILY

AMANZING FOOD FACTS

■

The French are credited with the propagation of the cherry trees along the St. Lawrence River to the Great Lakes and down to Detroit. The Grand Traverse region is the center of the cherry industry in Michigan.

■ *What makes them different?* The sour, pie or red tart cherry originates from the morella cherry, which has a slightly tart taste. It is usually smaller in size than the sweet cherry with a softer, tender skin and red color.

The sour cherry is harvested mechanically, which dislodges the fruit from the stem. (Sweet cherries are harvested with the stem.) The exposed cherry flesh from this technique makes them highly perishable and, therefore, they must be processed immediately. Very few sour cherries reach the fresh fruit market; most of the harvest is used commercially for baking, jams and preserves, juices and canning.

■ *What about commercial processing?* The commercial processing of the cherry adds preservatives, sugar, gels, starches and other elements of modern food chemistry which, unfortunately, alter the true cherry flavor. Even cherry

TODAY'S LESSON: It's easy to like the sweet cherry varieties, but it takes a little more work to fall in love with tart cherries.

sodas use almond extract as the "cherry" flavor. In many cases, the true cherry flavor is bleached out with the added flavorings and dyes. I hope that increased consumer interest will inspire cherry processors to develop a purer product that captures the cherry's true beauty.

■ *What about dried cherries?* Cherries of both tart and sweet varieties can be dried, although the Montmorency sour cherries are predominantly used for drying in Michigan. Eight pounds of whole cherries yield 1 pound dried, pitted cherries. The dried cherry offers the taste buds an incredible true cherry flavor.

■

SOUR CHERRY TART

Makes an 11-inch tart

1   Walnut Pastry shell (see accompanying recipe)
½   cup sugar
2   large eggs, lightly beaten
2   large egg yolks
1   teaspoon vanilla extract
    Pinch of salt
1   cup half-and-half, scalded
½   cup kirsch or cherry brandy
4   tablespoons (½ stick) unsalted butter
3   cups sour cherries, pitted
    Confectioners' sugar

Preheat the oven to 375 degrees. Line the tart shell with foil, shiny side down. Fill with pie weights or dried beans, then bake until set, about 20 minutes. Remove the beans and foil, and continue baking until browned, about 15 minutes.

In a medium bowl, combine the sugar, eggs, egg yolks, vanilla and salt. Add the hot half-and-half, then the kirsch. Strain the custard through a fine sieve and reserve. In a large skillet over high heat, melt the butter, then add the cherries. Cook until the cherries are warm and the juices have thickened to coat the fruit, about 5 minutes. Spoon the cherries into the tart shell, then pour the custard over the cherries. Bake until the custard sets, about 10 minutes. Cool on a rack. Dust the tart with confectioners' sugar and serve.

Nutrition details per serving
Calories .722
Percent of calories from fat 63%
Fat: .52 gm
Protein: . . . . .9 gm
Carbohydrate: . . . . .50 gm
Cholesterol: . . . . .245 mg
Sodium: . . . . .231 mg
Diabetic exchange: 1 milk, ½ fruit, 1⅓ bread, ⅜ meat, 9⅛ fat.

■

WALNUT PASTRY

Makes an 11-inch tart

½ cup walnuts

½ cup confectioners' sugar

24 tablespoons (3 sticks) unsalted butter

1 large egg

2 tablespoons grated lemon rind

¼ teaspoon salt

2 cups pastry flour

In a food processor, grind the nuts and sugar together until fine. Transfer to a mixing bowl. Add the butter and, using a mixer, whip until light. Add the egg, lemon rind and salt. Add the flour, mixing until just combined. Transfer the dough to a piece of parchment, and flatten into a disk. Cover with another piece of parchment, and refrigerate until firm, at least 8 hours. Dust the dough with flour, then roll the dough out between the sheets of parchment to a thickness of ¼ inch. Fit into an 11-inch tart pan, trim, and finish edges.

Refrigerate at least 30 minutes before baking (instructions in recipe for Sour Cherry Tart).

Cook's note: Keep the pastry dough cool for easy handling.

To order dried Michigan cherries, contact American Spoon Foods, PO Box 566, Petoskey, Mich. 49770; or call 1-800-222-5886, 9-5 weekdays.

■

Cherries originated in China around 4000 B.C. and traveled to Greece and across Europe. They were introduced to North America by the first settlers. Cherry is one of the most universally grown fruit trees.

BLACKBERRIES ADD A TASTE OF WINE

AMAZING FOOD FACTS
■

There are 100-200 species of blackberries, many with unique tastes and textures. Horticulturists continue to develop new, improved blackberries, such as thornless, ornamental and yellow, red and purple variations.

■ *How many varieties are there?* Some of the most intense flavors come from the blackberry and its close relatives, a group that defies a catchall description of their qualities. They range in size from a tiny thimble to about thumb-size; in flavor from intensely sweet to wine-like or tart; in texture from crunchy and firm to light and delicate. They come with many names, including Crackleberries, Flymboy, Nagoonberry, Logans and Wineberries.

■ *Health advantages:* Blackberries are high in potassium and vitamin A.

■ *How to select:* Choose berries that have deep color and a dry surface. They should be ripe and supple, never soft and mushy, although overripe berries are perfect for making sorbets, ice cream and preserves.

TODAY'S LESSON: It seems most folks are familiar with raspberries, but few can identify their darker relatives. Blackberries always were harder to locate in the thick underbrush than their more brightly colored cousins, but for me it was worth risking poison ivy to enjoy their deep, rich flavor.

■ *How to clean:* Carefully lay the berries out on a cookie sheet or shallow dish to sort out imperfect ones. Refrigerate with ventilation until ready to serve. Wash the berries under cold trickling water only moments before serving and allow to drain well in a colander.

■ *How to cook:* I prefer the cooked flavors of blackberries. You can sweeten tart or under-ripe berries with sugar, although I prefer maple sugar or light syrup. To spark up lackluster flavor, add a touch of balsamic vinegar along with the maple sweetener. Cook berries only lightly, because the delicate fruit will turn to mush otherwise.

■ *Mix and match:* Blackberries have a wine-like flavor that complements rack of veal, roasted or grilled duck and squab. Build the background flavor of the blackberries in the sauce, adding a splash of red wine to boost the acid balance if necessary. Strain the seeds from the sauce, adding fresh berries at the last second just to warm before serving.

The blackberry flavor accentuates roasted sweet shallots, chives, smoky bacon or Italian pancetta and prosciutto. Spices such as peppercorns, coriander, cloves and mace work well. Other good companions are fresh, stronger herbs with forest-like scents — rosemary, sage, thyme and savory — but fry the herbs first to crisp the texture and lighten the strong flavor.

■ *You can keep it simple, too:* Of course, the most direct way to enjoy blackberries is plain for breakfast or with a splash of whipped cream for dessert.

■

BLACKBERRY BRIOCHE PUDDING

Makes 8 servings

8   cups cubed fresh brioche (or other sweet egg bread)

2   pints fresh blackberries or related dark berries

6   whole eggs, beaten

3   egg yolks, beaten

1   cup granulated sugar

2   tablespoons vanilla extract

1½ cups milk, scalded

1½ cups light cream (half-and-half), scalded

    Confectioners' sugar to dust

8   scoops French vanilla ice cream

8   large sprigs fresh mint for garnish

Preheat oven to 350. In a buttered 9-by-13-inch baking dish, place half the cubed brioche evenly across the bottom. Cover with half the blackberries. Repeat with remaining brioche and blackberries.

In a medium bowl, combine eggs, yolks, sugar and vanilla. Gradually add hot scalded milk and cream until combined. Pour the mixture over the blackberries and brioche. With a spoon or spatula, push down on the brioche until most of the cream mixture has been absorbed.

Bake on the lower rack until firm and golden, about 25-30 minutes. Test by inserting a skewer or pick into the center. The center should be hot, and the skewer should come out clean. Remove to a cake rack to cool slightly.

To serve, cut the warm pudding into squares. With a spoon, transfer to serving plates. Dust with confectioners' sugar sifted through a fine mesh strainer. Put a scoop of ice cream beside the pudding. Garnish with a sprig of mint and serve.

Nutrition details per serving
Calories 1,015
Percent of calories from fat 16%
Fat: .18 gm
Protein: . . . . .33 gm
Carbohydrate: . . . . .172 gm
Cholesterol: . . . . .299 mg
Sodium: . . . . .1,266 mg
Diabetic exchange: ⅜ milk, ½ fruit, 8¼
bread, ⅛ meat, 2⅞ fat.

BOUNTIFUL OPTIONS WITH BLUEBERRIES

AMAZING FOOD FACTS

■

Blueberries are probably the easiest fruit to prepare and serve. There is no peeling, pitting, coring or cutting — just chill and rinse before serving.

■ *When to pick:* Blueberries are sweetest in the afternoon; during the night, they convert the day's sugar to other components. Harvesting in the midday sun is hot for you and the berry, resulting in quicker spoilage. Pick in late afternoon — after the heat has peaked in the field and in the berry. When picking, frequently move the picked berries to a shaded area (they were shaded under the plant's leaves) or to a cooler to avoid overheating and splitting the berries.

■ *How to pick:* To pick blueberries by hand, select the darkest berries and roll the individual berry between thumb and forefingers to release from stem. Open containers that attach to your belt are best for keeping both hands free for the picking. Refrigerate the berries as soon as possible. Take the berries home inside your air-conditioned vehicle rather than in your oven-like trunk.

TODAY'S LESSON: Blueberry picking and eating season is just about my favorite time of the year. Michigan's superior berry-growing soil means the state leads the United States in cultivated blueberry production.

■ *The easy way out:* For a shorter drive and less laborious collection, great blueberries are arriving at your local farmer's market and neighborhood supermarket.

■ *How to select:* Choose supple, plump, dark berries. Taste to ensure superior sweet, rich flavor. Avoid shriveled, greenish or cracked berries.

■ *How to store:* Choose carefully and consume within a few days. Tent with plastic wrap to prevent moisture loss and store in the coldest part of your refrigerator (best at 32 degrees).

■ *Serve fresh:* Blueberries are great served fresh with a little cream, a splash of bourbon or a scoop of ice cream. Wash just before serving and spin dry in your lettuce spinner or roll gently on paper toweling. Toss with spirits, creams and sugars just before serving to ensure a firm texture; all these substances tend to soften the berries if they are allowed to marinate. Serve slightly chilled for refreshing pronounced flavor.

■ *Give them a deep chill:* If summer temperatures hit high records, try squeezing lots of fresh lime juice over the blueberries in a metal bowl with a dusting of sugar to balance the acidic bite. Place the bowl in the freezer. Stir the berries every 15 minutes until just freezing or al dente to the bite, about 2-3 hours. Serve with lots of fresh mint for the coolest dessert of the season.

■ *How to cook:* Blueberry flavor really comes forward when berries are cooked in light batters such as pancakes and muffins. For pancakes, add the berries to the hot pan to cook for just one minute, then add the batter. The blueberry flavor will be stronger, and the presentation is superior. For baked goods, remember that wild berries are far superior to the larger cultivated varieties. Blueberries can also be sauteed in a little butter to develop their flavor, dusted with a little sugar and a splash of citrus or even bourbon to make a terrific sauce for ice creams. They may be sauteed for savory dishes, but remember to wear an apron: They occasionally

burst from the heat and spray their deep colorful juices.

■ *Save until later:* Fresh blueberry flavor can be captured in vinegar for use all year round. Fill a quarter of a glass container with blueberries and cover with hot white or red wine vinegar. Allow to steep until cool. Cover and refrigerate for at least one month. Use for delicate salad dressings to impart a fruity blueberry flavor.

■

BLUEBERRY CREPES WITH BOURBON & ICE CREAM

Makes 4 servings

¾ cup sifted flour
  Pinch of salt
1 tablespoon sugar
1 teaspoon freshly grated nutmeg
3 large eggs, lightly beaten

½ cup milk
½ cup bourbon (or substitute milk)
8 tablespoons melted unsalted butter, divided
1 pint of wild blueberries, cleaned and dry
4 scoops of your favorite vanilla ice cream or frozen yogurt
  Powdered sugar to dust for garnish
4 sprigs mint for garnish

In a medium bowl, combine the flour, salt, sugar and nutmeg. Slowly mix in the eggs. Add the milk and bourbon, mixing until smooth. Add 4 tablespoons of the melted butter. Allow the mix to stand at room temperature for about 15 minutes before cooking. In a nonstick 8-inch pan, heat 1 tablespoon of the remaining butter over medium-high heat. Add a fourth of the blueberries and cook for 1 minute to heat. Add about a fourth of the crepe batter to cover the entire bottom of the pan. Cook until golden

brown, about 2 minutes. Carefully turn over, making sure not to tear, and cook for another minute. Flip the crepe back over onto an ovenproof platter. Don't worry about the loose berries; they will be on the inside of the crepe when presented. Keep warm in an oven on low heat and repeat the procedure to make three additional crepes.

To serve: Place the crepe on a large plate, smooth side down. Spoon the ice cream in an oval shape across the center of the crepe. Roll the crepe around the ice cream to enclose. Transfer to the center of the serving plate, dust with powdered sugar, garnish with mint and serve immediately.

Nutrition details per serving
Calories 633
Percent of calories from fat 51%
Fat: .37 gm
Protein: . . . . .11 gm
Carbohydrate: . . . . .49 gm
Cholesterol: . . . . .223 mg
Sodium: . . . . .469 mg
Diabetic exchange: ⅛ milk, ¾ fruit, 2¼ bread, ⅓ meat, 6⅛ fat.

AMAZING FOOD FACTS

■

The peach originated in China, dating to about 2000 B.C., traveling through Persia about 1500 B.C. to the Mediterranean, and then to America with the Spanish in the 1600s.

HAVE A PEACHY SUMMER

■ *Health advantages:* Peaches are a great source of potassium and vitamin A.

■ *How to enjoy:* When perfectly ripe, peaches are sublime eaten out of hand. The wonderful fresh flavor usually inspires the cook to slice the raw peaches and serve them with shortcake or other simple preparations.

■ *Too tart?* A dusting of sugar may enhance the flavor. I prefer bar, or superfine, sugar. Sugar will draw moisture and slightly break down the texture of the peaches, so add it just before serving.

■ *How to cook:* Peaches are usually cooked in cobblers, tarts and pies, which concentrates the sweetness but eliminates the delicate fragrance. Poaching in a sugar syrup has been the best method for capturing the peach flavor and texture, but some of the flavor escapes to the liquid. To poach, combine equal parts of sugar and water

TODAY'S LESSON: Why drink water for refreshment when there are juicy summer peaches? Harry Cipriani of Harry's Bar in Venice had the same idea when he made the first Bellini cocktail. Ripe peaches were pureed and silkenly mingled like music with prosecco, a light sparkling wine, to make a drink that's hard to beat. Ripe peach puree is also terrific blended with sparkling water.

and bring to a slow simmer. Add the ripe fruit and rotate occasionally to ensure even cooking until tender, about 7-10 minutes. Check for doneness by delicately inserting a skewer into the peach; when the skewer is inserted with no resistance, it's done. Remove the cooked fruit to chilled poaching liquid to stop the cooking and hold until serving.

To dry-poach, select ripe peaches free of bruises, open

scars and cuts. The peaches may be washed but must be thoroughly dried before cooking. Place the salt in a 4- to 6-inch-deep ovenproof vessel. There should be enough salt to completely bury the peaches. Heat the salt as high as your oven goes, preferably 450-500 degrees. Carefully remove the vessel containing the salt from the oven, remembering that it is extremely hot! Remove part of the salt to another pan. Put the peaches into the remaining salt, making sure they touch neither the pan nor each other. Add hot salt to completely cover the peaches and return to the oven. Cook until done, about 7-10 minutes. To check the peaches, remove the pan from the oven and carefully dig out one peach. Gently squeeze the peach; it should be supple yet not soft. You will able to squeeze the peach without burning your hand, but be careful not to touch the salt. If necessary, cover again with the salt and return to the oven. When done, dig out the peaches without damaging the skins. Carefully brush off the salt with a soft towel and allow to cool to room temperature on a platter. Do not puncture or cut the peaches, for the juices will be released and bleed, resulting in very grainy fruit. Do not let the peaches cool in the salt, for they will taste salty.

■ *How to serve:* Dry-poached peaches may be served at room temperature or slightly chilled. The skin of the peach may be cut near the stem and easily

peeled away, or the fruit may be served intact. Light sauces or ice creams will enhance the peach.

■

DRY-POACHED PEACHES WITH WHITE CHOCOLATE ICE CREAM

Makes 4 servings

1 3-pound box kosher salt
4 large ripe peaches
½ cup maple syrup (the real stuff)
¼ cup Amontillado sherry
4 scoops White Chocolate Ice Cream (see recipe on page 284)
4 sprigs fresh mint for garnish

Preheat oven to 450. Select an ovenproof dish or pot just large enough to accommodate all four peaches. Put the salt in the dish and place in the oven for at least 1 hour to thoroughly heat. Remove the dish from oven. Carefully remove two-thirds of the salt to another pan. (Remember, the salt is 450 degrees!) Position the peaches on the remaining salt so that they do not touch

each other, the bottom or the sides of the dish. Completely bury the peaches with the hot salt you took out. Return the dish to the oven and cook until the peaches are supple and tender, about 10 minutes. Remove from the oven and carefully remove the salt from around the peaches, making sure not to damage the skin. Transfer to a plate. Carefully brush remaining salt from the peaches. Allow to cool.

In a small bowl, combine maple syrup and sherry. Reserve. With a paring knife, make a small incision near the stem of each peach, peel back the skin and discard. Position the peach in the center of the serving dish, stem side down. Scoop the ice cream and place it next to the peach. Garnish with the sprig of mint. Spoon the maple-sherry sauce over the peach at the table or just before serving.

Nutrition details per serving
Calories .427
Percent of calories from fat 63%
Fat: .30 gm
Protein: . . . . .7 gm
Carbohydrate: . . . . .33 gm
Cholesterol: . . . . .229 mg
Sodium: . . . . .85 mg
Diabetic exchange: ¼ milk, 1 bread,
⅓ meat, 5½ fat.

■

There are two principal peach types — freestone and clingstone, which describe the fruits' attachment to the stone, as the pit is called. The clingstone has firmer flesh.

■

Nectarines are actually a fuzzless variety of peaches. They are usually smaller but have all other peach characteristics.

AMAZING FOOD FACTS

■

Figs were thought to be sacred by the ancients. They were also considered signs of peace and prosperity.

■ *What is a fig?* The fresh fig, with its tender skin protecting soft, supple white flesh filled with crunchy seeds, bears little resemblance to the dried fig. They are great eaten for a snack, perfect with a smoked ham or salad as an appetizer, sublime with duck as a main course and profound as a dessert.

■ *Health advantages:* Figs are high in potassium and vitamin A.

■ *How many varieties are there?* There are many varieties of figs, although most commercial production is from four principal types. The Smyrna, or Calimyrna, fig is green in color and rounded in shape, with most production taking place in early summer. The tear-shaped Kadota is green-gold in color. There are two Mission varieties that range in color from dark purple or black to green with an elongated tear shape.

■ *A fruit with peculiarities:* In most varieties, both male and

TODAY'S LESSON: As the soft winds of summer begin to blow, they bring the first fresh figs of the season. Fresh figs have been treasured for more than 6,000 years for their delicate flesh and fruity flavor and as a natural source of sugar. Increased production and distribution have recently raised the popularity of fresh figs.

female flowers are found inside the fruit at the base. But the Smyrna variety has only female flowers and thus relies on the wild caprifig trees for pollination. Pollination is accomplished by tiny ⅛-inch wasps that enter a small pore at the base of the fruit. For this reason, care should be taken when eating raw figs; slice them into wedges first.

■ *How to select:* Figs are supple when ripe. To hasten ripening, rub the base, the fatter part of

the fruit, with a little olive oil and leave at room temperature. Avoid soft, wrinkled figs, which are overripe.

■ *How to store:* Store figs at room temperature to ripen and under refrigeration after ripening.

■ *Serving suggestions:* I can think of nothing that goes so well with champagne for a special breakfast or simply roasted for the sublime finish to a great meal. Fresh figs make any course unusual.

BAKED FIGS WITH HONEY & BOURBON

Makes 8 servings

¾ cup pure honey

¾ cup bourbon

16 large figs

1 cup heavy cream

2 tablespoons balsamic vinegar (or substitute good red wine vinegar)

4 Almond-Pistachio Tuiles (see accompanying recipe)

4 sprigs mint for garnish

Preheat oven to 375 degrees. In a small bowl, combine the honey and the bourbon. Place figs in a medium-size oven-proof pot large enough to accommodate all the figs. Bake on the lower rack of the oven, basting frequently with honey and bourbon mixture. Cook until tender, about 45 minutes. Remove from oven. Transfer figs carefully to a plate to cool. Pour the basting juices into a medium skillet and add the cream. Bring to a boil over medium high heat, cooking until thick enough to coat back of spoon, about 15 minutes. Remove from heat. Add vinegar. Spoon the sauce onto a serving plate. Position four figs per serving in the center of the sauce. Place a tuile atop the figs. Garnish with mint and serve.

Nutrition details per serving
Calories 1,348
Percent of calories from fat 35%
Fat: . . . . .55 gm
Protein: . . . . .28 gm
Carbohydrate: . . . . .177 gm
Cholesterol: . . . . .82 mg
Sodium: . . . . .297 mg
Diabetic exchange: 2⅝ fruit, 2⅓ bread, ½ meat, 10⅓ fat.

ALMOND-PISTACHIO TUILES

Makes 8 servings

Unsalted butter for parchment

1½ cups all-purpose flour

¾ cup sugar

¾ cup sliced toasted almonds

½ cup pistachios, roasted, skins rubbed off, coarsely chopped

4 large egg whites

Preheat oven to 300 degrees. Line a sheet pan with buttered parchment. In a large bowl, combine the flour, sugar, almonds, pistachios and egg whites. Fold together until well mixed. Spread the batter on the prepared sheet pan. Place in the upper third of oven and bake until the edges begin to brown, about 20 minutes. Remove from oven. While still hot, trim the edges of the tuiles with a sharp knife to form triangles. Remove to a cake rack to cool. Reserve at room temperature.

Nutrition details per serving
Calories .283
Percent of calories from fat 33%
Fat: . . . . .11 gm
Protein: . . . . .8 gm
Carbohydrate: . . . . .41 gm
Cholesterol: . . . . .0 mg
Sodium: . . . . .129 mg
Diabetic exchange: 1¼ bread, ¼ meat, 2 fat.

Figs were brought to North America by the Spanish Franciscan missionaries who set up Catholic missions in California.

MANGO:
A TROPICAL TREAT

AMAZING FOOD FACTS

■

Mango trees are evergreens that grow 50-60 feet tall in tropical regions. The tree will fruit four to six years after planting. They require hot, dry periods to set and produce a fruit crop, resulting in widely varying yields.

■ *Where do they come from?* Seventy percent of the mangoes sold in the United States come from Mexico, and they arrive in U.S. markets in June and July. The rest come from Haiti and Florida.

■ *What do they look like?* Mangoes can be heart- or kidney-shaped, or round, oval or thin. They can be red to yellow to dull green, with orange flesh. They can be as small as plums or as large as 5 pounds.

■ *Advantages:* Mangoes are high in vitamins A and C and potassium. They are also high in sucrose. Compared to apples, they have higher solids, twice the sugar, one-tenth the acid and the same amount of protein. When underripe, mangoes are high in malic and tartaric acids, which leave a chalky taste in the mouth.

■ *The principal varieties:*
Keitt: oval and large, green-skinned with yellow and red

TODAY'S LESSON: The mango, king of tropical fruits, has a sweet, delicate flavor and tender flesh. It is as common and popular in warmer climates as the apple is in the North. The mango is loved for its many uses — underripe in salads and ripe in salsas, chutneys, preserves and desserts such as pies, tarts, ice creams and sorbets.

highlights, juicy, fiberless flesh except near the seed, and rich sweet flavor.
Tommy Atkins: oblong with rounded base, large and red with almost fiber-free juicy flesh.
Haden: oval and large, crimson to pink skin with yellow highlights, juicy, low-fiber flesh with low acid flavor.
Irwin: elongated and medium weight, orange-yellow skin with red highlights, fiberless mild flesh and small stones or seeds.

Kent: oval and large, greenish-yellow skin, fiberless, rich and juicy flesh.

■ *How to select:* Select mangoes much the same way you would avocados, their close relatives. The flesh should give a little when gently squeezed. The skin should be taut without bruises and soft spots. Sniff the stem end. The mango should have a pleasant fragrance. Better fragrance means better flavor. Avoid discolored fruit with pitted spots.

■ *How to ripen:* Wrap in newspaper or bury in shredded paper and keep in a warm — not hot — spot, which will help maintain the humidity and temperature. Check the mango every day or two for fragrance and supple texture. Refrigerate when ripe.

■ *How to prepare:* The mango stone or seed resembles the shape of the mango. To remove the seed, cut the outer fleshy halves from the fruit, leaving the inch or so of center fruit attached. The flesh may be scored and the skin inverted to gain easy access to the fruit, or it may be peeled with a paring knife.

■ *Mix and match:* The mango is ready to be added to your favorite dishes, from salads to desserts. Mangoes make great salsas for grilled fish when paired with roasted sweet peppers, tomatoes and other bright flavors and fresh herbs.

■

MANGO-CASHEW ICE CREAM

Makes 8 servings or 1¼ quarts

8   large egg yolks
1¼ cups sugar
    Pinch of salt
1   teaspoon vanilla extract
1   cup half-and-half, scalded
1   cup heavy cream, scalded
3   large ripe mangoes, seeded, peeled and cut into pieces
2   limes, juiced

2   cups toasted unsalted cashews, coarsely chopped

In a medium saucepan, combine the yolks, sugar, salt and vanilla. Whisk in the half-and-half and heavy cream. Stir over medium-low heat until the custard thickens enough to coat the back of a spoon, about 10 minutes; do not boil. Remove from heat, and combine with the mangoes and lime juice in a blender. Puree until smooth, about 5 minutes. Strain through a fine sieve. Cover and refrigerate until well chilled.

Process the custard in an ice cream maker according to the manufacturer's instructions until thickened. Add the cashews. Freeze in a covered container overnight. If frozen solid, soften slightly before serving.

```
Nutrition details per ½-cup serving
Calories . . . . . . . . . . . . . . . . . . .634
Percent of calories from fat . . . . . . .65%
Fat: . . . . . . . . . . . . . . . . . . . . .46 gm
Protein: . . . . . . . . . . . . . . . . .17 gm
Carbohydrate: . . . . . . . . . . . . .40 gm
Cholesterol: . . . . . . . . . . . . . .265 mg
Sodium: . . . . . . . . . . . . . . . . .44 mg
Diabetic exchange: ⅛ milk, 1 fruit, ¾ meat,
9 fat.
```

■

The mango is related to the cashew and the pistachio as well as to poison ivy and sumac. When immature, it may be an irritant, although these qualities diminish as the fruit ripens.

■

The leaves are high in vitamin C. The bark is high in tannins and is used for tanning leather.

THE CREAM OF ICE CREAMS

■ *What kinds of ice cream to make:* America is rich in fruits of many origins. Tree fruits such as apricots, cherries, peaches, nectarines, plums and figs are full of flavor. The berry family is at its peak. Vine fruits — melon, cantaloupe and watermelon — reflect flavor and character as at no other time of year.

■ *Where did sorbet and ice cream originate?* Sorbets were thought to originate in China before being passed to the Persians and on to the Italians. All of this took place a century or two before ice cream was invented. The origin of ice cream is unclear but is believed to be found in the French court in the mid-17th Century.

■ *Innovations to please the palate:* Americans refined the product with the invention of the first hand-cranked ice cream machine in 1846. This machine generated smaller

TODAY'S LESSON: The temperatures of July bake summer fruits to perfumed glory. But with the extreme heat of summer, the fruits are at their best for only a fleeting moment, perfect to be captured in the frozen splendor of ice creams and sorbets.

crystals of ice produced by the introduction of air. Our innovative ancestors invented ice cream cones in 1904, Eskimo Pies of chocolate-coated ice cream in 1919, and the Good Humor Bar — ice cream on a stick — in 1924.

■ *How it is made:* The three basic phases of ice cream making are preparing the mix, freezing and hardening. The basic mix is composed of fruits or spices, fats from cream for richness, sugar and air, which interrupts the frozen solids and liquids for that special ice cream texture.

■ *The basics:* The basic mix is heated to help dissolve the sugar and kill off bacteria. It is then chilled for quick, efficient freezing and better texture.

■ *Deep freezing:* The freezing procedure is quite simple in a self-contained refrigerated machine such as a Minigel. Fill the container to two-thirds to allow for air intake and expansion, and proceed according to manufacturer's specifications.

If you use a traditional machine, which uses ice and salt for freezing, prepare the proper freezing brine of eight parts ice to one part salt to start. As the ice cream mix begins to freeze and become thicker, increase the salt to one part per three parts of ice, which will lower the brine temperature to approximately minus 4 degrees.

When the ice cream is thick enough to stop the mechanical action, add a couple of hand-fuls of salt to further lower the brine temperature. Allow the ice cream to remain in this brine to harden. You can serve the ice cream at this point or transfer it to your freezer.

■ *How cold to keep it?* The ideal temperature of the freezer should be minus 10 degrees, and the ice cream should stay at this temperature during storage to preserve the fine texture and delicate flavor. Before serving, the ice cream should be tempered to 10-20 degrees to soften slightly.

■

PEACH ICE CREAM

Makes 1 quart

3   cups very ripe, peeled, pitted and chunked peaches

2   cups whipping cream, scalded

6   egg yolks

¾   cup sugar

Dash of salt

1   teaspoon vanilla

¼   cup Southern Comfort

Combine the peaches and hot cream in blender and puree until smooth.

Combine the egg yolks, sugar, salt and vanilla in a medium saucepan. Whisk in puree. Stir over medium-low heat until custard thickens enough to coat the back of spoon, about 10 minutes. Do not boil. Remove from the heat and strain through fine sieve into medium bowl. Add Southern Comfort. Cover and refrigerate until well chilled.

Process custard in ice cream maker according to manufac-turer's instructions. Transfer to container. Cover and freeze overnight. If frozen solid, soften slightly before serving.

Nutrition details per serving
Calories .315
Percent of calories from fat 72%
Fat: . . . . .26 gm
Protein: . . . . .4 gm
Carbohydrate: . . . . .19 gm
Cholesterol: . . . . .241 mg
Sodium: . . . . .28 mg
Diabetic exchange: ⅓ fruit, ⅓ meat, 4⅓ fat.

■

Americans eat more than 750 million gallons of ice cream a year, or 15 quarts per person.

GRANITAS

■ *What exactly is a granita?* A granita is a fruit or other liquid beverage that has been frozen while occasionally stirred, producing a coarse, icy dessert. It is much rougher than a sorbet.

■ *Why they taste so good:* Granitas have less sugar than sorbets, resulting in a purer, less sweet flavor. They seem to capture more of the natural flavor of fresh fruits with their simple, clean and direct taste.

■ *Health advantages:* Granitas are made from fresh fruit or fruit juices, sugar, occasionally a little water and a squeeze of lemon. Their natural vitamins and minerals are captured without any fat.

■ *Selecting your fruit:* Choose the ripest, best-tasting fruit possible. The flavor in the fruit will be the flavor you get in your granita. Fruit that even seems a little overripe will be even better for your granita.

TODAY'S LESSON: Like sorbets, their French cousins, Italian granitas are a cool refresher on a hot summer day. Granitas are the easiest of the frozen desserts to make with a couple of new techniques.

■ *Preparing your fruit:* There are two types of fruit for making granitas — those that are processed raw because of their eat-from-the-hand ripeness and firmer fruits which are improved by a light poaching. Here's how the groups break down:

Raw fruit types: berries, papayas, mangos, citrus, pineapple, kiwi and melons — mostly fruits with high acid and moisture content.

Cooked fruit types: apricots, plums, peaches, pears, cherries, passion, Asian pears, coconut and quince. The stone fruit family and the firmer tropical fruits improve with a little poaching to soften and bring the flavor forward. Cooking also helps set the color and prevent browning.

■ *The cooking begins:* The fruit is seeded and cut into small even pieces and combined with sugar and in some cases a little additional water or fruit juice. The mixture is brought to a simmer and cooked until the fruit is tender. It is then pureed until smooth and strained to remove any pulp. Additional seasonings are added, and it is ready to freeze.

■ *The cooking does not begin:* For the raw fruit types, the fruit and sugar are pureed until smooth, then strained.

Additional seasonings are added, and they are ready to freeze.

■ *To freeze:* The traditional method calls for pouring the liquid into a shallow pan in the coldest part of your freezer, then allowing the mix to begin to freeze. As the liquid begins to form ice crystals, usually on the bottom, sides and top, they are broken up and stirred into the granita. This process continues occasionally for a few hours until an icy thick slush forms, at which time it is ready to serve and enjoy.

■ *The drawback:* Besides the time consumption of stirring when the granita is ready, it must be enjoyed within about a 30-minute time frame, or the mixture will freeze solid.

■ *Tricks of the trade:* The new method is the best way to get the texture and flavor with half of the work and is ready when you are. Make your liquid granita mix as described above and pour into ice cube trays to freeze.

The cubes are then placed, one layer deep, in a food processor and pulsed about 10-12 times to achieve the icy granita texture. The granita is ready to enjoy! The even cubes, food processor and not too many cubes in a batch are the secrets to the perfect texture. Do not overwork the granita, or it will turn to a slush like you'd find at the carnival.

■ *Serving suggestions:* I like to serve granitas in a frozen martini glass with a sprig of mint as garnish. Another great presentation, especially for citrus, is to cut about a quarter off the end of the fresh fruit, squeeze and scoop out the juice and pulp, then freeze the citrus shell. Make the granita, then stuff the frozen orange or lemon shell with the granita. Serve with a sprig of mint.

■ *Mix and match:* Although the pure fruit flavors are stellar, try a blend of fruits for some outrageous flavor combinations such as papaya-lime, passion-coconut and any others your wild imagi-

nation might like. Make each of the flavors separately, then blend a couple of tablespoons and try before you make a batch of your masterpiece that no one else may eat.

■ *Try your technique:* Try each of the recipes, matched to suit your fruit type, and beat the heat of summer in granita style.

■

APPLE CIDER GRANITA

Makes 2 cups

2 cups apple juice
½ cup superfine sugar
Lemon juice to taste
Fresh mint sprigs for garnish

In a small saucepan, combine the juice and the sugar. Heat over medium-high heat while stirring until the sugar is completely dissolved, about 2-3 minutes. Remove from the heat and add the lemon juice to taste. Transfer the mix into ice cube trays

and freeze until firm. If not using immediately, transfer the frozen cubes into a sealed freezer-proof locking-style bag.

To serve: Place one layer of the granita cubes in a food processor. Pulse the processor to achieve coarse crystals. Serve immediately in a frozen martini glass or bowl garnished with a sprig of mint.

Nutrition details per ½-cup serving
Calories 118
Percent of calories from fat 1%
Fat: . . . . .4 gm
Protein: . . . . .trace
Carbohydrate: . . . . .30 gm
Cholesterol: . . . . .0 mg
Sodium: . . . . .4 mg
Diabetic exchange: 2 fruit. Not recommended for diabetics.

■

PEACH GRANITA

Makes 2 cups

1   pound fresh ripe
    peaches, pitted,
    peeled and cut into
    medium dice
½   cup superfine sugar
1   cup water
    Lemon juice to taste
    Fresh mint sprigs for
    garnish

In a small saucepan, combine the peaches, sugar and water. Bring to a simmer over medium-high heat, cooking until the peaches are tender and the sugar is completely dissolved, about 6 minutes. Remove from the heat and transfer to a blender. Puree until smooth. Strain through a fine sieve to remove the pulp. Add the lemon juice to taste. Transfer the mix into ice cube trays and freeze until firm. If not using immediately, transfer the frozen cubes into a sealed freezer-proof locking-style bag.

To serve: Place one layer of the granita cubes in a food processor. Pulse the processor to achieve coarse crystals. Serve immediately in a frozen martini glass or bowl garnished with a sprig of mint.

Nutrition details per ½-cup serving
Calories .107
Percent of calories from fat 1%
Fat: . . . . .trace
Protein: . . . . .1 gm
Carbohydrate: . . . . .28 gm
Cholesterol: . . . . .0 mg
Sodium: . . . . .trace
Diabetic exchange: 1¾ fruit. Not recommended for diabetics.

■

WATERMELON GRANITA

Makes 1 quart or 8 servings

3   pounds ripe sweet
    watermelon, trimmed
    of rind and seeds
½   cup fresh lime juice
1   cup sugar
    Mint sprigs for
    garnish

In a blender, combine the watermelon and lime juice, pureeing until smooth. Transfer to a saucepan, add the sugar and bring to a simmer over high heat. Remove from heat after one short boil. Strain through a coarse sieve to ensure a smooth texture. Refrigerate until cool, about 1 hour.

Pour the mixture into a large, shallow metal pan that has been placed level in the coldest part of your freezer. Stir every 15 minutes with a fork to break up the large ice crystals until no liquid remains, about 2-3 hours. Spoon into chilled bowls or glasses, garnish with mint and serve.

Nutrition details per ½-cup serving
Calories .128
Percent of calories from fat 3%
Fat: . . . . .4 gm
Protein: . . . . .1 gm
Carbohydrate: . . . . .32 gm
Cholesterol: . . . . .0 mg
Sodium: . . . . .4 mg
Diabetic exchange: 2¼ fruit. Not recommended for diabetics.

■

MELON GRANITA

Makes 2 cups

1½ pounds fresh ripe
    melon or cantaloupe,
    seeded, trimmed of all
    rind, and cut into
    medium dice
¼   cup superfine sugar
    Lemon juice to taste
    Fresh mint sprigs for
    garnish

In a blender, combine the melon and sugar. Puree until smooth. Strain through a fine sieve to remove the pulp. Add the lemon juice to taste. Transfer the mix into ice cube trays and freeze until firm. If not using immediately, transfer the frozen cubes into a sealed freezer-proof locking-style bag.

To serve: Place one layer of the granita cubes in a food processor. Pulse the processor to achieve coarse crystals. Serve immediately in a frozen martini glass or bowl garnished with a sprig of mint.

Nutrition details per ½-cup serving
Calories .57
Percent of calories from fat 4%
Fat: . . . . .trace
Protein: . . . . .1 gm
Carbohydrate: . . . . .14 gm
Cholesterol: . . . . .0 mg
Sodium: . . . . .7 mg
Diabetic exchange: 1 fruit. Not recommended for diabetics.

FRUIT SORBET
BEATS THE HEAT

**AMAZING
FOOD FACTS**
■

Lightly flavored
sorbet is often
served between
courses to clear
or refresh the
palate.

■ *Why it tastes so good:*
Summer fruit that is tree-ripened is best eaten raw at that moment or captured in a frozen sorbet. Whatever the flavor combinations, freezing with sugar syrup seems to enrich the flavor.

■ *Advantages:* Sorbets and even Popsicle-style treats made from these formulas are mostly good, healthy fruit with a little sugar. They contain no fat yet have the flavor and texture to satisfy summer dessert cravings. They are also very easy to make. They freeze quickly in molds and flat pans that are stirred, or processed in a sorbet machine.

■ *Tricks of the trade:* These are so easy to make that there are only a couple of tricks. Shop for overripe fruit at your local farmer's or fruit market. This fruit is considered too ripe to eat out of hand, but the sweet taste and scent are the best for these frozen treats. Take your

TODAY'S LESSON: Nothing cools you down like the pure flavor of frozen sorbets. These chillers are usually made of fresh fruit puree and a little sugar water, then quickly frozen. The more unusual flavorings include tea, espresso, coffee, herbs, citrus, chocolate and even wines.

time to get the sugar balance right. Too much sugar, and the sorbet will be loose and soft. Too little sugar turns them into ice bricks. Another trick: A good shot of fresh lemon juice will keep flavor fresh and balance the sugars for taste and texture. Don't cheat and use lemon concentrate; it is not worth the trouble.

■ *Preparing your fruit:* Peel and seed the fruit, making sure all the juices are captured. If the fruit tends to brown quickly, add a good squeeze of lemon juice while you prepare the

rest of the ingredients. Puree in a blender until smooth, straining through a fine sieve.

■ *Preparing the sugar syrup:* Although recipes may vary slightly, I prefer a more concentrated sugar syrup so less water is inadvertently added to the fruit puree. Try 1 cup water to ¾ cup sugar, heated with a touch of lemon juice in a clean saucepan. Bring to a short boil to make the syrup. In the sorbet, the sugar prevents large, hard crystals from forming and freezing solid.

■

Unlike sherbet, sorbet never contains any milk or milk products. Sorbet has a lighter, softer consistency than sherbet.

■ *A star is born:* Add the sugar syrup to the fruit puree or flavoring base until the right concentration is achieved. Try following recipes while using your own taste buds and a little experimentation to find the correct mix. Test by freezing a little of the mix before committing the entire batch to the deep freeze. Adjust syrup until the right texture is achieved.

■ *Get freezing:* Choose your method.

Frozen treats on a stick — in imitation of Popsicles — are easy to make in a mold. Try new exotic flavors instead of the artificial ones. I love chocolate-espresso to cool me off late at night. My kids like to stick with the fruit flavors, such as guava, orange-passion and mango-coconut.

Sorbets use a slightly sweeter mix, frozen in an ice cream machine. More sugar makes smaller crystals form when sorbet freezes. The constant action of the machine also contributes to the small crystals and the smooth, almost silky texture. The best is served right from the machine for the chilly, melt-in-your-mouth tex-

ture and flavor. It is great the next day and should be fairly smooth and scoopable if the sugar concentration is correct.

■ *Serving suggestions:* Any way you serve it is great. A crunchy cookie will enhance the flavor and increase the satisfaction for something sweet. Remember to freeze the serving bowls or freezer-proof glasses as well for a stunning presentation and to help keep the sorbets from melting quickly.

Try serving different flavors of sorbet in the same dish to mix tastes. A scoop of vanilla or other mild ice cream such as macadamia is a perfect but more filling counter to the tart, bright sorbet.

■ *Mix and match:* Flavor combinations in the sorbet and frozen delicacies are terrific, and it seems just about any will work. Try spices infused into the mixes, such as green peppercorn with papaya, or ginger with mango or orange. The combinations taste incredible even if they sound a little odd.

■

PEACH SORBET

Makes ½ quart or 4 servings

1 cup sugar
½ cup water
   Juice of 1 lemon
1 pound peaches, peeled, pitted

In a small saucepan, combine sugar, water and lemon juice. Bring to a simmer over high heat. Remove from heat.

In a blender, combine peaches and sugar syrup. Puree until smooth. Strain through a fine sieve. Process the fruit mixture in an ice cream maker according to manufacturer's instructions. Freeze until firm, at least overnight.

Cook's note: This recipe uses less water than normal because of the juiciness of peaches.

Nutrition details per ½-cup serving
Calories 248
Percent of calories from fat 1%
Fat: . . . .1 gm
Protein: . . . . .1 gm
Carbohydrate: . . . . .64 gm
Cholesterol: . . . . .0 mg
Sodium: . . . . .1 mg
Diabetic exchange: 4¼ fruit. Not recommended for diabetics.

CHOCOLATE SORBET

Makes 1½ quarts

14 ounces extra-
   bittersweet chocolate

4 cups coffee, as strong
   as you like

2 cups sugar

2 ounces extra-
   bittersweet chocolate,
   shaved

4 ounces white
   chocolate, shaved

In the top of a double
boiler, over simmering water,
melt the chocolate. Stir until
smooth.

In a medium saucepan,
combine coffee and sugar
over medium heat. Cook
until sugar is dissolved, then
remove from heat. Whisk
the coffee mixture slowly
into the melted chocolate,
making sure the chocolate
doesn't lump. Strain through
a fine sieve.

Process in an ice cream
machine, according to the
manufacturer's instructions,
until just about solid. Add
the chocolate shavings, then

freeze in a container until
firm, at least overnight.

Cook's note: This rich sorbet is the best of both worlds
— rich flavor without cream
or milk products.

Nutrition details per ½-cup serving
Calories 551
Percent of calories from fat 50%
Fat: .35 gm
Protein: . . . . .8 gm
Carbohydrate: . . . . .72 gm
Cholesterol: . . . . .2 mg
Sodium: . . . . .15 mg
Diabetic exchange: 6¼ fat.

PEAR-RASPBERRY SORBET

Makes 1 quart

3 pounds fresh pears,
   peeled, quartered

½ cup fresh lemon juice

1¼ cups sugar

2 cups raspberries

In a blender, puree the
pears and lemon juice until
smooth. Transfer to a
saucepan, add the sugar and
bring to a simmer over high
heat. Remove after one short
boil. Stir in the raspberries.
Strain through a very fine
sieve, then process the mixture in an ice cream maker,
according to manufacturer's
instructions. Freeze until
firm, at least overnight.

Nutrition details per serving
Calories 211
Percent of calories from fat 2%
Fat: . . . . .6 gm
Protein: . . . . .1 gm
Carbohydrate: . . . . .54 gm
Cholesterol: . . . . .0 mg
Sodium: . . . . .trace
Diabetic exchange: 1½ fruit, 2 bread.

STRAWBERRY-RUM SORBET

Makes ½ quart

1 pound very ripe
   strawberries, stemmed

1 cup sugar

½ cup water

¼ cup fresh lime juice

½ cup rum

In a heavy saucepan, com-
bine the sugar and water.
Bring to a simmer over
medium heat. Add the strawberries and cook until the
fruit is soft, about 2 minutes.

Transfer to blender and
puree until smooth. Add the
lime juice and rum. Strain
through a fine sieve, then
process in an ice cream
maker, according to the
manufacturer's instructions.
Freeze in a container until
firm, at least overnight.

Nutrition details per serving
Calories 295
Percent of calories from fat 1%
Fat: . . . . .4 gm
Protein: . . . . .7 gm
Carbohydrate: . . . . .59 gm
Cholesterol: . . . . .0 mg
Sodium: . . . . .2.9 mg
Diabetic exchange: ⅓ fruit, 3½ bread.

AUTUMN

INSIDE THE CHILI PEPPER

■ *What is a chili, and what does it have to do with a pepper?* Chilies and peppers of the peppercorn family are exactly the same. The peppercorn family is unrelated to the vegetable pepper plant.

■ *Why they taste so good:* All chili peppers have a green vegetable flavor when raw. Cooking to remove the skin enhances the sweet flavor characteristics and builds the rich, fuller taste. The skin of a chili is pretty solid when raw but becomes more coarse and tough when the cooking process softens the flesh underneath. Removing the skin allows the tender, sweet, rich flesh to shine through.

■ *Why do they taste hot?* Some varieties of chilies — such as jalapenos, some poblanos, serranos and the hottest habaneros — develop more heat or spicy bite than the sweet bell peppers. Beside the varietal differences, the development of capsaicin, which is the spicy hot bite of the chili, is directly related to the nighttime growing temperature. The hotter the night, the hotter the pepper.

■ *Why do people like the hot bite?* The spicy bite is pure pleasure to some and a total irritant to others. The heat of the chili initially causes slight discomfort, but after a few bites, the brain releases endorphins, which create a sense of pleasure to overcome the hot sensation.

■ *What's with all these colors and shapes?* All chilies begin green, then mature to their final colors. Just about all chilies ripen to red or yellow. Green bell peppers will turn red if allowed to mature. Some chilies are picked and eaten in their green immature form, while others are allowed to ripen fully. Fully ripened chilies generally have flesh the same color as the skin. But the newer purple, black and white varieties develop a different-colored skin from the flesh. For instance, if you remove the skin of a purple chili, it will be green underneath. Use these skin-deep beauties raw with their skins on for salads.

■ *Skinning the chili:* There are several ways to skin a chili. Here are the most effective:

Open gas flame. This is one of my favorites because it works well while developing the flavor of the chili flesh. Place chilies on the gas burner grate over a high flame, allowing the skin to cook until

TODAY'S LESSON: The best methods to get under the skin and to the delicate flesh of chili peppers.

black. Turn the chili with tongs to ensure complete blackening of the skin. Do not cook the chili until it turns ash black and feels hollow, for there won't be anything left.

Open electric flame. Similar to but less effective than gas. Follow the same technique, turning more frequently to get even blackening.

Grill. Place chilies on the red-hot grill and allow the skin to blacken as described above. This is a good technique for developing the smoky flavor.

Broiler. This is similar to the grill method but tends to steam the flesh slightly. Cut the chilies in half lengthwise, place them skin side up on a broiler pan and cook until the skin turns black.

Oven roasting. This technique will remove the skins but does not develop the flavor as much as open flame and grilling. Prick the skins of the chilies; place them on a rack in a preheated 550-degree oven for about 7 minutes or so until the skin blisters. Rotating the chilies is not necessary in this technique.

Frying or oil technique. Oil blistering is effective for removing the skin without much heat penetration to the flesh, the best method for keeping the chili al dente for salsa and for preserving the more raw flavor. This method is also great for odd-shaped chilies with ridges and grooves, which the oil easily penetrates. Make a couple of small pricks in the skin as a precaution against exploding oil. Carefully place the chilies in a fry basket, submerge in 400-degree oil and cook for about 2 minutes, until the skin blisters. Make sure the oil is hot before submerging the next batch.

■ *Tricks of the trade:* The trick to flavor development is half in the skin blistering as described and, most importantly, in what you do afterward. Plunging the chili in ice water will chill the skin and loosen its grip on the meat for easy removal. But the best sweet flavor is produced by placing the hot chilies in a bowl and covering them with plastic wrap so they steam each other. Let the chilies slowly cool to room tempera-

ture, about 15-30 minutes. This process finishes cooking the chilies to a sweet taste and texture, almost like candy. If you don't have a bowl, use heavy zipper-locking plastic bags.

■ *Cleaning the chilies:* Once they have properly cooled, hold the chilies under running cold water over a strainer or fine colander. Rub, starting at the stem end, to release the skin, which will collect in the colander. Slit the chili with a paring knife and remove the core and veins.

■ *Watch out for that chili bite!* The hot chili bite goes beyond the palate to anything it touches, including your hands. Hot chili bite will transfer from your hands to your eyes or anywhere else you touch, so be careful. Wear rubber gloves.

■ *The cooking begins:* The properly cleaned chili won't need much, if any, additional cooking time. Add chilies to your sauce and dishes in the last few minutes for best results.

■

Chilies have a history that stretches back 10,000 years. The debate still rages over whether the Spanish colonists brought the first seeds to the Southwest from Mexico in the late 1500s or the Pueblo Indians had long before traded seeds with the Toltecs of central Mexico.

■ *Try all the flavors:* Chilies come in all sizes, colors, flavors and, of course, degrees of hot spicy bite. Experiment with all the wonderful varieties to enhance your late summer and autumn menus.

■

GRILLED CHILI PEPPERS & AUTUMN VEGETABLE SANDWICH

Makes 2 servings

2 sweet red bell chili peppers (or substitute yellow)

1 small eggplant, peeled and sliced ¼ inch thick

Sea salt or granulated salt to taste

2 tablespoons olive oil, divided

Coarse ground black pepper to taste

1 small red onion, peeled, ends removed, sliced thick

1 medium zucchini, ends removed, sliced

¼ inch thick on the bias

4 slices hearty peasant-style bread

2 tablespoons Dijon-style mustard, divided

2 tablespoons home-made mayonnaise, optional

4 slices garden-ripe tomatoes

4 leaves arugula or Bibb lettuce, washed, dried

Preheat grill to red hot. Place the chilies on the grill. Cook each side until completely black, about 3-4 minutes, depending on the size of the chilies. Transfer to a bowl and cover tightly with plastic wrap. Allow to cool to room temperature, about 15 minutes.

Meanwhile, generously salt the eggplant slices and place on a rack or colander to drain, about 15 minutes.

Prepare a colander under cold running water. When the chilies are cool, place under the water and rub the skin, beginning at the stem end, to remove the skins. Slit the chili with a paring knife and remove the seeds and

veins, reserving the meat on a paper towel.

Rinse the eggplant under running cold water to remove the salt. Pat dry with paper toweling. Rub the surfaces with 1½ tablespoons olive oil and place on the grill, cooking until tender, about 4 minutes. Turn over and finish cooking, about 3 minutes. Season with salt and pepper.

Rub the onion with a touch of the olive oil, place it on the grill and cook until al dente, about 3 minutes. Turn over to finish cooking, about 3 minutes. Season with salt and pepper to taste.

Place the zucchini on the grill and cook until tender, about 2 minutes per side. Season with salt and pepper to taste.

Grill the slices of bread to crisp. Remove to the plate for assembly. Spread 1 table-spoon of the Dijon-style mustard on each of 2 bread slices. Spread the mayonnaise on the remaining 2 slices. Divide the eggplant, chili peppers, zucchini, tomato slices, onions and greens atop the bread. Season with additional pepper if you like. Top with the remaining slices of bread, spear with 2 skewers per sandwich and cut on an angle. Serve with crisp tart pickles, homemade chips or potato salad of your choice.

Nutrition details per serving
Calories 337
Percent of calories from fat 43%
Fat: .16 gm
Protein: . . . . .8 gm
Carbohydrate: . . . . .43 gm
Cholesterol: . . . . .1 mg
Sodium: . . . . .485 mg
Diabetic exchange: 2½ vegetables, 2 bread, 2¾ fat.

BRUSSELS SPROUTS – MILD AT HEART

■ *What are they?* Brussels sprouts are related to cabbages. The numerous buds grow on tall stalks. The vegetable is often found in local farmer's markets harvested with the stalk. Brussels sprouts are quite hearty; they'll not only endure a deep, chilling frost, but their flavor actually improves with the cold. They usually are among the last vegetables to be harvested each year. Brussels sprouts and the cabbage family contain goitrins, compounds that interfere with the absorption of iodine. Iodine is essential to the thyroid gland. The goitrins cannot start a thyroid problem but may aggravate an existing one. Large, mature cabbage is higher in goitrins than the small, immature brussels sprouts.

■ *How to select:* The smallest brussels sprouts are the mildest and sweetest. Select firm, deep green sprouts, preferably still on the stalk. Avoid yellowing

TODAY'S LESSON: Brussels sprouts are a tasty autumn garden treat.

buds and outer leaves, shriveled stems, wilted or soft flesh, or sprouts that show rot or insect damage.

■ *How to store:* Although they store well under refrigeration — up to three weeks — their flavor is most delicate when they are fresh-picked.

■ *How to prepare:* When ready to cook, break or cut the sprouts from the stalk. Pull off the loose outer leaves. Soak in cold salted water to drive out any hitchhiking insects. Trim the stem flat. Cut a small cross through the stem into the heart, about ¼ inch to ½ inch deep, to facilitate even cooking.

■ *How to cook:* Cook in simmering salted water until tender but still crisp, about 4 minutes for medium-size buds. Drain and serve, or cool under running cold water if the sprouts are going to be used in another preparation, such as a casserole. The brussels sprouts should still be bright green when properly cooked. The cooked texture should be like that of al dente pasta, tender but firm to the bite.

■ *Tricks of the trade:* Brussels sprouts are high in sulfur-containing compounds. Their principal flavor comes from mustard oils, which are the source of the strong scent and taste found in mustard seed, horseradish and radishes. Traditional methods of cooking for hours and hours produced the strong odors and flavors that forever scared many people away from brussels sprouts and the cabbage fam-

Brussels sprouts are available from late August through March.

Brussels sprouts are high in vitamins A and C and are a fair source of iron.

ily. So the secret is to cook until just tender and sweet, never mushy.

■ *Mix and match:* Season brussels sprouts with a little salt. Use lots of freshly ground black pepper and a pinch of ground nutmeg. Brussels sprouts are enhanced by cheese, butter and cream sauces. The flavor of toasted nuts, such as almonds, pecans and chestnuts, complements their taste. Try a light dusting of these. Brussels sprouts hold their shape well in casseroles and gratins. After combining the ingredients, cook only until thoroughly heated. Blend the sprouts with cooked potatoes and puree in the food processor for a light, rich flavor. Brussels sprouts also make wonderful cole slaw.

GRATIN OF BRUSSELS SPROUTS & POTATOES

Makes 8 servings

1 pound brussels sprouts

1 pound baking potatoes, peeled

1 cup heavy cream

1 teaspoon salt

¾ teaspoon freshly ground white pepper

¼ teaspoon freshly ground nutmeg

2 tablespoons unsalted butter

½ cup snipped fresh chives

½ cup grated Parmesan cheese

Preheat the oven to 350. Remove loose outer leaves from the brussels sprouts. Trim the stem flat. Cut a cross through the stem into the heart, about ¼ inch to ½ inch deep, depending on size of sprout.

Bring a large pot of water to a boil. Add brussels sprouts and salt to taste, cooking until just tender, about 4 minutes for

medium-size sprouts. Drain and cool under running cold water. Spread out on paper towels to dry. Slice sprouts about ¼ inch thick and reserve. Slice all the potatoes to the thickness of potato chips. Combine cream, salt, pepper and nutmeg in a small bowl. Rub an 8-by-8-by-2-inch baking dish with butter. Cover the bottom of the dish with a single layer of potatoes, allowing them to overlap slightly. Pour some of the cream mixture lightly over the potatoes. Repeat with the brussels sprouts. Sprinkle with a layer of chives and Parmesan. Repeat layering steps until completely assembled. Top with remaining cheese. Cover pan with aluminum foil, dull side out. Bake on the lower rack of the oven for 25 minutes. Remove foil and continue baking until brown, about 15-20 minutes. Remove to a cake rack to cool slightly. With a sharp knife, cut into portions and serve.

Nutrition details per serving
Calories 228
Percent of calories from fat 61%
Fat: .16 gm
Protein: . . . . .6 gm
Carbohydrate: . . . . .17 gm
Cholesterol: . . . . .49 mg
Sodium: . . . . .438 mg
Diabetic exchange: 1 vegetable, ¾ bread, ⅜ meat, 2⅛ fat.

FENNEL GOES WITH EVERYTHING

■ *What it is:* Fennel, a member of the carrot family, has feathery leaves that resemble dill, celery-like stalks and a bulbous base.

■ *What it tastes like*: The delicate, sweet, anise-like flavor of fennel goes with just about everything. It is a natural match with all the flavors of the Mediterranean basin, such as tomatoes, peppers, onion, garlic, olives, capers, such hard cheeses as Parmesan and Romano, olive oil, lamb, sausages, poultry and fish.

■ *How do you use it?* Fennel can be served raw, marinated, roasted, sauteed, pureed, braised, even fried. The tender stems can be stringed to remove the coarser fibers and enjoyed just as you would celery sticks: in Bloody Marys, or stuffed with cheeses or olive spreads. The bulb may also be cut into sticks or wedges for dipping and stuffing. The stalks and the bulb are milder and more tender than celery.

TODAY'S LESSON: Capturing the wonderful flavor of fennel from raw to roasted.

■ *How do you enjoy it raw?* Raw fennel is terrific as a simple salad for late summer and fall. Remove the coarser outer leaves, cut the bulb into quarters and slice paper thin. Leave the stem core attached to hold the slices. Dress with salt, freshly ground pepper, a splash of lemon juice or good vinegar and extra-virgin olive oil. Add raw sliced artichoke cut just like the fennel but immediately rubbed with lemon juice to retard browning, as well as tomatoes, roasted or raw red bell peppers, onions, roasted whole garlic cloves, capers and olives.

■ *Enjoy fennel as soup:* The outer coarse parts of the bulb and the tender stalks are perfect for soup. Pair fennel with onions, garlic, shallots, light stock and potatoes for natural thickening, cooking all until tender. Puree the soup in a blender; season with salt, fresh pepper and a good dose of fresh lemon juice. Save the greens for garnish along with a few fried shallots to frame this masterpiece.

■ *As puree:* Fennel is also great pureed with potatoes. Select the most tender parts of the bulb, or strain after pureeing. Season the potatoes with butter for a rich flavor or a good olive oil. Top with a sprig of fennel greens and a dusting of finely grated Parmesan.

■ *To serve cooked:* To serve fennel as a vegetable, roast or braise.
   To roast: Trim the bulb of the coarse outer leaves, then

■

Fennel stimulates the appetite, refreshes the palate and aids in digestion. It contains few calories. In ancient Greece, Olympic athletes ate it as part of their training regimen.

quarter it. Toss with a little olive oil, season with salt and pepper, and place in an ovenproof roasting dish. Add a splash of white wine or water, cover and cook until tender in a preheated 400-degree oven for about 45 minutes. Remove from the oven and serve with a splash of balsamic vinegar or a squeeze of lemon. Sprinkle with a little Parmesan or Romano cheese, and dust with fresh chives or fennel greens.

To braise: Place the trimmed fennel in an ovenproof vessel and cover with seasoned stock. Add garlic, onions and other nutrients for fuller flavor. Cover tightly with aluminum foil and a lid and place on the lower rack of an oven preheated to 350 degrees. Cook until tender when checked with a skewer, about 1 hour. Remove and allow to cool slightly before serving. Serve with a splash of the cooking liquids, a splash of olive oil or a pat of butter and any herb garnish you like.

To saute: Fennel is a great addition to just about any sauteed vegetable dish. Julienne the fennel bulb so it will cook in about the same time as the other vegetables. Fennel will remain crisp under heat unless immersed in liquids.

■ *Tricks of the trade:* My favorite method of preparing fennel captures all the delicate flavor of this vegetable. Trim the fennel as described for raw fennel salad, but slice ¼ inch thick. In a medium bowl, combine the fennel, a few whole garlic cloves, a couple of tablespoons of good olive oil, salt and freshly ground black pepper, mixing well to combine. Lay out a piece of aluminum foil twice the size of a cookie sheet, shiny side up. Spread the fennel and garlic evenly on half the foil. Fold the remaining section of the foil over the fennel and tightly crimp all the edges to seal tightly. Place on a cookie sheet and bake in an oven preheated to 400 degrees for about 45 minutes. Remove from oven and allow to cool on a cake rack before opening. When you tear the foil open, collect the fennel and the juices into a bowl. This makes a wonderful warm or room-temperature appetizer served with a few black olives and tiny capers. For another variation, add sliced vine-ripened tomatoes, a drizzle of balsamic vinegar and shaved Parmesan cheese for one of the simplest and best-tasting dishes you'll ever enjoy.

■ *Try your technique:* Any way you slice it, the tender fennel bulb is a show stopper.

■

FENNEL & TOMATO SALAD

Makes 4 servings

2 large fennel bulbs
8 whole cloves garlic, peeled and sliced thin
¼ cup virgin olive oil
Salt to taste
Coarsely ground black pepper to taste
3 large vine-ripened tomatoes, peeled and cut into 12 slices
¼ cup balsamic vinegar
¼ cup black tiny Nicoise olives, pitted
½ cup Parmesan cheese sliced paper thin and cut into 1-inch strips

Preheat oven to 400 degrees. Remove ½ cup of the better fennel leaves from the stalk and reserve for garnish. Remove the larger ribs from the fennel bulb. Cut the bulb vertically into quarters. With a sharp knife, cut the fennel ⅛ inch thick, leaving strips attached to the core. In a medium bowl, combine the fennel, garlic and olive oil, and season with salt and pepper.

On a cookie sheet, lay a piece of aluminum foil twice the size of the pan, shiny side up. Distribute the seasoned fennel quarters across half of the foil, keeping it about 2 inches away from the edges. Fold the extra foil over the fennel and seal the edges.

Place the cookie sheet on the bottom rack of the oven. Cook for 45 minutes. Remove and allow to cool on a cake rack before opening the foil.

Arrange 3 slices of tomato in a fan on each of four serving plates. Add the balsamic vinegar to the fennel mixture and divide atop the tomatoes. Distribute the olives and fennel greens over the plates. Top with the shaved Parmesan cheese and serve.

Nutrition details per serving
Calories 265
Percent of calories from fat 63%
Fat: . . . . .20 gm
Protein: . . . . .8 gm
Carbohydrate: . . . . .18 gm
Cholesterol: . . . . .10 mg
Sodium: . . . . .646 mg
Diabetic exchange: 2⅔ vegetables, ¾ meat, 3 fat.

■

Fennel is available in all seasons but summer. November and December are its peak months.

HUBBARD SQUASH HAS GIANT TASTE

AMAZING FOOD FACTS

■

Hubbard squash is frequently used in place of pumpkin in recipes because of its similar moisture content and meaty quality. Hubbard squash can be used in any recipe calling for pumpkin.

■ *How to select:* Dark green varieties seem to have the most intense flavor. Select by trying to dig your fingernail into the skin. The skin should be hard and should not indent or scrape away under the pressure. Softer skin signifies immature Hubbards, which are edible but have a very bland taste. Look also for a hard stem that's not spongy.

■ *How to store:* Store Hubbard squash in a well-ventilated, dry area, about 50 degrees. The squash will store well for three or four months — about as long as winter lasts. Stored at room temperature, they will not last as long. If the stem and skin soften, cook immediately.

■ *Don't forget the seeds:* The seeds are a great treat. Wash them under cold running water to remove all the fibers. Combine the seeds and 1 tablespoon of salt in a medium saucepan. Cover with water

TODAY'S LESSON: Giant Hubbard squash has delicate, smooth flesh with a rich full flavor and a high yield — characteristics that in many cases have pushed the pumpkin right out of its can. The fresh squash is sublime for the table as well as in applications usually reserved for pumpkin. Hubbard squash has a sweet rich flavor and good storage qualities. The round shape with bumpy skin comes in blue, light and dark green, red-orange and even gold. It makes a very attractive ornamental centerpiece for your holiday feasts; afterward it is a culinary treasure for the next meal.

and bring to a simmer, cooking until tender, about 15 minutes. Transfer to a fine sieve and drain. Transfer to a bowl and toss with 2 tablespoons olive oil to coat. Spread across a

cookie sheet and bake at 350. Stir seeds every 10 minutes until crisp and golden, about 30 minutes. Allow to cool, then enjoy. Store in an airtight jar at room temperature.

How to cut and cook the big squash: The largest Hubbard squash may be imposing to the average cook, considering that they can grow as large as pumpkins. The easiest way to prepare the Hubbard is to first cut it down to size. With a large sharp knife or cleaver, cut off the stem end. Turn the squash, cut side down, onto the cutting board to keep from tipping and rolling during trimming. With the knife, cut straight down through the squash to the board to split into two pieces. Cut the halves to 1-pound size pieces for easy cooking.

The cooking begins: Baking Hubbard squash seems to intensify the flavor. Place the 1-pound squash pieces skin side up in an ovenproof baking dish. Add a cup of water or white wine and bake at 375 for about 45 minutes. Larger squashes may be baked in their full half-globes for presentation and stuffing purposes, but cooking will take longer.

Steaming the squash pro-duces a lighter texture and flavor in about half the time of baking. Cut the squash into ½-pound pieces and place cut side down in the steamer tray or basket. Boil the water, cover and steam until tender, about 15-20 minutes.

Microwaving is a fast and effective way to enjoy the Hubbard squash in a fraction of the traditional cooking time. Place the 1-pound or smaller pieces in a micro-wave dish. Add ½ cup of water and cover very tightly in plastic wrap, then puncture to release excess steam or pressure. Microwave at high power for about 6-9 minutes or until tender. Be careful not to burn yourself on the steam! Remove from the oven and allow to rest for 3-4 minutes before serving.

BAKED HUBBARD SQUASH WITH HONEY

Makes 4 servings

1	medium-sized Hubbard squash
1	cup wildflower honey
12	cassia buds (or substitute 2 cinnamon sticks)
1	cup water
2	tablespoons balsamic vinegar
4	tablespoons unsalted butter, cut into teaspoon-size pieces
	Salt to taste
	Freshly ground black pepper to taste
¼	cup snipped fresh chives

Preheat oven to 375. Cut the stem end off the Hubbard squash. Turn the squash cut side down onto the cutting board. With a sharp knife, cut straight down through the squash to the board, splitting in two. Remove the seeds (save for toasting if you like). Cut the halves into 1-pound pieces.

Lay two pieces cut side down (skin side up) in an oven-proof baking dish. Wrap the remaining squash in plastic wrap and store under refrigeration for up to 4 days.

In a small bowl, combine honey, cassia buds or cinnamon, and water. Pour into the baking dish with the squash. Place the baking dish on the lower rack of the oven and cook until tender, about 45 minutes. Remove to a cake rack to rest. Carefully pour the cooking liquids through a fine sieve into a medium skillet. Cook over medium-high heat, until the liquids are reduced to coat the back of a spoon, about 4 minutes. Add vinegar and remove from heat. Scoop the squash from the skin into the serving dish.

Dot squash with butter, season with salt and pepper and sprinkle with chives. Pour the honey sauce over squash or serve in a side sauce boat.

Nutrition details per serving
Calories .443
Percent of calories from fat 24%
Fat: . . . . .13 gm
Protein: . . . . .4 gm
Carbohydrate: . . . . .87 gm
Cholesterol: . . . . .15 mg
Sodium: . . . . .391 mg
Diabetic exchange: 1 bread, 2½ fat.

VEGETABLES IN PARCHMENT

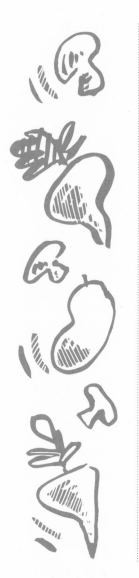

■ *What exactly is parchment?* Parchment paper is a thick, clean paper that stands up to the heat of cooking and is used primarily for pastry. Although many people know it for preparing sweets, it is perfect for cooking vegetables and even fish. If you don't have parchment paper, substitute aluminum foil.

■ *Why it tastes so good:* The parchment wrapper seals in the juices and steam generated through cooking. These flavors are concentrated back onto the vegetables as they cool, resulting in some of the healthiest and best-tasting food around.

■ *Advantages:* I prefer this technique because it results in full, uncompromising flavor, and little or no fat.

■ *Selecting the vegetables:* The ones best accentuated by this technique are mild and higher in moisture, including fennel, celery, artichokes and members

TODAY'S LESSON: Cooking in parchment is a wonderful, easy way to capture all the natural flavors of vegetables in the oven.

of the onion family. The more delicate flavors of some vegetables are often lost in other methods of preparation.

■ *Mix and match:* Think not of a solo vegetable flavor but of an ensemble orchestrated for a wonderful dish. For example, combine artichokes, fennel and garlic with a little thyme to scent.

■ *Preparing your vegetables:* Start by trimming or peeling vegetables of your choice. Cut the vegetables into about ¼-inch slices. Complementary vegetables such as shallots, onions and garlic are best more finely cut so that they cook faster and release their flavors into the primary vegetables.

Combine vegetables in a

medium bowl. Splash with a little very good olive oil, which adds flavor but also helps transfer the heat from the oven through the parchment and into the vegetables. Season with sea salt and freshly ground black pepper, add a sprig or two of herbs and you're in business.

■ *Seal in parchment:* Cut a piece of parchment large enough to hold vegetables on one half. Fold the parchment in half and cut the unfolded edges into a round shape. Distribute the vegetables evenly over half the parchment. Fold the top section over and crease firmly. Hold the edges together and fold up a small section of the rim. Crease it, and fold it up again. Hold down this double

Folding parchment

Use a generous amount of paper, at least twice the size of the food portion. Roll the edges of the parchment tightly as you work, so the edges stay sealed as the parchment puffs up when baked. There is no right way or wrong way to fold/roll the edges, so whatever works for you is fine.

For an individual portion, use a piece of paper 1-foot square folded in half.

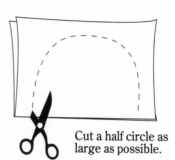

Cut a half circle as large as possible.

Open and place food near the crease, folding half over the food.

Starting at the top, hold both edges together and fold up a small section of the rim.

Crease and fold again.

While holding this double-fold in one hand, fold up an adjacent piece the same way.

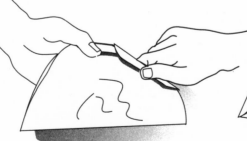

Each fold should overlap the previous to produce a tight seal.

Continue folding until the entire edge is secure.

fold as you fold up the adjacent section in the same way. Each fold should slightly overlap the previous fold for the most secure seal. When using foil, use the same technique, placing the dull side down on the counter. Distribute the vegetables on the lower half, fold over and crimp the edges to seal, then place on a cookie sheet.

For even cooking, keep the packages small and avoid overcrowding the vegetables. A couple of smaller packages will cook much faster and more thoroughly than one large one.

■ *The cooking begins:* Bake on the lower rack of the oven until tender, about 30-45 minutes depending on the thickness and density of vegetables. Remove from the oven and allow to cool until the steam has dissipated to keep the flavors.

■ *Tricks of the trade:* For the best, most even cooking, carefully turn the parchment pouches over halfway through cooking. Seasoned

oils with basil, rosemary, garlic or even the exotic flavors of curry will enhance the vegetables.

■ *Serving suggestions:* The vegetable medley is ready to eat right from the parchment, with the remaining juices poured back over the vegetables as their own little glaze. If you wish, top with a little finely grated Parmesan cheese and a few fresh herbs.

The vegetables can also be a great start for pasta and grain dishes. The concentrated flavors of the vegetables come alive when blended with these normally bland ingredients. Just adjust the seasonings to compensate for the larger volume. Then you have a complete healthy and satisfying meal all in one.

■ *Try your technique:* Cooking in parchment is terrific for the holidays, especially Thanksgiving. Wrapping vegetables makes the cooking easy and eliminates those messy pots.

■

WILD MUSHROOMS, PARSNIPS & BUTTERNUT SQUASH

Makes 4 large servings

1 pound wild mushrooms, preferably chanterelles, portobellos or shiitakes, cleaned, sliced ¼ inch thick

4 small parsnips, peeled and sliced ⅛ inch thick

1 small butternut squash, peeled, seeded and sliced ¼ inch thick into long sheets, then cut into julienne strips

12 whole garlic cloves, peeled, ends removed, thinly sliced

3 tablespoons extra-virgin olive oil

Sea salt and freshly ground black pepper to taste

1 tablespoon fresh rosemary leaves

2 tablespoons snipped fresh chives

¼ cup finely grated aged Parmesan cheese, optional

1 sprig rosemary or parsley for garnish

Preheat oven to 400 degrees.

In a large bowl, combine the mushrooms, parsnips, butternut squash, garlic and olive oil. Season with sea salt and generous doses of black pepper. Add rosemary leaves and chives. Seal mixture in parchment, following the guidelines set out previously. Place the parchment pouch on a cookie sheet.

Bake on the lower rack of oven until tender, about 45 minutes. Remove from oven and allow about 10 minutes to cool slightly. Transfer to a serving dish, top with Parmesan cheese if desired. Garnish with rosemary or parsley if desired.

Nutrition details per serving
Calories 193
Percent of calories from fat 57%
Fat: . . . . .12 gm
Protein: . . . . .5 gm
Carbohydrate: . . . . .19 gm
Cholesterol: . . . . .4 mg
Sodium: . . . . .96 mg
Diabetic exchange: ¼ medium fat meat, 1 vegetable, ¾ bread, 2 fat.

INFUSE FLAVOR INTO OILS

■ *Why they taste so good:* Essential or volatile oils are the components in herbs, spices and vegetables that carry the flavor. Seasoned oils will absorb, preserve and radiate their pronounced flavors to food.

■ *Advantages:* In an oil, the bounty of summer and autumn is easily captured for several months under proper refrigeration.

Infused oils are generally more pronounced in taste than sauces, allowing a little to go a long way to spice up the flavor of a dish. Although they do contain fat, infused olive or canola oils are low in saturated fats and cholesterol, especially when compared with a cream-based sauce.

■ *Choose your oil:* Olive oil is my favorite for infusing with ingredients that are complemented by the olive flavor, such as tomato, garlic, rosemary, basil and thyme, to

TODAY'S LESSON: The best flavors of summer herbs, vegetables and spices can be captured in oils to enjoy in the coming months.

name a few. Canola oil is more neutral in flavor, which works well for more delicately flavored ingredients.

■ *Choose your technique:* There are three primary techniques to infuse the flavor into the oil: cold, warm and hot oil infusion. This means that the seasoning ingredient is introduced into the oil at different temperatures, which will produce different flavors and concentrations.

Cold infusion introduces the ingredients into the oil at room temperature. Then they are allowed to mature under refrigeration. This technique produces the most delicate flavor, takes a few weeks to produce and has the shortest refrigerated shelf life, as the

ingredients are not cooked.

Warm infusion heats the oil to 200 degrees before it is blended with the seasoning ingredients, which are slightly cooked by the heat in the oil. This technique produces more pronounced flavors, matures more quickly and has a longer shelf life under refrigeration.

Hot infusion combines or cooks the seasonings in 250-degree or hotter oil, which results in strongly flavored oil with a longer shelf life. This oil may be bitter from the heating of the oil and cooking of the seasonings.

■ *Tricks of the trade:* For the best flavor, dry seasoning should be rehydrated with a little hot water before infusing. Vegetables are best roasted or

cooked by techniques that concentrate and enhance their natural sweet flavor. They may be cooked in the oil or separately before combining with the oil.

■ *Serving suggestions:* The most direct way to enjoy these infused oils is to substitute them for ordinary oil in your favorite recipes. Best are salad dressings, mayonnaise or aioli. Or enhance mashed potatoes with rosemary oil instead of butter. A little brush of the infused oil will pick up many ingredients destined for the grill. High-temperature cooking with these oils should be avoided, because the oil will tend to burn and cause a bitter flavor.

The infused oils can be rich in flavor — rich enough to drizzle directly onto your dish as you would a sauce. A simple salmon fillet, grilled and then drizzled with basil oil and a splash of balsamic vinegar, is satisfying both to the eye and to the taste buds.

■ *Mix and match:* A couple of complementary infused oils

can be served together with terrific results, such as basil oil and sun-dried tomato oil. Blending infused oils of different flavors gets tough, since the flavors tend to become muddy and generally less palatable.

■ *Store properly:* Keep your infused oils in the refrigerator for up to a year. If they become cloudy in the refrigerator, don't worry; they will clear at room temperature.

■

TOMATO SALAD WITH BASIL-INFUSED OIL

Makes 4 servings

4   medium ripe tomatoes, washed, cored, divided

1   large red onion, peeled, ends removed, sliced into 8 thin slices, divided

12   little fresh mozzarella balls (available in many grocery stores), divided

¼   cup balsamic vinegar, divided

½   cup Basil-infused Oil, divided (see accompanying recipe)
Coarsely ground black pepper

4   sprigs fresh basil or other herb for garnish, divided

Slice tomatoes into 3 slices each. Arrange 3 slices of tomato with 2 slices of onion between them in an arc on 4 serving plates. Position 3 mozzarella balls on the plates next to the tomatoes. Spoon 1 tablespoon of vinegar over the tomatoes and onion on each plate. Spoon 2 tablespoons of Basil-infused Oil over the tomatoes and mozzarella on each plate. Sprinkle with black pepper, garnish each plate with basil sprigs or herb of choice and serve.

Nutrition details per serving
Calories 301
Percent of calories from fat 81%
Fat: .27 gm
Protein: . . . . .7 gm
Carbohydrate: . . . . .10 gm
Cholesterol: . . . . .22 mg
Sodium: . . . . .132 mg
Diabetic exchange: 1½ vegetables, ¾ meat, 4½ fat.

■

BASIL-INFUSED OIL

Makes 1 pint

2   cups extra-virgin olive oil

½   cup chopped fresh basil leaves and stems

4   cloves garlic, minced fine

1   teaspoons freshly ground black pepper
Pinch of sea salt

In a food processor, combine the olive oil, basil, garlic, pepper and salt, pulsing to chop the basil and mix the ingredients thoroughly. Transfer to a saucepan and warm to about 200 degrees over medium heat. Transfer to a clean glass jar and allow to cool at room temperature. Cover and refrigerate for about a week to allow the flavor to mature.

Nutrition details per serving
Calories 121
Percent of calories from fat 100%
Fat: .14 gm
Protein: . . . . .trace
Carbohydrate: . . . . .trace
Cholesterol: . . . . .0 mg
Sodium: . . . . .8 mg
Diabetic exchange: 3 fat.

POLENTA MAKES A RICH SIDE DISH

■ *Where did it come from?* Polenta originated with the simple staple dish of the ancient Roman legions called *puls* or *pulmentum*. Originally, it was a mush made of millet or spelt (a primitive wheat), the common grains of the period.

■ *What is it made of?* Today, yellow cornmeal is the traditional choice for making polenta, although blue, white and red cornmeals are also quite delicious. Different-color cornmeals absorb moisture differently, so if you're tempted to substitute, remember that you might have to add more cornmeal. Three grinds of cornmeal are used in making polenta.

Finely ground cornmeal makes thinner, more delicate polenta, but it's most susceptible to forming lumps during cooking. To prevent lumps, add 20 percent of the cornmeal in your recipe to the cold, salted water and bring to a simmer before adding the

TODAY'S LESSON: Polenta is the Italian equivalent of mashed potatoes — a wonderfully earthy comfort food. It's now finding a following even at non-Italian restaurants.

remainder. Fine cornmeal cooks the quickest.

Coarsely ground cornmeal makes thicker polenta and can be served immediately or chilled for later cooking. It takes the longest to cook, so be patient and don't rush.

Medium cornmeal may be used for thinner or thicker recipes but will yield a slightly different texture.

■ *How to select:* Cornmeal is best when freshly ground. Check the expiration date or harvest date on the package to ensure freshness. Old cornmeal has poor absorption qualities and often a bitter taste.

■ *Choose your weapon:* Traditionally, polenta is made in an unlined copper pot with a convex bottom called a *paiolo* and is stirred with a *tarello*, a wooden paddle. You can use a heavy saucepan with a thick bottom and a cool handle. The saucepan should have twice the capacity as the liquid called for in your recipe to prevent splashing. Select a flat wooden spoon or paddle for stirring. Rubber spatulas initially work well but part under the long, hot temperatures.

■ *Choose your liquid:* Water is standard. For a richer, fuller flavor, stocks such as beef, poultry and game may be used to replace part or all of the

Polenta can be made with coarse or fine cornmeal or a blend of the two. Polenta made with coarse cornmeal typically provides the best texture for grilling or sauteing. Polenta made with fine cornmeal is generally served loose.

water. Milk is also used with stocks for a softer, more delicate flavor. For thin polenta, use 2 quarts of water per pound of cornmeal. For thick polenta, use 1½ quarts of water per pound of cornmeal.

■ *Add flavorings:* Seasoned vegetable purees, such as pumpkin, red or spicy peppers, sweet potato, and garlic and fennel, may be added for flavor, up to a quarter of the liquid volume. Cook the vegetables and puree with as little moisture as possible. Measure the amount of puree and substitute it for the same volume of liquid in your recipe. Adjust the polenta texture by adding a little water if too thick.

■ *How to prepare:* Bring the liquids to a boil, add the seasonings and spices (traditionally only salt). Lower the heat to a slow simmer and slowly add the cornmeal by handfuls, making sure each addition is mixed well. Add the vegetable purees, increase the heat to simmer, and constantly stir, scraping the sides and bottom. Vegetable purees should be added now. Cook until thick-

ened enough to support the weight of the spoon standing straight up and the polenta comes away from the spoon, about 20 minutes.

■ *Tricks of the trade:* When done, thin polenta is often enriched with cheeses such as Parmesan, Romano, Gorgonzola (blue-type) and mozzarella, dotted with butter or enhanced with wild mushrooms and truffles. It is immediately poured from the saucepan onto a wooden board. The polenta is allowed to set for a couple of minutes, garnished with herbs, cut with a string or knife and served.

■ *Let's get fancy:* Thicker polenta is poured into a parchment-lined sheet pan or loaf pan, smoothed and refrigerated. Once the polenta has firmed, it is unmolded and cut into slices from the loaf pan or whimsical shapes from the sheet such as stars, moons, diamonds and triangles. Finish by:

Grilling: Brush the surface of the polenta with olive oil and place on the grill. Cook

until seared, about 3 minutes, then turn over until hot, about 2 more minutes. Close the top on the grill if so equipped or cover with a pan lid or inverted saute pan to help the polenta heat more quickly.

Sauteing: Heat a nonstick pan over medium-high heat. Add a little butter or olive oil. Carefully place the polenta in the pan, cooking until golden, about 3 minutes. Turn over with a metal spatula and cook until hot, about 3 more minutes. Remove to paper toweling to drain.

Frying: Heat 3 inches of canola or corn oil in a heavy skillet to 325 degrees. Add the polenta, cooking until golden, about 3 minutes. Remove to paper toweling to drain. Keep warm in the oven.

The grand finale: For all three methods above, finish further by brushing the crisped polentas with a little butter or extra-virgin olive oil and dusting them with herbs and Parmesan or Romano cheese before serving.

Baking: Layer the slices in an ovenproof dish with butter, herbs and cheese. Bake at 350 degrees until hot.

■ *Serving suggestions:* Polenta can be added to other dishes, such as spinach, braised meats and dried and fresh beans, as a rich, starchy accompaniment.

■

RED PEPPER & FRESH CORN POLENTA

Makes 4-6 servings

4   large red peppers, roasted, peeled and seeded

2   cups milk, divided

2   cups poultry stock

½   teaspoon salt
    Pepper to taste

2   tablespoons paprika, hot

2   cups yellow cornmeal, coarsely ground

2   cups fresh corn

½   cup freshly snipped chives

¼   cup unsalted butter, divided

¼   cup finely grated Parmesan cheese

Preheat the oven to 400 degrees. In a food processor, puree the peppers with ¼ cup of the milk until smooth. In a large saucepan, combine the remaining milk, the stock, salt, pepper and paprika. Bring to a simmer over medium-high heat, then gradually whisk in the cornmeal. Add the pepper puree. Stir with a spatula or wooden spoon until the polenta is thick enough to allow the spoon to stand up in it, about 20 minutes. Add the corn, chives and 2 tablespoons of the butter, stirring until incorporated. Adjust the salt and pepper to taste. Pour the polenta mixture into a parchment-lined sheet pan, 12 inches by 16 inches by 1 inch. Smooth and level the surface, cover with plastic wrap and refrigerate until firm, a minimum of 4 hours. Remove the plastic wrap. With a knife or cookie cutter, cut the polenta into desired shapes (triangles, rectangles, diamonds, moons, etc.), then invert pan to unmold. Refrigerate until ready to cook. In a nonstick skillet, heat the remaining butter over high heat. Carefully add the polenta, and cook until seared, about 2 minutes. Turn over to brown lightly,

about 2 minutes. Remove to paper toweling to drain. Place the polenta on the serving plate while hot. Top with grated Parmesan cheese and serve with your favorite main course.

Nutrition details per serving
Calories .340
Percent of calories from fat 30%
Fat: .11 gm
Protein: . . . . .10 gm
Carbohydrate: . . . . .50 gm
Cholesterol: . . . . .29 mg
Sodium: 583
Diabetic exchange: ⅓ milk, 2⅙ bread,
¼ meat, 1⅓ fat.

■

Polenta made with coarse cornmeal can be sliced and used instead of bread in a sandwich and can be toasted, baked or fried.

GRAINS AND BEANS ARE A HEARTY COMBO

TODAY'S LESSON: Autumn brings the bounty of the field to the pantry with grains and dried beans.

■ *Why they taste so good:* The flavor of beans and grains comes alive when soaked and then cooked until tender. Grains develop a broader, richer flavor when toasted through sauteing, but beans are best when cooked with stronger-scented vegetables and herbs. Served alone or together, they have a nutty, rich, earthy flavor.

■ *Advantages:* Grains and beans provide the necessary dietary protein intake for a third of the world's population. Grains and beans also are high in carbohydrates, which provide us with energy. Their only fat comes from food added during cooking.

■ *Tricks of the trade:* For best results, cook grains and beans separately, then combine before serving.

Toast grains by sauteing in a little oil until hot to the touch before adding hot liquids.

Soak beans before cooking to allow them to rehydrate. Soaking makes beans easier to cook in less time, helps retain nutrients and leaches out some of the indigestible sugars that may produce gas.

Season grains and beans with salt and spices after the liquid is added so that the flavors cook in. For grains, cover tightly for a pilaf; with beans, loosely cover and finish in a 375-degree oven. This provides slow, even cooking and prevents scorching.

■ *The cooking begins:* Start beans first. Combine soaked beans, liquids to cover, vegetables and herbs to season. Bring to a simmer over high heat. Transfer to a preheated oven and cook until tender, 2½-3 hours. Remove from heat and add a little acid such as vinegar or wine to hold the texture.

For rice and some grains, the pilaf method works best by preheating a pan with oil. Add any vegetables and saute until tender. Add the grains and cook until hot. Add hot liquids and any seasonings according to your recipe. Cover the surface of the grains with foil and seal with a lid, cooking until done, generally 15-20 minutes.

Other grains require different techniques, so follow the instructions on the package or use your favorite cookbook.

■ *Try your technique:* This Red Lentil & Wild Rice Pilaf recipe is fast because the lentils can be cooked right with the grains.

RED LENTIL & WILD RICE PILAF

Makes 8 servings

6   cups light vegetable stock, divided

½   cup extra fancy wild rice

    Sea salt

    Freshly ground black pepper

2   tablespoons virgin olive oil or butter, divided

2   cloves garlic, minced fine

1   small red onion, cut into ¼-inch dice

1   tablespoon fresh thyme leaf

1   cup long-grain white or brown rice

2   ounces dried red lentils

¼   cup chopped parsley

1   little bunch of parsley or thyme for garnish

In a small saucepan, heat 2 cups of the stock to a simmer over medium heat. Add the wild rice and season the stock to taste, cooking until tender, about 35 minutes. Drain and reserve the rice. Preheat the

oven to 375.

Bring the remaining 4 cups of stock to a boil. Meanwhile, in an ovenproof skillet or saucepan with a tight-fitting lid, heat 1 tablespoon of the olive oil over medium high heat. Add the garlic, cooking until golden, about 3 minutes. Add the onion, cooking until the edges begin to brown, about 5 minutes. Add the thyme and white or brown rice, cooking until the rice is hot to the back of your hand,

about 3 minutes. Remove from the heat and add the boiling stock. Stir in the lentils. Return to the heat and bring to a simmer. Season with salt and pepper to taste. Cover with heavy-duty aluminum foil over the edge of the saucepan and bring the foil down to the surface of the liquid, crimping the edges to seal well. Seal with the lid and transfer the pan to the lower rack of the oven, cooking until all the liquid has been absorbed, about 15-20 minutes.

Transfer to a large bowl. Add the wild rice, parsley and remaining olive oil or butter. Check the seasoning one final time. Transfer to your serving dish, garnish with the sprigs of herbs and serve.

Nutrition details per serving
Calories .121
Percent of calories from fat 26%
Fat: .3.6 gm
Protein: . . . . .3.7 gm
Carbohydrate: . . . . .19 gm
Cholesterol: . . . . .0 mg
Sodium: . . . . .146 mg
Diabetic exchange: ¼ vegetable, 1¼ bread, ⅓ fat.

Kamut, like spelt, is an ancient strain of non-hybrid wheat. It has larger kernels and more protein than hybrids and is processed into cereals, noodles and crackers.

VEGETABLES UPDATE AN ANCIENT GRAIN

AMAZING FOOD FACTS

■

Quinoa was brought to the United States from South America in the form of a 50-pound bag of seeds. The grain was planted on 5 acres in Colorado in 1982. Quinoa was harvested that fall and every fall since.

■ *What is it?* Quinoa (pronounced KEEN-wah) is an ancient grain that originated in the Andes region of South America. It was one of three staples of the Incas, along with maize (corn) and the potato. Although it was a significant source of protein in the Inca diet, it was overlooked by the Spanish explorers.

■ *What it tastes like:* It tastes light and nutty with an earthy tone.

■ *Health advantages:* Quinoa contains between 16 percent and 20 percent protein — higher than the 14 percent of wheat, 9.9 percent of millet and 7.5 percent of rice. It's also much more digestible. All these protein statistics may seem like no big deal to you, but consider this: A third of the world's dietary protein originates from grains and legumes. The meat-, milk- and egg-rich protein we get in the

TODAY'S LESSON: In case you haven't discovered it, let me tell you about quinoa, an age-old grain that is migrating from health-food stores to grocery store shelves. Some are even calling it the grain of the future.

United States has been shown to contribute to heart disease.

■ *How to prepare:* Quinoa is very simple to prepare. Add it to twice the volume of boiling salted water, simmering until tender and all the water is absorbed, about 15 minutes. The directions call for covering the pot, but I get better results by very slowly simmering with the lid removed. Add garnishes of nuts and fresh herbs and serve. Spices are best added to the boiling water so that they may evenly disperse through the dish.

■ *A pilaf of quinoa:* I prefer to prepare the quinoa with the rice pilaf technique. Heat a small amount of olive oil in a saucepan. Add the dry quinoa and cook until hot. Add twice the volume of boiling salted water, with spices if you like, cover and place on the lower rack of an oven heated to 350 degrees for 12-15 minutes, until tender. Carefully remove from the oven, remembering the handle and lid are very hot, stir in the garnishes and serve.

■ *Mix and match:* Vegetables may be added to the cooking

quinoa. Cut vegetables into a smaller dice so that they may finish cooking about the same time as the quinoa. Firmer vegetables such as young carrots, beets, parsnips, beans, broccoli, celery root, members of the onion family and even potatoes make a wonderful combination if cut very small. Softer leafy vegetables such as spinach, chards, mustards, greens and herbs are best chopped very fine and added in the last few minutes of cooking time to preserve the full flavor. Garnish vegetables to add at the end of the cooking are roasted sweet or hot peppers, tomatoes, sauteed mushrooms, roasted fennel and many more. These vegetables should be introduced at the end just to heat, not to actually cook with the quinoa.

■ *Serving suggestions:* Quinoa is great served warm or cold. After the quinoa is cooked, transfer it to a large broad dish and spread evenly across. Allow to cool. Break up large lumps, if they occur, with a wide-tined fork. The cooled quinoa is terrific in green and vegetable salads.

■ *Try your technique:* Only time will tell if quinoa takes over the role of the other grains in feeding the world, but for now you will find me enjoying the flavor, texture and extra clean protein. I think you'll like it, too.

■

QUINOA & VEGETABLE RISOTTO

Makes 4 servings

2   cups quinoa
¼   cup virgin olive oil, divided
1   red onion, peeled, ends removed, diced
2   whole cloves garlic, finely minced (optional)
4   cups light vegetable stock or water, brought to a boil
    Salt to taste
    Black pepper to taste
1   cup mushrooms, cleaned, sliced
1   large red pepper, seeded and diced
1   cup baby haricots verts, or French green beans, trimmed and cut into 2-inch sections, blanched in boiling water until al dente
½   cup chopped fresh basil leaves
½   cup grated Parmesan or Romano cheese
4   sprigs fresh basil or herbs for garnish

Place the quinoa in a fine strainer and rinse under running cold water to remove any residue of the bitter husks. Allow to drain thoroughly. In a large saucepan, heat half of the olive oil over medium-high heat. Add the onion and the garlic, cooking until translucent and tender. Add the quinoa and cook until hot. Remove from the heat and carefully pour the boiling vegetable stock or water over the quinoa. Return to the heat and bring to a simmer. Season with salt and a generous dose of black pepper. Cook until just about all the liquids are reduced, about 8 minutes.

Meanwhile, in a skillet, heat the remaining olive oil. Add the mushrooms, cooking until browned on the edges, about 4 minutes. Add the peppers and cook until al dente. Transfer the mushrooms and the peppers to the quinoa saucepan and combine. Add the blanched haricots verts to the quinoa. Cook until the quinoa is softened but not mushy. Add the basil. Transfer to soup bowls. Top with grated cheese. Garnish with the sprig of herbs and serve immediately.

Nutrition details per serving
Calories 527
Percent of calories from fat 37%
Fat: . . . . .22 gm
Protein: . . . . .18 gm
Carbohydrate: . . . . .66 gm
Cholesterol: . . . . .10 mg
Sodium: . . . . .398 mg
Diabetic exchange: 1¼ vegetables, 3¼ bread, ¾ meat, 3⅛ fat.

NUTS ADD RICH, TOASTY GOODNESS

■ *Health advantages:* Nuts are a good source of vitamin E, an antioxidant that helps keep LDL-cholesterol from being oxidized in the blood. Oxidized LDL-cholesterol has a greater tendency to clog arteries than does nonoxidized LDL-cholesterol.

■ *How to select:* The high fat content of the meat makes nuts susceptible to rancidity. When you're buying nuts, smell them first to make sure they're fresh. They'll smell slightly musty if they're rancid. Another way to tell may be to look at the expiration date on the package.

■ *How to store:* Store nuts in an airtight glass container in a dark, cool, dry area. For best results, use nuts quickly and repurchase only when needed.

■ *To toast:* Place shelled nuts on a cookie sheet on the lower shelf of an oven heated to 300 degrees for at least 25 minutes.

TODAY'S LESSON: Nuts once were used more than they are today. In the fall, when the temperature dips and nuts reach maturity, people used to forage and store nuts for winter. Some kinds of nuts, such as acorns and chestnuts, are high in starch and were ground as a flour for simple breads and porridges. Today nuts are no longer a dietary staple. Unlike nut trees, which often take years to reach maturity and produce, other plants yield food more quickly and inexpensively.

Watch for them to turn a light tan color. Avoid fast toasting at higher temperatures, to prevent scorching of the exterior before the inside becomes crisp. Transfer nuts to another cookie sheet to cool after toasting.

■ *Infused flavor:* To infuse the nut flavor into liquids for

desserts, ice creams and sauces, toast more deeply, or until the color becomes like coffee with cream and the nut scent is quite forward. Don't allow the nuts to turn dark brown or develop a bitter scent.

To bake: For nut breads, chop the nuts in a food processor with flour. The flour will absorb the oils and intensify the nut flavor throughout the bread. Then proceed with your regular recipe. Add toasted nuts to batters at the last minute to prevent the nuts from absorbing moisture and softening. For the crispest results, top desserts with nuts just before serving.

GRILLED BEEF TENDERLOIN WITH HAZELNUTS

Makes 4 servings

2 cups veal or poultry stock

1 cup red wine

2 cups hazelnuts, roasted, skinned and coarsely chopped

2 tablespoons ground fennel seed

2 tablespoons cracked black peppercorns

2 tablespoons olive oil

4 beef tenderloin steaks, 8 ounces each

½ cup Jack Daniels, optional

   Salt to taste

   Black pepper to taste

¼ cups scallion greens, diced

4 sprigs mint for garnish

Preheat oven to 550 or highest setting. In a medium saucepan, combine stock and red wine. Bring to a simmer over medium-high heat, cooking until thickened to coat the back of a spoon, about 10 min-utes. In a small bowl, combine hazelnuts, fennel and black pepper. Rub oil on surface of steaks. Press top and bottom of steaks into nut mixture so that the mix adheres to meat. Place steaks in nonstick ovenproof skillet. Position on lower rack of oven, cooking until desired doneness is reached or until meat thermometer inserted to center of steak registers 130 for medium-rare. Allow to rest 3 minutes before serving. Meanwhile, return sauce to simmer. Add the Jack Daniels if desired. Adjust seasonings with salt and black pepper. Spoon sauce onto lower half of serving plate. Sprinkle scallions over sauce. Position steaks in center of sauce. Garnish with mint sprig and serve.

Nutrition details per serving
Calories 1,091
Percent of calories from fat 65%
Fat: . . . . .80 gm
Protein: . . . . .72 gm
Carbohydrate: . . . . .16 gm
Cholesterol: . . . . .189 mg
Sodium: . . . . .1,016 mg
Diabetic exchange: 9 meat, 10¾ fat.

Acorns and chestnuts are rich in starch and have been used for centuries as a grain substitute by the poor, who grind them into a coarse flour for porridge or to make flat breads.

THE COMFORT
OF MASHED POTATOES

■ *The root of the matter:* The root vegetables we are talking about are the potato, sweet potato, parsnip and celery root.

■ *Groundless fears about root vegetables:* Many people think mashed spuds are fattening and provide little, if any, nutritional value. Not true. Potatoes and other root vegetables are highly nutritious, because they store the plant's energy for rebirth the following year. As for fat, we add that in the form of butter, sour cream, bacon bits and cheese.

■ *So how do we keep these mashed roots healthy?* For the richest flavor, you can't beat good old fattening butter. But we can control the fat and not skimp on flavor. I add no-fat or low-fat yogurt instead of butter for a creamier taste, a small amount of olive oil for texture, and herb- and spice-infused oils for amazing flavor. The healthiest approach is to add fruit purees. Try a little apple-

TODAY'S LESSON: The silky, luscious puree of root vegetables, most commonly known as mashed potatoes, is a homey comfort food that satisfies down to your soul. I'll show you ways to make the most of mashing, with innovative twists to excite the palate and lower the fat.

sauce or pear sauce for great results. Purees of other vegetables also will work if they have some body to them. Roasted pumpkin, onion, garlic, sweet bell peppers and corn are good.

■ *Handle with care:* Root vegetables require proper handling and storage to be at their best. Select only firm, dense roots without bruises and cuts. Store under refrigeration or in a cool, well-ventilated, dark place. For extended storage, keep the roots from touching.

■ *The cooking begins:* Wash, peel and cut the roots into a 1-inch dice. A mixture of roots is fine to cook together as long as they are cut the same size. Submerge them in a large amount of cold water in a pot. Adding starchy roots to hot or boiling water instantly seals the outside, which inhibits cooking and results in uneven starch development — that means lumps! Bring to a simmer over medium-high heat and cook until tender, about 15-30 minutes depending on the variety of the roots.

■ *Steep trick:* Turn off the heat and allow the roots to steep in the water for a couple of minutes before mashing to reduce the liquid that must be added to satisfy the potato starches. If you drain immediately, the mashed roots will be drier and tighter. Drain the roots and transfer to a large bowl.

■ *How to be a mash master:* Everyone has a technique, but here's the lowdown.

The pro technique starts by placing the roots in a ricer, a tool that squeezes the root through tiny holes. It's like a giant garlic press. This is an extra step that results in absolutely the best texture. Then whip the roots with a strong hand mixer and follow with any seasonings, liquids and enrichments.

The hand method of mashing to death also works, but it results in a more irregular texture. Mash until smooth before adding liquids. A mixer also can be used following this late, slow addition of liquids.

Using a food processor

requires adding at least part of the extra ingredients at the start of the pureeing process. Avoid using blenders, because their action causes a stringy, tough texture.

■ *Serving suggestions:* If you need to hold the mashed roots for a few minutes while you finish the rest of the meal, keep them in a warm oven in an ovenproof dish. Heat is the essential ingredient to a great puree, so choose a vessel that keeps it in.

■ *Mix and match:* The flavor of potatoes is enriched by the other, more intense fla-

vors of the other root vegetables. Try combinations such as potatoes and celery root or parsnips.

■ *Try your technique:* I'll be serving Mashed Potatoes & Celery Roots with Crispy Shallots this Thanksgiving. Try it for a special meal or make an everyday meal very special.

■

BAKED PUMPKIN FILLED WITH PARSNIP & POTATO PUREE

Makes 8 servings

1   small pie pumpkin, about 8-9 inches in diameter

    Salt to taste

    Freshly ground black pepper

¼   cup maple sugar (or substitute light brown sugar)

3   pounds fresh parsnips

1   pound baking potatoes

8   tablespoons (1 stick) unsalted butter (or substitute extra-virgin olive oil or, to eliminate fat, cooking liquid or vegetable stock)

½   teaspoon freshly ground nutmeg, optional

½   cup whipped fresh chives, optional

Preheat oven to 375. Cut top off pumpkin. Scoop out the seeds and coarse inner fibers. Season cavity with salt, pepper and maple sugar. Place pumpkin upright in ovenproof baking dish with top next to it. Bake until tender but with the body still firm enough to support the filling, about 45 minutes. Remove from oven and keep warm.

Meanwhile, peel parsnips and potatoes; cut into 2-inch dice. Place in large pot and cover with cold water about 1 inch over the tops of the roots. Bring water to simmer over medium-high heat. Season with salt to taste. Cook roots until very tender. Turn off heat; allow roots to sit in water for about 5 minutes. Transfer roots to a colander and drain. Transfer to a food processor. Add butter. Season with salt and pepper to taste. Puree until smooth, but do not overwork. Taste to ensure puree is properly seasoned; add nutmeg if desired. Fold in chives. Keep warm.

To serve: Reheat pumpkin shell if necessary in oven. Place shell on serving platter. Pumpkin top may shrink, so place carefully. Fill pumpkin with hot root puree; replace top. Spoon the puree out, scooping a little of the baked pumpkin to complement.

Nutrition details per serving
Calories 292
Percent of calories from fat 16%
Fat: . . . . .5 gm
Protein: . . . . .5 gm
Carbohydrate: . . . . .60 gm
Cholesterol: . . . . .0 mg
Sodium: . . . . .345 mg
Diabetic exchange: 6 vegetables, 1¾ bread, ⅛ fat.

■

MASHED POTATOES & CELERY ROOTS WITH CRISPY SHALLOTS

Makes 8 servings

½   cup virgin olive oil
1   cup fresh rosemary leaves, divided
1   cup all-purpose flour
1   tablespoon paprika
1   cup shallots, peeled, ends removed, cut into 1-inch dice
    Canola oil for frying
3   large russet potatoes, peeled, eyes removed, cut into 1-inch dice
3   large celery roots, trimmed even with paring knife, peeled, cut into 1-inch dice
1   tablespoon salt
2   teaspoons freshly ground black pepper
2   cups applesauce
1   cup low-fat yogurt

In a small saucepan, heat the olive oil to 325 degrees over medium-high heat. Add ½ cup of rosemary leaves, cooking until crisp and the oil stops bubbling around the leaves, about 3 minutes. Using a small, fine sieve, transfer rosemary to paper toweling.

Repeat with remaining ½ cup rosemary in batches. When completed, allow the rosemary-scented olive oil to cool. In a medium bowl, combine the flour and the paprika, mixing well. Add the shallots and mix thoroughly until completely coated. Remove the shallots to a cookie sheet to hold while preparing the next step.

Fill a medium saucepan to a depth of about 2 inches with the canola oil and bring to 325 degrees over medium-high heat. Shake the shallots to remove excess flour, then carefully add them to the oil. Cook until golden and crisp, about 3 minutes. Transfer with a slotted spoon to paper toweling to cool. Allow the oil to cool and store for frying purposes.

In a large pot of cold water, combine the potatoes and the celery root. Bring to a simmer over high heat and cook until tender, about 15 minutes. Turn the heat off and allow to sit for 3 minutes before proceeding. Drain in a colander. Transfer in batches to a ricer, and process the fine roots, salt and pepper with a stationary or hand mixer until smooth. Add the applesauce and yogurt, whipping until smooth. Transfer to a warm serving dish. Drizzle a few tablespoons of the rosemary-scented olive oil over the surface of the puree. Sprinkle the crispy shallots and rosemary over the top of the puree. Serve immediately while piping hot.

Nutrition details per serving
Calories 350
Percent of calories from fat 37%
Fat: .15 gm
Protein: . . . . .6 gm
Carbohydrate: . . . . .50 gm
Cholesterol: . . . . .2 mg
Sodium: . . . . .859 mg
Diabetic exchange: ¼ milk, ⅓ vegetable, ½ fruit, 2½ bread, 2¼ fat.

BAY SCALLOPS ARE A TENDER TREAT

■ *What is a bay scallop?* The bay or cape scallop is named after the shallow water bodies of the mid- to northern Atlantic seaboard, which give birth to and nurture these shellfish. This scallop is held in esteem because of its sweet, fresh flavor and ultra-silky texture. Its large cousin, the sea scallop, is dredged from sea beds as deep as 900 feet. Sea scallops are much larger and firmer in texture and more savory. Calico scallops are tiny cousins from southern waters. They are steamed to open, resulting in a cooked texture similar to a pencil eraser.

■ *Do you eat the whole thing?* The entire scallop is edible, but what most people recognize as the scallop is actually the adducter muscle. This translucent, cylinder-like muscle opens and closes the scallop's shell.

■ *Why it tastes so good:* Bay scallops are best from northern

TODAY'S LESSON: The small bay or cape scallop is the rarest and most delicate of the scallop family. Cooking these tiny delicacies requires split-second timing over perfect heat to create silky, tender treasures.

waters, which slowly nurture them to maturity. The rich marine life on which they feed produces a delicate sweet flavor.

■ *Advantages:* The small scallops cook in just a minute or so. They are low in calories, fat and cholesterol.

■ *Tricks of the trade:* The secret of cooking bay scallops is medium-high heat, in a heavy nonstick or seasoned skillet, with whole butter, for just a few seconds. Every surface must be exposed to cook properly, so don't crowd the scallops. The heat that is quickly transferred into the scallop will

lightly brown the exterior, seal in the sweet juices and cook the scallop all in about 1 minute, plus or minus a few seconds. I do mean seconds, because the scallops will continue to cook even after they are removed from the pan. Extra seconds will result only in a rubbery texture.

■ *How to pick good ones:* Bay scallop season opens in late September and picks up as the weather cools, running through the holidays before demand outstrips supply. Select translucent, not white, scallops. They should smell sweet, never fishy.

AMAZING FOOD FACTS

■

Bay scallops average 100 per pound. Sea scallops average 30 to the pound.

■

Bay scallops are available on the East Coast in the fall; sea scallops' peak season is mid-fall to mid-spring.

■
The color of scallops can range from pale beige to creamy pink. If scallops are stark white, it is a sign that they have been soaked in water. Soaking in water is a marketing ploy to increase the weight of scallops before they are sold.

Make sure you clean the scallops. It's easy to do, and if you don't you'll regret it. Simply pull off the small rectangular strip of fiber, often called the foot, which used to connect the scallop meat to the shell. The foot is easy to identify and in some cases may not be present. When cooked, the foot becomes like a piece of rubber. The foot may be added to the sauce or stock for flavor but must be strained to remove before serving.

■ *Preparing your garnishes:* Stick with subtle, complementary herbs and seasonings that will enhance the flavor, not overpower it. Herbs such as tarragon, chives, parsley and chervil are naturals and are best when fresh, not dried. The flavors of shallots, white wine and lemon broaden the natural sweet balance.

■ *The cooking begins:* Select a heavy nonstick or well-seasoned skillet and preheat over medium-high heat. The stored heat in the pan is essential for cooking quickly and preventing steaming.

■ *Cooking is fast and easy:* Have all the ingredients ready — scallops, garnishes and side dishes ready on warm serving plates. Add the sweet butter to the pan and allow it to melt. The butter will foam a little, start to recede and then begin to brown, indicating the temperature is right and the nutty flavor has developed. Add the scallops, making sure they do not crowd in the pan, and allow to sear on the first side for about 30 seconds. Shake the pan a little bit to roll the scallops around, and brown the remaining surfaces for another 30 seconds or so. Season with a touch of salt and pepper and a splash of lemon or white wine, toss in the herbs, and they're done. Immediately drain or spoon the scallops directly onto the serving plates. Don't wait a second; serve immediately.

■ *How else can you cook scallops?*
Broiling is best, with a splash of good olive oil or melted butter and a dusting of salt, fresh pepper and spices. Preheat the broiler to the highest setting. Place the scallops

on a broiler pan and place under the broiler, leaving the oven door open slightly to vent. Cook for 4 minutes, or just until slightly resilient.
Frying can be a treat, but choose a light, thin batter such as tempura to allow the scallop flavor and texture to come through. Dip the scallops in the tempura batter, allow the excess to drain and place in clean oil heated to 360 degrees. Cook for about 2 minutes, or until the scallops ever so slightly begin to hiss. Remove to paper towels to drain.

■ *Serving suggestions:* Scallops are perfect with a splash of lemon and a sprinkle of herbs. They are also terrific with a good fresh herb tartar sauce or a few toasted almonds.

■ *Try your technique:* My favorite recipe for scallops with chives, lemon and black pepper is simple.

BAY SCALLOPS WITH FRESH TARRAGON & LEMON

Makes 4 servings

4   tablespoons unsalted butter

1½ pounds bay scallops, cleaned

1   lemon, juiced

Sea salt

Freshly ground black pepper

2   tablespoons fresh tarragon leaves

2   tablespoons snipped fresh chives

4   sprigs tarragon or other herb for garnish

Place a large, heavy, non-stick skillet over medium-high heat. When warm, add the butter, cooking until the foam recedes and it begins to turn brown. Add the scallops, making sure they do not crowd the pan, and cook until seared, about 30 seconds. Shake the pan a little to roll the scallops and sear all the surfaces of the scallops, lightly browning about 30 additional seconds. Add the lemon juice and season with a pinch of salt and a generous shot of black pepper. Add the tarragon and chives, toss and divide onto four warm serving plates. Garnish with sprig of tarragon or herbs and serve.

Nutrition details per serving
Calories 264
Percent of calories from fat 46%
Fat: .13 gm
Protein: . . . . .33 gm
Carbohydrate: . . . . .6 gm
Cholesterol: . . . . .106 mg
Sodium: . . . . .377 mg
Diabetic exchange: 3 meat, 2¼ fat.

BAY SCALLOPS WITH ALMONDS

Makes 4 servings

1   cup dry white wine, preferably chardonnay

½   cup fish fumet (fish stock) or clam juice

1¼ cups heavy cream

Salt to taste

Freshly ground white pepper to taste

2   tablespoons unsalted butter

1½ pounds bay scallops, foot removed and cleaned as necessary

¼   cup snipped fresh chives

½   cup blanched sliced almonds, toasted

4   sprigs fresh chives for garnish

In a medium-size saucepan, combine the wine and fish fumet or clam juice. Bring to a simmer over high heat, cooking until reduced to ½ cup, about 6 minutes. Add the cream and cook until thickened to coat the back of a spoon, about 10 minutes. Salt and pepper to taste. Remove from the heat. In a large nonstick skillet, heat the butter over high heat. Add the scallops and cook until browned and well seared, about 2 minutes. Stir scallops and finish cooking until slightly firm, about 1 minute, depending on the size. Season with salt and pepper to taste. Transfer to a colander to drain. Add the scallops to the sauce, mixing to coat. Spoon the scallops into the center of the serving plates. Top with chives and almonds. Position the garnish chives into the top of the scallop mound and serve immediately.

Cook's note: The tender scallops are best accentuated with a crispy vegetable such as snow peas.

Nutrition details per serving
Calories 629
Percent of calories from fat 59%
Fat: .42 gm
Protein: . . . . .45 gm
Carbohydrate: . . . . .12 gm
Cholesterol: . . . . .198 mg
Sodium: . . . . .1,007 mg
Diabetic exchange: ½ vegetable, 5⅔ meat, 7¾ fat.

SUNFLOWER SEEDS TAP THE HEAT

AMAZING FOOD FACTS

■

Sunflowers are native to the Americas and probably got their start in Peru. Native Americans discovered they could crush and boil sunflower seeds and skim a particularly nourishing oil from the surface.

■ *Who eats sunflower seeds?* Sunflower seeds are an important foodstuff for all the population of the Plains, from the tiniest game birds to prairie dogs, deer, moose and antelope. Indians and early settlers gathered sunflowers for the seeds' high oil content and protein. Sunflower seeds are still a popular energy-rich snack today, but they are raised commercially mostly for their edible oil, perfect for dressings and cooking.

■ *How to harvest:* The seeds are easiest to harvest from a whole mature flower. Dry the flower in the sun, covering it to protect it from birds and squirrels until the seeds are easily released. Collect the seeds in a towel, closing the edges together to form a pouch; tie with a string to hold. Beat the towel on a hard surface to break the husks loose from the kernels. Once the husks have been split, transfer the kernels and husks to a bucket of water.

TODAY'S LESSON: The late summer sun's heat brings to fruition the seeds for the next generation. Plants spend September gathering the last nutrients from the sun and soil while hardening their seed shells to protect against the winter frost. The sunflower is a beautiful testimonial to this life cycle. Head bowing in reverence to its namesake, it is a gorgeous flower surrounding a seed-filled center.

Stir vigorously and allow to soak for about 30 minutes. The kernels will sink to the bottom while the husks rise to the surface. Strain the separated kernels into a colander.

■ *How to cook:* Dry on a cookie sheet in an oven heated to 250. Remove from oven and allow to cool to room temperature. Store in an airtight jar in a cool place out of direct sunlight.

■ *A meal of seeds?* To make sunflower meal, combine 1 part dried kernels with 3 parts all-purpose flour in your food processor and run until a fine meal is obtained. Sift before using for a finer texture. Substitute an equal volume of sunflower meal for the flour in your favorite muffin, pancake or sweet bread dough for a nutty, rich flavor. Add whole or chopped sunflower kernels for additional flavor and texture.

■ *A sunflower garnish:* For a terrific garnish for salads, pastas and even desserts, toast sunflower kernels on an ungreased cookie sheet at 325 until light tan, about 12 minutes. Cool to room temperature. The kernels will be crunchier after cooling.

■ *Breading:* Use chopped toasted kernels as a coating instead of breading for broiled fish. Place the cooled toasted kernels in a food processor, pulse on and off until a coarse chop is achieved. Do not sift, because the fine crumbs help seal the fish. Add 1 or 2 tablespoons of flour if the meal is moist. Season the mix with salt, pepper and herbs such as chives, parsley and paprika to complete the coating. Broiling works better than baking, because the kernels tend to absorb the moisture from baking.

■ *Sunflower oil:* Sunflower oil is fruity and light from the first pressing. Just as with

olive oils, the quality can vary greatly. Be selective and taste the oil to ensure quality. Sunflower oil is best in dressings because of its neutral flavor. It can be used in cooking, but do not heat beyond 340 degrees because it will break down. Use for light, low-temperature sauteing and low-temperature baking.

■

PICKEREL WITH SUNFLOWER CRUST

Makes 4 servings

3 tablespoons freshly squeezed lemon juice

½ cup extra-virgin olive oil, divided

½ cup nonpareil capers

¼ cup snipped fresh chives (or substitute chopped parsley)

Salt to taste

Freshly ground black pepper

1½ cups sunflower kernels, toasted

½ cup bread crumbs

1 tablespoon paprika, mild or hot, to taste

½ cup chopped parsley

4 pickerel fillets, about 8 ounces each, trimmed of skin and all bones

Sprigs of parsley for garnish

Preheat broiler. In a medium-size bowl, combine lemon juice, 1 tablespoon of the olive oil, capers and chives. Season with salt and a generous dose of black pepper. Set aside. In a food processor, combine the sunflower kernels, bread crumbs, paprika and chopped parsley. Pulse, on and off, to chop to a fine texture. Transfer to a shallow dish for breading. Rub the surfaces of the pickerel with the remaining olive oil. Press each fillet into the sunflower mixture to coat completely, then place on a broiler pan. Place the fish under the broiler and cook until done, about 6-8 minutes, depending on the thickness of the fillet. It is not necessary to turn the fillet. Center fillet on the serving plate. Stir lemon-caper sauce and spoon a little across each fillet. Garnish with a sprig of parsley and serve.

Nutrition details per serving
Calories 994
Percent of calories from fat 64%
Fat: . . . . .73 gm
Protein: . . . . .65 gm
Carbohydrate: . . . . .28 gm
Cholesterol: . . . . .195 mg
Sodium: . . . . .481 mg
Diabetic exchange: ⅓ bread, 8¾ meat, 12⅓ fat.

CAPO DE TUTTI CAPONS

■ *What is it?* The capon, with its moist and tender flesh, is the king of the chicken family. Capons are roosters desexed at around 2 weeks of age. This makes for a hungry yet peaceful bird that will fatten over a 5-month period on about 50 pounds of premium grain. The mature capon will weigh in from 6-15 pounds, with a high percentage of white breast meat.

■ *Where do they come from?* Capons are difficult and expensive to raise and are often overlooked by the average consumer. Capons are found in specialty markets, and from farms and local markets around the holidays. More available and less expensive is the caponette, a fattened hen.

■ *How to select:* When buying capons, select large birds with oversized breasts. Avoid capons with torn skin or whitish flesh. The skin and surfaces of the bird should be pristine, never sticky or slimy. The smell

TODAY'S LESSON: As the temperatures of fall begin to drop, I always anticipate the capon's arrival to market.

should be sweet, never strong or sour. If the capon has been freshly harvested, it is best to refrigerate it overnight before cooking.

■ *Don't forget the liver:* The capon liver is a delicacy unto itself. Clean and saute over high heat for a treat.

■ *To roast:* Roasting is the best method for cooking capon. Preheat the oven to 425. Remove the neck, liver and gizzard from the cavity. Thoroughly wash the capon inside and out with cold running water. Dry with paper toweling. Season the cavity with salt and pepper and add herbs, garlic, onions or citrus from your recipe. It is preferable not to stuff capons and other large birds, because of

the possible development of bacteria at low internal temperatures. Truss the capon with the legs tight to the body and the wing tips under the neck. Place in a roasting pan or on a wire rack in an ovenproof pan. Place the roasting pan with the capon on the lower rack of the oven. Cook for 15 minutes at 425, then turn the oven down to 350 to finish. Baste every 15 minutes to ensure even browning. Check the capon with an instant or meat thermometer inserted into the thickest part of the thigh after 1 hour. When done, the thermometer should read 175. Remove the capon from the oven and allow to rest for 10 minutes before carving. Cut the trussing twine away from the bird. Carve the capon just as you would a turkey. You will find the breast to be extremely moist and the legs and thighs superb. Save the small pieces for the best chicken salad or club sandwich in the world.

■ *Tricks of the trade:* For the crispest skin, rub all the surfaces of the capon with 2 tablespoons of poultry fat. The fat will develop the best flavor on the bird and promote even browning. If you prefer, you can substitute a little butter or olive oil, which also will enhance the browning and crisping.

■ *To crimp:* Capons are most tender when crimped, a cooking technique quite similar to poaching. In a large pot, bring enough light poultry stock or water to cover the capon to a simmer. Add onion, leek, carrot and spices to your taste. Over high heat, add the capon and return the stock to a boil. Lower the heat to just maintain the slowest possible simmer. Cook the capon for about 1¼ hours or until a thermometer inserted in the thickest part of the thigh reads 175. Turn the heat off and move the

pot to an inactive burner. Allow the capon to rest for 10 minutes before carving. The capon will be silky in texture and will melt in your mouth.

■ *Soup's on:* Strain the stock for the best-tasting soup base you'll ever have. Add noodles, a few of your favorite vegetables and the last of the meat from the capon's frame.

■

ROAST CAPON WITH CRAB APPLES & THYME

Makes 6 servings

1   capon, about 9 pounds, rinsed well
    Salt to taste
    Freshly ground black pepper to taste (be generous)
2   bunches fresh thyme, leaves and stems separated; reserve 6 large sprigs for garnish
2   tablespoons poultry fat (see cook's note), or substitute butter or olive oil
24 medium to large crab apples

2   tablespoons butter
½   cup light brown or maple sugar

Preheat the oven to 425. Salt and pepper the cavity and skin of the capon. Place the thyme stems in the cavity. Truss the capon with the legs tight to the body and the wings behind the neck. Rub the poultry fat across all surfaces of the capon. Sprinkle thyme leaves across the surface of the capon. Place the capon in an ovenproof skillet. Place the skillet on the lower rack of the oven, cooking until the capon begins to brown, about 15 minutes.

Lower the heat to 350. Rub the skin of the crab apples with the butter. Roll the crab apples in the sugar and place in an ovenproof pan. Add the pan to the oven while the capon is cooking. Cook the crab apples until tender as tested by a skewer through the center. Remove and keep warm until the capon is ready to be served. Baste the capon with the pan drippings every 15 minutes. The capon will be done in about 1½ hours

total cooking time, depending on the exact weight of your bird, or when an instant meat thermometer inserted in the thigh reads 175 and the juices run clear. Remove from the oven. Pour the cooking fat and juices into a glass measuring cup, skim off the fat and reserve the juices. If the juices are caramelized in the pan, add ½ cup stock or wine to reconstitute. Carve the capon. Divide onto 6 warm serving plates. Spoon the juices over the capon. Position the warm crab apples around the capon. Garnish with thyme and serve.

Cook's note: The fat pads may be removed from near the tail of the capon, placed in a small pan, covered with cold water and cooked until only the liquid fat remains, about 30-45 minutes. Strain and store in a clean glass jar under refrigeration for up to 1 week.

Nutrition details per serving
Calories 1,711
Percent of calories from fat 47%
Fat: .·. . . . . .87 gm
Protein: . . . . .193 gm
Carbohydrate: . . . . .25 gm
Cholesterol: . . . . .709 mg
Sodium: . . . . .562 mg
Diabetic exchange: ½ fruit, 1¼ bread, 28 meat, 1⅓ fat.

EVERYTHING'S DUCKY

■ *But isn't it fatty?* Duck has the reputation of being a fat meat, but beneath the skin and fat insulation is wonderful, protein-rich meat that is lower in cholesterol than chicken, beef, lamb or pork.

■ *Which ducks are which?* There are more than 100 species, but most domesticated ducks sold in the United States are the mildly flavored Pekin variety. Their arrival in 1873 met with instant success because they grow quickly to a tender maturity. In recent years, some of the Muscovy and Barbary have been sold because of their large meaty breasts. The canvasback is held in highest regard as the best wild duck. Its flesh and flavor are legendary.

■ *Isn't duck expensive?* Duck is more expensive than chicken but less than pheasant, quail, partridge and guinea fowl. One large whole duck, about 4½ pounds, will feed four. The growing popularity of ducks

TODAY'S LESSON: Although many people think duck is tough, when properly cooked it is as delicate and tender as filet mignon.

has brought individual pieces to the butcher's case. Serve one 8-ounce boneless breast of duck per person. Duck legs and thighs are the best buy. Buy about 12 ounces per person because of the bone for stews or the weight you need for making pastas and pizzas.

■ *How to cook:* The breast, thighs and legs of the duck all require different cooking times. The breast of the whole duck will be done in about half the time it takes to completely cook the legs and thighs. The breast is most tender when cooked medium-rare to medium (slightly pink), while the thighs and legs are best when cooked past medium. A whole roasted duck is a delectable treat, but by the

time the legs and thighs are done, the breast will be a little on the dry side.

■ *Divide and conquer:* The best technique is to separate the breasts, thighs and legs from the skeleton. This will allow you to cook each piece separately to achieve the best results. For example, the breast may be sauteed or grilled while the legs and thighs are roasted, grilled or even braised for a wonderful combination of textures and flavors.

■ *Just the breasts:* The easiest and fastest way to a terrific duck dinner is to purchase just the breasts. Trimmed of all skin and fat, they saute in about 8 minutes. Allow 2-3 minutes before slicing or serving.

■ *Just the thighs:* The thighs and legs are cheaper than the breast and have the richest flavor. They can simply be roasted at 400 degrees until done, about 40 minutes. Trim the excess fat and serve. The roasted meat is best removed from the bone and diced for duck salads, duck tortillas and duck pizzas. The skin may be discarded or crisped for a garnish. Thighs and legs braised in stock are tender and moist. Sear until golden, cover with seasoned stock and add onions and herbs to highlight the duck flavor. Bring the stock to a simmer, cover with foil and transfer to a 350-degree oven. Cook until tender, about 1 hour and 45 minutes. Remove the pot to the back of the stove and allow the thighs and legs to cool in the stock. Discard the skin, remove the meat from the bone and use in moist dishes such as ravioli, pastas and stews.

■ *How about that liver?* The duck liver is considered a delicacy. The liver is larger than a chicken's, with a

stronger flavor. Clean the liver and saute over medium-high heat. Season with salt, pepper and spices and serve with onions, apples and sage. Duck livers are also a favored ingredient in pates and terrines.

■ *Mix and match:* Pair the duck with bright, high-acid sauces such as citrus or wine and spices to balance the rich natural flavor.

■

DUCK BREAST WITH CHERRIES & SAGE

Makes 4 servings

1 cup whole shallots

1 cup dried tart cherries

1 cup dry red wine

¼ cup balsamic vinegar

1 cup poultry stock

   Salt to taste

   Freshly ground black pepper

½ cup canola oil

½ cup fresh sage leaves

4 boneless, skinless duck breasts, trimmed of all fat, about 10 ounces each

Preheat the oven to 425. Place shallots in a small ovenproof pan. Place on lower rack of oven and cook until tender, about 30 minutes. Allow to cool, then peel.

In a medium-size saucepan, bring cherries, red wine, vinegar and stock to a simmer over medium-high heat. Cook until thick enough to coat the back of a spoon, about 15 minutes. Adjust seasonings with salt and pepper to taste. Add the baked shallots to the sauce. Set aside and keep warm.

In a small saucepan, heat canola oil to 375 degrees. Add sage leaves and cook until crisp, about 2 minutes. Remove with a strainer or slotted spoon to paper towels to drain.

Reserve oil. (Sage may be used without frying if you prefer, but use only half or to taste.)

In a medium, nonstick, ovenproof pan, heat 1 tablespoon of the reserved oil until hot. Cook the duck breasts until seared well, about 2 minutes. Turn over to sear about 1 minute. Drain excess fat from the pan and place duck on lower rack of the oven. Cook until medium-rare, about 6 minutes (or longer if desired). Transfer to a plate to rest for 2 minutes before cutting. Spoon sauce onto warm serving plates. Slice each breast, on a slight angle perpendicular to the length, into 4 or 5 pieces. Lay the sliced duck in a fan shape across the sauce. Sprinkle sage and sauce across the duck.

Nutrition details per serving
Calories 532
Percent of calories from fat 59%
Fat: . . . . .35 gm
Protein: . . . . .34 gm
Carbohydrate: . . . . .12 gm
Cholesterol: . . . . .0 mg
Sodium: . . . . .408 mg
Diabetic exchange: ⅛ vegetables, 4⅔ meat, 5½ fat.

■

ROAST DUCK WITH TANGERINES

Makes 4 servings

2   5- to 6-pound ducks
7   large tangerines, peeled (Dancy is the juiciest)
2   cups poultry stock
2   lemons, peeled and quartered
½   cup dry red wine, preferably cabernet sauvignon
4   tablespoons green peppercorns, optional
2   tablespoons unsalted butter
    Salt to taste
    Coarsely ground black pepper to taste
¼   cup snipped fresh scallion greens

Preheat oven to 425. Place the ducks on a rack in a roasting pan on the lower shelf of the oven and cook for 20 minutes. Turn the oven down to 350 and cook until the breast is medium-rare, about 15 minutes. Remove the ducks from the oven and allow to cool slightly. Cut the breasts from the ducks and return the legs and carcasses to the oven, cooking until medium, about 45 minutes. Remove from oven, carve legs from carcasses and trim the fat from the breast and legs. Cut 4 of the tangerines into quarters, and divide the remaining tangerines into clean segments. In a medium-size saucepan over medium-high heat, bring the stock to a simmer. Cook until reduced to ½ cup, about 8 minutes, then add the quartered tangerines, the lemons and the red wine. Cook until thickened to coat the back of a spoon, about 10 minutes, and strain through a fine sieve into another saucepan. Return to a simmer over high heat, add the green peppercorns, then whisk the butter into the sauce, cooking until thickened, about 4 minutes. Adjust the salt and pepper to taste, reduce the heat to low, and add the tangerine segments and scallion greens. Crisp the legs and breasts in a 450-degree oven for 8-10 minutes. Thinly slice breasts. Spoon half the sauce onto warm serving plates. Position the leg and breast meat over the sauce. Spoon the remaining sauce with the tangerine segments over the duck. Serve.

Cook's note: This technique for cooking ducks keeps the breast medium-rare and the legs well done. For a well-done duck, continue cooking the whole duck at 350 for 1 hour after turning down the temperature.

Nutrition details per serving
Calories 1,400
Percent of calories from fat 72%
Fat: . . . . .111 gm
Protein: . . . . .74 gm
Carbohydrate: . . . . .20 gm
Cholesterol: . . . . .325 mg
Sodium: . . . . .518 mg
Diabetic exchange: 1 fruit, 10 meat, 16 fat.

TOP TURKEY SECRETS

■ *Why it tastes so good:* The tender skin can be roasted to a golden crisp while the meat remains moist and fork-tender. The flavor of the bird is concentrated by the combination of initial high heat, necessary to develop the roasted flavor, and the low-temperature penetration necessary to cook the innermost regions delicately without driving out natural moisture.

■ *Tricks of the trade:* There are a number of important techniques for producing the perfect bird, but the most important is the proper cooking temperature. It is essential to preheat the oven to 425-475 degrees — the hotter the better — and to start the turkey at this temperature for about 45 minutes.

■ *Preparing the turkey of your dreams:* Remove any parts from the cavity and use or discard them. Rinse the bird, inside and out, under cold running

TODAY'S LESSON: Only a few times a year do you cook a bird as big as the traditional roast turkey, so even a good cook doesn't get to practice. I'll show you all the insider tricks for preparing a perfect bird.

water. Pat dry with paper towels. Season the cavity and truss the bird with kitchen twine for even cooking. Rub the skin with butter or olive oil.

■ *Prepare your glaze:* Combine maple syrup and a dark alcohol for the best results. The maple syrup draws the moisture from the skin and helps develop a crisp skin. The brandy, bourbon, scotch or such contains caramelized flavor profiles that enhance the roasted flavor (the alcohol is driven off during cooking).

■ *Prepare your stuffing:* Make your favorite stuffing, but I suggest you bake it in an oven-

proof dish, not the bird's cavity. Filling the bird with stuffing causes irregular heat penetration; the stuffing may never get hot enough to kill bacteria, which may result in food poisoning. Cook your stuffing separately, adding any extra pan juices from the bird to the stuffing for moisture if you wish.

■ *Roast the turkey:* Start the bird at 425-475 degrees for 45 minutes, then lower the temperature to 375 degrees to penetrate and cook the bird thoroughly. Baste the bird with the glaze every 20 minutes or so. Cook until a thermometer inserted into the thickest part

AMAZING FOOD FACTS

■

Most U.S. turkeys are a variety called White Hollands, which have been bred to produce a maximum amount of white meat. Most Americans prefer white turkey meat to dark.

■

Although turkeys can weigh up to 70 pounds, those heavier than 20 pounds are becoming less commonly available. Females usually weigh 8-16 pounds. A fryer-roaster weighs 5-8 pounds. Smaller, more compact turkeys are great for smaller families and for making turkey an everyday food instead of a holiday specialty.

of the thigh reads 160 degrees and the juices run clear; the time will vary by the size of the bird. Remove the turkey from the oven and allow it to rest for about 15 minutes before carving. This allows the internal juices to stabilize.

■

ROAST BREAST OF TURKEY WITH APPLE CIDER

Makes 4 servings

1 turkey breast, boneless with skin on, about 4 pounds
   Salt
   Freshly ground black pepper
1 cup honey
3 cups fresh apple cider, divided
2 cups poultry stock
½ cup red wine vinegar
2 tablespoons unsalted butter (or substitute olive oil)
2 large Granny Smith or good cooking apples, quartered, core

removed, peeled and sliced thin
¼ cup snipped fresh chives

Preheat the oven to 450. Place the turkey breast on a roasting rack in an ovenproof skillet. Season well with salt and pepper. In a small bowl, combine the honey and 1 cup of the cider. Brush the honey-cider mixture over the turkey breast. Place the skillet on the lower rack of the oven and cook for 15 minutes. Lower the oven temperature to 375 and continue to cook, basting the turkey breast with the honey-cider mixture every 15 minutes. Cook until a meat thermometer inserted in the thickest part of the breast reads 170 degrees, about an additional 1-1¼ hours for a 4-pound breast. Remove the skillet and allow the turkey to rest for at least 10 minutes before slicing.

While the turkey is cooking, combine the stock and the remaining 2 cups of cider in a medium saucepan. Bring to a simmer over high heat and cook until reduced to coat the back of a spoon, about 20 minutes. Add the vinegar and cook again until thickened, about 5 minutes. Season with salt and pepper to

taste. Reserve the sauce.

When the turkey is done, heat a large nonstick skillet over high heat. Add the butter and the sliced apples, cooking until the apples are golden, about 8 minutes. Add the sauce to the apples and reduce to coat the apples. If the sauce becomes too thick, add a little water or white wine. Adjust salt and pepper to taste. Stir in half of the chives. Remove from the heat.

Slice the breast against the grain, perpendicular to the length of the breast. Lay the slices on the serving platter. Spoon a little sauce over the turkey and sprinkle with the remaining chives. Serve the remaining sauce in a sauce boat.

Cook's note: If you prefer a paler, softer skin on the turkey, tent the skillet with aluminum foil, dull side out, when the oven is turned down to 375. Continue to baste, but replace the foil tightly after each basting.

Nutrition details per serving
Calories 1,190
Percent of calories from fat 28%
Fat: .36 gm
Protein: . . . . .131 gm
Carbohydrate: . . . . .81 gm
Cholesterol: . . . . .343 mg
Sodium: . . . . .563 mg
Diabetic exchange: 2⅓ fruit, 18½ meat, ⅓ fat.

ROAST TURKEY WITH MAPLE GLAZE, PEARS & BOURBON

Makes 8 servings

1   16-pound turkey
1   tablespoon salt
1   tablespoon freshly ground black pepper
1   tablespoon chopped fresh rosemary
2   tablespoons unsalted butter
1   cup pure maple syrup
¾   cup Markers Mark bourbon, divided
2   cups poultry stock
2   tablespoons butter
8   medium pears, preferably Comice, peeled, cored, sliced into wedges
1   cup Maple-Ginger Butter (see accompanying recipe)

Preheat oven to 475 degrees with rack in the lower third of the oven. Rinse turkey and dry with paper towels. Sprinkle cavity with salt, pepper and rosemary. Truss turkey, then rub the entire skin with butter.

Place turkey in a roasting pan and roast for 45 minutes, breast side up. Reduce temperature to 375 degrees. Combine syrup and ¼ cup of bourbon, and baste turkey with it frequently. Cook until an instant meat thermometer inserted into the thickest part of the thigh reads 160 degrees, about 1½-2 hours. (Start cooking your favorite stuffing about a half hour before the turkey is finished.) Transfer turkey to a heated serving platter.

In a medium saucepan, bring poultry stock to a simmer, cooking until reduced by three-quarters, about 10 minutes.

In a large skillet over high heat, melt butter for the sauce, add pears and saute for 3 minutes. Add stock and the remaining ½ cup of bourbon, cooking until the sauce coats the back of a spoon, about 3 minutes. Whisk in the Maple-Ginger Butter. Remove to a metal bowl, and continue whisking for 1 minute to stabilize before serving. Transfer to a sauce boat. Serve the sauce and turkey immediately.

Nutrition details per serving
Calories 2,162
Percent of calories from fat 39%
Fat: .90 gm
Protein: . . . . .255 gm
Carbohydrate: . . . . .56 gm
Cholesterol: . . . . .876 mg
Sodium: . . . . .1,508 mg
Diabetic exchange: 2 fruit, ¾ fat.

MAPLE-GINGER BUTTER

Makes ¾ cup

¼   cup peeled and diced fresh ginger
¼   cup granulated white sugar
1   cup water
8   tablespoons (1 stick) unsalted butter
¼   cup maple syrup

In a small saucepan, combine the ginger, sugar and water. Bring to a simmer over medium heat and cook until tender, about 30 minutes. Transfer to a blender and puree until smooth. Strain through a medium sieve.

With a mixer, in a small bowl, mix the butter until light. Add the ginger puree and maple syrup, mixing well. This can be made 3 days in advance and stored, covered, in the refrigerator.

Nutrition details per serving
Calories 89
Percent of calories from fat 40%
Fat: . . . . .4 gm
Protein: . . . . .trace
Carbohydrate: . . . . .14 gm
Cholesterol: . . . . .11 mg
Sodium: . . . . .4 mg
Diabetic exchange: ½ bread, ¾ fat.

ROAST TURKEY

Makes 8 servings

1 fresh turkey, about 16 pounds

1 teaspoon salt

1 teaspoon freshly ground black pepper

1 bunch fresh thyme, chopped

4 tablespoons unsalted butter, softened

¼ cup single-malt scotch

1 cup pure maple syrup

1 cup heavy or whipping cream

2 teaspoons grated orange rind

¼ cup coarsely chopped toasted black walnuts or other walnuts

1 teaspoon pure vanilla extract

¼ cup snipped fresh chives

Salt and black pepper to taste

1 bunch thyme, or parsley and chives, for garnish, optional

Ornamental harvest vegetables such as gourds, baby Indian corn and dried chilies, for garnish, optional

2 cups light stock or water, if needed

Preheat oven to 475. Place rack in the lower third of oven.

Remove and discard the giblets from the cavity. Rinse the turkey inside and out under cold running water. Pat dry with paper towels. Sprinkle the cavity with salt, pepper and thyme. Truss the bird with kitchen twine to secure the legs and wings. Rub the entire skin of the bird with butter. Place the turkey, breast side up, on a rack in an ovenproof roasting pan.

In a small bowl, combine scotch and maple syrup. Reserve for basting. Place the turkey in the oven; cook until well seared, about 45 minutes. Reduce temperature to 375 degrees. Baste the breast and the legs of the bird about every 20 minutes with scotch-syrup mixture until all the liquid is used. Continue basting with the pan drippings until the turkey is done. Turkey is done when a meat thermometer inserted in the thickest part of the thigh reads 160 degrees and the juices run clear — about 1½-2 hours. Remove from oven and allow to rest about 15 minutes before carving to allow the juices to settle.

Meanwhile, prepare sauce: Collect the juices from the roasting pan in a clear measuring cup. Remove the fat from the juices and discard. Transfer the juices to a small saucepan and bring to a simmer over medium-high heat. Add the heavy or whipping cream and cook until reduced enough to coat the back of a spoon, about 8 minutes. Add the orange rind, walnuts, vanilla extract and chives, removing pan immediately from the heat. Adjust the seasoning with salt and black pepper to taste. Transfer to a sauce boat and keep warm until serving.

Present the turkey garnished with thyme or parsley and chives, and ornamental harvest vegetables such as gourds, baby Indian corn and dried chilies. Serve the warm sauce on the side to serve over the turkey when carved.

Cook's note: If the roasting pan is dry and no liquids are obtained for the sauce, add 2 cups of light stock or water to the pan and heat if necessary to dissolve the pan drippings, then proceed with the recipe.

Nutrition details per 8-ounce serving with skin and without bone
Calories .755
Percent of calories from fat 49%
Fat: .41 gm
Protein: . . . . .65 gm
Carbohydrate: . . . . .28 gm
Cholesterol: . . . . .243 mg
Sodium: . . . . .467 mg
Diabetic exchange: 8½ lean meat, 1¾ fruit, 4 fat.
Diabetics: Omit maple syrup.

STUFFING WITH STYLE

■ *The basics:* Bread is the backbone of stuffing. High-quality breads of all kinds are now easily available, so isn't it time to replace bland bread cubes with real crusted bread as the basis of your recipe? Then add wild mushrooms, fresh herbs, varieties of onions and maybe even a red pepper or two, which will lend not only flavor but also color. Why not use specialty breads to add flavor? Substitute a combination of whole wheat, black or pumpernickel and a little sourdough for the standard white in your recipe. Other favorite store-bought breads might work well together for your stuffing, but you might want to experiment with the combinations before making a whole batch. I use three of my favorite specialty breads: black walnut, five-onion and rosemary. These breads all have quite distinct flavors that complement one another. To this bread base, I add sauteed onions, wild mushrooms, fresh fennel bulb,

TODAY'S LESSON: Let's play with the basic ingredients of stuffing and polish up some techniques to raise traditional standards. Your stuffing recipe may have gone unchanged for generations in your family. Perhaps this is the only time of year it is made. Or the family recipe may have been replaced with an instant version for convenience.

seasoned stock and fresh chives and sage.

■

WALNUT, ONION & ROSEMARY STUFFING

Makes 8 servings

½ cup olive oil

2 cups diced red onions

2 cups wild mushroom pieces (chanterelles, hedgehogs or cepes)

2 teaspoons salt

1 teaspoon fresh ground black pepper

2 tablespoons chopped fresh rosemary

2 tablespoons chopped fresh sage

2 tablespoons snipped fresh chives

2 tablespoons chopped fresh parsley

1 loaf Walnut Bread (see accompanying recipe), diced and allowed to dry overnight

1 loaf Five-Onion Bread (see accompanying

recipe), diced and allowed to dry overnight

1 loaf Rosemary Bread (see accompanying recipe), diced and allowed to dry overnight

Butter for dish

Poultry stock to moisten

In a large heavy skillet, warm olive oil over medium-high heat. Add onions and saute until soft, about 5 minutes. Add mushrooms and saute until golden, about 6 minutes. Add salt, pepper, rosemary, sage, chives and parsley, and allow to heat through, about 1 minute.

Remove to a large bowl. Mix in the bread and enough stock to moisten the mixture. Transfer to a buttered 12-by-8-by-2-inch baking dish and cover with aluminum foil, shiny side down. Refrigerate until ready to bake. Bake in a preheated 375-degree oven until hot, about 30-45 minutes.

Cook's note: The walnut, five-onion and rosemary breads may be replaced with other nut, onion and herb breads, or with breads of your choice.

Nutrition details per serving
Calories 1,252
Percent of calories from fat 42%
Fat: . . . . .59 gm
Protein: . . . . .29 gm
Carbohydrate: . . . . .158 gm
Cholesterol: . . . . .0 mg
Sodium: . . . . .1,152 mg
Diabetic exchange: 1¾ vegetables, 8¾ bread, 11⅓ fat.

■

ROSEMARY BREAD

Makes 1 small loaf

1 package dry yeast

¼ cup sugar

1 cup lukewarm water (110 degrees)

2½ cups all-purpose flour, sifted

¾ teaspoon salt

½ tablespoon coarsely ground black pepper

¾ cup fresh rosemary

¼ cup extra-virgin olive oil

In a small bowl, combine the yeast, sugar and water.

Allow the yeast to activate and foam.

In a food processor, combine the flour, salt and pepper. Add ½ cup of the rosemary, chopping until very fine. Add the yeast mixture and process until a ball forms; work just until the dough pulls away from the side of the bowl. Add the remaining rosemary and the olive oil. Remove immediately to an oiled bowl, cover with a clean cloth and allow to rise in a warm, draft-free place until double in size. Punch down.

Place a baking stone on the lower rack of the oven and preheat the oven to 400 degrees. Form the dough into a round ball. Cover with a clean cloth and allow to rise in a draft-free place to 1½ times in volume, about 10 minutes. Place on the stone in the oven. Bake for 10 minutes. Reduce heat to 350 degrees and continue to bake until golden, about 25 minutes.

■

FIVE-ONION BREAD

Makes 1 small loaf

1 package dry yeast

¼ cup sugar

1 cup lukewarm water (110 degrees)

¼ cup extra-virgin olive oil, divided

1 cup red onion, diced

1 cup leeks, cleaned and diced

6 cloves fresh garlic, chopped

1 cup scallions, diced

¼ cup snipped fresh chives

4 cups all-purpose flour, sifted

¾ teaspoon salt

½ teaspoon coarsely ground black pepper

In a small bowl, combine the yeast, sugar and water. Allow the yeast to activate and foam.

In a large skillet, heat 2 tablespoons of the olive oil over high heat. Add the onion, leek and garlic, cooking until tender, about 5

minutes. Add the scallions and chives. Remove from the heat and reserve.

In a food processor, combine the flour, salt and pepper. Add 2 cups of the onion mixture, chopping until very fine. Add the yeast mixture and process until a ball forms; work just until the dough pulls away from the side of the bowl. Add the remaining onion mixture and the olive oil.

Remove immediately to an oiled bowl, cover with a clean cloth and allow to rise in a warm, draft-free place until doubled in size. Punch down.

Place a baking stone on the lower rack of the oven and preheat the oven to 400 degrees. Form the dough into a round ball. Cover with a clean cloth and allow to rise in a draft-free place to 1½ times in volume, about 10 minutes. Place on the stone in the oven. Bake for 10 minutes. Reduce heat to 350 degrees and continue to bake until golden, about 25 minutes.

■

WALNUT BREAD

Makes 1 small loaf

1 package dry yeast
¼ cup maple syrup
1½ cups lukewarm water (110 degrees)
2 cups all-purpose flour, sifted
1 cup whole wheat flour, sifted
¾ teaspoon salt
½ teaspoon coarsely ground black pepper
3 cups walnut pieces, divided
2 tablespoons extra-virgin olive oil

In a small bowl, combine the yeast, syrup and water. Allow the yeast to activate and foam.

In a food processor, combine the flours, salt and pepper. Add 2 cups of the walnuts, chopping until fine. Add the yeast mixture and process until a ball forms; work just until the dough pulls away from the side of the bowl. Add the remaining walnuts and the olive oil. Remove immediately to an oiled bowl, cover with a clean cloth and allow to rise in a warm, draft-free place until doubled in size. Punch down.

Place a baking stone on the lower rack of the oven and preheat the oven to 400 degrees. Form the dough into a round ball. Cover with a clean cloth and allow to rise in a draft-free place to 1½ times in volume, about 10 minutes. Place on the stone in the oven. Bake for 10 minutes. Reduce heat to 350 degrees and continue to bake until golden, about 15 minutes.

GET A RISE OUT OF BISCUITS

■ *Why they taste so good:* Biscuits are leavened by baking soda or baking powder. That lets more butter, shortening and flavoring be added to the batter than in a yeast-risen bread. The texture is delicate because of the short mixing time, which does not develop the gluten or resilient texture necessary for yeast-leavened products.

■ *Advantages:* Biscuits are fast and easy. Leftovers such as peppers, scallions, herbs and even onion ends can be added to the batter.

■ *Tricks of the trade:* Start biscuits with chilled butter, shortening and liquid ingredients to produce the most delicate texture. Keep the dough cool while working to slow the development of gluten, which will make the biscuits tough.

■ *Make it rise:* Baking soda and baking powder produce a gas during cooking that causes the biscuits to rise. Baking soda requires an acid such as buttermilk or lemon juice; baking powder requires only moisture and heat. Baking powder is the better all-around choice, but it loses its potency quickly in the cupboard. Check expiration dates.

■ *Prepare flavoring and garnish ingredients:* Flavored biscuits are terrific. They may contain vegetables, herbs, cheeses, spices and even prepared meats. Or they can go sweet with sugar, a shot of vanilla extract and cinnamon or nutmeg.

For variety, divide the recipe into several batches and season each differently.

TODAY'S LESSON: Nothing is as good as a biscuit right from the oven. The light texture and subtle flavor warm your soul, especially on cool autumn evenings.

Vegetables are best diced into small pieces to disperse evenly. Saute or cook the vegetables until tender, since baking time is too short to soften them.

Herbs are best chopped into coarse pieces, then added raw to the dough.

Dry spices may be added to the other dry ingredients, or to the vegetables during cooking.

Meat products such as sausage, ham and prosciutto should be cooked if raw and cut into small pieces before being added to the batter. You may want to compensate for their fat by reducing the amount of butter or shortening.

■ *The mixing begins:* Start by combining the dry ingredients, then cut in butter or shortening until only pea-size pieces remain. If your recipe calls for beaten egg, add it before the liquid ingredients and garnishes. Stir until just combined. Immediately turn onto a floured surface, and knead a few times to ensure an even texture. Roll and cut.

■ *The cooking begins:* Bake on the upper rack of an oven preheated to 400-425 degrees until golden brown, usually no more than 20-25 minutes. Cool on a cake rack a few minutes before serving.

■ *Serving suggestions:* Biscuits are good with just about everything, especially sopping up gravies and cooking juices.

■

ONION, CHEDDAR & CHIVE BISCUITS

Makes 12 biscuits

1   stick unsalted butter (8 tablespoons), divided

1   medium red onion, peeled, ends removed, cut into ¼-inch dice

½   cup sherry vinegar

   Salt to taste

   Freshly grated coarse black pepper to taste

2   cups all-purpose flour

1   tablespoon double-acting baking powder

2   tablespoons sugar

½   teaspoon salt

1   teaspoon black pepper

½   cup snipped fresh chives

1   cup grated sharp aged cheddar cheese

½   cup light cream, half-and-half or ice water

   Additional cream or ice water, optional

In a medium skillet, melt 2 tablespoons butter over high heat. Add onion and cook until tender and slightly brown around edges, about 10 minutes. Add the sherry vinegar and cook until reduced to coat the onions, about 3 minutes. Season with salt and pepper to taste.

In a medium bowl, combine the flour, baking powder, sugar, ½ teaspoon salt and 1 teaspoon black pepper. Cut the remaining 6 tablespoons of butter into the flour mixture until reaching pea-sized pieces. Add the chives, onions, cheddar cheese and cream, mixing until just combined into a ball. If the dough is still crumbling, add 1 tablespoon at a time of cream or ice water until the dough ball forms.

Preheat oven to 400 degrees. Turn the dough onto a floured surface and knead a dozen or so times to make it smooth. Dust the top of the dough ball with additional flour and roll to about ½ inch thick. Cut the biscuits with a floured metal cutter, or use a floured drinking glass. Transfer the biscuits to a greased baking sheet. Gather and press together the scraps, roll and cut additional biscuits. Bake about 20 minutes or until golden.

Remove from the oven to cake rack to cool for at least a few minutes before serving. If allowed to cool, reheat before serving. Store in a sealed zipper-style plastic bag.

Nutrition details per serving
Calories 417
Percent of calories from fat 52%
Fat: . . . . .24 gm
Protein: . . . . .10 gm
Carbohydrate: . . . . .41 gm
Cholesterol: . . . . .69 mg
Sodium: . . . . .315 mg
Diabetic exchange: ¼ vegetable, 2 bread, ¾ meat, 4¼ fat.

CLASSIC CHUTNEYS

■ *What exactly is a chutney?* The name "chutney" comes from the Hindu term meaning "to taste." It originated in India as a preserving process for fruits and vegetables, both as pickles and as a condiment. It is an easy and tasty method of extending the flavors of summer and spicing up a meal.

■ *What's it made of?* Green as well as ripe firm fruit, usually with a vegetable for contrast, is poached until softened, then combined with spices, often spicy hot chili.

■ *Why it tastes so good:* The concentration of the fruit and vegetable juices with a balance of vinegar and sugar provides a very rich flavor which enhances the taste of many foods.

■ *Advantages:* Chutneys perfectly capture the bounty of the season as well as late-maturing fruits and vegetables. Even immature fruits and veg-

TODAY'S LESSON: Chutney, the venerable combination of fruits and savory vegetables framed by spices, can be just as exciting today as it was in the India and Britain of old.

etables become tender and rich in a chutney.

■ *Tricks of the trade:* Blend sweet but firm fruit with green fruit for the best flavor and texture. Cook the spices in the mix to intensify their flavors while minimizing the amount needed.

■ *Selecting your ingredients:* Just about any firm fruit will work. Apples, pears, peaches, mangos, papayas, cherries and melons are just a few. Vegetables such as tomatoes, onions and carrots add flavor and texture. Dried fruits such as raisins, apricots and currants are popular. Nuts such as almonds, walnuts and pista-

chios add interesting texture and flavor.

■ *Spices are nice:* Fresh ginger is chutney's favorite, along with the standard cumin, cloves, nutmeg, allspice and turmeric, which provides the yellow coloring. The heat comes from chili peppers, fresh or dried, as well as peppercorns. The traditional master seasoning is mustard; best is the strong English dry variety or whole toasted seeds.

■ *Preparing your fruit:* Peel, seed as necessary and dice your fruits. Immature green fruits should be diced small or cooked separately to ensure that all the fruit reaches a similar texture, not mush. Vegetables should be cut similarly, although they may be sauteed and softened to allow the flavors to concentrate.

■ *The cooking begins:* There are three techniques for chutney — two traditional and one modern:

Method 1. Combine all the ingredients in a mixture of vinegar and sugar and cook for a few hours until they become tender, highly concentrated and naturally thickened. This method produces a darker, more intense and softer-textured traditional chutney.

Method 2. Cook fruit and vegetables until tender by poaching in a sugar syrup enriched with vinegar. Then mix with a cooked sauce of vinegar, sugar and spices. This method is best for retaining more distinct texture and fruit flavors.

Method 3. Start by sauteing the vegetables, then cook the spices until devel-

oped. Add the fruit, vinegar and sugar, cooking until tender and concentrated, about 15 minutes. This nontraditional technique is the fastest; the chutney is ready to enjoy immediately and is the lightest in color and concentration.

■ *Cool and store:* Transfer the chutney into clean glass containers, process by canning, seal or refrigerate. The flavors will continue to develop under proper conditions for many months to come.

■ *Serving suggestions:* Chutney can be the basis of a substantial meal when served mixed with or over an assortment of grains and vegetables. Over fish, poultry and meat, the pungent rich flavors and tart tones are fulfilling. Chutneys are best served at room temperature or slightly warm to release the full flavors.

■ *Mix and match:* Try mixing multiple fruit and vegetable combinations for an endless assortment of condiments to spark up your favorite foods.

■

PEAR, PAPAYA & SWEET PEPPER CHUTNEY

Makes 1 quart

2 tablespoons olive oil

2 cups large-diced red onions

2 cups large-diced sweet red bell pepper

2 tablespoons fresh ginger root, peeled and diced fine

1 teaspoon dried hot red chili flakes, or to taste

2 teaspoons ground cumin

1 teaspoon ground turmeric, for yellow color

½ teaspoon ground Sichuan pepper

6 large, firm, ripe pears, peeled, cored and diced

1 firm papaya, peeled, seeded and diced

2 cups white wine vinegar

1 cup brown sugar

Salt and freshly ground black pepper to taste

In a skillet large enough to hold all ingredients, heat the olive oil over high heat. Add the onions and cook until they start to become tender, about 4 minutes. Add the diced pepper, ginger, chili flakes, cumin, turmeric and Sichuan pepper, cooking for about 3 minutes. Add the fruit, vinegar and sugar, stirring well to dissolve.

Return to a boil and turn down the heat to maintain a simmer. Cook until the fruit is tender and juices reduced until thickened to coat the back of a spoon.

Remove from the heat, season as necessary with salt and black pepper. Allow to cool, transfer to a clean container, cover and refrigerate.

Serve as a condiment to a grilled, light-flavored, firm fish such as mahimahi.

Nutrition details per serving
Calories .35
Percent of calories from fat 14%
Fat: .6 gm
Protein: . . . . .trace
Carbohydrate: . . . . .8 gm
Cholesterol: . . . . .0 mg
Sodium: . . . . .2 mg
Diabetic exchange: ½ fruit.

THE APPLE
OF YOUR KITCHEN

■ *Multiple personalities:* Cooked apples can be silky with a delicate texture or seared crunchy on the outside with a soft, firm center or left extra crunchy. Go for a texture that accentuates the main ingredient of your dish. For example, for a crunchy breast of duck, choose a technique that will give you a silky or delicate apple. The most common techniques are the following.

For crunchy cooked apples: Saute in a broad skillet or saute pan over high heat. For a crisp texture, add the apples without crowding to a very hot pan with just a touch of canola or corn oil, cooking to lightly brown the edges, about 3-4 minutes. This works best with diced apples, because heat is applied quickly to all the surfaces. You can use sliced apples, but they will need to cook longer for the texture to change from raw to merely crunchy. When done, quickly transfer apples to a strainer. If

TODAY'S LESSON: Apples impart a rich wine tone to duck, pheasant, poultry and the red meats of lamb, beef and game. Apples stand up to sauteing, roasting, grilling and even frying. The firm texture becomes more like a starchy vegetable than a tender fruit.

you don't, the pan juices will soften the crunch.

For tender cooked apples: For a softer-textured apple, sear over high heat to brown the apples slightly, then turn down the heat to allow them to cook thoroughly. Depending on the variety of apple, some juice may be released. The juice can be reduced to just coat the apples, or it can be collected and added to your sauce. If the apples brown too much, even at lower temperatures, add a splash of cider, white wine or water. It will enhance both the silky texture and the flavor.

You can increase the browning by adding maple or granulated sugar. The sugar itself will brown and cling to the apples. Add just 1 tablespoon to a 12-inch saute pan to get the best results. To balance the additional sweetness of the sugar, add 1 or 2 tablespoons of cider or red wine vinegar to the pan in the last few seconds of cooking.

To fry: Fry in wedges or diced in the form of fritters. Select apples with low moisture so the batter stays attached during cooking. High-moisture apples will release their juices and result in soggy batter, which may fall off the apple. The apple wedges or rings should be about ¼ inch thick so they will cook in the same time as the batter. If you want thicker slices, precook by sauteing, then lightly bread and fry. Fry in lighter oils such as canola to allow the natural apple flavor to come through best.

■ *Serving whole apples:* Small apples and edible crab apples are terrific when simply oven-roasted in their skins. They may be served whole, glazed with sauce or dusted with complementary spices in the last minutes of cooking. The whole roasted apple can be cored easily from the bottom, stuffed with a wild mushroom ragout and served with the apple shape preserved. The presentation is a show stopper, and the ragout inside will surprise your guests. Whole apples may be stuffed before baking, but the internal temperature is too low to do much more than warm or melt soft cheese. Stuffings that con-

tain poultry, meat and associated juices should be avoided, because of potential bacterial contamination.

■ *Instead of potatoes:* Apples also can be cut in large wedges, tossed in a little light oil or butter, seasoned with salt, pepper and fresh herbs, then roasted in a 400-degree oven until browned and tender — just like potatoes. Stir occasionally to ensure even browning and cooking. Do not cover with foil or the apples will steam and taste quite boring.

■ *Puree until smooth:* Although savory apples stand on their own, they are great additions to your favorite recipes. Try a puree of celery root and potatoes with applesauce. A puree of apples and a jolt of cider will pick up just about any savory sauce. A compote of seared apple will add flavor and texture to your next gratin or scalloped potatoes. Although not as starchy, apples can go just about anywhere a potato goes. Try a

Popular apples

Type	Origin	Use
Golden Delicious	Virginia, 1916	Eat fresh, bake
Jonathan	New York, 1800	All-purpose
McIntosh	Ontario, 1796	Eat fresh, bake
Red Delicious	Iowa, 1872	Eat fresh, Waldorf salad
Cortland	New York, 1915	Bake, applesauce
Empire	New York, 1966	Eat fresh, bake
Idared	Idaho, 1942	Cook, desserts
Lodi	New York, 1924	Applesauce
Paulared	Michigan, 1967	Eat fresh, bake, sauce
Rome Beauty	Ohio, 1830	Bake
Winesap	N. Y./N.J., before 1800	Bake, cider

Antique apples (19th Century favorites)

Type	Origin	Use
Chenango Strawberry	New York, 1850	Eat fresh, cook
Grimes Golden	Virginia, 1800	Eat fresh
Golden Russet	Unknown, before 1870	Eat fresh, desserts
Northern Spy	New York, 1800	Cook, desserts
Primate	New York, 1840	Cook, desserts
Snow Apple "Fameuse"	France, 1730	Eat fresh
Wealthy	Minnesota, 1860	Applesauce, cook
Wolf River	Wisconsin	Bake
Yellow Transparent	Russia, 1880	Applesauce

few apples in your next pot of leek and potato soup, better known as vichyssoise.

■ *Try your technique:* This autumn, discover the more savory personalties of apples. The flavor combinations are limited only by your imagination.

■

APPLE, POTATO & LEEK SOUP

Makes 8 servings

2 tablespoons unsalted butter (or substitute olive oil), divided.

1 large onion, peeled, ends removed, diced

1 large leek, trimmed, cleaned well and diced

4 large potatoes, peeled, diced

6 large apples, peeled, diced

10 cups poultry stock (or substitute water and 1 bouillon cube), cold

Salt to taste

Freshly ground white pepper to taste

1 lemon, juiced

1 tablespoon superfine sugar (or substitute white granulated)

1 tablespoon cider vinegar

¼ cup fresh snipped chives

In a large pot, melt 1 tablespoon of the butter over high heat. Add the diced onion and leek, cooking until translucent, about 15 minutes. Add the potatoes, all but 2 cups of the diced apples and the cold stock. Season with salt and pepper to taste. Bring to a simmer and cook until tender, testing for doneness by inserting a skewer into the vegetables, about 45 minutes. Pour the soup into a colander over another pot to separate the vegetables and stock.

Ladle the vegetables into a blender or food processor fitted with the metal blade until about half full. Add cooking liquids to cover. Place the lid on the blender and carefully puree until smooth. Pour into a fine sieve and strain into another pot. Repeat with the remainder of the vegetables. Add

more cooking liquids if the soup is too thick, or place the soup over heat and bring to a simmer to cook until thickened to your desired consistency. Season with salt, pepper and lemon juice to taste.

In a medium nonstick pan, heat the remaining butter over high heat. Add the remaining apples, cooking until seared and beginning to brown. Sprinkle the tablespoon of sugar over the apples and continue cooking until golden. Add the vinegar and remove from heat. Set aside for garnish.

Ladle the hot soup into a tureen or serving bowl. Spoon the diced apple garnish into the center of the soup. Garnish the top of the soup with chives.

Nutrition details per serving
Calories 208
Percent of calories from fat 6%
Fat: . . . . .1.5 gm
Protein: . . . . .3.8 gm
Carbohydrate: . . . . .48 gm
Cholesterol: . . . . .2.7 mg
Sodium: . . . . .155 mg
Diabetic exchange: ⅓ vegetable, 1 fruit, 2 bread, ¼ fat.

■

BREAST OF CHICKEN WITH ROASTED APPLES

Makes 4 servings

5 whole small apples

½ cup maple syrup

4½ cups apple cider, divided

1 tablespoon unsalted butter

4 boneless chicken breasts, about 8 ounces each

1 cup poultry or veal stock

2 tablespoons cider vinegar

2 tablespoons Calvados or brandy (or substitute apple cider)

Salt to taste

Freshly ground nutmeg to taste

Pinch of black pepper

¼ cup snipped fresh chives

4 sprigs chives or other fresh herbs as garnish

Preheat oven to 375. In an ovenproof baking dish, place the whole apples standing upright. Combine the maple syrup and 2½ cups of the apple cider and pour over the apples. Bake about 35 minutes, until tender, basting with the liquids about every 15 minutes. Remove and cool enough to handle. Remove the core from the apples with a melon baller.

Transfer the basting juices to a small saucepan and bring to a simmer. Cook until reduced to coat the back of a spoon, about 3 minutes. Spoon the reduced basting juices over the apples to coat. Keep warm while cooking the chicken.

In a large skillet, heat the butter over medium-high heat. Add the chicken, skin side down, and cook until well browned, about 3 minutes. Turn over and cook until browned, about 3 minutes. Add the stock and remaining 2 cups of cider. Reduce the heat to low, cover and let simmer for 10 minutes. Remove the lid and return to a boil. Cook until the liquid thickens to coat the back of a spoon, about 10 minutes. Remove the chicken to a dish and keep warm.

Transfer the liquid from the pan to a blender. Peel 1 apple. Cut into a rough, small dice and add to the blender. Add the vinegar and the Calvados. Season with salt, nutmeg and a generous pinch of black pepper. Carefully place the lid on the blender and slowly puree until smooth. Quickly strain through a fine sieve.

To serve: Position 1 apple on each serving dish. Cut the breast of chicken into thin long slices with a sharp knife. Lay the slices of chicken breast onto the plate, slightly overlapping the apple. Spoon the sauce over the chicken and the apple. Sprinkle chives over the chicken. Garnish the plate with the sprigs of chives and serve.

Nutrition details per serving
Calories 814
Percent of calories from fat 32%
Fat: .30 gm
Protein: . . . . .52 gm
Carbohydrate: . . . . .90 gm
Cholesterol: . . . . .116 mg
Sodium: . . . . .416 mg
Diabetic exchange: 4⅓ fruit, 7 meat, 1⅓ fat.

■

APPLE FRITTERS

Makes 18 fritters

1   tablespoon unsalted butter
1   cup red onion, diced
2   cups apples, cored, peeled, diced
1   tablespoon superfine sugar (or substitute granulated)
¼   teaspoon nutmeg
½   cup chopped scallion greens
2   egg yolks
⅓   cup of low-fat milk
1   cup all-purpose flour
¼   teaspoon salt
2   egg whites, whipped to soft peaks
    Corn oil for frying

In a large nonstick skillet, heat the butter over high heat. Add onions, cooking until translucent, about 5 minutes. Add the apples and sugar, cooking until lightly browned on the edges, about 7 minutes. Transfer to a large bowl. Stir in the nutmeg and the scallion greens. In a medium-size bowl, combine the yolks and the milk, then mix in the flour and salt. Combine with the apples and onion mixture until well coated. Fold in whipped egg whites.

Line baking sheet pans with parchment. Spoon the fritter batter into 2½-inch rounds on the parchment. If the batter is too loose, adjust its texture with additional flour. Freeze until firm, at least 4 hours.

Fill a large skillet with corn oil to a depth of 2 inches. Bring oil to 350 degrees over high heat. Remove the fritters from the parchment, then place directly into the oil. Cook until browned, about 2 minutes. Turn over to finish cooking, about 2 minutes. Remove to drain on paper toweling. Keep warm in a low oven until ready to serve.

Nutrition details per serving
Calories 161
Percent of calories from fat 18%
Fat: . . . . .3 gm
Protein: . . . . .6 gm
Carbohydrate: . . . . .27 gm
Cholesterol: . . . . .75 mg
Sodium: . . . . .124 mg
Diabetic exchange: ⅛ vegetable, ⅜ fruit, 1 bread, ⅓ meat, ½ fat.

ANTIQUE APPLES OFFER UNIQUE TASTE TREATS

AMAZING FOOD FACTS

■

Apples are generally grown at altitudes of less than 600 feet, where summer temperatures are high and rainfall low. Low rainfall prevents the developing apple from being attacked by fungal disease.

■ *What are they?* These lesser-known varieties haven't been commercial hits because of their irregular sizes, shapes and colors, low crop production and delicate handling requirements. And that's too bad, because they commonly have superior flavor and texture.

■ *Advantages:* These apples are most often completely tree-ripened for better flavor as well as higher nutritional content.

■ *My favorite for eating fresh:* The Famous Snow Apple — ancestor of the McIntosh — with its pure white flesh. The Strawberry Chanengo, Pink Pearl, Chieftain, Gala, Holly and Winter Banana are a few other antique varieties that might change your opinion of what a great apple tastes like.

■ *How to store:* Apples are kept at room temperature at the local market and in your favorite fruit bowl. For commercial apples, picked imma-ture and transported to their destinations, keeping them at room temperature helps ripen them. Once ripened, they should be stored in the refrigerator. Local tree-ripened varieties picked at their peak should be refrigerated immediately to preserve them.

■ *How to use:* Lodi or Yellow Transparent, Wolf River, Cortland and Empire are my favorites for sauces and butters. For baking — which requires a variety with flesh that remains firm during the cooking — I like Granny Smith, because of the tart bright flavor. Jonathan, Greening, Northern Spy and Spigold all perform well in pies.

TODAY'S LESSON: In recent years, antique apple varieties have become especially popular, and for good reason.

WHERE TO FIND UNUSUAL APPLES

Applesource, Route 1, Chapin, Ill. 62628; 1-217-245-7589.

Kilcherman Christmas Cove Farm, 11573 N. Kilcherman Rd., Northport, Mich. 49670; 1-616-386-5637.

Tree-Mendus Fruit Farm, East Eureka Road, Eau Claire, Mich. 49111; 1-616-782-7101.

APPLE TART WITH NUTMEG-VANILLA ICE CREAM

Makes 1 10-inch tart

2   tablespoons unsalted butter

1¼ cup sugar, divided

¼   cup fresh lemon juice

½   cup water

½   cup blanched, sliced almonds

8   Greening apples, peeled, cored and cut into ¼-inch slices

½   pound puff pastry (use your recipe, or buy frozen)

Nutmeg-Vanilla Ice Cream (see accompanying recipe)

Mint sprigs to garnish

Preheat the oven to 400. Rub a 10-inch nonstick, ovenproof skillet with butter and set it aside. In a medium-size saucepan, combine 1 cup of sugar, the lemon juice and water. Bring to a simmer over high heat and cook until light caramel in color, or until temperature reaches about 320 on a candy thermometer. Add the almonds and stir to coat. Pour into buttered skillet. Layer the apples over the almond-caramel sauce in the skillet, sprinkling a little of the remaining sugar on each layer. Roll out pastry to ⅛ inch thick. Lay over the apples. Trim the pastry ½ inch from the edge of the skillet. Bake on the lower rack of the oven until pastry is golden, about 30 minutes. Remove from the oven and carefully invert onto a serving platter. To serve, cut into slices, top with a scoop of ice cream and garnish with mint.

Nutrition details per serving
Calories 381
Percent of calories from fat 36%
Fat: . . . . .16 gm
Protein: . . . . .3 gm
Carbohydrate: . . . . .61 gm
Cholesterol: . . . . .4 mg
Sodium: . . . . .233 mg
Diabetic exchange: 1⅓ fruit, ¾ bread, 3 fat.

NUTMEG-VANILLA ICE CREAM

Makes 1 quart

2½ cups half-and-half

1   nutmeg, crushed fine

1   cup sugar

8   large egg yolks
    Pinch of salt

¼   cup vanilla extract

½   cup heavy cream

In a heavy saucepan, bring the half-and-half to just short of a boil, about 185 on a food thermometer. Add the nutmeg. Remove from heat. Let cool completely. Combine the sugar, egg yolks and salt in a medium-size bowl. Stir in the half-and-half mixture, then return to a saucepan. Stir over medium-low heat until thickened to coat the back of a spoon, about 10 minutes; do not boil. Remove from heat and whisk in the vanilla and heavy cream. Strain through a fine sieve. Cover and refrigerate until well chilled. Transfer the custard to an ice cream maker and process according to the manufacturer's instructions. Freeze in a covered container overnight to mellow the flavors. If frozen solid, soften slightly before serving.

Nutrition details per serving
Calories 329
Percent of calories from fat 54%
Fat: . . . . .19 gm
Protein: . . . . .5.3 gm
Carbohydrate: . . . . .31 gm
Cholesterol: . . . . .261 mg
Sodium: . . . . .210 mg
Diabetic exchange: ¼ milk, 1⅓ bread, ½ meat, 3½ fat.

ALL-AMERICAN PIES

■ *Why they taste so good:* Pies capture ripe fruit flavor in a delicately scented, flaky pastry.

■ *Advantages:* Pies use the season's abundant ripe fruit. And while the pastry contains fat, the proportion of fruit filling to crust can result in a smaller fat content than in less satisfying desserts.

■ *The trick to a great pie is the pastry:* Pie pastry should be flaky yet able to maintain the pie shape during cutting and serving. The secret to perfect texture is retarding the development of gluten, which produces the elastic texture observed in bread dough. To limit gluten development, chill flour, butter, lard or shortening and mix ingredients together as quickly as possible. Chill the dough and let it rest before rolling the dough into a crust.

TODAY'S LESSON: Perfect fruit pie.

■ *Choosing ingredients:* For best results, use pastry flour or all-purpose flour.

Fat is very important. It tenderizes the dough by coating the starch granules, keeping gluten from developing, while larger pieces of fat separate layers of dough to provide flakiness.

Unsalted butter is my choice because of its flavor and lower saturated fat content than lard or shortening. It produces a finer, slightly less flaky texture than lard. (You should use less moisture with butter.)

Lard gives the flakiest texture. It has a stronger flavor that's best with robust fruit. It also is higher in saturated fats.

Solid vegetable shortening performs closer to lard with less flavor and similar saturated fat considerations.

■ *Modern tricks:* A food processor cuts preparation time.

Collect all the ingredients. Place the flour and half of the butter, lard or shortening into the processor bowl and combine well, about 10 seconds. Add the remaining butter, lard or shortening and pulse for about 5 seconds to combine less thoroughly than the first mixing. Add water and pulse for 5- 8 seconds. Add more water and pulse briefly as needed until the dough just starts to hold together. Turn the crumbly dough onto a piece of parchment paper or plastic wrap, then press into two rounds about 6 inches or so in diameter. Wrap and refrigerate for about 20 minutes before continuing.

On a floured cool countertop, use a rolling pin to roll the dough for the bottom into a circle, working from the center out. Make it the size of the pie tin, plus about 2 inches. Fold the circle in half and then half again, so you can easily put it in the pie tin. Place the point of the pastry in the center of the tin and unfold. Carefully press the pastry to fill the bottom of the tin, then lift the edges to fill the sides of the tin.

Fill the crust quite full with fruit, since the fruit will condense when cooked. Add any flavoring over the fruit at the last second to prevent the bottom pastry from becoming soggy.

For the top crust, roll out the other pastry circle, fold into quarters and make cuts about 1 inch long for ventilation when cooking. Place atop the pie, unfold and center the pastry. Trim off the excess, and crimp the edges to seal. Brush a mixture of egg yolk and cream over the pastry to glaze. A light dusting of the crust with coarse sugar will make it glisten after it's baked.

■ *The presentation:* A lattice top made from scalloped pastry strips is beautiful, especially over brightly colored fruit fillings. Try different crimping techniques and tools on the edges. Or decorate the top crust with pretty shapes,

such as leaves, cut from extra bits of pastry and attach with the egg wash. Protect them from overbrowning with a little piece of foil.

■ *The baking begins:* Bake the pie on the lower rack of a preheated oven for thorough cooking. Test the filling for doneness with a pastry needle or metal cooking skewer.

Cool on a cake rack. Pies are generally best served warm or at room temperature. Berry and moist fruit fillings are often better when served just slightly chilled to allow the natural texture of the fruit to solidify.

■ *Serving suggestions:* Apple pie with ice cream is the traditional way, but try some new approaches. Frozen yogurt is a lower-fat approach; so is mixing vanilla yogurt with whipped cream. Experiment with different combinations, such as almond ice cream with peach pie, ginger ice cream with apple pie or even rich, dark chocolate sorbet with raspberry pie. Who says pie is boring?

Pie crimping

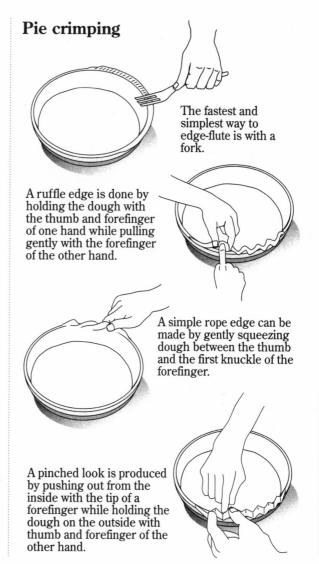

The fastest and simplest way to edge-flute is with a fork.

A ruffle edge is done by holding the dough with the thumb and forefinger of one hand while pulling gently with the forefinger of the other hand.

A simple rope edge can be made by gently squeezing dough between the thumb and the first knuckle of the forefinger.

A pinched look is produced by pushing out from the inside with the tip of a forefinger while holding the dough on the outside with thumb and forefinger of the other hand.

■

APPLE & GINGER PIE

Makes 1 10-inch pie

1 cup unsalted butter (2 sticks), divided

2 cups sifted all-purpose flour

1 teaspoon salt

8-10 tablespoons ice water

2 tablespoons fresh ginger root, shredded fine

2 cups sugar (more if apples are too tart), divided

2 teaspoons ground nutmeg

3 pounds tart Granny Smith Apples, peeled, cored and sliced

1 egg yolk

¼ cup half-and-half or light cream

2 tablespoons coarse granulated sugar

Vanilla ice cream (optional)

Sprigs of fresh mint for garnish

Preheat oven to 425 degrees. In a food processor, combine ½ cup of the butter, the flour and salt, mixing until well incorporated, about 10 seconds. Add ¼ cup more butter, pulsing the processor to achieve a coarser texture, about 5 seconds. Add the water just until the dough begins to form. Transfer and divide the crumbly dough onto two pieces of parchment paper or plastic wrap. Press each into a small circle, wrap and refrigerate for at least 20 minutes before proceeding.

In a small pan, combine the shredded ginger, 1 cup of the sugar and 1 cup of water. Bring to a simmer over medium-high heat, cooking until tender, about 10 minutes. Transfer to a fine sieve and drain. In a small bowl, combine the remaining 1 cup sugar and the nutmeg. Add the ginger mixture, blending well.

Roll the first pastry disk out to ¼ inch thick on a floured counter. Place in a pie tin, allowing the edges to fall over the sides of the tin. Place half of the apples in the pie, then sprinkle with half of the ginger-sugar mixture. Repeat with the remaining apples, sugar mixture and remaining butter.

Roll out the second pastry disk to the same thickness. Fold in half, then half again. Make three cuts, through all the layers, on the two long sides of the wedge of pastry. Place the pastry on top of the apples and unfold. Trim and crimp the edges to seal.

In a small bowl, combine the egg yolk and cream. Brush the top of the pie with the mixture. Cut decorative shapes from the trimmed pastry and arrange atop the center of the pastry. Brush with the egg glaze as well. Sprinkle the top of the pie with the coarse sugar. Position a small piece of aluminum foil over the decorations.

Place the pie on the lower rack of the oven for 15 minutes, then turn the temperature down to 375 degrees and remove the protective foil. Continue baking for 30 minutes or until golden. Cool on a cake rack. Slice and place on serving plates. Scoop ice cream and position next to the pie. Garnish with mint sprig and serve.

Nutrition details per serving
Calories 627
Percent of calories from fat 35%
Fat: . . . . .26 gm
Protein: . . . . .4 gm
Carbohydrate: . . . . .101 gm
Cholesterol: . . . . .92 mg
Sodium: . . . . .275 mg
Diabetic exchange: 1¾ fruit, 1⅓ bread, 4¾ fat.

SEAL AUTUMN FLAVOR INTO BAKED FRUIT

■ *What kinds of fruit can you bake?* Baking is best for firmer fruits, such as apples, pears, bananas, papayas and even peaches, which will maintain their structure as they are cooked. Softer fruits, such as plums, must be handled with more care but still will yield sublime desserts. My favorites are peaches during summer and pears in autumn and winter.

■ *Why they taste so good:* Although the dry heat of baking may dehydrate moist fruits severely, the encompassing heat tends to concentrate all the wonderful ripe flavor.

■ *Advantages:* Baking fruit is easy, clean and fast. It can be done without added fat. The fruit can be baked whole without removing skin or seeds. A splash of wine, vinegar or citrus with a little honey, syrup or sugar makes a quick sauce.

TODAY'S LESSON: Baking is one of the easiest and most gratifying ways to capture the flavor of autumn fruits.

■ *Tricks of the trade*: Leave the skin on and baste with sugar or a light sugar syrup to help seal in the moisture. Basting is critical for peeled fruit, which tends to shrivel up and turn tough.

■ *Pick your pear:* Perfect pears are picked when they're still slightly green; they can finish ripening off the tree to prevent the flesh from turning mealy. Choose pears that are firm but not hard, without cuts, bruises or soft areas. Buy them about 3-6 days before you need them, and ripen them in a paper bag large enough so they won't touch each other. Add an apple to hasten ripening, and cut a few holes in the bag for ventilation.

Store out of direct sunlight at room temperature. Test daily until the pears become supple under light pressure. Some pears will change from a dark green, unripe color to yellow or even bluish-red, but other varieties don't change color at all. Refrigerated pears can hold their just-ripe state for up to 5 days; let the fruit come to room temperature before baking. My personal choice for baking is the softer Comice, but Bartlett, Bosc and Anjou are quite good, too.

■ *Preparing your fruit:* If you prefer fruit without the peel, rub the peeled surface with lemon juice or vinegar to inhibit browning. Then proceed with one of these two methods:

AMAZING FOOD FACTS

■

Mother Nature protected the easily bruised pear by making it better when picked while still hard. Unlike most fruit, it improves both in texture and in flavor after it's picked.

There are more than 5,000 varieties of pears grown throughout the world in temperate climates. France in particular is known for the superior flavor of its pears.

Core the fruit with a small melon baller. The hole can be stuffed with a mix of crushed cookies and other sweet treats. Core most fruits from the bottom to preserve their natural sensuous shape; some juices will escape neatly into your sauce during baking.

Cut the fruit in half lengthwise, remove seeds or stones and bake with the cavity upright for the shortest cooking time. The cavity can be filled with sweets as mentioned above.

■ *The cooking begins:* Place the fruit in a shallow ovenproof pan — not aluminum, which may react with the fruit acids. Place the pan on the lower rack of a preheated 400-degree oven. Begin basting the fruit immediately, and continue basting throughout cooking. Test the fruit with a small metal skewer to judge its heat and the resistance of the flesh. When it's done, the fruit will heat the metal skewer in 60 seconds and the flesh will have little, if any, resistance. Remove the pan to a cake rack to cool.

■ *Quick sauce:* Although the pan basting juices are a sauce in themselves, they may be balanced with acid such as vinegar or citrus if they're too sweet. To enrich the sauce, collect the juices and syrup in a saucepan, add an equal amount of whipping cream and bring to a boil. Reduce the sauce until it's thick enough to coat the back of a spoon. Allow it to cool to room temperature, or chill it for an interesting contrast to the warm fruit.

■ *Serving suggestion:* The natural shape of fruit is gorgeous on the plate, so let simplicity be your guide.

■ *Try your technique* on my favorite, Baked Pears with Honey & Balsamic Vinegar Sauce. The recipe includes a couple of my usual tricks, such as stuffing the pear with Amaretti cookies for an extra surprise.

BAKED PEARS WITH HONEY & BALSAMIC VINEGAR SAUCE

Makes 4 servings

4   large Comice or other baking pears
    Juice of 1 lemon
1   cup crushed Amaretti cookies
2   egg yolks
2   tablespoons light brown sugar
2   tablespoons red wine
1   cup honey
¼   cup balsamic vinegar
1   tablespoon toasted poppy seeds
4   sprigs fresh mint

Preheat oven to 375. Using a melon baller, remove the seed core of the pears through the bottom. Trim the bottom flat to ensure pears will stay upright during baking. Rub all cut surfaces with lemon juice. In a small bowl, combine the crushed cookies, egg yolks, brown sugar and red wine. Divide the mixture and place in the cavity of the pears. Immediately place the pears in an ovenproof baking dish. In another small bowl, combine the honey and vinegar. Pour the mixture over the pears, then place them in the oven on the lower rack. Baste frequently during cooking until tender, about 1 hour for large pears. Add a little water if your basting juices start to become too thick. Remove the dish to a cake rack to cool. To serve, place each pear in the center of a serving plate. Collect the basting juices and transfer to a small saucepan. Reduce the juices over medium heat until thickened enough to coat the back of a spoon. Spoon the juices evenly over the pears. Sprinkle the poppy seeds over the pears and the sauce. Garnish with mint sprigs and serve.

Nutrition details per serving
Calories .444
Percent of calories from fat 9%
Fat: . . . . .4 gm
Protein: . . . . .2 gm
Carbohydrate: . . . . .108 gm
Cholesterol: . . . . .6 mg
Sodium: . . . . .44 mg
Diabetic exchange: ¼ bread, 6¾ fruit, ½ fat.

COMICE PEARS BAKED WITH HONEY

Makes 4 servings

4   large Comice pears
1   cup wildflower honey
½   cup bourbon (or substitute white wine or water)
2   cups whipping cream
3   tablespoons balsamic vinegar
½   cup pistachio nuts, blanched, skinned and toasted
4   sprigs mint

Preheat oven to 400. Place the pears in an ovenproof dish large enough to accommodate them without touching each other. Combine the honey and the bourbon (or substitute) and spoon over the pears. Bake on the lower rack of the oven, basting the pears every 15 minutes with the honey mixture. Cook the pears until they are tender, about 1 hour. Remove the pears to a plate and let cool. Transfer the cooking juices and honey mixture to a saucepan. Add the cream and bring to a simmer over medium-high heat. Cook until thickened to coat the back of a spoon, about 12 minutes. Remove from the heat, add the balsamic vinegar and keep warm until ready to serve.

To serve, position the pear in the center of the serving plate. Spoon the sauce over the pear, sprinkle with the pistachios, garnish with mint and serve.

Nutrition details per serving
Calories 1,012
Percent of calories from fat 49%
Fat: . . . . .57 gm
Protein: . . . . .9 gm
Carbohydrate: . . . . .108 gm
Cholesterol: . . . . .163 mg
Sodium: . . . . .262 mg
Diabetic exchange: 2 fruit, 11 fat.

BUTTER UP
WITH FRUIT

■ *What's a fruit butter?* Fruit butter gets its name from the texture of the puree, which is almost like regular butter. It has different texture and a more concentrated flavor than applesauce.

■ *Why it tastes so good:* Cooking the fruit before adding sugar concentrates the flavor and allows for a creamier texture as the moisture is evaporated. The best butters are enhanced by cooking in cider, which further intensifies the flavor.

■ *Advantages:* Fruit butters can be stored in the refrigerator for as long as 2 months.

■ *Tricks of the trade:* Start preparation by selecting the same or complementary flavor of fruit cider — apple butter with apple cider, for instance. Bring the cider to a boil, cooking until reduced to half before adding fruit.

TODAY'S LESSON: Fruit butters capture the flavors of fall in a spread that can be enjoyed for months to come.

■ *Preparing your fruit:* Select ripe fruit. Slightly overripe fruit will also work well, but avoid any bruised, brown spots. Peel, core or seed, then cut into small pieces for fast, even cooking.

■ *The cooking begins:* Add fruit to the boiling-reduced cider, cooking slowly until tender, about 30-40 minutes depending on fruit. Transfer to a food processor or blender and puree. Pass the puree through a fine sieve and return to another cooking pot.

■ *Sugar and spice make it nice:* Select complementary spices to add a special zing. The most common are cinnamon, nutmeg, vanilla and allspice. Choose whole spices for the least addition of color, and

remove before serving. Ground spices are easy to use but will darken the butter.

Use white, light or dark brown sugar to add flavor and color. Once sugar and spices have been added, slowly simmer 30-45 minutes. Remember to stir often to prevent sticking and scorching.

■ *Seal the flavor in:* Transfer the finished butter to a clean glass jar with a tight-fitting lid. Allow to cool, then refrigerate for up to 2 months.

■ *Serving suggestions:* Treat like jams, preserves and jellies and use on toast and pastry. Fruit butters can also be served with savory dishes, such as apple butter over a grilled pork chop. When making the butter for savory dishes, choose comple-

mentary spices such as green peppercorns and herbs.

■ *Mix and match:* Try blending fruits and flavors such as apples and pears, pumpkin and pears, or peaches and Asian pears. Taste-test the combinations first by tasting slices of fruit with a pinch of the spices or seasonings. If it tastes good raw, it probably will taste great cooked.

■

APPLE-PEAR BUTTER

Makes 1½ quarts

6 cups apple cider

2 pounds ripe apples, peeled, cored and cut in medium dice

2 pounds ripe pears, peeled, cored and cut in medium dice

2½ cups light brown sugar

2 teaspoons ground cinnamon

2 teaspoons freshly grated nutmeg

2 tablespoons pure vanilla extract

¼ cup cognac, optional

In a large, acid-resistant pot, bring the cider to a boil over high heat. Cook until reduced by half, about 10 minutes. Add the diced apples and cook for about 5 minutes. Add the pears and continue cooking the fruit until soft and tender, about 30-40 minutes. Transfer to a food processor and puree until smooth. Transfer to a fine sieve and strain into another acid-resistant pot to finish cooking.

Return the fruit puree to a simmer. Add the sugar, cinnamon and nutmeg, and stir until thoroughly dissolved. Simmer slowly while occasionally stirring to keep from scorching. Cook until very thick, about 30 minutes. Remove from the heat, add the vanilla and, if desired, the cognac. Allow to cool at room temperature. Transfer to a clean glass jar with a good sealing lid. Store under refrigeration for up to a couple of months.

Nutrition details per 1-tablespoon serving
Calories 41
Percent of calories from fat 2%
Fat: . . . . .trace
Protein: . . . . .trace
Carbohydrate: . . . . .10 gm
Cholesterol: . . . . .0 mg
Sodium: . . . . .2 mg
Diabetic exchange: ¾ fruit. Not recommended for diabetics.

PUMPKIN EXALTS SOUPS AND MORE

■ *Why it tastes so good:* Pumpkins mature with a rich deep flavor that overshadows the weaker, lesser cousins of the winter squash family. Slow roasting caramelizes the natural sugars and concentrates that wonderful autumn flavor.

■ *Health advantages:* Pumpkin is rich in vitamin A and potassium, with very few calories.

■ *Which pumpkin is for you?* Larger isn't necessarily better. Maturity is the secret to flavor. Look for a golden pumpkin that makes a good hollow sound when thumped.

■ *When to buy:* Pumpkins disappear after Halloween. Store in a cool, dry, dark spot for up to a couple of months.

■ *Preparation:* The tiny miniature pumpkins are the easiest to open, with a quick slice around the top. Spoon out the few fibers and seeds. Season the interiors and return the top

TODAY'S LESSON: Modern times have stereotyped the pumpkin as a jack-o'-lantern. But the noble pumpkin's talents extend from delicate soup to wonderful vegetable dishes — even to breads and desserts. I'll explore them all with you.

before baking. Medium-sized pumpkins may be prepared just like the little guys.

Medium pumpkins are perfect for serving whole, filled with pumpkin and other starchy vegetable purees, or for pumpkin soup. Cut them into small pieces to use for purees and small garnishes.

For larger pumpkins, start by cutting the top out of the pumpkin as you would for carving a jack-o'-lantern. Then invert the pumpkin and cut the bottom out to remove most of the fibers and seeds. Carefully slice down through the pumpkin to yield long

wedges. Scrape the remaining fibers from the meat and discard.

■ *What do you do with them?* Let's categorize options by cooked textures.

Puree: Soft and sensuous is the only way to describe the flesh after cooking. The puree will spark life into many other dishes as well. Here are a few to get you started.

Soup: Cook the pumpkin pieces in your soup stock and puree along with the other vegetables at the end. Light stocks and flavors of the onion family are very complementary.

Ravioli: Savory pumpkin joined with wild mushrooms, a few shallots and a little cheese will change your life. Pumpkin fillings are a natural for just about any flavor of vegetable- or meat-filled ravioli.

Tamales, polenta and other grains: The pumpkin puree will liven up these simple dishes as well. Add the puree as a portion of the liquid in the recipe.

As a vegetable: The pumpkin puree stands well alone, but it also will lift the simple characteristics of root vegetables such as potato, celery root, turnips and parsnips. Try adding cooked whole cranberries to the pumpkin puree or even sauteed wild mushrooms or other roast vegetables for garnish.

Breads and muffins: Add the puree as part of the moisture in quick breads for a terrific flavor. Muffins and other bat-ter-style baked goods are perfect to show off the rich pumpkin flavor, especially with dried fruits and intense spices. When baking, try replacing the fat in your recipes with pumpkin puree.

Dessert: Pumpkin pie is the most obvious choice, but puree is also perfect for mousse, tarts, cakes and cookies. Jam and preserves are terrific when prepared with the pumpkin puree.

Solid textures: For rich flavor without a bite, cook the pumpkin until tender, but not falling apart. Cook chunks of pumpkin, then cut them into the desired shape and size. You can also cook the chunks until tender and then grill to add a smoky flavor. Try these pieces of pumpkin garnished in salads, pastas, risottos, grains and savory sauces for game. You'll love the subtle flavor and firm texture.

■ *Save the seeds:* Separate the seeds from the fibers and rinse seeds under cold running water until clean. Dry on paper towels for a day or two. Toast by tossing in a little canola oil and season with salt. Spread out over a cookie sheet and toast in a 300-degree oven until golden and crisp, about 20 minutes.

■ *How to prepare:* I prefer baking. The slower, even tempera-

■

In medieval Ireland, beets and turnips were carved into lanterns and placed on gateposts to ward off evil spirits on All Hallow's Eve. When Irish immigrants arrived in the New World, they discovered how easy it was to scoop out and carve the plump, soft-centered pumpkin.

ture is easy to control and concentrates the flavor. Boiling cooks swiftly, but the pumpkin flesh tends to absorb the water and the flavor gets dissipated. Steaming works better than boiling, but there is less caramelized flavor.

■ *What about microwaving?* Generally, pumpkins cook pretty well in the microwave. Tent them with plastic wrap, and be sure to add additional moisture, such as water, to the container holding the pumpkin chunks. The liquid will help steam the pumpkin as well as help prevent the flesh from drying out. Small, whole pumpkins cook well with moisture added to the cavity and the lid replaced to trap the steam inside. Be careful when removing the lid after cooking because there may be a blast of steam.

■

SWEET PIE PASTRY

Makes enough for 1 pie

2 cups all-purpose flour, sifted

½ cup granulated sugar

1 cup butter, cut into marble-sized pieces

2 egg yolks

¼ cup half-and-half

In a food processor, combine the flour and sugar. Add the butter and pulse until cut into the flour. In another bowl, whip together the yolks and half-and-half until smooth. Slowly add the egg mixture to the food processor. Pulse the processor to just get the pastry to combine. Remove the pastry to a parchment-lined cookie sheet and flatten the dough into a rectangle. Cover with plastic wrap and refrigerate for at least 2 hours. To roll, remove dough from the refrigerator and place on a cool, floured countertop.

Roll the dough to ¼ inch thick and cut to fit your desired pie tin. Proceed with your favorite pie recipe.

Nutrition details per serving
Calories 387
Percent of calories from fat 58%
Fat: . . . . .25 gm
Protein: . . . . .4 gm
Carbohydrate: . . . . .36 gm
Cholesterol: . . . . .118 mg
Sodium: . . . . .240 mg
Diabetic exchange: 1½ bread, 5 fat.

■

PUMPKIN-PECAN PIE WITH NUTMEG & CINNAMON

Makes 1 10-inch pie

1 Sweet Pie Pastry recipe (see accompanying recipe)

⅓ cup granulated white sugar

1 cup water

½ lemon, juiced

1 cup light corn syrup

¼ cup light rum

¼ cup unsalted butter

3 eggs

⅓ cup brown sugar

1 teaspoon freshly ground nutmeg

1 teaspoon ground cinnamon

¾ cup pumpkin puree

2½ cups pecans

4 sprigs mint for garnish

Vanilla ice cream

Preheat the oven to 350. Roll out the pastry dough and press into the pie tin. Crimp the edges. In a heavy saucepan, combine the granulated sugar, 1 cup of water and the lemon juice. Cook over high heat to dark caramel, or about 350 degrees on a candy thermometer. Add the corn syrup, mixing well. Add the rum and the butter and cook for 2 minutes. Remove the pan from the heat.

In a bowl, combine the eggs, brown sugar, nutmeg and cinnamon. Slowly add the syrup from the pan while constantly whisking.

In another bowl, combine the pumpkin and the egg and syrup mixture, stirring until homogeneous. Pour the filling into the bottom of the pie tin. Arrange the pecans evenly over the top. Bake on the middle rack of the oven until the filling is set and the pie is golden, about 45 minutes. Remove to cake rack until solid, about 4 hours. Cut, garnish with mint and serve with vanilla ice cream.

Nutrition details per serving
Calories 516
Percent of calories from fat 52%
Fat: .31 gm
Protein: . . . . .5 gm
Carbohydrate: . . . . .55 gm
Cholesterol: . . . . .87 mg
Sodium: . . . . .110 mg
Diabetic exchange: ⅓ meat, 5¾ fat.

■

PUMPKIN & SHALLOT SOUP

Makes 8 servings

2   tablespoons unsalted butter

2   cups sliced shallots

2   pounds cleaned pumpkin meat

2   cups diced parsnips, peeled

8   cups light vegetable or poultry stock

1   teaspoon nutmeg
    Salt and freshly ground black pepper to taste

1   cup snipped fresh chives

¼   cup toasted hazelnuts, chopped coarse

In a large pot, melt the butter over medium-high heat. Add the shallots, cooking until translucent, about 5 minutes. Add the pumpkin and parsnips, cooking until lightly browned, about 10 minutes. Add the stock and bring to a simmer. Cook until the pumpkin and the parsnips are tender, about 30 minutes.

Working in batches, puree the vegetables in a blender. Strain through a medium sieve into a saucepan to remove any remaining fibers. Season with nutmeg, salt and a generous dose of black pepper. Add the chives. Serve by ladling into warm bowls. Garnish with hazelnuts sprinkled across the top and serve.

Nutrition details per serving
Calories 175
Percent of calories from fat 35%
Fat: . . . . .7 gm
Protein: . . . . .8 gm
Carbohydrate: . . . . .22 gm
Cholesterol: . . . . .8 mg
Sodium: . . . . .797 mg
Diabetic exchange: 2 vegetable, 1 bread, 1 fat.

■

PUMPKIN, CRANBERRY & BLACK WALNUT BREAD

Makes 2 loaves, 18 half-inch slices per loaf

12 ounces fresh cranberries

4   cups sugar, divided

2   cups water
    Butter for preparing loaf pans

2½ cups all-purpose flour

2   cups whole wheat flour

1   tablespoon baking powder

1   teaspoon baking soda

4   eggs

2   cups pumpkin puree

1   teaspoon salt

½   pound unsalted butter, softened at room temperature

4   cups black walnut pieces

1   egg yolk mixed with ¼ cup light cream for glaze

In a medium saucepan combine the cranberries, 2

cups of the sugar and 2 cups of water, bringing to a simmer over medium-high heat. Cook until tender and sweet, about 15 minutes. Drain.

Preheat oven to 350 degrees. Butter two 9-by-5-inch loaf pans. Sift the flours, remaining sugar, baking powder and soda together into a large bowl. Combine the eggs, pumpkin and salt in another bowl. Add the moist ingredients into the dry, mixing until smooth. Mix in the butter, 1 tablespoon at a time. Add the cranberries and the walnuts.

Divide the batter between pans and smooth the tops with a spatula. Brush the loaves with the egg yolk-cream glaze and bake until golden brown, about 45 minutes. Invert onto cake racks and allow to cool before slicing.

Nutrition details per one ½-inch slice serving
Calories 294
Percent of calories from fat 46%
Fat: .15 gm
Protein: . . . . .5 gm
Carbohydrate: . . . . .38 gm
Cholesterol: . . . . .47 mg
Sodium: . . . . .155 mg
Diabetic exchange: 1½ fruit, 1 bread, 2¾ fat. Not recommended for diabetics.

Indians living
in the
mountains of
Mexico
cultivated the
forerunner
of the pumpkin
some 7,000
years ago.

PUMPKIN, MAPLE & GINGER PIE

Makes 8 servings

Pastry:

2   cups all-purpose flour, sifted

½   cup granulated sugar

1   cup butter, cut into marble-size pieces

2   egg yolks

¼   cup half-and-half

Filling:

2   cups Fresh Pumpkin Puree (see accompanying recipe)

¼   cup Ginger Puree (see recipe on page 112)

1   cup pure maple syrup

3   eggs, beaten

1   teaspoon ground cinnamon

½   cup maple sugar (or substitute granulated sugar)

Sprigs of mint for garnish

Vanilla ice cream or frozen yogurt, optional

To prepare pastry: In a food processor, combine flour and sugar. Add butter and pulse until cut into the flour.

In another bowl, whip together the egg yolks and half-and-half until smooth. Slowly add the egg mixture to the food processor. Pulse the processor just to get the pastry to combine. Remove the pastry to a parchment-lined baking sheet and pat the dough into a thick rectangle. Cover with plastic wrap and refrigerate for at least 2 hours.

Preheat oven to 350 degrees. Grease a 10-inch pie pan. Remove pastry dough from refrigerator. Place on a cool, floured work surface. Roll dough to ¼ inch thick and press into a greased 10-inch pie pan; crimp edges.

To prepare filling: In a medium bowl, combine pumpkin puree, ginger puree, maple syrup, eggs and cinnamon; stir until smooth. Pour the filling into the prepared pie shell. Bake on the middle rack of the oven until the filling is set and the pie crust is golden, about 45 minutes. Remove to a cake rack to cool until solid, about 4 hours.

To serve: Fold aluminum foil around the top edge of the pie crust to shield against the heat. Sprinkle the top of the pie with maple sugar. Place the pie under the broiler, heating until

the sugar caramelizes, about 2 minutes. Remove the foil. Cut the pie into 8 wedges, garnish with mint and ice cream or yogurt if desired.

Cook's note: The sugar may be caramelized on the top of the pie by using a creme brulee iron as well.

Nutrition details per serving
Calories 636
Percent of calories from fat 38%
Fat: .27 gm
Protein: . . . . .8 gm
Carbohydrate: . . . . .93 gm
Cholesterol: . . . . .198 mg
Sodium: . . . . .276 mg
Diabetic exchange: ½ vegetable, 3¼ bread, ¾ meat, 5¼ fat.

FRESH PUMPKIN PUREE

Makes 4 cups

1   small to medium pumpkin

¼   cup granulated sugar, optional

1   cup water

Preheat oven to 400 degrees. Cut the top and bottom off the pumpkin. Cut down through the sides of the pumpkin to make large wedges. With the edge of a spoon, scrape the fibers and seeds from the pumpkin flesh. Transfer the pumpkin to an ovenproof dish, flesh side up. Sprinkle with sugar if desired. Add 1 cup water to the dish and place on the lower rack of the oven. Bake until tender, about 30 minutes. Remove from oven; let it sit until cool enough to handle.

Scoop the pumpkin flesh from the rind and place in a food processor. Puree until smooth. Strain through a coarse sieve to remove remaining fibers. If the puree is very loose and wet, transfer to a nonstick skillet and heat until simmering over medium-high heat. Cook until thick like mashed potatoes.

■

GRILLED MUSHROOM & PUMPKIN RAGOUT

Makes 4 appetizer servings

½ pound pumpkin meat, peeled

1 cup water

¾ pound wild mushrooms, such as portobellos or chanterelles, sliced

¼ cup extra-virgin olive oil

2 cloves garlic, minced

Salt and freshly ground black pepper

3 tablespoons balsamic vinegar

¼ cup chopped fresh parsley

Preheat oven to 350 degrees. Place pumpkin in an oven-proof dish with 1 cup water and bake until tender but not mushy, about 15 minutes. Remove from oven and allow to cool. Preheat grill or broiler.

In a medium bowl, combine the mushrooms, olive oil, garlic and the cooled pumpkin, mixing to coat evenly. Remove pumpkin slices and place on the grill. Allow to cook until seared well, about 4 minutes. Turn over and repeat until warm, about 4 minutes. Remove to a cutting board and cut into large dice. Transfer to a bowl.

Put the mushrooms on the grill and cook until seared, about 3 minutes. Turn them, cooking until done, about 1 minute. Add to the pumpkin bowl. Season with salt and pepper to taste. Add the vinegar and parsley, tossing to combine evenly. Divide into the center of serving plates and serve.

■

Pumpkin plants produce male and female flowers. Bees transfer pollen from the male to the female blossoms, which develop into pumpkins.

THE SWEET SIDE OF WINTER SQUASH

AMAZING FOOD FACTS

■

Red Kuri has a squat shape, like a spinning top. It is deep reddish-orange outside and deep yellow-orange inside, like the curry spice blend.

■

Buttercup usually has a flattened round shape with a beanie top in both deep green and orange.

■ *Why they taste so good:* My favorites are the Red Kuri, Buttercup, Kabocha, Turbans and the fun miniature pumpkins masquerading as Jack-Be-Littles and Munchkins. These squashes are much deeper in flavor than some of the more common varieties. They have compact, rich flesh that enables the cook to go beyond the standard preparation of pureeing.

■ *Advantages:* Winter squashes are high in vitamins and potassium.

■ *Add a little spice:* Winter squashes are complemented by nutmeg, mace, cinnamon or maple sugar. The more exotic flavors of ginger, cardamom, vanilla and even roasted chili peppers in the form of paprika also work well.
 Because the sweet flavor of the squash can become a little flat, splash on a little acid — wine or a few drops of a good balsamic, sherry or cider vine-

TODAY'S LESSON: When many people think of squash, they think mostly of the common butternut and acorn varieties that are so widely available. But winter squashes come in 300 edible and ornamental varieties to tease the senses of sight, smell and taste.

gar. Use acids sparingly; they should remain undetectable.

■ *How to cook:* Winter squashes often are just pureed. Instead, cook the squash until just about done, still slightly firm but not falling apart. Remove the skin, dice, then saute to finish with other vegetables and seasonings for a perfect side dish or vegetable stuffing. Or cook, peel and grill the squash for a smoky flavor, then add to your favorite salad or entree.

■ *Mix and match:* Winter squash is terrific in many other

dishes, such as vegetable risotto, pastas, chowders and breads. Pumpkin bread is the base for my favorite Thanksgiving turkey stuffing. Winter squash also is terrific in baked custards, creme brulees, creme anglaise sauces, ice creams and, of course, pies, tarts and flans. The flavor of pumpkin is a natural with caramelized sugars, gingers and other sweet spices when balanced by a few drops of lemon juice.

RED KURI & GINGER CREME BRULEE

Makes 8 servings

1½ cups fresh ginger, peeled, diced

½ cup fresh lemon juice, plus 2 tablespoons, divided

2 tablespoons granulated sugar

2 cups heavy cream

½ cup half-and-half

10 large egg yolks

½ cup superfine sugar

1 tablespoon vanilla extract

¾ cup Red Kuri squash (or other favorite squash), cooked and pureed

¼ cup light brown sugar

To make ginger puree: In a small saucepan, combine diced ginger, ½ cup of the lemon juice and granulated sugar. Bring to a boil, lower to simmer and cook until tender, about 30 minutes. Cool slightly.

Transfer mixture to a blender or food processor fitted with the metal blade and puree until smooth. Strain. Makes 1 cup. Reserve 1 tablespoon for recipe. Store remainder in a tightly covered container in the refrigerator for up to 1 month. Can be used in other recipes, including baking and sauces.

To make creme brulee: Preheat the oven to 300 degrees. In a medium-size saucepan, heat the cream and half-and-half over medium heat until just below the boiling point. Remove from the heat and set aside.

In a large mixing bowl, combine the egg yolks, superfine sugar and vanilla; beat rapidly with a wire whisk until light and fluffy. Slowly add the hot cream, pureed squash and 1 tablespoon of the ginger puree while continuing to whisk until smooth. Add the remaining 2 tablespoons of lemon juice. Strain through a fine sieve. Fill custard dishes to ¼ inch below the top edge.

Place the custard cups in a 9-by-13 pan. Carefully fill the pan with water to within ¼ inch of the custard cup rims. Place pan in the lower third of the oven. Cook until lightly tanned on top and a skewer inserted into the center is hot to the touch, about 15-20 minutes. Remove to a cake rack and allow to cool. Cover with plastic wrap and chill for at least 8 hours before serving.

At serving time, preheat the broiler.

Evenly divide the brown sugar across the tops of the custards. Place the custards under the broiler, allowing the tops to caramelize but not burn. (A brulee iron also works well; preheat it until white-hot for the best effect.) Allow to cool for several minutes before serving.

Nutrition details per serving
Calories 407
Percent of calories from fat 66%
Fat: .30 gm
Protein: . . . . .6 gm
Carbohydrate: . . . . .30 gm
Cholesterol: . . . . .353 mg
Sodium: . . . . .42 mg
Diabetic exchange: ⅜ vegetable, ½ meat, 5⅓ fat.

Kabocha is a very large Japanese variety, usually orange.

Turban squash is named for its shape, a low rounded body with a smaller extended cap. It has a variety of different colorations and a creamy, mild flesh.

The miniature Jack-Be-Littles and Munchkins range from golden yellow to deep orange.

WINTER

AMAZING FOOD FACTS

■

The volatile oils in orange skin are extremely flammable, as demonstrated by twisting an orange peel near an open flame.

■

People who are near orange trees in bloom can have adverse respiratory reactions.

ORANGES: MORE THAN JUST JUICE

■ *Where do they come from?* Florida is the largest producer of oranges and their hybrids. California oranges are thicker-skinned to protect against a drier climate. That's an easy way to identify the source of the fruit.

■ *Health advantages:* The juice, though high in vitamin C, contains only 25 percent of the fruit's total vitamins. The peel and albedo (white section between the skin and the inner fruit) are much higher in vita-min concentrations.

■ *Variety of uses:* The juice is great for satisfying a winter thirst, but it also has many cooking applications. Reduce the juice, concentrating its acidic qualities, and you've got a flavorful marinade to replace vinegar in your favorite dress-ing. In fact, since orange juice vinaigrette is less tart than vinegar, you'll need less salad oil to balance the flavors, mak-ing a vibrant dressing that is

TODAY'S LESSON: Oranges add a bright burst of citrus flavor while replacing heavy sauces and high-calorie seasoning agents. And we're talking more than just juice.

lower in fat. You can also use reduced orange juice blended with a little reduced stock as a sauce for meat.

■ *How to peel:* The orange seg-ments may be removed easily by cutting the skin and albedo from the inner orange with a knife. Slice into the segment with the knife blade parallel to the dividing membranes on both sides of the section to release the clean fruit. Squeeze the remaining membranes after the segments are removed to capture all of the orange value.

■ *How to store:* Keep citrus fruit under mild refrigeration or in a cool, well-ventilated area. Very

cold refrigeration can produce brown spots on the skin (it won't hurt the taste), so keep oranges in the vegetable crisper. Do not store in plastic bags, which trap moisture that promotes the growth of mold. Refrigerate the segments in juice to ensure they stay plump and rich. Segments — an ele-gant, colorful addition to just about any dish — are perfect for garnishing a salad or a dessert.

■ *Cooking oranges?* In heated preparations, add the segments at the last second to just warm but not cook them, to preserve that fresh flavor.

■ *Tricks of the trade:* One of the tricks in cooking with oranges is figuring out how many to buy to produce the amount of juice or segments called for in a recipe. Here's my rule of thumb: Three medium oranges produce 1 cup of juice; two produce 1 cup of bite-size pieces; 1 produces 10 segments. Each orange will produce 4 teaspoons of grated rind, 1 tablespoon of fine zest.

■ *Use the skin, too:* The skin is the most underused part of the orange. It can be substituted for lemon in espresso and as seasoning for milks and creams. It also makes a great candy. Candied orange rind is my favorite snack candy, with its slight sweet tinge followed by a pure orange punch. Just blanch a large julienne of orange rinds to soften, then bury in granulated sugar. The zest, or fine strips of rind, is great to spark the flavor of muffins and sweet baked pastries. It's also terrific in sauces and hot preparations.

■

ORANGE, RED ONION & WINTER GREENS SALAD

Makes 4 servings

1 cup fresh orange juice

2 tablespoons red wine vinegar

¼ cup extra-virgin olive oil

¼ cup snipped fresh chives

Salt to taste

Coarsely ground fresh black pepper

2 large heads Belgian endive

2 bunches watercress, lower third of stems removed

2 small heads baby frisee, cut into bite-size pieces, about 3 cups (or substi-tute young curly endive)

1 small red onion, finely julienned

4 large oranges, separated into segments

In a small saucepan, bring the orange juice to a simmer over medium-high heat, cooking until reduced to ¼ cup. Remove and allow to cool to room temperature. In a small bowl, combine the reduced orange juice, vinegar, olive oil and chives. Season to taste with salt and pepper. Remove the larger outer leaves of the Belgian endive and arrange about 6 leaves outward on the serving plates. Cut the remaining endive into bite-size pieces. In a medium-size bowl, combine the bite-size Belgian endive, watercress, baby frisee, onion and orange segments. Add the dressing and toss. Distribute the salad mixture in the center of the endive.

```
Nutrition details per serving
Calories . . . . . . . . . . . . . . . . . . . .266
Percent of calories from fat . . . . . . .45%
Fat: . . . . . . . . . . . . . . . . . . . . . .14 gm
Protein: . . . . . . . . . . . . . . . . . . .4 gm
Carbohydrate: . . . . . . . . . . . . . .35 gm
Cholesterol: . . . . . . . . . . . . . . . .0 mg
Sodium: . . . . . . . . . . . . . . . . .289 mg
Diabetic exchange: ⅛ vegetable, 1¾ fruit,
2¾ fat.
```

■

Excessive contact with the volatile oils in orange peel can produce dermatitis. People who eat orange rinds often suffer skin irritation around the mouth.

■

Sawdust from the wood of orange trees is used to polish jewelry.

MINESTRONE IS A HEARTY MEAL

■ *What is minestrone?* Minestrone is Italy's traditional vegetable soup. It is made with a minimum of three different vegetables and cooked until it shouts of combined rich flavors.

■ *Why it tastes so good:* Minestrone combines lots of vegetables in ways that create a rich, full-bodied, satisfying flavor. Usually, sweet root vegetables are balanced with bitter greens. The starches help to thicken the soup slightly while absorbing all the wonderful flavors of the vegetables and seasonings.

■ *Tricks of the trade:* In most recipes, the vegetables are first sauteed, or at least sweated, to release their liquids, concentrate their flavors and caramelize their sugars. This step is crucial. Without it, the soup will taste just like boiled vegetable water.

■ *Preparing your vegetables:* Start with a couple of members of

TODAY'S LESSON: Let's unlock the secrets to one of the best vegetable soups in the world, minestrone.

the onion family, such as garlic, shallots, leeks, scallions and, of course, sweet onions. Sweeter vegetables such as carrots, fennel and celery will round out the base flavors. Then come the garnishes of zucchini, summer squash, winter squash, tomatoes and peppers. Add leafy vegetables such as savoy cabbage, spinach, kale, radicchio, endive, chicory and escarole. Choose your starches from pasta, beans — whether fresh or dried — rice, dumplings or potatoes. Finally, herbs will establish the style of minestrone you are making. Basil, chives and summer savory are the sweeter summer group; fennel greens, parsley, rosemary and oregano make up the winter group.

Clean, trim and cut all the vegetables into medium to

small dice. Cut leafy greens into chiffonade or a julienne cut. Pick herbs from their stems.

■ *The cooking begins:* Start by heating a little olive oil in the soup pot over medium-high heat. Add the onion-family vegetables and cook until golden. Next add the sweet vegetables, cooking until they start to brown as well. Then add the hearty garnishes and leafy greens and cook just until they begin to wilt. Add light stock, broth or water and bring to a simmer. Add half the herbs and reserve the rest to finish the soup just before serving. Cook for about 3 hours to develop the flavor, but do not add any more liquid. Cook the beans, pasta, potatoes, dumplings and rice separately until al dente. Add to the soup when just about finished.

■ *Finishing the minestrone:*
Seasoning the minestrone with a little salt and a generous shot of freshly ground black pepper will round out the flavors. The remaining herbs are added into the hot soup just before serving.

■ *Serving suggestions:*
Minestrone is best enjoyed in a large, flat-rimmed soup bowl in order to fascinate the eye and excite the palate with varied colors and shapes. A little Parmesan and great olive oil may be offered to each guest's own taste.

■

WINTER VEGETABLE MINESTRONE

Makes 16 servings

½ cup olive oil

4 cloves garlic, peeled, ends removed, finely minced

2 large onions, peeled, ends removed, diced

1 large carrot, peeled, ends removed, diced

1 bulb fennel, trimmed and diced, optional; reserve the greens

½ pound spinach, stems trimmed, well washed, dried, julienned

1 small head kale, washed, trimmed, julienned

1 cup flat leaf parsley, washed, dried, chopped, divided

1 cup chopped fennel greens (from the fennel above), divided

6 quarts vegetable stock

Sea or granulated salt to taste

Freshly ground black pepper to taste

1 medium celery root, washed, ends removed, peeled, diced

4 medium parsnips, washed, ends removed, peeled, diced

1 small butternut squash, peeled, seeded and diced

1 medium head radicchio, washed, dried, core trimmed and julienned

¼ pound dried red lentils, rinsed, sorted

½ pound stelline (star-shaped) pasta, or substitute another small pasta

½ cup Parmesan cheese, grated

Crusty peasant bread

In a large soup pot, heat olive oil over medium-high heat. Add the garlic and cook, stirring, until golden, about 3 minutes. Add the onions and cook until browned, about 5 minutes. Add the carrot and the fennel bulb, cooking until they begin to brown, about 5 minutes. Add the spinach, kale, ½ cup parsley, ½ cup fennel greens, cooking until they wilt, about 3 minutes. Add the vegetable stock and bring to a boil over high heat, adjusting the temperature to a slow, even simmer. Season with a little sea salt or granulated salt and black pepper. Cook for 1 hour.

Add the celery root, parsnips and butternut squash, and cook for 30 minutes. Add the radicchio and the red lentils and continue cooking for another 15 minutes.

Meanwhile, bring a medium pot of water to a boil. Season with salt and add the pasta. Cook until al dente, about 4-8 minutes depending on the variety you have chosen. Transfer to a colander and drain. Rinse under warm running water. Allow to drain.

When the lentils are tender, add the pasta and the remaining ½ cup parsley and ½ cup fennel greens. Adjust the seasonings with salt and pepper. Serve with Parmesan cheese on the side and crusty peasant bread.

Nutrition details per serving
Calories 235
Percent of calories from fat 31%
Fat: . . . . .8 gm
Protein: . . . . .9 gm
Carbohydrate: . . . . .30 gm
Cholesterol: . . . . .2 mg
Sodium: . . . . .92 mg
Diabetic exchange: ¼ medium-fat meat, 1¾ vegetable, 1½ bread, 1¼ fat.

GET TO THE ROOT OF SOUP

TODAY'S LESSON: With the cold weather setting in, it's time for soup, especially my personal favorites, those made with the root vegetables of potato, parsnip, celery root and sweet potato.

■ *Is it difficult?* Root vegetable soups are some of the most elegant and easiest soups to prepare. These cooked vegetables can thicken a soup naturally. That eliminates the need for a messy and high-fat roux (cooked flour and butter) or corn or arrowroot starch thickeners. Blended with members of the onion family, root vegetables puree to a wonderful silky texture that doesn't need a drop of cream. Their earthy flavors satisfy your soul and fortify your spirit against the chill of winter.

■ *Why it tastes so good:* Potatoes, parsnips, celery root and sweet potatoes are at their best — sweeter and more full-flavored — after a frost. Slow cooking in a soup concentrates their flavors.

■ *How to select and store:* Select firm roots that show no signs of rot, mold or slime. Store potatoes in a cool, dry and well-ventilated area and the parsnips and celery root in the refrigerator.

■ *How to prepare:* All root vegetables should be peeled and evenly diced for cooking in a soup. The smaller the dice, the faster the cooking time.

■ *The cooking begins:* Start your soup by sauteing onions, leeks or shallots until translucent. Add the roots of your choice, cover with cold stock or use water with a bouillon cube. Bring to a simmer over high heat, then turn the temperature down to a slow simmer. Cook until all the vegetables are very tender, almost falling apart. Drain the vegetables in a colander, reserving the liquid.

Place some of the vegetables in a blender and add enough of the cooking liquids to puree until smooth. Repeat with the remaining ingredients. Strain through a fine sieve to achieve the best texture.

■ *Add a splash of color:* Colorful garnishes are also attractive. A little puree of sweet red pepper or green scallions will make your soup look like you slaved all day. After finishing the soup, return 1 hot cup to the blender, add a roasted and cleaned red pepper or trimmed scallion greens, and puree until smooth. Reserve the garnish until serving.

■ *Too thick or thin?* If the soup is too thick, add additional cooking liquids, stock or water. If the soup is too thin, return it to the stove and simmer until the excess moisture is eliminated. Season with salt, freshly ground pepper and herbs of your choice.

■ *Presentation is everything:* To present the soup, ladle it into a bowl or terrine, and top with a swirl of the brightly colored scallion and/or pepper puree. Add the fried garnish, and prepare for applause!

■

PARSNIP & POTATO SOUP

Makes 8-10 servings

2   tablespoons unsalted butter (or substitute olive oil)

1   large onion, ends removed, peeled, diced

6   large parsnips, peeled and cut into 1-inch dice

3   large potatoes, peeled and cut into 1-inch dice

10 cups poultry stock (or substitute water and 1 bouillon cube)

    Salt to taste

    Freshly ground white pepper to taste

2   lemons, juiced, to taste

1   bunch scallion greens, white base removed

1   red bell pepper, roasted, peeled, seeded and diced

4   cups all-purpose flour

2   tablespoons mild paprika

1   small red onion, peeled and sliced paper thin

    Canola or corn oil for frying

In a large soup pot, melt the butter over high heat. Add the diced onion and cook until translucent, about 10 minutes. Add the parsnips, potatoes and stock. Season with salt and pepper to taste. Bring to a simmer, and cook until tender, about 30 minutes, testing for doneness by inserting a skewer in the vegetables. Pour the soup into a colander over another soup pot to separate the vegetables and stock. Ladle the vegetables into a blender until about half full. Add the cooking liquids to cover. Place the lid on the blender, and carefully puree until smooth. Pour into a fine sieve, and strain into another pot. Repeat with the remainder of the vegetables. Add more cooking liquids if soup is too thick, or place soup over heat and bring to a simmer to cook until thickened to desired consistency. Season with salt, pepper and lemon juice to taste.

For garnishes: Ladle 1 cup of hot finished soup into the blender with the scallion greens. Puree until smooth, adding a little cooking liquid as necessary. Set aside. Repeat the same technique with the red pepper, and reserve. In a medium bowl, sift together the flour and the paprika. Add the thinly sliced onions, and mix well to completely coat all the surfaces of the onions. Let sit for about half an hour, occasionally mixing the onions to ensure an even coating. Shake the excess flour from the onions, and transfer to a cookie sheet. Fill a deep skillet with canola oil to a depth of 2 inches. Heat to 360 as indicated by a fryer thermometer. Add a quarter of the onions to the skillet; cook until golden, about 2-3 minutes. Remove onions from the oil to a plate lined with paper towel. Repeat with the remaining onions in batches.

To serve: Return the soup to a simmer. Ladle the soup into the serving bowls or terrines. Decoratively spoon the green scallion and red pepper purees across the top of the soup for a festive holiday look. Top with the fried onions, or serve them on the side.

Cook's note: The soup may be made up to 3 days before serving, but garnishes are best made the same day as serving. For simplicity, the soup also may be garnished with just the diced chives and/or peppers. The colors are great, and it takes less time.

Nutrition details per serving
Calories 385
Percent of calories from fat 5%
Fat: . . . . .2 gm
Protein: . . . . .9 gm
Carbohydrate: . . . . .84 gm
Cholesterol: . . . . .2 mg
Sodium: . . . . .135 mg
Diabetic exchange: 4⅙ vegetables, 3⅔ bread, ¼ fat.

FIND EARTHY FLAVOR IN WINTER GREENS

■ *What are winter greens?* Winter greens include a couple of groups: the leafy kind, such as spinach, broccoli rabe, purslane, kale, turnip and collard greens; and the more compact Belgian endive and radicchio.

■ *Why they taste so good:* The cooler growing temperatures cause slow, concentrated growth that is full of earthy rich flavor — strong enough to handle spicy dressings and splashes of bright vinegar along with garnishes of smoky fish and meats.

■ *Health advantages:* Winter greens are very high in vitamins C and E and many mineral concentrations.

■ *How do you prepare them?* Try spinach, Belgian endive and radicchio in salads. The rest of the greens are pretty rough on the palate when served raw. The coarser greens are best warmed and wilted, or cooked.

TODAY'S LESSON: Winter greens flourish in cool temperatures. Although they can make a substantial salad, the coarser texture is best tamed by wilting in warm salads or cooking.

Here are the best techniques for cooking:

Warm salads are made by cooking the garnishes, adding the dressing until hot, then pouring over the greens to mix. The hot dressing wilts even the toughest greens, rendering them soft and silky.

Boiling will convert most greens to a tender texture similar to that of cooked spinach. Boil the water, then pour the hot water over the greens. The greens should be in a large pot that is not being heated. Stir until tender and cooked, about 1 minute. Drain in a colander, squeeze out excess water, season and serve. The drawback to

boiling is the loss of vitamins, minerals and some flavor.

Sauteing the leafy greens is terrific for capturing all the flavor and nutrition. In a large nonstick skillet, heat olive oil or butter until warm. Add the greens, cooking until tender and juices just coat the leaves. This method works great on broccoli rabe, which tends to become very bitter when cooked in water. You can turn these sauteed greens into a meal by adding cooked pasta and a few other meat or vegetable garnishes. Just toss and serve.

Braising works best on compact heads of greens such as

radicchio and Belgian endive. Split the heads if they are very large. Place in a pan. Cover with vegetable stock, season well, cover with both aluminum foil and a lid, cooking until tender in a 375-degree oven. The braised vegetables may be served with a splash of lively vinaigrette as a room-temperature appetizer or as an accompanying vegetable to any main course. The braising seems to sweeten the flavor and turn the texture silky. Braising is very popular in Europe but is not pursued here because of the slightly longer preparation time.

Grilling has come into vogue in recent years and is best with tight heads, which prevent the leaves from burning up. Use Belgian endive or radicchio cut into quarters or eighths, tossed in olive oil and seasonings. Place directly on the grill. Cook until slightly

browned before turning over. Avoid flame-ups, which will give greens a burnt flavor. Cook until al dente or tender, splash with a bright vinaigrette and a few herbs, and serve. The hearty combination of the

earthy and smoky flavors is perfect for a cool winter day.

■ *Tricks of the trade:* Soaking in water makes radicchio, endive and broccoli rabe bitter, so clean only by rinsing under

running cold water. Even though the greens have coarse leaves, they quickly decline just like more tender lettuces, so select the freshest and use them quickly.

■ *Seasonings:* Try fuller flavors of stronger vinegars, smoky bacon or pancetta, mustards, pronounced peppercorns and spices to highlight the greens' earthy flavor. Stronger smoked fish and meats, game birds and red meats along with wild mushrooms and members of the onion family are great garnishes.

■ *Try your technique:* Fire up that grill or cheat with your broiler on Grilled Endive, Radicchio & Mushroom Salad to try these new flavors.

■
Winter greens are usually higher than summer greens in concentration of vitamins, which are essential to balance your winter diet.

GRILLED ENDIVE, RADICCHIO & MUSHROOM SALAD

Makes 4 servings

4   heads Belgian endive, cut into quarters lengthwise, washed, dried

1   head radicchio, cut into quarters, washed, dried

½   pound wild mushrooms, such as portobellos or shiitakes, stems trimmed and cut into large bite-size pieces, cleaned

½   cup virgin olive oil

4   cloves garlic, peeled, ends removed, finely minced

    Sea salt to taste

    Freshly ground black pepper to taste

¼   cup flat parsley leaves, washed, dried

3   tablespoons balsamic vinegar (or substitute aged red wine vinegar)

2   tablespoons grained mustard

4   large paper-thin slices Parmesan cheese, optional

Preheat grill or broiler. In a large bowl, combine endive, radicchio, mushrooms, olive oil and garlic. Mix well to combine. Season with sea salt and a generous dose of black pepper. Lay the endive together on the grill and repeat with the radicchio and mushrooms so that they will cook evenly. Cook until they are golden and begin to become tender, about 3 minutes. Turn over the pieces of endive and radicchio while mixing up the mushrooms to finish cooking until tender on the remaining side, about 3 minutes. As the vegetables become tender, transfer back to the bowl. When all are cooked, add the parsley into the bowl and toss. In a small bowl, combine the vinegar and the mustard, mixing until combined. Add to the bowl of grilled vegetables and toss to combine. Adjust the seasonings as necessary with salt and pepper to taste. Artistically distribute the vegetables on serving plates. Top with the shaved Parmesan cheese and serve.

Nutrition details per serving
Calories 237
Percent of calories from fat 59%
Fat: . . . . .15 gm
Protein: . . . . .9 gm
Carbohydrate: . . . . .22 gm
Cholesterol: . . . . .0 mg
Sodium: . . . . .222 mg
Diabetic exchange: 4 vegetable, 3 fat.

BEANS STAND OUT IN CHILI AND SOUP

TODAY'S LESSON: Legumes are among humanity's earliest cultivated plants. The family members are principally the lentil, the pea, the chickpea, the broad bean, the mung, the soy and the common bean. The flavor of black beans is so rich that it is a star of soups, vegetable stews and chilies — without the meat or poultry stocks often needed to prop up other types of beans.

■ *Where do they come from?* The common bean *(Phaseolus vulgaris)* is native to southern Mexico and has been cultivated for 7,000 years. It adapted well to different climates and spread easily into all areas of South and North America.

■ *How many varieties are there?* The common bean was developed into hundreds of varieties, among them navy, pinto, kidney, black turtle, pink and the black-eyed pea. Recently, more unusual bean varieties with variegated colors and different textures have been introduced. Examples are the cranberry bean, yellow eye and, my friend even in name, the rattlesnake bean.

■ *A native Michigander:* The Michigan legume crop is the largest in the nation, at more than 55 million pounds a year. Our most famous are the white navy bean and the wonderful black turtle bean. The Saginaw Valley and Thumb account for the largest production.

■ *Health advantages:* Beans are about 22 percent protein, 60 percent carbohydrates and 1-2 percent fat, and are high in iron and vitamin B.

■ *How to select:* Choose beans that are plump, not wrinkled. Smell to detect any odd odors. If you're buying from a bulk container, check the cleanliness of the beans and look for weed chaff and small stones.

■ *How to prepare:* Beans take a considerable time to cook. Soak them overnight in your refrigerator (or up to 48 hours) to soften and shorten cooking time. Or, if you're in a hurry, add 1 cup beans to 3 cups boiling liquid. Return to a simmer for 2 minutes, then turn off the heat and allow the beans

The gas-producing molecules can be reduced by soaking the beans, rinsing before cooking and boiling in large amounts of liquid. Large amounts of water will dilute them but will also dilute the nutritious elements.

to soak for 1 hour before beginning your recipe.

■ *The cooking begins:* Drain the excess soaking liquid, then rinse under cold running water, place them in a large pot and cover with fresh liquid. Add about 1 tablespoon salt per pound of beans. Chilies or hot peppers will add a nice glow. Add other spices to your own taste. To hasten the cooking, add ½ teaspoon baking soda for every quart of water. Any more than that, however, and you could get a bland taste. Do not add any type of acidic seasonings such as vinegar, citrus juice or salsas before or while cooking. The acids will reinforce the hard texture, and the beans won't cook properly. Add acids only when they're at the desired texture. If you are using the beans as a garnish, cook the beans separately until tender and then add to the finished soup or chili. The beans will not continue to soften. When properly seasoned, bring beans to a simmer and cook until tender. Use a "flame tamer" or burner insulator after reaching a simmer to help prevent scorching.

Occasionally stir the pot to prevent beans from sticking to the bottom and scorching. Add more liquid as necessary to keep the beans covered. Excess liquid can always be removed. The beans need liquids to cook and soften, so more liquid is better than less.

■ *Tricks of the trade:* Bring the beans to a simmer in an oven-proof pot or skillet, then place them on the lower rack of an oven preheated to 350 degrees, and bake until tender. The even heat of the oven prevents scorching and develops a tender texture. Add a little vinegar to spark up the flavor and lock in the perfect texture.

■ *Plan ahead:* If you're so inclined, by all means make beans ahead. Cooled and refrigerated overnight, their flavor develops even more depth.

VEGETABLE BLACK BEAN CHILI

Makes 12-16 servings

½ pound dried black turtle beans, soaked and drained

2-3 quarts water

2 tablespoons virgin olive oil

2 cups diced onions

1 tablespoon dried chili powder

2 large dried pasilla chilies or peppers (or substitute hot peppers of your choice), optional

1 tablespoon salt

Freshly ground black pepper to taste

4 cloves garlic, roasted, minced (see roasting directions on next page)

¼ cup fresh lime juice

2 cups fresh corn kernels (or substitute frozen corn, but thaw before adding to the chili)

½ cup low-fat sour cream or yogurt

½ cup grated sharp cheddar cheese

½ cup snipped fresh
scallion greens

Place beans in a large pot and cover with 2-3 quarts water. Soak overnight. Drain. Or bring water and beans to a boil, reduce heat and simmer for 2 minutes. Allow to soak 1 hour. Drain. In a large pot over high heat, add the olive oil and the onions, sauteing until tender, about 3 minutes. Add the chili powder and cook for 1 minute. Add the beans and the pasillas or hot peppers. Fill the pot with cold water until the beans are covered by 1 inch. Add 1 tablespoon salt and black pepper to taste. Bring to a simmer, reduce heat to medium and cook until the beans are tender, about 1½-2 hours. Remove the pasillas or hot peppers. Stir in the garlic and lime juice. Adjust the salt and pepper to taste if necessary. Add the corn and cook until hot, about 3 minutes. Ladle into warm bowls. Top with low-fat sour cream or yogurt, cheddar cheese and scallion greens. Serve immediately.

To roast garlic: Preheat oven to 400. Coat the out-

side of a whole or partial head of garlic with olive or corn oil and place it in an ovenproof skillet. Roast on the lower rack of the oven until the skin is brown and the garlic is tender, about 30-60 minutes. Set aside to cool.

Roasted garlic, which has a mild flavor, can be spread on crusty bread as an appetizer or refrigerated for up to 3 days and used in any recipe that calls for garlic.

Nutrition details per serving
Calories .67
Percent of calories from fat 25%
Fat: . . . . .2 gm
Protein: . . . . .2 gm
Carbohydrate: . . . . .11 gm
Cholesterol: . . . . .0 mg
Sodium: . . . . .412 mg
Diabetic exchange: ⅜ vegetable, ½ bread, ⅓ fat.

■

NAVY BEAN SOUP WITH SHALLOTS & PARMESAN

Makes 16 servings

2 tablespoons virgin olive oil

2 cups diced shallots

1 bulb fresh fennel, trimmed and julienned (optional); trim and chop fennel greens and reserve for garnish

1 pound dried navy beans, soaked in water overnight and drained

16 cups cold poultry stock (or water with good bouillon cubes, but reduce salt in recipe)

1 smoked ham hock (optional)

1 tablespoon salt
Freshly ground black pepper to taste

½ cup balsamic vinegar

4 cloves garlic, roasted and minced

½ cup snipped fresh chives (or substitute scallion greens)

½ cup grated Parmesan cheese

Heat the olive oil in a large pot over high heat, and saute the shallots and fennel until tender, about 3 minutes. Add the beans, stock and ham hock. Add 1 tablespoon salt and pepper to taste. Bring to a simmer, reduce heat to medium and cook until the beans are tender, about 3½-4 hours. Remove the ham hock, then stir in the vinegar and garlic. Adjust the salt and pepper to taste if necessary. Remove from heat and stir in the fennel greens and chives. Ladle into warm bowls, top with Parmesan and serve immediately.

Nutrition details per serving
Calories 88
Percent of calories from fat 28%
Fat: .2.8 gm
Protein: . . . . .4 gm
Carbohydrate: . . . . .12 gm
Cholesterol: . . . . .2.5 mg
Sodium: . . . . .474 mg
Diabetic exchange: ½ vegetable, ⅜ bread, ¼ meat, ⅜ fat.

AMAZING FOOD FACTS

■

In the Middle East, couscous is cooked to a texture that will enable a loose ball to be formed so that it can easily be eaten with the right hand.

COUSCOUS IS A COMFORT FOOD

■ *What it is:* "Couscous" is the name of the national dish of Morocco and of the tender grains of coarse wheat used in it. The wheat is steamed and served with vegetable or meat stew.

■ *Where it comes from:* Many variations are found in Tunisia, Algeria and much of the Middle East. Each incorporates the natural foods and products of the different regions. Couscous is an integral part of the fabric of these rich cultures. Most supermarkets carry couscous as a regular staple, usually in the specialty food section.

■ *Why does it taste so good?* The traditional Moroccan couscous is best described as combining the spice of chili with the sweetness of onions and raisins in such a balanced way that the meats, vegetables and grains mesh in perfect harmony.

TODAY'S LESSON: Grains are an important part of a balanced diet, providing fiber, minerals, protein and carbohydrates. Enjoy the best grain the world has to offer — couscous.

■ *How to cook:* To cook couscous as a side dish, heat olive oil in a heavy, shallow skillet over medium-high heat. Add the dry grains and cook until hot, about 3 minutes. Turn off the heat, add hot stock or broth and stir to saturate. Allow to steep and plump, letting sit until thoroughly cool. Break up the clumps with your hands or a whisk. Reheat by steaming or sauteing in olive oil. Spices such as turmeric, paprika, chili powder and saffron enhance the nutty grain flavor. Mix them well into the stock to make sure they disperse throughout the couscous when cooked. Vegetables such as sweet peppers, mushrooms, scallions, onions, fennel and

garlic are best finely diced and sauteed in the olive oil before adding to the couscous when it is reheated. Add fresh herbs after reheating so they will retain their fresh flavors. Be sure to choose your vegetables, spices and herbs to complement the main course.

■ *Serving suggestions:* The dish is very adaptable into everyday menus as a complete meal or a side dish. The coarse semolina wheat can be cooked by the traditional steaming method or handled like a rice pilaf.

FAST CRACKED SPICY WHEAT (COUSCOUS) PILAF

Makes 8 servings

4   cups boiling Vegetable Stock (see accompanying recipe)
1   tablespoon paprika
1   teaspoon turmeric powder
    Salt and pepper to taste
¼   cup olive oil
½   cup shallots, peeled and diced
1   large red pepper, peeled, seeded and diced
1   large green pepper, peeled, seeded and diced
1   box couscous (approximately 15-17 ounces)
1   cup diced scallion greens

In a medium saucepan, bring the vegetable stock to a boil. Add the paprika, turmeric and any other spices of your choosing. Season with salt and pepper to taste. Keep simmering on low. In a large heavy skillet, heat the olive oil over medium heat. Add shallots, cooking until translucent, about 5 minutes. Add the peppers, cooking for just 1 minute. Turn heat to high and add couscous. Stir until coated with olive oil and very hot. Remove the skillet from the heat. Add the seasoned stock and stir to distribute the liquid. Allow the grain to absorb the stock and swell until no liquid remains, about 5 minutes. Stir the scallions into the pilaf. Season again with salt and pepper as necessary. Keep warm until serving.

Nutrition details per serving
Calories .392
Percent of calories from fat 17%
Fat: . . . . .8 gm
Protein: . . . . .9 gm
Carbohydrate: . . . . .58 gm
Cholesterol: . . . . .0 mg
Sodium: . . . . .46 mg
Diabetic exchange: 2⅓ vegetabless, 2¾ bread, 1⅓ fat.

VEGETABLE STOCK

Makes about 10 cups

2   large leeks, cleaned of sand, diced
2   large onions, diced
1   cup shallots, chopped
1   large carrot, diced
1   celery root, peeled and diced
12 cups (or more) water
3   cups dry white wine
1   bunch parsley stems
2   bay leaves
2   tablespoons whole black peppercorns

Combine the vegetables with the water and wine in a stock pot. Bring to a simmer, skimming the surfaces occasionally. Add the parsley stems, bay leaves and peppercorns. Return to a simmer, cooking for 4 hours, adding more water if necessary to keep the ingredients covered. Strain. Refrigerate for up to 3 days or freeze for up to 1 month.

Nutrition details per serving
Calories 99
Percent of calories from fat 2%
Fat: . . . . 0.2 gm
Protein: . . . . .2 gm
Carbohydrate: . . . . .12 gm
Cholesterol: . . . . .0 mg
Sodium: . . . . .63 mg
Diabetic exchange: 1½ vegetabless, ¼ meat.

Couscous is traditionally made with millet flour, but it may also be made with crushed rice and other North African grains.

LENTILS FOR SOUPS AND SALADS

■

Lentils are about 25 percent protein — similar to many leaner cuts of red meat. Lentils are 60 percent carbohydrates and only 1 percent fat.

■ *Where do they come from?* They originated in southwestern Asia and quickly spread throughout the Middle East, into Egypt, India and Asia, finally reaching central Europe by the Bronze Age. Today, the largest consumer of lentils is India, with more than 50 varieties cultivated there. Lentils — latecomers to this country, arriving in 1916 — are produced in eastern Washington and northern Idaho. The lentil is an annual plant that grows to 20 inches tall in a bush-like shape. Small pods that grow from the branches contain one or two edible seeds.

■ *How many varieties are there?* The two varieties produced in the United States are the yellow Chilean, which is tan to brown, and the coral-colored Red Chief. Smaller red varieties are grown in Egypt and the Middle East. Green lentils are usually found in eastern Europe and other cooler climates.

TODAY'S LESSON: Lentils were one of the first crops to be cultivated, as early as 7000 B.C. They are still important as a versatile starch, a base for soup or stew and a salad nutrient.

■ *What do they taste like?* Lentils have an earthy but plain taste, like other beans. Add acids such as vinegar, citrus or wine to brighten the flavors; add herbs and spices to build depth of flavor. Remember, adding acid to the lentils will reinforce their textures, keeping them firmer to the bite. Add these ingredients after your optimum texture has been reached.

■ *How to cook:* There are two ways to cook lentils. The first is to soak the lentils overnight. Soaking softens the lentils, and some of the skins float to the surface for easy removal. The soaked lentils are rinsed, covered with water, brought to a simmer, then cooked until tender, about 25 minutes. I prefer to soak first because it saves time when preparing the rest of the meal. The second approach is to add the dried lentils to water and simmer until tender, about 1 hour — about twice as long as cooking soaked lentils. But this is still less cooking time than for other legumes.

■ *How to use lentils:* Lentils are most commonly used for soups. They are cooked until tender, pureed, usually in a blender, strained and served. Straining removes the indigestible skin and refines the soup's texture. The soup may be served with a whole lentil garnish by reserving a quarter of the lentils when just softened. Puree the remaining lentils, then add to your seasoned soup base. This gives you the best of both textures — the whole lentil and the silky puree. Lentil purees can be made by following the directions for soup, but puree with less moisture than the recipe calls for. Adding diced potatoes (up to half the volume of the lentils) when you begin simmering will let you prepare a delicate lentil-scented potato puree. Enrich with butter, olive oil or such nut oils as walnut or hazelnut. Garnish with herbs and serve as the starch in your meal.

■ *Serving suggestions:* My favorite use for lentils is in salads. Simmer the lentils just until tender, then drain. Mix them with your favorite vinegar, such as balsamic, and enrich with a splash of olive oil. Season with salt, black pepper and fresh herbs. A little roast garlic or fresh sweet onion can be terrific. This salad is perfect as

is, or you can mix in some of the heartier greens of winter, such as endive, radicchio, watercress and baby mustard. The coarser greens will enhance the delicate texture of the lentil. Serve as an appetizer, salad or side dish. A lentil salad is especially wonderful with smoked meats, fish and terrines or pates.

■

LENTIL & WINTER GREEN SALAD

Makes 4 servings

¼ pound red lentils, soaked in water overnight and drained (or mix and match lentil colors)

1 large onion, quartered

½ cup balsamic vinegar or sherry vinegar

1¼ teaspoons salt

¾ teaspoon freshly ground black pepper

½ cup virgin olive oil

2 tablespoons snipped fresh thyme, optional

½ cup snipped fresh scallion greens

Salt and pepper to taste

3 cups bite-sized pieces of mixed winter greens, such as radicchio, Belgian endive or romaine

¼ cup finely grated Parmesan cheese

In a medium-size saucepan, combine the lentils and onion. Cover

with salted water and bring to a boil over medium-high heat. Reduce the heat to low and simmer until the lentils are tender, about 25 minutes. Remove the onion and discard. Drain the lentils and let cool. In a medium-size bowl, combine the lentils, vinegar, salt, pepper and olive oil. Add the thyme and scallions. Add more salt and pepper to your own taste. Add the greens and toss to combine. Distribute to serving plates. Garnish with Parmesan cheese and serve.

Nutrition details per serving
Calories 356
Percent of calories from fat 73%
Fat: . . . . .29 gm
Protein: . . . . .6 gm
Carbohydrate: . . . . .19 gm
Cholesterol: . . . . .5 mg
Sodium: . . . . .794 mg
Diabetic exchange: ⅛ vegetable, ⅜ bread, ⅓ meat, 5⅔ fat.

INVITE A LOBSTER TO DINNER

AMAZING FOOD FACTS

■

Lobsters take about seven years to grow to a weight of 1 pound. It takes another four years to grow each additional pound.

■ *Why it tastes so good:* Lobsters shed their hard exterior shells every spring. This makes them mushy during the summer and early autumn. Late autumn and winter lobsters are at their prime, with hard shells full of tender meat.

■ *Select your lobster:* The freshest lobsters are the best. Select lively, fresh lobsters with rockhard shells from very cold water tanks. Big lobsters look like a feast, but 1- to 1½-pound lobsters are more tender.

■ *Choose your technique:* To boil, steam, broil or bake?

Boiling in salt water is best for instant heat penetration. Fill a very large stock pot with water and bring to a rapid boil. Add a good shot of salt, more than you think you should. It will seem salty but will prevent the lobster from losing natural salt. The salt will not penetrate the shell.

TODAY'S LESSON: What could be better during the holidays than a tender, sweet and delicate lobster?

Add lobsters, cover with a lid and return to a boil. Cook for about 7-8 minutes per pound. Serve by cutting in half lengthwise, removing the sand sack located near the mouth and the intestinal tract and cracking the claws. Garnish with herbs and serve with drawn butter and lemon.

Steaming over boiling salted water cooks the lobster in its own juices since water does not leak into the shell. Steaming is best done in a large vessel where there is enough steam to cook the lobsters quickly and thoroughly. Carefully place lobsters in a steamer, cover and cook 8 minutes per pound. Allow a couple of additional minutes per pound if you are cooking several lobsters. Serve as for boiled lobster.

Broiling produces the firmest and driest flesh. Cut the lobsters in half lengthwise, remove the sand sack and intestinal tract and crack the claws. Position lobsters cut side up, dust with bread crumbs or seasonings and add a little butter or olive oil. Broil until firm, 7-8 minutes.

Baking can be accomplished at a high heat of 450 degrees, similar to broiling, or very slowly at 350 degrees. Prepare the lobster as you would for broiling and cook on the lower rack of the oven. Cooking time is 10-12 minutes per pound at high temperature, 15-18 minutes at low temperature.

1 tablespoon grated lemon rind

3 cups heavy cream
   Salt to taste

4 1¼- to 1½-pound lobsters

¼ cup snipped fresh chives

2 ounces sturgeon caviar, Beluga or Sevruga grade
   Freshly ground black pepper

4 sprigs fresh herbs for garnish

Choose a stock pot large enough for all of the lobsters and fill to ¾ capacity with water. Cover and bring to a simmer over high heat. Meanwhile, in a large saucepan, melt the butter over medium-high heat. Add shallots and cook until translucent, about 4 minutes. Add white wine and lemon juice, cooking until reduced to ¼ cup, about 5 minutes. Add lemon rind and cream; cook until reduced to coat the back of a spoon, about 8 minutes. Transfer to a fine sieve, strain into a clean saucepan and reserve. Add salt to the stock pot for the lobsters. Add lobsters, cover and return to a

■ *How about cooking lobster just for the meat?* Boil lobsters for about 4 minutes per pound, then remove to a colander and allow to cool at room temperature. Split the lobster, remove meat from the tail, claws and arms. Finish cooking in sauce or gently reheat in melted butter.

■ *Try your technique:* For an elegant holiday lobster dish, try Maine Lobster with Citrus & Caviar Sauce.

■

MAINE LOBSTER WITH CITRUS & CAVIAR SAUCE

Makes 4 servings

2 tablespoons unsalted butter

¾ cup shallots, peeled, ends removed, minced

2 cups dry white wine

½ cup freshly squeezed lemon juice

boil. Start timing when water returns to a boil. Cook about 7 minutes per pound (about 9 minutes for the 1¼-pounders and 10½ minutes for the 1½-pounders). Carefully remove lobsters with tongs and transfer to a colander to drain. Allow to cool slightly before cutting. Return the sauce to a simmer. Remove from the heat and stir in chives and caviar. Adjust the seasonings with black pepper and salt if necessary. Transfer to a sauce boat and keep warm. Cut lobsters in half lengthwise. Remove and discard the sand sack found in the mouth area and the intestinal tract. Crack claws and arms with a mallet or cleaver. Position the lobster in the center of the plate with claws and arms on either side. Garnish with herbs. Spoon a little sauce over the tail meat and serve the remainder in a sauce boat on the side. Serve immediately.

Cook's note: This is a very elegant sauce and is well presented with meat removed from the shell and mixed with the sauce. To do this, cook lobsters about 4 min-

utes per pound, remove to a colander and allow to cool. Split the lobsters and extract the meat from the shell and claws. To serve, combine the meat with the sauce base, heating until cooked through, about 3 minutes. Finish the sauce with chives, caviar and seasonings.

Nutrition details per serving
Calories 719
Percent of calories from fat 67%
Fat: . . . . .54 gm
Protein: . . . . .42 gm
Carbohydrate: . . . . .15 gm
Cholesterol: . . . . .386 mg
Sodium: . . . . .910 mg
Diabetic exchange: ¼ milk, 3¾ lean meat, ¾ vegetable, ½ fruit, 10 fat.

■

BROILED LOBSTER WITH ALMONDS & CHIVES

Makes 4 servings

¼ cup fresh lemon juice

½ teaspoon salt

¼ cup extra-virgin olive oil

¼ cup melted unsalted butter (or substitute additional olive oil)

½ cup snipped fresh chives (or substitute scallion greens)

Tabasco or cayenne pepper to taste

¼ cup minced toasted almonds

¼ cup plain bread crumbs

1 tablespoon paprika

4 1½-pound live lobsters, halved lengthwise, with sand sack and intestinal tract removed

4 lemon halves, ornately cut

4 sprigs chives (or substitute scallions)

In a small bowl, combine the lemon juice and salt. Slowly whisk in the olive oil and melted butter in a thin stream. Add the chives and adjust the Tabasco to your taste. In a food processor, combine the almonds, bread crumbs and paprika. Chop the mix until a fine powder is produced. Position the oven rack 4 inches from the broiler and preheat to 425 degrees. Arrange the lobsters, cut side up, on the broiler pan. Stir the vinaigrette and

spoon 2 tablespoons over each lobster half, then sprinkle with the bread crumb mixture. Broil until the lobster meat is opaque and the topping golden brown, about 10 minutes. Transfer lobster to the serving plates, and garnish with lemon and chive sprigs. Serve immediately, and pass the remaining vinaigrette separately.

Nutrition details per serving
Calories 946
Percent of calories from fat 37%
Fat: . . . . .38 gm
Protein: . . . . .133 gm
Carbohydrate: . . . . .13 gm
Cholesterol: . . . . .679 mg
Sodium: . . . . .327 mg
Diabetic exchange: 3 bread, 18 meat, 6 fat.

POACH MOISTURE AND TASTE INTO FISH

■ *How does this method work?* Place the fish on top of a thin bed of vegetables in a skillet, splash with fish stock and white wine, then cover with parchment. Heat the skillet until the liquids begin to boil, then transfer the skillet to a preheated oven to finish cooking. Serve with pan juices finished into a sauce.

■ *Why it tastes so good:* Cooking fish in liquid preserves that moist, delicate and slightly resilient texture. A small amount of liquid concentrates the naturally rich flavor.

■ *Advantages:* This style of cooking is quick, and there are no added fats.

■ *Selecting your fish:* This technique works best on less dense fish such as pickerel, whitefish, sole, salmon, mahimahi and snapper. Oily fish such as bluefish, and dense fish such as swordfish or tuna don't work

TODAY'S LESSON: An old French technique for poaching fish in the oven results in a light and delicate texture in just a little splash of moisture. The fish is not only lean and healthy but also absolutely delicious.

as well — it is difficult for the high heat to penetrate the fish.

Choose thinner fillets from ½ to ¾ inch thick. Thicker fillets take too long to cook, causing the moisture to escape and the fish to dry out; fillets thinner than ½ inch cook too fast.

■ *Tricks of the trade:* The flavor of the fish depends on which vegetables you cook with it. Select companions such as shallots, leeks, carrots, fennel or sweet peppers for their flavor and color. Cut them into a fine julienne so they will cook and release their flavor in a short time. The poaching liquids — wine, citrus juice and

stock — also influence the flavor of the dish. For the best sauce, combine these liquids and any of the vegetable garnish trimmings in a separate saucepan and simmer until reduced by half to concentrate flavor. Strain out any garnish vegetables and allow the reduced liquids to cool before combining with the fish.

■ *Get started:* Start with a small nonstick skillet that will comfortably hold the fillets. Sprinkle the pan with a fine julienne of vegetables. Top with the seasoned fish and add wine, fish stock, clam juice or vegetable stock to about half the thickness of the fish. Cover

AMAZING FOOD FACTS

■

Poaching the fish on the bone preserves more of the fish's natural flavor. The bones are easily removed after cooking.

with parchment, crimping the edges down into the skillet to ensure good protection while cooking. The fish may be refrigerated at this point until you are ready to cook.

■ *The cooking begins:* Preheat the oven to 425 degrees to ensure fast cooking. Place the skillet over high heat and bring the liquid to a simmer; then immediately transfer the skillet into the oven to finish cooking the fish, about 3-5 minutes. When done, remove the fish to a hot serving plate and serve, or keep warm if making a sauce. Return the skillet to a boil over high heat, cooking until the juices are reduced to coat the back of a spoon, about 3 minutes. Season the sauce and add any garnished herbs before spooning over the fish.

■ *Serving suggestions:* The delicate flavor of the fish is best enhanced with crunchy vegetables and silky grains. Choose colorful and complementary accompaniments.

■

SALMON POACHED WITH SHALLOTS & PARSNIPS

Makes 4 servings

4   medium parsnips, peeled, sliced ⅛ inch thick, reserve stems

2   cups white wine

2   cups light vegetable or fish stock

1   bunch parsley stems, washed, leaves reserved

1   cup shallots, peeled, ends removed, cut ⅛ inch thick, reserve skins and ends

2   carrots, peeled, ends removed, sliced thin, cut into ⅛-inch julienne, reserve ends and peels

4   salmon fillets, boneless and skinless, fatty tissues trimmed

Sea salt and freshly ground black pepper to taste

3   tablespoons snipped chives

Preheat oven to 425 degrees. Cut 2 of the parsnips into julienne strips

and the remaining 2 into 1-inch pieces. Bring a medium saucepan of water to a boil over high heat. Add the julienne parsnips, cooking until just al dente, about 1 minute. Using a slotted spoon, remove to a sieve and immediately cool under cold running water. Reserve. Add the remaining parsnip chunks to the boiling water, cooking until tender, about 4 minutes. Transfer to a sieve and drain. Transfer the parsnips chunks to a food processor, puree until smooth and reserve. In an acid-resistant saucepan, combine the white wine, vegetable or fish stock, parsley stems and vegetable trimmings from parsnips, shallots and carrots. Bring to a simmer over medium-high heat, cooking until reduced to 2 cups, about 10 minutes. Pour through a fine sieve, collecting the reduced liquids and discarding the vegetables. Allow to cool.

Spread the shallots, carrots and parsnips across the bottom of a nonstick skillet. Position the salmon over the vegetables, allowing a little room between each fillet. Season with salt and pepper.

Pour the cooled liquids over the vegetables to a depth half the thickness of the salmon. Cover tightly with a piece of parchment. Place the skillet over high heat and bring to a simmer, about 3 minutes. Transfer the skillet to the lower rack of the oven and cook until desired degree of doneness, about 3-5 minutes depending on the thickness of the salmon. Carefully remove the skillet from the oven and return to a burner. Remove and discard the parchment. Place the salmon on hot serving dishes. Bring the cooking liquids to a boil over high heat. Add the parsnip puree and cook until reduced to coat the back of a spoon, about 3 minutes. Add the chives and adjust the seasonings. Spoon the sauce and garnishes over the salmon. Garnish with parsley sprigs and serve.

Nutrition details per serving
Calories 317
Percent of calories from fat 25%
Fat: . . . . .9 gm
Protein: . . . . .34 gm
Carbohydrate: . . . . .24 gm
Cholesterol: . . . . .61 mg
Sodium: . . . . .332 mg
Diabetic exchange: 3¾ lean meat, 1¾ vegetable, ¼ bread.

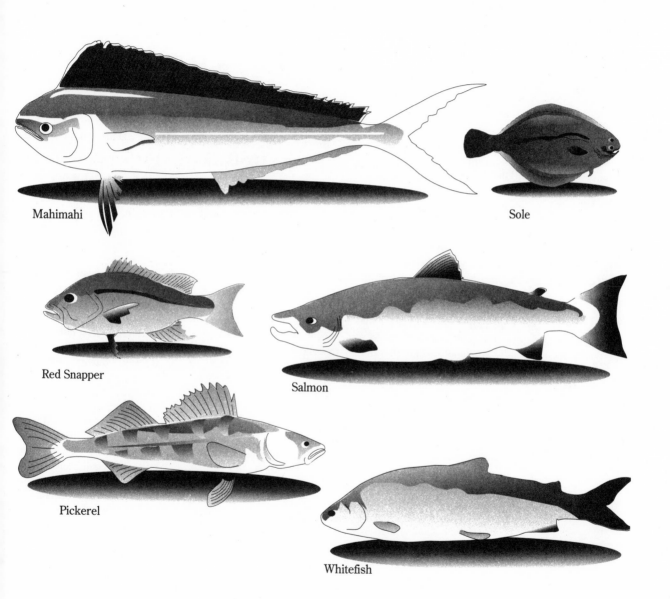

Mahimahi

Sole

Red Snapper

Salmon

Pickerel

Whitefish

GRAPEFRUIT ADDS ZEST

■ *What exactly is a grapefruit?*
The grapefruit — the johnny-come-lately of the citrus family — might have been an accident. Grapefruit actually are thought to be an accidental hybrid of the pummelo, the largest citrus fruit, and the orange.

■ *Where does it come from?*
Once discovered, the grapefruit rose quickly in popularity. From the first commercial production in Florida in 1875, consumption has rocketed to 14 million boxes of fresh fruit annually.

■ *How many varieties are there?*
The four principal varieties of grapefruit in peak production from Florida during the winter months are:
Duncans. They are large and round with a pale yellow color. Their skin usually is quite thin, and they are the best for juice. They contain 30-50 or more medium to large seeds.
Marsh Seedless (or White

TODAY'S LESSON: The grapefruit is probably the most underused member of the citrus family; it's ready to be discovered.

Marsh). They have a smooth yellow skin, an oblate shape and a flatter end. They are medium to small in size, with no seeds, or just a few. The fruit has a rich bright flavor and a delicate texture.
Thompson (or Pink Marsh Seedless). They are oblate, medium-sized grapefruits with a smooth light yellow skin. The fruit is light buff in color, with pink blushes that are most intense during the peak months of January and February. The juice is fragrant and bright-flavored but colorless. There are at most 3-5 seeds.
Redblush (Marsh Red, Red Seedless and Ruby or Ruby Red Seedless). These are quite similar to the Thompson, but with a redder color, especially

in the flesh. The flavor is rich and bright and the fruit is virtually seedless.

■ *Why do they taste so good?*
Pink and white grapefruit are equally tart. Yet most people prefer the pink because of the perceived sweeter taste.

■ *Health advantages:* Pink grapefruit contains more beta-carotene, which is responsible for the reddish hue. Beta-carotene has been linked to lower rates of cancer. Both white and pink grapefruit contain 80-105 milligrams of vitamin C, which exceeds the recommended daily allowance of 60 milligrams.

■ *How to select:* Select grapefruit by the weight and fragrance, not the color. Choose those that are large, heavy and supple. Hard grapefruit will be dry and low in juice. Check the stem end; the collapse of the end is a sign of deterioration. All citrus fruit should be consumed quickly, because they do not continue to ripen after picking.

■ *How to store:* Keep citrus fruit under mild refrigeration or in a cool, well-ventilated area. Very cold refrigeration can cause brown spotting of the skins (a visual detriment only), so keep citrus in the vegetable crisper. Do not store in plastic bags, because they trap moisture that promotes the growth of mold.

■

MAHIMAHI WITH GRAPEFRUIT

Makes 4 servings

2   tablespoons mild paprika
2   tablespoons corn oil
8   escallops of mahimahi, about 3 ounces each
2   cups fish stock or clam juice
½   cup scallion greens, diced
½   cup parsley, chopped
1   cup fresh grapefruit segments, pink or white
    Salt
    Freshly ground white pepper
    Pinch of cayenne pepper
2   tablespoons unsalted butter, optional
2   tablespoons zest of grapefruit rind
4   sprigs parsley for garnish

Preheat broiler to 475. In a small bowl, combine the paprika and corn oil to form a smooth paste. Rub the paprika mixture on all surfaces of the fish. Reserve fish in refrigerator. In a medium, acid-resistant saucepan, bring the fish stock to a boil over high heat and reduce to ½ cup, about 12 minutes. Remove from the heat. Arrange the mahimahi on a broiler pan. Place under the broiler and cook until done, about 6-8 minutes. Remove from the oven and keep warm. To finish the reserved sauce, return it to a boil over high heat. Add the scallions, parsley and grapefruit segments, cooking until thickened, about 1 minute. Adjust the seasonings with salt, white pepper and a pinch of cayenne pepper. Whisk in the butter and remove from the heat. Spoon the sauce onto the serving plates. Position 2 escallops, slightly overlapping, on the sauce. Top with the grapefruit zest, garnish with parsley sprigs and serve.

Nutrition details per serving
Calories 366
Percent of calories from fat 36%
Fat: . . . . .15 gm
Protein: . . . . .33 gm
Carbohydrate: . . . . .25 gm
Cholesterol: . . . . .132 mg
Sodium: . . . . .954 mg
Diabetic exchange: 2¾ vegetables, ⅓ fruit, 4¾ meat, 2½ fat.

■

The grapefruit's ancestor is the pummelo, an ancient Asian fruit. Legend tells us that a 17th Century British sailor, Capt. Shaddock, brought the first pummelos to the West Indies. The fruit was known as "shaddocks."

STEAMY MUSSELS MAKE A SUMPTUOUS FEAST

**AMAZING
FOOD FACTS**

■

Good-quality
mussels smell
like a salty sea
breeze. Like
clams and
oysters, they
need to be kept
alive until
they're cooked.

■ *What it is:* The blue mussel *(Mytilus edulis)* has a smooth oval shell and is deep blue to almost black. The two shells form an external skeleton to protect the pale to orange-hued delicate meat. Green-lipped or green mussels *(Mytilus canaliculus)* have ridges with a pale to dark green color. The meat has a more pronounced flavor, with an orange to greenish hue.

■ *Advantages:* The tender meat of moules — as they're called in Europe — is high in protein, carbohydrates, vitamin A and minerals. Mussels make a great meal for company at a small price.

■ *How to select:* For the meatiest mussels, select those that are larger and heavy. They should smell like a salty sea breeze, never of old smelly fish. Shells should be firmly closed, well rinsed and moist. I prefer farmed mussels to wild mussels because of their better meat yield and flavor.

■ *How to store:* A plastic bag is fine for carrying mussels home from the market, but it will suffocate the little guys overnight. Store mussels in a colander placed in a bowl, all covered with wet paper toweling, in the bottom of your refrigerator. To take up less space, they can be wrapped loosely in damp newspaper and left out until dinner or even overnight. Do not submerge in fresh water or cover with ice.

■ *How to cook:* Steaming is best. Use an acid-resistant pot with a

TODAY'S LESSON: A pot of mussels steamed with a splash of wine or vermouth, dusted with snipped parsley and a few chopped shallots, then bathed in melted butter will make a Belgian's heart skip a beat.

tight-fitting lid. Combine a little wine or vermouth with a splash of water, any member of the onion family and aromatics such as thyme, peppercorns, parsley stems and a bay leaf. Place the mussels inside and a simmer over medium-high heat. Cook for 3-5 minutes or until the mussels begin to open. Remove the mussels as they open and transfer them to warm serving dishes while the slower ones finish. Discard mussels that refuse to open. Pour the steaming juices through a very fine sieve. Season and pour over the mussels. Sprinkle with fresh spices such as parsley, thyme and chives. Dress with a splash of melted butter over or on the side. Serve immediately.

■ *To prepare for casseroles:* To gather the meat for pastas and casseroles, steam as described. The meat may be removed from the shells after cooking and kept moist by covering with the strained steaming liquids. They may be prepared hours ahead, but refrigerate until you use them.

■ *How many do you need?* Three pounds of fresh mussels in their shells will yield approximately 1 pound, or 2 cups, of steamed meat. For mussel appetizers in the shell, plan on 12 per person. As a main course, you'll need 24-30 to satisfy the average appetite. For shelled mussels in pasta or casseroles, figure on ½ cup, or 4 ounces, per person. I always add ½ pound to adjust for the ones that don't open and must be discarded plus another ½ pound to snack on while cooking.

■ *Presentation is everything:* When it's time to serve,

spread a newspaper or red-checked tablecloth across the table and top with basic napkins. Put a large bowl in the center for the shells. Add a candle in an old wine bottle. Select a dry, crisp white wine such as a Sancerre or Alsacian Gewurztraminer. In Europe, the traditional steamed mussels are always served with frites (french fries). Select the skinniest french fries. Serve the steamy mussels in covered bowls or soup plates to capture the wonderful aroma. Position large plates of seasoned french fries within easy reach.

■ *How to eat from the shell:* Join your guests and use the traditional eating technique. Begin with an open mussel shell with the hinges still intact. If the mussel is still attached, pluck the meat with your fingers. Then keep the first shell and use it like tweezers to empty the remaining mussels. The technique is easy and is better than any fork.

■

MOULES

Makes 4 servings

4 pounds mussels

½ cup unsalted butter (1 stick)

2 cups dry white wine, preferably chardonnay

1 cup water

½ cup shallots, cleaned, ends removed, diced

½ bunch fresh parsley steams, rinsed, dried

Freshly ground black pepper to taste

4 sprigs fresh thyme or 1 teaspoon dried, crumbled

1 bunch Italian (flat) parsley, washed, patted dry with paper toweling or spun dry, cut with scissors into coarse pieces

Wash the mussels under running cold water and scrub as necessary with a coarse brush to remove any dirt. Do not allow the mussels to be submerged in fresh water or they will die. Press on any open mussels to see

if they will close. Discard all mussels that do not close. Remove the "beard" by pulling gently with your fingers, or with a pair of clean needle-nose pliers. Reserve the mussels in a colander in your sink covered with wet paper toweling while you prepare the steaming liquid. In a small saucepan, melt the butter. Let it stand for about 5 minutes. Spoon the foamy top from the yellow butter fat and discard. Spoon the yellow butter fat into another small pan and keep warm. Discard the whitish liquid that remains at the bottom of the saucepan.

In a large stainless steel or acid-resistant pot, combine the white wine, water, shallots, parsley stems, thyme and a generous dose of freshly ground black pepper. Add the mussels. Cover the pot, place over high heat and bring to a boil. Cook the mussels until most have opened. Remove the mussels to warm serving bowls and keep covered while the remaining mussels finish cooking. Discard any mussels that do not open. Remove the pot from the heat. Pour the steaming liquids into a pan or bowl through a very fine sieve. Distribute the steaming liquids over the mussels in their serving bowls. Spoon the butter over the mussels or serve on the side. Dust the mussels with the Italian parsley.

Nutrition details per serving
Calories 751
Percent of calories from fat 41%
Fat: .34 gm
Protein: . . . . .68 gm
Carbohydrate: . . . . .24 gm
Cholesterol: . . . . .316 mg
Sodium: . . . . .1,342 mg
Diabetic exchange: ⅜ vegetable,
¼ bread, 8 meat, 4 fat.

■

STEAMED SHRIMP, MUSSEL, OYSTER & ARTICHOKE STEW

Makes 6 servings

3 cups dry white wine

2 cups heavy or light whipping cream

2 cups bottled clam juice

2 medium red onions, cut into a medium dice

6 garlic cloves, peeled, ends removed, finely minced

12 small new potatoes, redskins or similar, washed, eyes removed, quartered

½ tablespoon paprika

12 baby artichokes, trim outer tougher leaves and stem, then cut into quarters lengthwise and rub the cut surface with lemon juice

Sea salt or granulated salt to taste

3 dozen large mussels, debearded and scrubbed clean

12 medium oysters, scrubbed clean

24 jumbo shrimp (U-15 size), shelled and deveined (about 1¼ pounds)

1 large pinch saffron threads, optional

¼ cup fresh basil, washed, dried, chopped; or substitute 2 tablespoons dried basil and 2 tablespoons fresh chopped parsley

¼ cup fresh flat-leaf parsley, washed, dried, chopped, divided

Generous dose of crushed hot red pepper flakes, optional

In a large acid-resistant soup or stock pot with a tight-fitting lid, combine the white wine, cream and clam juice. Bring to a boil, uncovered, over medium-high heat. Add the onions, garlic, potatoes and paprika, cooking until tender, about 10 minutes. Add the artichokes and cook for 5 minutes. Season with salt to taste. Add the mussels and oysters, place the lid on the pot and cook until mollusks begin to open, about 5 minutes. As the mollusks open, transfer them to another pot, removing the shell half without the meat while keeping the shell with the meat warm. When almost all of the mollusks have opened, remove and discard any unopened shells. Remove the lid, add the shrimp to the pot and allow to cook until the shrimp turn opaque, about 2 minutes. Return the mollusks to the pot and allow the shellfish to finish cook-

ing together, about 2 minutes. Remove from the heat. Stir in the saffron, basil and half of the parsley. Transfer to a large, hot serving bowl or deep platter, or to individual serving dishes. Dust with the remaining parsley and sprinkle with pepper flakes if desired. Serve immediately.

Cook's note: "U-15" is the industry term used to indicate the size of the shrimp. It means the shrimp are large enough that there are fewer than 15 shrimp to a pound.

Nutrition details per serving
Calories 745
Percent of calories from fat 41%
Fat: .34 gm
Protein: . . . . .41 gm
Carbohydrate: . . . . .73 gm
Cholesterol: . . . . .270 mg
Sodium: . . . . .904 mg
Diabetic exchange: ¼ milk, 3½ lean meat, 3¾ vegetables, 2¼ bread, 5¾ fat.

SQUID PRO QUO

TODAY'S LESSON: Calamari has a wonderful, slightly resilient texture and sweet, almost nutty flavor. Let's unlock the secrets of cooking calamari fried and in terrific stews and chowders.

■ *What exactly is calamari?* "Calamari" is the Italian name for the extremely popular mollusk known as squid. Squid is related to octopus and cuttlefish but is much smaller, more tender and delicate.

■ *Why it tastes so good:* When cooking, handle calamari's wonderful, delicate character and flavor carefully to achieve the perfect texture. Calamari is rubbery when undercooked and becomes dry and tough if overcooked.

■ *Health advantages:* Calamari is very nutritious, 18 percent protein, with only a third the cholesterol of shrimp. There are about 156 calories in a 6-ounce serving.

■ *Tricks of the trade:* Carefully apply heat, and cut the calamari into similar-sized pieces for even cooking.

■ *Buying your calamari:* Calamari is terrific fresh but also great frozen. It freezes well, maintaining superior flavor and texture. For the most tender texture, buy the smallest squid; the larger ones can get just a little tough.

■ *Preparation:* Most frozen squid comes cleaned and ready to cook. Thaw under cold running water or overnight in the refrigerator. To clean, hold the sack in one hand and with the other grab the tentacles and separate. Remove the quill-like bone from the sac and thoroughly rinse under cold running water. Cut the tentacles into even-sized pieces and the body into ¼-inch rings. Submerge in ice water to blanch white, then drain and prepare according to your recipe.

■ *The cooking begins:* Short cooking is best for my tastes. The best, most direct way to enjoy calamari is to dredge in seasoned flour, submerge in hot oil and cook until it begins to hiss. Stir-frying and sauteing also produce terrific calamari. Grilling works best with large, even pieces of calamari flattened for quick heat penetration. Short cooking times are also great for stews, chowders, risotto and pasta. The trick to introducing calamari into these dishes is to add them in the last couple of minutes of cooking. The final heat of the ingredients will carry over into

Because the name "squid" does not appeal to American consumers, it is sometimes sold as "calamari" (the Italian name).

the small, delicate pieces of calamari and cook them to a silky, moist texture.

Long cooking is best with large or whole calamari, which take longer for the heat to penetrate; they slowly tenderize while the dish cooks. This method is perfect for dishes that are cooked in 45-60 minutes, the same time the calamari reaches its peak texture.

■ *Serving suggestions:* Calamari is complemented with sauces and condiments from the simplest squeeze of lemon to the hottest salsas. The natural mild flavor goes with just about everything.

■ *Try your technique:* Try the simple but wonderful ragout (stew) of calamari and red lentils. The texture of the silky calamari against the slightly firm lentils with the visual red, white and green colors is a terrific light meal or a simple starter.

RAGOUT OF CALAMARI & RED LENTILS

Makes 4 servings

2 tablespoons virgin olive oil

2 cloves garlic, peeled, ends removed, minced

1 medium onion, peeled, ends removed, finely diced

2 teaspoons thyme leaf

1 cup dry white wine

2 cups vegetable or fish stock

6 ounces dried red lentils
    Salt and freshly ground black pepper to taste

1 pound small calamari, cleaned, body cut into rounds and the tentacles quartered lengthwise

¼ cup snipped fresh chives

¼ cup finely grated Reggiano Parmesan cheese

4 sprigs chives for garnish, optional

In a large nonstick skillet, heat olive oil over medium-high heat. Add the garlic and

cook until golden brown, about 2 minutes. Add the onions and cook until lightly browned, about 5 minutes. Add the thyme, white wine and vegetable or fish stock, and bring to a boil over high heat. Add the lentils, cooking until al dente (firm to the bite) and the liquids have been reduced to coat the beans, about 15 minutes. Season with salt and pepper to taste. Add the calamari and chives, cooking until opaque, about 1-2 minutes; do not overcook. Remove from heat. Spoon ragout into warm soup plates. Sprinkle with a little more black pepper and Reggiano Parmesan cheese. Garnish with sprigs of chives if desired and serve.

Nutrition details per serving
Calories .358
Percent of calories from fat 26%
Fat: .10 gm
Protein: . . . . .33 gm
Carbohydrate: . . . . .32 gm
Cholesterol: . . . . .268 mg
Sodium: . . . . .149 mg
Diabetic exchange: 2 lean meat, 1 vegetable, 2 bread, 1½ fat.

■

CRISPY CALAMARI & SHALLOTS

Makes 4 appetizer servings

1   pound squid, cleaned
    Canola oil for frying
2   cups all-purpose flour
2   tablespoons paprika
1   teaspoon salt
¾   teaspoon freshly ground white pepper
1   lime, sliced paper thin
2   large eggs, lightly beaten
1   cup milk
1   cup shallots, thinly sliced into little rings
¼   cup freshly squeezed lime juice
    Hot red pepper flakes, optional
½   cup cilantro leaves, rinsed, patted dry

Cut the wings from the squid's body and slice into ¼-inch-thick strips. The remaining cone-shaped body is cut perpendicular to its length to yield ¼-inch-thick rings. The tentacle bunch is divided into 2-4 pieces, depending on size.

Fill a large, heavy, deep skillet with the oil to a depth of 3 inches. Heat over medium-high heat to 350 degrees.

In a medium-size bowl, sift together flour, paprika, salt and pepper. Add the lime slices and coat evenly. Transfer lime slices to a cookie sheet and set aside.

In another medium-size bowl, combine eggs and milk. Drench squid and shallots in the egg and milk mixture and shake off excess. Dredge in the seasoned flour, coat evenly and shake to remove excess.

Gently slide the squid, shallots and lime into the oil, stirring occasionally. Fry until golden, about 3 minutes. Drain on paper towels for 1 minute. Transfer to a large bowl. Sprinkle with the lime juice. Season with salt and red pepper flakes, toss with cilantro and serve.

Nutrition details per serving
Calories 455
Percent of calories from fat 14%
Fat: .7 gm
Protein: . . . . .31 gm
Carbohydrate: . . . . .66 gm
Cholesterol: . . . . .379 mg
Sodium: . . . . .652 mg
Diabetic exchange: ¼ milk, 1¼ vegetables, ¼ fruit, 3 bread, 3 meat, ⅖ fat.

Cleaning squid

Reach into the body as far as you can, grasping the innards while holding the outer sac.

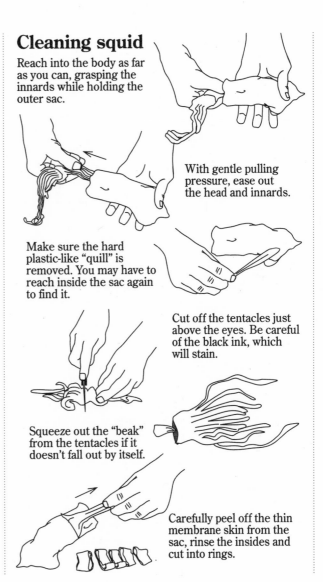

With gentle pulling pressure, ease out the head and innards.

Make sure the hard plastic-like "quill" is removed. You may have to reach inside the sac again to find it.

Cut off the tentacles just above the eyes. Be careful of the black ink, which will stain.

Squeeze out the "beak" from the tentacles if it doesn't fall out by itself.

Carefully peel off the thin membrane skin from the sac, rinse the insides and cut into rings.

SPICES DRESS FISH CAJUN-STYLE

■ *Why it tastes so good:* Blackened fish uses a spice mixture to create what is almost a breading for the fish. This mixture, when cooked over very high heat, seals the fish to hold in moisture and flavor while toasting the spices to release their wonderful fragrances.

■ *Health advantages:* Although the technique traditionally calls for the sweetness of butter to bind the spices, this recipe allows the fish to be made with olive oil.

■ *Tricks of the trade:* Deep-chill fish before coating it with the spice. The very cold fish helps to attract the butter or olive oil and the spice.

■ *Select your fish:* The traditional fish for this dish had been the redfish or red drum, native to the Gulf of Mexico, but with growing numbers of Cajun restaurants, the fish became almost impossible to find. So

TODAY'S LESSON: Enrobing sweet fish fillets with blackened, spicy flavors is a popular Cajun standard. It has gone beyond being a regional food to become a regular request in many restaurants. I'll show you the secrets of enjoying this technique at home.

choose pompano, mahimahi, swordfish or salmon.

■ *How to prepare:* Prepare the fish by cutting it into fillets no more than ½ inch thick. This way the fish cooks quickly, finishing before the spice mixture is burnt and bitter. Cut thicker fillets into escallops by slicing them on a 30-degree angle for an even thickness. Remove all skin, fatty tissue and bones.

■ *Blend the spices:* The best and easiest blackened fish spice mix is Chef Paul Prudhomme's Louisiana Cajun Magic, at local supermarkets. You can also

make your own blend. The primary spices are paprika, onion and garlic powders, hot red pepper, white and black pepper, thyme and oregano, all balanced with a pinch of salt. Experiment with a small batch and taste it on fish before committing expensive spices to your formula. Mix the spice blend in a bowl, then store in a sealable bottle.

■ *Preparing your skillet:* Heat a heavy cast-iron skillet over medium-high heat until it turns almost white-hot. The pan can't be too hot; be careful when handling it.

■ *Butter or olive oil?* Butter used sparingly offers a rich, sweet flavor but adds more saturated fats. Extra-virgin olive oil, which is viscous at cold temperatures, is the best alternative. Standard cooking oils are too thin to adhere to the cold fish, resulting in an irregular spice crust.

■ *The cooking begins:* Dredge the deep-chilled fillets in the melted butter or olive oil, pausing for 30 seconds or so for the excess to fall back into the dish. Place on a plate of the spice blend and pack the surface well to secure the spice. Turn the fish over to coat the remaining surfaces. Lift the fillets and allow the excess spices to fall onto the plate. Repeat with the remaining fish. Carefully place the fish in the hot skillet, making sure not to crowd. The pan will smoke immediately, so make sure the hood fan is on full blast. Cook the fish for 2 minutes, then turn it over to finish cooking, about 2 additional minutes, depending on thickness.

■ *Serving suggestions:* Simple blackened fish is a treat by itself, but a pat of butter is the traditional moistener for the top. A wedge of lemon will offer a clean, tart counterpoint.

■ *Try your technique:* Blackened Mahimahi with Papaya-Citrus Salsa will warm your taste buds.

■

BLACKENED MAHIMAHI WITH PAPAYA-CITRUS SALSA

Makes 4 servings

8   escallops of mahimahi, about 2½-3 ounces each, trimmed of all skin, fat and bones

1   ripe papaya, peeled, halved, seeded and diced

2   large oranges, trimmed of all rind, segments cleanly removed

1   lime, juiced

1   small red onion, diced fine (about ½ cup), to taste

2   tablespoons diced green onions, green part only

2   tablespoons chopped cilantro

   Salt and freshly ground black pepper to taste

¼   cup olive oil

   Paul Prudhomme's Blackened Redfish Magic (or see the recipe for Blackened Spice Mix on page 256)

4   sprigs cilantro for garnish

Deep-chill the mahimahi in the freezer for about 30-60 minutes before cooking; do not let it freeze. In a medium bowl, combine the papaya, orange segments, lime juice, red onion (to your taste), green onions and cilantro. Season with salt and black pepper to taste. Reserve under refrigeration. Place a large, heavy cast-iron skillet over medium-high heat and allow to warm until white-hot, at least 15 minutes. Remember to use heavy insulated cooking gloves, long tongs or a long-handled spatula, and turn on the exhaust fan to high.

Pour the olive oil into a shallow medium-size pan or plate. Pour the spice mixture into another shallow pan or plate. Remove the fish from the freezer. Dredge each escallop through the olive oil on both sides to coat evenly, holding it above the oil for a few seconds to allow the excess to drop back into the pan. The oil coating should be very thin. Lay the escallop onto the spices and apply light pressure to adhere the spices to the fish. Turn over to completely enrobe both sides of the escallop with the spices. Lay the spice-coated escallop on a cookie sheet while repeating the coating process with the remaining fish. Carefully lay the escallops in the hot skillet without overlapping or crowding. Cook the fish until the spice mixture browns, about 2 minutes. Turn over and finish cooking, about 2-3 additional minutes, depending on the thickness of your fish. Remove to hot serving plates with a spatula, placing 2 slightly overlapping escallops on the center of each plate. Divide the salsa in a band across the escallops or serve on the side. Garnish with the cilantro sprigs and serve immediately.

```
Nutrition details per serving
Calories . . . . . . . . . . . . . . . . . . . .343
Percent of calories from fat . . . . . . .43%
Fat: . . . . . . . . . . . . . . . . . . . . . .16 gm
Protein: . . . . . . . . . . . . . . . . .30 gm
Carbohydrate: . . . . . . . . . . . . . .21 gm
Cholesterol: . . . . . . . . . . . . . .104 mg
Sodium: . . . . . . . . . . . . . . . . .374 mg
Diabetic exchange: 2½ lean meat, ½ vegetable, 1¼ fruit, 2½ fat.
```

■

BLACKENED SPICE MIX

Makes ½ cup

4 tablespoons mild paprika

4 teaspoons sea salt, or substitute granulated table salt

2 teaspoons garlic powder

4 teaspoons onion powder

½ teaspoon ground hot red pepper

2 teaspoons ground black pepper

2 teaspoons ground coriander

1 teaspoon dried thyme leaves

1 teaspoon dried oregano leaves

In a food processor combine paprika, salt, garlic powder, onion powder, red pepper, black pepper, coriander, thyme leaves and oregano leaves. Pulse to combine well. Store in a clean airtight glass jar. Keeps for about 3 months if it is moisture-free and cool.

```
Nutrition details per serving
Calories . . . . . . . . . . . . . . . . . . . .16
Percent of calories from fat . . . . . . .25%
Fat: . . . . . . . . . . . . . . . . . . . . . .trace
Protein: . . . . . . . . . . . . . . . . . .1 gm
Carbohydrate: . . . . . . . . . . . . . .3 gm
Cholesterol: . . . . . . . . . . . . . .0 mg
Sodium: . . . . . . . . . . . . . . . . .949 mg
Diabetic exchange: No exchange.
```

BRAISE-WORTHY MEATS

■ *Why braising tastes so good:* Browning the meat produces a rich, caramelized flavor. Covered with a light stock, it is flavored and moistened during cooking. The long, slow process dissolves the tougher connective tissues and meat bundles, leaving only the most tender meat. The meat's juices escape to mingle with the cooking liquids and create a robust flavor marriage of all the ingredients.

■ *Advantages:* Although it takes time to prepare meat for braising, the oven does all the work. Cooking in liquids such as a stock or seasoned broth requires only a little oil for browning. Trim the meat to remove excess fat for a lean dish.

■ *Select your cuts of meat:* Try veal shanks, which produce the famous Italian osso buco, for a really special dinner. Beef short ribs, briskets and corned beef are also terrific. Similar

TODAY'S LESSON: Veal shanks, beef short ribs and many other less tender cuts of meat are braised for some of the most satisfying dishes you will ever taste.

cuts in lamb, along with rabbit and game, are worth trying.

■ *Preparing to braise:* Heat a large heavy skillet that can hold all the meat. Brown the meat, then reserve. Add complementary vegetables and cover with hot, light stock or seasoned broth. Return to a slow simmer.

■ *Tricks of the trade:* Season the stock with salt and pepper. Too little seasoning will draw the natural flavors out of the meat and will result in a bland, boring dish. Add spices and herbs to round out the flavor. Cover the surface of the simmering stock in the skillet with a couple of sheets of aluminum foil.

Place the shiny side down, directly touching the surface of the liquid, to ensure the food will braise, not steam. Cover the skillet with an oven-proof lid to help hold the foil tightly in place.

■ *The cooking begins:* Put the skillet on the lower rack of a preheated 350-degree oven. Cook for 1¾ hours before testing for doneness. Remove the skillet from the oven to the stovetop. Remove the lid and gently pull back the foil. Insert a metal skewer; there should be little or no resistance when the meat is done. When done, remove from oven and let cool. Do not remove the meat from the stock; it must stay in

■

The properly cooked braised veal shank is the moistest cut of veal. After cooking, it is perfect for dicing as a filling for ravioli, canneloni and tortellini.

the liquid or it will become dry and tough. To serve later, cool meat in the stock and store overnight. Reheat in the cooking liquids and serve.

■ *To make a sauce:* Try a sauce to enhance the flavor of the meat. Remove a quarter to a third of the cooking liquids and strain into a saucepan. Bring the liquids to a boil over high heat and cook until reduced to coat the back of a spoon. Add any sauce garnish you choose and adjust the seasonings.

■

BRAISED VEAL SHANKS OSSO-BUCO STYLE

Makes 4 servings

½ cup chopped flat parsley leaves

2 lemons, rind finely grated, all the white inner membrane trimmed, sliced, 4 slices reserved for garnish, the remaining fruit diced, divided

3 garlic cloves, peeled, ends removed, finely minced, divided

1 tablespoon anchovy paste; or 2 anchovy fillets, finely mashed

3 tablespoons olive oil

4 lean veal shanks, fat trimmed

1 large onion, peeled, ends removed, cut into ⅛-inch dice

1 large carrot, peeled, ends removed, cut into ⅛-inch dice

2 cups dry white wine

1 can (32 ounces) Italian plum tomatoes, drained, seeded and crushed

1 quart light veal stock; or substitute vegetable or light poultry stock

   Sea salt to taste; or substitute granulated

   Freshly ground black pepper

4 sprigs parsley, washed, dried, for garnish

Preheat oven to 375 degrees. On a cutting board, combine the chopped parsley, grated lemon rind, half of the garlic and the anchovy paste. Chop with a chef's knife to combine the ingredients thoroughly. Transfer to a small bowl, cover with plastic food wrap and reserve in refrigerator. In a

large, deep, heavy, ovenproof skillet, heat the oil over medium-high heat. Add the veal shanks and cook until seared and browned, about 3 minutes. Turn the veal shanks on their sides and continue browning. Turn again until all the surfaces have been seared and browned, about 6 minutes total. Remove to a plate to reserve. Add the onion, carrot and remaining garlic, cooking until browned on all surfaces, about 5 minutes. Add the chopped lemon and the white wine, cooking until the wine is about evaporated, about 5 minutes. Return the veal shanks to the skillet and nestle them among the vegetables. Add the tomatoes and the hot stock to cover the meaty part of the shanks. Return to a simmer and adjust the seasoning generously with salt and pepper to taste. Cover the skillet with a couple of sheets of aluminum foil, dull side up, directly on the surface of the stock and crimped over the edge of the skillet to create a good seal. Cover the skillet with a snug-fitting ovenproof lid.

Place the skillet on the lower rack of the oven and cook until tender, about 1¾ hours. Check the shanks by inserting a skewer. It should pass through the veal without resistance. Remove the skillet from the oven and allow to cool for about 10 minutes before proceeding. Carefully remove the veal shanks to a plate, making sure they don't fall apart. Cover with plastic wrap to keep warm and moist. Return the skillet to high heat and bring the liquids to a boil, cooking until the liquids are thick enough to coat the back of a spoon, about 6 minutes. Add the chopped parsley mixture to the sauce and lower the heat to a simmer. Return the shanks to the sauce to heat for 2 minutes while basting with the sauce. To serve, position each shank in the center of the serving plate. Spoon the sauce over the veal shanks. Garnish with a slice of lemon atop the meaty part of the shank and a sprig of parsley beside it.

Nutrition details per serving
Calories 436
Percent of calories from fat 31%
Fat: .15 gm
Protein: . . . . .36 gm
Carbohydrate: . . . . .24 gm
Cholesterol: . . . . .117 mg
Sodium: . . . . .797 mg
Diabetic exchange: 4½ meat, 3 vegetables, ⅓ fruit, 2 fat.

■

VEAL SHANKS WITH CAPERS & CHIVES

Makes 4 servings

½ cup olive oil, divided

4 veal shanks (12-14 ounces each), tied around middle

2 large fennel bulbs, trimmed and cut in half

8 cups apple cider or juice

2 cups veal stock or to cover, depending on size of shanks (bouillon can be substituted)

Salt

Freshly ground black pepper

½ cup cider or red wine vinegar, divided

½ cup nonpareil capers, drained

¼ cup snipped fresh chives

1 tablespoon cracked black pepper, optional

2 Belgian endives, cut widthwise into ¼-inch pieces

3 cups mache or watercress, cleaned and roots removed

1 large head radicchio, core removed and leaves cut into julienne or chiffonade

Place 2 tablespoons olive oil and veal shanks in large ovenproof skillet. Cook over high heat until browned on all sides. Transfer shanks to plate and discard any remaining oil. Arrange shanks and fennel in skillet. Add cider and stock. Bring to a boil over high heat. Season to taste with salt and pepper.

Float sheet of foil, dull side down, on surface of stock. Cover skillet with lid and place on lower rack of oven. Bake at 350 degrees about 1¾ hours or until meat is tender. Shanks are done when skewer inserted into thickest section is removed without resistance. Remove 3 cups braising liquid to medium saucepan. Bring to simmer over high heat and cook until thickened to coat the back of spoon, about 12 minutes. Add ¼ cup vinegar. Season to taste with salt and pepper. Add capers and

chives and keep warm. Combine remaining ¼ cup vinegar and remaining olive oil in small bowl. Season to taste with cracked black pepper and salt. Remove fennel from liquid, drain and cut into ½-inch dice. Place in large bowl along with dressing, endive, mache and radicchio, tossing well. Transfer veal shanks to serving plates. Remove strings. Divide salad among separate salad plates. Spoon caper sauce over shanks.

Nutrition details per serving
Calories 684
Percent of calories from fat 40%
Fat: .32 gm
Protein: . . . . .34 gm
Carbohydrate: . . . . .76 gm
Cholesterol: . . . . .115 mg
Sodium: . . . . .375 mg
Diabetic exchange: ¼ vegetable, 4½ fruit, ¼ bread, 4½ meat, 5¾ fat.

WONTON WAYS

■ *Why they taste so good:* The simple egg dough is rolled so thin you can almost see through it. When it's this thin, it allows the filling to heat and cook while capturing all the wonderful flavors inside.

■ *How they are cooked:* These skins allow cooking by frying, steaming or boiling.

■ *Advantages:* Wonton or dumpling wrappers are perfect to encase vegetables, meats, poultry, fish and shellfish and even leftovers.

■ *Tricks of the trade:* Since the wontons or dumplings are cooked only long enough to thoroughly heat the filling, it is always best to cook the ingredients for the filling first, allow them to cool to room temperature, then chop or dice them. Be generous with your seasonings for the fillings since the wrapper is bland and some of the flavor will dissipate during the cooking.

TODAY'S LESSON: One of the most versatile ingredients of Asian cooking is the wonton wrapper. This simple combination of flour, egg, water and salt is made into a tight dough, then rolled paper-thin to encase an infinite combination of taste sensations.

■ *Selecting your wrappers:* There are many different sizes of wrappers. Wontons for frying are usually 3¼-inch squares of super-thin dough. There are about 90 per pound. Dumplings for steaming are 3¼-inch rounds. They are also super-thin, almost translucent, and also about 90 per pound. Dumplings for boiling are thicker, 3½-inch rounds that are tougher in order to stand up to all that movement during cooking. They come 60 to a pound. Spring rolls are 7- to 8-inch squares, usually made without egg so that the texture is more like paper when cooked. They tear easily, so buy extra. They come 30-35 per pound.

■ *Preparing your filling:* Cook your filling ingredients until just about done for meat, poultry and fish, and until al dente for vegetables. Allow to cool before chopping or dicing small, to prevent the filling from tearing through the wrappers. Combine the ingredients and season well.

■ *Filling wontons or dumplings:* Thaw the frozen wrappers overnight in the refrigerator. Lay the wrappers out on a flat surface. Spoon a small amount of the filling in the center; do not overfill, because the filling expands when cooked and may break out of the wrapper. Moisten the edges of the wrapper with water, fold over the filling and seal with slight pressure from your fingertips. Transfer to a cookie sheet lined with parchment and dusted with corn starch; refrigerate until ready to cook.

■ *The cooking begins:* Place the wontons in the fryer and cook until golden. Dumplings can be placed in a steamer or dropped into simmering water, cooking until hot and tender. The moist heat methods make the wrappers quite tender, so remove them from the pot carefully and serve tenderly.

■

BARBECUE SHRIMP, SCALLION & GINGER WONTONS

Makes 4 servings

2 tablespoons olive oil
1 clove garlic, peeled, ends removed, minced
1 small fresh ginger root, peeled, 1 tablespoon chopped fine and the remaining root sliced thin, divided
1 bunch green onions, washed, ends removed, green and white parts separately diced
1 red bell pepper, washed, cored, seeded, finely diced
1 pound shrimp, peeled and deveined
¼ cup barbecue sauce of your choice
Salt to taste
Tabasco or habanero sauce to taste
24 wonton wrappers, 3½ inches square
Corn starch
½ cup red wine vinegar
½ cup dry white wine
2 tablespoons natural soy sauce
2 tablespoons sugar, or to taste
Canola oil for frying
¼ cup fresh cilantro leaves, washed, dried, chopped

To prepare filling: In a large nonstick skillet, heat the olive oil over high heat. Add the garlic and the chopped ginger root, cooking until golden, about 3 minutes. Add the white and half of the green diced onions and the red pepper and cook until tender, about 2 minutes. Add the shrimp and cook until opaque, about 2 minutes. Remove from heat and transfer to a large bowl, allowing to cool to room temperature. When cool, remove the shrimp and cut into a medium dice, just larger than the rest of the ingredients. Return the shrimp to the bowl. Add the barbecue sauce and season with salt and hot sauce to your taste.

To fill wontons: Lay the wontons on a flat surface. Place about 1 tablespoon of filling in the center of each wrapper. Moisten the edges of the wrapper with water. Fold the wrapper over the filling to make a triangle and seal the edges with your fingertips. Transfer to a parchment-lined cookie sheet dusted with corn starch. Refrigerate until ready to cook.

To prepare sauce: In a small saucepan, combine the sliced ginger root, vinegar and wine. Bring to a simmer over medium-high heat. Remove from heat and add the soy sauce and sugar. Allow to cool to room temperature. Strain through a fine sieve to remove the ginger, if you prefer.

To cook the wontons: Heat the canola oil in a large, deep skillet, filled to a depth of 2 inches, to 375 degrees as indicated by a deep fat or candy thermometer. Carefully slide the wontons into the oil and cook until golden on all sides, about 4 minutes. Remove with a slotted spoon to paper towel to drain for 1 minute. Transfer to a bowl and toss with the remaining green onions and cilantro. Put the sauce in a bowl in the center of a large serving platter. Place wontons on the platter, surrounding the sauce. Serve immediately.

Nutrition details per serving
Calories 630
Percent of calories from fat 29%
Fat: .20 gm
Protein: . . . . .34 gm
Carbohydrate: . . . . .76 gm
Cholesterol: . . . . .172 mg
Sodium: . . . . .1,342 mg
Diabetic exchange: 2¼ lean meat, ¾ vegetable, 4½ bread, 3 fat.

EGG-WHITE OMELETS RING IN A HEALTHY YEAR

■ *What are lean omelets?* The fat in eggs comes from the yolk. Eliminate them and you still can make a great omelet.

■ *Why they taste so good:* An omelet's texture comes from the egg white. Much of the flavor comes from the yolk, so when you eliminate it, compensate by adding fresh herbs and spices before cooking. Stuff a cooked omelet with vegetables and low-fat cheese.

■ *Tricks of the trade:* Select the appropriate size pan for the number of eggs you are cooking. A pan that's too large makes an omelet like a pancake; one that's too small yields an omelet too thick to cook through. Use a 5-inch pan for two eggs, a 6-inch for three eggs and upward as the party demands.

■ *Preparing your eggs:* Set out three small to medium bowls. Crack the egg on the side of a bowl and open into the cradle

TODAY'S LESSON: Many people ring in the new year with resolutions to live a healthy life. Start your regimen with terrific lean omelets.

of your hand, letting the white fall between your fingers into the bowl without breaking the yolk. Transfer the yolk to one bowl and the white to another. Repeat, separating the eggs over the empty bowl to prevent yolk from getting into the egg whites.

Whisk the whites until pale but not foaming. Season with fresh herbs such as chives, parsley, tarragon or a few scallions. Add a touch of black pepper, paprika or your other favorite spices. Use only a pinch of salt.

■ *Prepare your fillings:* Cheese is the all-time favorite, but select low-fat or nonfat cheese. Sharper cheeses have more pronounced flavor, so less is

needed to satisfy your palate.

Vegetables such as sweet peppers, onions, fennel, garlic and winter squashes are best oven-roasted or grilled without fat until tender. Keep warm or reheat before adding to the omelet. Cooked skinless poultry can be added at the last second.

■ *The cooking begins:* Heat your nonstick pan over medium heat, brushing the surface with just a drop of oil to moisten. Pour the whites into the pan and cook until they begin to congeal. Slide a rubber spatula under the eggs and let the uncooked whites from the top of the omelet run to the pan surface. Repeat until the eggs are solid. Flip the eggs over in the pan to cook the top. (If you don't feel comfortable doing that, place the pan momentarily under a hot broiler.) Fill half the pan with the filling.

Remove from heat and place the lip of the pan on the serving plate, quickly inverting the pan in a smooth motion to enclose the filling, and place the omelet on your plate. Sprinkle with any garnish herbs or spices and serve.

■ *Serving suggestions:* A great omelet has a comforting, tender texture best complemented by crisp, crunchy breakfast breads. Brush with jams and preserves.

■ *Mix and match:* Choose from herbs, spices, vegetables and lean meats. The best combinations are simple: one main herb with a couple of vegetables and, at the most, one cheese.

■

SWEET ROASTED PEPPER & EGG-WHITE OMELET

Makes 2 servings

1 red pepper, roasted, peeled, seeded and diced

1 green pepper, roasted, peeled, seeded and diced

2 cloves roasted garlic, optional

2 tablespoons fresh sweet basil, washed, chopped

Freshly ground black pepper to taste

Sea salt to taste, divided

6 large egg whites

1 teaspoon paprika

1 bunch scallion greens, washed, diced

Canola oil to moisten pan

2 sprigs basil or parsley, washed, dried, for garnish

In a nonstick skillet over medium heat, combine the red and green peppers, roasted garlic and basil, cooking until hot, about 5 minutes. Season with black pepper and salt to taste. Keep warm. In a medium bowl, whisk the egg whites, paprika and salt to taste until light and frothy but not foamy. Stir in the scallions.

Heat an 8-inch nonstick skillet over medium heat. Brush the pan with a drop or two of canola oil to just moisten the surface. Pour the egg whites into the pan, cooking until they begin to congeal. Slide a rubber spatula under the eggs and allow the uncooked whites to run under the omelet to the pan; repeat until eggs are solid. Flip eggs over in the pan to cook the top, or place pan momentarily under a hot broiler. Fill half the pan with the filling. Remove from heat and place the lip of the pan on the serving plate, quickly inverting the pan in a smooth motion to enclose the filling, and place the omelet on the plate. Garnish with the fresh herbs and serve.

Nutrition details per serving
Calories 129
Percent of calories from fat 20%
Fat: . . . . .3 gm
Protein: . . . . .16 gm
Carbohydrate: . . . . .10 gm
Cholesterol: . . . . .0 mg
Sodium: . . . . .230 mg
Diabetic exchange: 1¼ lean meat, 1¼ vegetable, ½ fat.

■

Omelets may be made with eggs other than chicken — particularly duck eggs, where the volume of the yolk is near equal to the volume of the white, making a richer-tasting omelet.

ROAST CHICKEN IS A WINTER WINNER

■ *What kind of chicken roasts best?* Winter calls for a heartier bird to roast than the young, delicate fryer. Roaster chickens range from 3½ to 6½ pounds and from 14 weeks to 8 months old. Their flesh is firm and full-flavored, perfect for roasting.

■ *Health advantages:* These days the skin is routinely removed before cooking. But the Nutritional Coordinating Center of Minneapolis has reported the fat content of average-size, oven-roasted chickens to be almost identical whether the skin was removed before or after cooking. Cook the chicken in its skin to develop the flavor and help maintain moisture, but ditch the fat by removing the skin before serving.

■ *How to select:* Select a roaster with smooth yellow skin free of tears, bruises or blemishes. The more mature roaster should have more fat visible

TODAY'S LESSON: Winter winds that blow through long, cold nights bring out our craving for rich, fulfilling flavors. Imagine a chicken roasting over a crackling fire, warming the room with its glow.

around its neck and interior cavity. Kosher, free-range or Amish roasters often have fuller flavor, moister and more tender meat than the average commercial roaster. These specialty birds cost more, but you generally can taste the difference. Avoid frozen roasters, which may be quite tough because of their maturity and the effect of freezing. You can keep a roaster refrigerated for a couple of days.

■ *How to prepare:* Remove the neck and other parts from the interior cavity. Rinse the bird well under running cold water. Pat dry with paper toweling. Season inside and out with sea

salt and a generous dose of fresh-ground black pepper. Truss the bird with kitchen twine to enhance even cooking, and place it on a roasting pan.

■ *How to cook:* Roasting can maximize the flavor of the bird through caramelization of the skin while the meat cooks to juicy tenderness. Start cooking the bird at around 400-450 degrees for 15-20 minutes, or sear it in a skillet on the stove to start the browning. Without that initial high heat, the chicken would be bland and very dull. Turn the oven down to 350-375 degrees to finish the cooking process for smaller roasters, 250-300 degrees for larger ones. Test the roaster by inserting an instant meat thermometer into the thickest part of the thigh; it should read 160-165 degrees when done. Let the roaster rest about 10 minutes at room temperature before carving, to allow the juices to settle.

■ *Seasoning the bird:* Heartier roasters taste best when seasoned with evergreen herbs such as rosemary. Such winter herbs tend to be quite strong and coarse, especially when served uncooked. They are best tamed by frying or sauteing in olive oil. The seasoned cooking oil can carry their flavor to dressings and other foods.

■ *Serving suggestions:* As long as you have the oven fired up, whole roasted garlic will please your palate and help protect against the winter cold. Figure one head of garlic per person, although some may favor two. Slice the heads of garlic in half on the equator, rub with a little olive oil and add to the roasting pan after the initial sear. Cook until very tender or mushy, 30-45 minutes. Remove from the oven and keep warm. Serve with earthy peasant bread, grilled or toasted with a touch of olive oil if you like. Serve the roaster with hearty root vegetables that match and fortify against the winter season. The combination is a winning, warming one.

■

ROAST CHICKEN WITH ROSEMARY

Makes 4 servings

½ cup extra-virgin olive oil
1 bunch fresh rosemary
1 5-pound roasting chicken
Salt to taste
Freshly ground black pepper to taste (be generous)
4 large bulbs garlic, cut in half on the equator
½ cup stock or wine, if needed

Preheat oven to 450. In a medium skillet, heat the olive oil to 300-325 degrees. Add the rosemary sprigs and cook till crisp, about 2 minutes, or until the oil stops bubbling around the rosemary. Drain the rosemary on paper towel. Remove the rosemary leaves from the stems, reserving 4 full sprigs for garnish. Allow the oil to cool. Thoroughly rinse the roaster inside and out under running cold water. Pat dry with paper toweling. Salt and pepper the cavity and skin. Truss it to ensure even cooking. Place the chicken in an ovenproof skillet. Rub ¼ cup of the rosemary oil across the skin. Place the roaster on the lower rack with the legs toward the back of the oven. Cook until the bird starts to brown, about 15-20 minutes. Turn down the heat to 350. Rub the surfaces of the garlic with a little of the remaining rosemary oil. Add the garlic to the roasting skillet and cook until tender, about 30-45 minutes. Remove the garlic and keep warm while continuing to cook the chicken until done, about an additional 40 minutes, until an instant meat thermometer inserted in the thigh reads 160 degrees and the juices run clear. Remove from the oven. Pour the cooking fat and juices into a glass measuring cup and retrieve the jus. If the juices are caramelized in the pan, add ½ cup stock or wine to reconstitute. Carve the chicken. Divide the pieces onto warm serving plates. Spoon the juices over the chicken and top with rosemary leaves. Position the garlic heads beside the chicken. Garnish with a sprig of crisped rosemary.

Nutrition details per serving (including skin)
Calories 1,102
Percent of calories from fat 52%
Fat: . . . . .63 gm
Protein: . . . . .128 gm
Carbohydrate: . . . . .6 gm
Cholesterol: . . . . .497 mg
Sodium: . . . . .911 mg
Diabetic exchange: 1¼ vegetables, 16 meat, 5¾ fat.

DRINK TO YOUR HEALTH

■ *Why they taste so good:* Most tropical fruits are high in acid, making them perfect thirst quenchers. They can be blended to make interesting flavor combinations that become out of this world with a sprinkling of spices.

■ *Health advantages:* Fruit juices are abundant in vitamins, but the predominant vitamin C is perfect to boost the immune system against winter colds.

■ *Tricks of the trade:* Nearly all fruit juice flavors can benefit from sweetening; the best method is to make a simple sugar-water syrup that is gradually mixed into the juice.

I prefer to make a spiced sugar syrup by adding cinnamon, vanilla, nutmeg or citrus peels. The combination of the juice and spice adds an extra dimension. You can also make a sugar syrup out of tea. First, brew the tea to a mild concentration. Remove the tea leaves

TODAY'S LESSON: Tropical fruits that arrive in winter – pineapples, bananas, passion fruit and, of course, citrus – make some of the best juices for invigorating your new year.

or bag, blend in the sugar and choose your fruit. Select the fruits to blend into a juice by primary flavor, secondary flavor or texture.

Primary flavor fruits, such as oranges, are used for the largest volume of juice and usually have a softer flavor and lower price. Secondary or seasoning fruits, such as passion fruit, intensify the primary flavor. A texture fruit has a solid flesh that is thicker than the blending fruit. Start with mostly orange juice, thicken with bananas and highlight with a little passion fruit. Then spice with a little citrus-vanilla sugar syrup. Serve well chilled with a sprig of mint.

■ *Preparing your fruit:* Wash, peel and seed the fruit. Process the fruits separately through a juicer or extractor. Blend the texture fruit and the secondary fruit together. Add the sugar syrup slowly until you achieve your desired level of sweetness.

■ *Serving suggestions:* All juice tastes best when chilled for at least 3 hours in the refrigerator or an hour in a snowbank. Serve over cubed or shaved ice. Remember, the juice will dilute as the ice melts. For a different approach, freeze juices in ice cube trays and serve the same or complementary juices over the cubes.

■ *Mix and match:* Try any combination of the more common tropical fruits such as pineapple, banana, papaya, orange, grapefruit and the incredibly wide citrus family. For more exotic flavors, try passion fruit, carambola, ceriman, cherimoya, guava, feijoa, kumquat, loquat, mango, pepino, sapote and tamarillo.

■ *Try your technique:* To get you started, try the simple Banana, Orange & Passion Fruit Drink.

■

BANANA, ORANGE & PASSION FRUIT DRINK

Makes 2½ quarts

16 juice oranges
1 lemon
2 cups granulated sugar
2 cups cold water
1 vanilla bean, split in half lengthwise; or substitute pure vanilla extract to your taste

4 large bananas, peeled, strings removed
1 cup passion fruit juice or puree, fresh or frozen
Sprigs of mint for garnish

Using a sharp vegetable peeler, cut the outer rind from the oranges and the lemon without the white inner membrane. Reserve rinds from oranges and lemon; set aside. Squeeze all the oranges into juice and chill. Squeeze the lemon into juice separately.

In a medium saucepan, combine the sugar, water and lemon juice. Bring to a simmer over medium-high heat. Add the orange and lemon rinds and the vanilla, returning to a simmer. Remove from the heat

and allow to cool to room temperature. Strain through a fine sieve, and discard the rinds. Reserve the sugar syrup in a clean glass container under refrigeration. It will keep for as long as a month.

In a blender, puree the bananas until smooth and fluid, mixing with orange juice as necessary. Transfer to a large bowl. Add the remaining orange juice and passion fruit juice or puree. While whisking, slowly add the sugar syrup until you have reached your desired level of sweetness. Chill well. Serve over ice or straight, garnishing with a sprig of mint.

Nutrition details per serving
Calories .277
Percent of calories from fat 2%
Fat: . . . . .1 gm
Protein: . . . . .2 gm
Carbohydrate: . . . . .70 gm
Cholesterol: . . . . .0 mg
Sodium: . . . . .4 mg
Diabetic exchange: 4½ fruit. Not recommended for diabetics.

FRUIT PUREES
ADD FLAVOR, NOT FAT

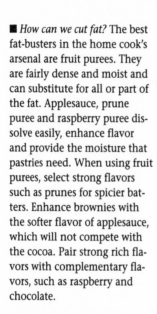

■ *How can we cut fat?* The best fat-busters in the home cook's arsenal are fruit purees. They are fairly dense and moist and can substitute for all or part of the fat. Applesauce, prune puree and raspberry puree dissolve easily, enhance flavor and provide the moisture that pastries need. When using fruit purees, select strong flavors such as prunes for spicier batters. Enhance brownies with the softer flavor of applesauce, which will not compete with the cocoa. Pair strong rich flavors with complementary flavors, such as raspberry and chocolate.

■ *Can I change your oil?* Even with lots of fruit puree, some pastries might seem a little rubbery without at least a little oil. In that case, use cholesterol-free oils such as canola or light olive oil. If you are still looking for that rich taste, replace butter with low-fat cream cheese.

TODAY'S LESSON: A trip to the bakery or supermarket shows that commercial bakers have gotten surprisingly good at eliminating fat and still coming up with a nice texture. But home cooks can cut the fat, too.

■ *The cooking begins:* Here are some baking guidelines and tips for experimenting with your favorite recipes.

Simmer fresh purees gently with a little sugar to taste until thickened to a heavy sauce consistency. Strain through a fine sieve to remove seeds and coarse parts that would adversely affect the pastry's texture.

Rehydrate dried fruits by covering with boiling water and allowing to steep a few hours before pureeing. Steep in hot wine or juices to enhance flavor. Strain through a fine sieve for smooth texture.

Replace up to 75 percent of fat with thick fruit puree, at room temperature.

LOW-FAT BROWNIES

Makes 10 servings

2   ounces baking chocolate

2   teaspoons vanilla extract

1½ cups sugar

¼   teaspoon salt

3   large eggs, lightly beaten

2   large egg whites, lightly beaten

¾   cup maple syrup or honey

1   cup unsweetened applesauce

¼   cup canola oil

1   cup cake flour, sifted

¾   cup cocoa powder

6   ounces extra bittersweet chocolate pieces, optional

    Confectioners' sugar

Preheat oven to 350 degrees. Line a 9-by-9-inch baking pan with parchment paper. In the top of a double boiler with water at a low simmer, melt baking chocolate with vanilla. Remove from stove and transfer to a large mixing bowl. Stir in sugar, salt, eggs and egg whites until smooth. Mix in syrup or honey, applesauce and canola oil. Sift together flour and cocoa over the batter and carefully fold in until smooth. Add bittersweet chocolate and gently combine. Do not overmix. Pour batter into prepared pan and bake for about 45 minutes or until a wooden pick comes out clean. Cool on rack. Dust with confectioners' sugar.

Nutrition details per serving
Calories 302
Percent of calories from fat 16%
Fat: . . . . .5 gm
Protein: . . . . .6 gm
Carbohydrate: . . . . .65 gm
Cholesterol: . . . . .64 mg
Sodium: . . . . .92 mg
Diabetic exchange: ½ medium-fat meat,
¾ bread, 3 fruit, ½ fat

Nutrition details per serving (with extra bittersweet pieces)
Calories 383
Percent of calories from fat 29%
Fat: . . . . .12 gm
Protein: . . . . .7 gm
Carbohydrate: . . . . .73 gm
Cholesterol: . . . . .64 mg
Sodium: . . . . .93 mg
Diabetic exchange: ½ medium-fat meat,
¾ bread, 3¾ fruit, 1¼ fat. May not be
suitable for diabetics.

CARROT MUFFINS

Makes 16 muffins

1½ cups pitted prunes

½   cup hot water

2   large eggs, lightly beaten

2   large egg whites, lightly beaten

¼   cup canola oil

2   teaspoons vanilla extract

2   cups light brown sugar

2¾ cups cake flour, sifted

2   teaspoons cinnamon

2   teaspoons grated nutmeg

1   tablespoon double-acting baking powder

¼   teaspoon salt

1½ cups carrots, peeled, ends removed, finely grated

½   cup pineapple, diced

¼   cup golden raisins, soaked in 1 cup orange juice for 1 hour to soften

Preheat oven to 350 degrees. Fill a 2½-inch muffin pan with paper liners. In a food processor fitted with metal blade, combine prunes, hot water, eggs, egg whites, canola oil and vanilla. Puree until smooth. Strain. Stir in brown sugar. Set aside in large bowl. In another large bowl, combine flour, cinnamon, nutmeg, baking powder and salt. Add dry mixture to batter, mixing just until smooth. Stir in carrots, pineapple and raisins. Divide batter into prepared pan. Bake until golden, about 30 minutes. Cool on rack.

Nutrition details per serving
Calories 263
Percent of calories from fat 15%
Fat: . . . . .4 gm
Protein: . . . . .3 gm
Carbohydrate: . . . . .54 gm
Cholesterol: . . . . .27 mg
Sodium: . . . . .190 mg
Diabetic exchange: ¼ vegetable, 1
bread, 2½ fruit, ¾ fat

SAP IS RISING ON SYRUP SEASON

AMAZING FOOD FACTS

■

American Indians were the first to collect maple sap and produce sugar.

■

Before they are tapped for sap, maple trees are usually 40 years old or more.

■ *Where does it come from?* The rock, or hard, maple is considered the best for producing syrup because of the high natural sugar level in the sap, 3 percent. The largest sap production comes from trees with a full, large crown of leaves. Severe winter weather, which freezes the roots, and late snow, which keeps the roots chilled, will lead to a heavy sap flow when the temperature rises above 40 degrees.

■ *How is it processed?* After the sap is collected, water is removed in a number of ways, but the process is completed by boiling to concentrate the sugar to about 68 percent. The color and flavor come from the browning of the natural sugars and amino acids, but the real quality is determined by the tree itself, the weather and the soil.

■ *What's the best?* The best-quality sap comes from the first flow of the season, when

TODAY'S LESSON: Thanks to freezing nights and warm days that start the sap flow, maple syrup production begins in mid-March and lasts until the trees bud, about four weeks.

the weather is still cold. As temperatures rise, the sap produces stronger and darker syrup — considered to be of a lower quality. When the tree begins to bud, the sap begins to carry substances that give the syrup a harsh burnt flavor, often compared to the taste of Tootsie Rolls. Maple syrup is found in three grades:

The highest grade of syrup is light amber, or Grade AA. It has a very light color, delicate texture and taste, and is best as a dessert topping or sauce.

Medium amber, Grade A, has a more pronounced color and flavor which is perfect for pancakes and waffles.

Dark amber, Grade A, is deeper in color with a full-bod-

ied caramel flavor and is best used as a sweetener in recipes.

■ *A substitute for sugar?* Maple sugar has a rich, full flavor when substituted for granulated or light brown sugar, especially for caramelizing on top of creme brulees. Remember, the maple sugar is less sweet, so adjust the quantity in your recipe to your taste.

■ *Why is it so expensive?* Pure maple sugar products are expensive because the sap from three to four trees is needed to produce 1 gallon of syrup. Birch and elm trees may be used but are less sweet, requiring many more gallons of sap to produce syrup. Commercial syrup products are usually made with corn syrups and so-called natural flavors to reduce the cost, but they miss the true maple flavor.

At the turn of the century, maple sugar and syrup were more popular than refined sugar but declined because of high prices. As spring arrives, it is a great time to get out of the house and experience maple sugaring.

■

MAPLE BRAN MUFFINS

Makes 8 servings

Butter for greasing muffin tin

1½   cups whole wheat flour
2   cups bran
⅛   teaspoon salt
1¼   teaspoon baking powder
1   tablespoon ground cinnamon
4   tablespoons (½ stick) unsalted butter
1   large egg
1¼   cups buttermilk

1   tablespoon vanilla extract
¾   cup maple syrup
½   cup grated coconut
¾   cup finely diced apples
¾   cup pineapple cut into ¼-inch pieces
¼   cup golden or regular raisins, soaked in orange juice, covered for 1 hour to soften and excess drained

Preheat oven to 350. Grease a muffin pan with butter. Combine the flour, bran, salt, baking powder and cinnamon in a large bowl. With a mixer on medium speed, cream the 4 tablespoons butter into the flour mixture. Mix in the egg, buttermilk and vanilla. Add the maple syrup just to combine; do not overwork. Fold in the coconut, apple, pineapple and raisins. Divide the batter into the muffin pan. Bake until golden. Test by inserting a skewer; it should be warm and clean when removed, about 30 minutes. Cool on a cake rack.

Nutrition details per serving
Calories .369
Percent of calories from fat 30%
Fat: . . . . .14 gm
Protein: . . . . .11 gm
Carbohydrate: . . . . .62 gm
Cholesterol: . . . . .43 mg
Sodium: . . . . .128 mg
Diabetic exchange: ¼ milk, ½ fruit, 2 bread, 2¼ fat.

■

It takes 40-50 gallons of sap to produce 1 gallon of syrup. An average rock maple tree produces 10-12 gallons of sap each season.

■

Maple sugar is made from syrup with high concentrations of sugar. The crystals that form are removed from the syrup and finely ground to simulate granulated sugar.

BISCOTTI LIGHTEN THE HOLIDAYS

■ *Why they taste so good:* Biscotti are intensely flavored cookies that are twice baked for a special crunchy texture. They're the perfect accompaniment to such spirits as marsala, the Italian sweet wine called Vin Santo, and grapa, the Italian white lightning. They are dipped in Vin Santo, like dunking doughnuts into coffee.

■ *What are biscotti made from?* Biscotti commonly are made with such nuts as hazelnuts, walnuts and pistachios. Nuts give an earthy depth and, in the case of the almonds, extra crunch. Spices also are important to biscotti. A strong shot of vanilla extract, licorice-scented anise seed, cinnamon and nutmeg will make biscotti linger on your palate. Spiced biscotti go well with a good brandy or cognac, and they help take the edge off some of the rougher alcohols. Even chocolate occasionally finds its way into biscotti. Cocoa may

TODAY'S LESSON: Not all the season's desserts need to overflow with fat and calories. For a lighter but satisfying treat, try the Italian specialty cookie biscotti.

be substituted for part of the flour for an overall chocolate flavor. A sweeter, more intense flavor comes from adding chocolate chips or shaved morsels. Chocolate-flavored biscotti with espresso or cappuccino are a great close to a holiday feast.

■ *How to bake:* After the biscotti batter is made, it is shaped into a long French baguette-style loaf, then baked at 350 for about 20-30 minutes, depending on size. The loaf is allowed to cool, then sliced ½- to ¾-inch thick on a slight diagonal with a serrated bread knife. These slices are placed on a cookie sheet and returned to the oven to bake until lightly golden, about 15 minutes.

■ *How to store:* Allow the cookies to cool completely before storing in a moisture-resistant tin or jar. They will keep for several weeks.

■ *Sensational gifts:* Biscotti make perfect holiday gifts. Wrapped in colored parchment or tissue paper and packed in a fancy box or tin, these simple treats take on an air of pure luxury.

BISCOTTI WITH ALMONDS, ORANGE & CHOCOLATE

Makes 12 servings

8 ounces unsalted butter (2 sticks)

1½ cups sugar

3 tablespoons finely grated orange rind

2 tablespoons pure vanilla extract

6 cups all-purpose flour

1 tablespoon baking powder

1 teaspoon salt

6 eggs, beaten

¼ cup Amaretto

2 cups sliced blanched almonds, lightly toasted

2 cups chocolate chips or pieces

Preheat the oven to 350 degrees. In an electric mixer bowl, combine butter, sugar, orange rind and vanilla, and beat until light and creamy. Sift together the dry ingredients. With the mixer on slow, add the dry ingredients to butter mixture until thoroughly combined. Slowly add the eggs and Amaretto. Add almonds and chocolate until just combined.

Remove the dough to a floured surface and form into two flat logs about 4 inches wide and the length of your cookie sheet. Lay the logs on buttered cookie sheets and place on the lower rack of the oven. Bake until lightly browned, about 45 minutes. Remove to a cake rack to cool. With a serrated knife, cut the loaves into ½-inch slices, placing the cut slices flat on the cookie sheet. Return them to the lower rack of the oven and cook until golden, 15-20 minutes. Remove the slices to a cake rack to cool. Store in an airtight container such as a sealed cookie jar or decorative cookie tin.

Cook's note: If the biscotti lose their crispness, repeat the crisping stage.

Nutrition details per serving
Calories 662
Percent of calories from fat 45%
Fat: .35 gm
Protein: . . . . .16 gm
Carbohydrate: . . . . .80 gm
Cholesterol: . . . . .111 mg
Sodium: . . . . .209 mg
Diabetic exchange: 3½ bread, ⅓ meat, 4¾ fat.

ADD SUNSHINE WITH LEMONS

AMAZING FOOD FACTS

■

A medium-size lemon contains 2-3 tablespoons of juice and 3 teaspoons of grated rind. It takes five to six lemons to make 1 cup of juice.

■

After pitting cherries or slicing beets, use lemon juice to remove the stains from your fingers.

■ *How many varieties are there?* Of the many varieties of lemons worldwide, the lemons that land on our supermarket shelves are mainly either Lisbon or Eureka. They are almost identical in size, shape, color and acid level. Both lemons have their largest harvest in late winter when the demand for the sunny fruit is the highest. The Meyer lemon recently has grown in popularity. It's is a hybrid produced by crossing a lemon with a mandarin orange. The result is larger and more golden in color than the parent lemon, with a moderate acidity and medium lemon flavor. The peel has little characteristic lemon essence.

■ *How are they grown?* Although each variety of lemon has a peak harvest, the lemon tree is really everbearing. This means the tree has blossoms, immature fruit and some ripe fruit on the tree almost all the time. Lemons often are picked green. The lemons are then cured at around 56 degrees for up to four months. In that time, the thinner yellow skin develops and the fruit pulp turns to juice.

■ *Advantages:* Lemons perform wonderful food chemistry. They retard the oxidation and slow the enzyme reactions that cause discoloring of cut fruits and vegetables. The acid inverts sugars for syrups and desserts and even "cooks" certain proteins in fish and shellfish without them ever seeing a stove.

■ *How to select:* Select lemons by feel more than by looks. Choose heavy lemons with tight smooth skins. Check the stem end to ensure a firm fruit. Squeeze the lemon to detect the slight "give" which indi-

TODAY'S LESSON: How to break the winter grays? Try the brightest flavor of the season: the lemon.

cates more juice. Lemons with blotchy skin, rusty patches and uneven shapes are still great when they pass the above test. Avoid soft, puffy-skinned, moldy and light lemons.

■ *How to store:* The biggest enemy of the fresh lemon is moisture loss through the skin. Store lemons in an airtight jar or heavy-duty zipper-style plastic bag under refrigeration and they will keep a few weeks.

■ *How to prepare:* To enjoy the lemon, scrub well under running cold water to remove the wax and post-harvest fungicides. Lemons are sprayed to prevent mold during curing and shipping. A mist of wax enhances the look for the supermarket and seals the surface for moisture retention.

■ *Don't forget the peel:* The lemon rind should not go unnoticed. The rind produces peel oil, which complements food and drink. It is probably more important in the production of furniture polishes, perfumes, shampoos and soaps.

■

LEMON TART

Makes 1 10-inch tart

2   cups fresh lemon juice, about 6 lemons

1½ cups granulated sugar

6   large eggs

6   large egg yolks

¼   cup lemon rind zest (the yellow part of the peel), finely chopped or grated

6   ounces unsalted butter, room temperature

1   10-inch prebaked Pastry Shell (see accompanying recipe)

Confectioners' sugar

Mint sprigs for garnish

Combine lemon juice and sugar in a heavy, medium-size, stainless steel saucepan. Bring to a boil over high heat, then simmer. Remove from heat. In a medium bowl, combine eggs, egg yolks and lemon zest. Whisk hot syrup into egg mixture. Pour custard back into saucepan. Return saucepan to medium heat. Constantly whisk custard while cooking. Occasionally stir with a rubber spatula to ensure custard is not sticking. Cook until thickened to coat the back of a spoon heavily. Remove from heat and whisk in butter tablespoon by tablespoon until silky smooth. Pour through a fine sieve into a bowl to cool for an instant. Fill pastry shell to the top. Refrigerate until firm, about

4 hours. To serve, dust the top with confectioners' sugar. Present each slice with a sprig of mint.

Nutrition details per serving
Calories 405
Percent of calories from fat 53%
Fat: . . . . .25 gm
Protein: . . . . .7 gm
Carbohydrate: . . . . .43 gm
Cholesterol: . . . . .366 mg
Sodium: . . . . .56 mg
Diabetic exchange: ⅓ fruit, 1 meat, 4⅓ fat.

■

PASTRY SHELL

Makes 1 10-inch start shell

2   cups all-purpose flour

6   tablespoons sugar
    Pinch of salt

12 tablespoons unsalted butter, chilled

1   large egg, beaten

In a medium-size bowl, combine flour, sugar and salt. Using pastry blender or two knives, cut in butter until mixture resembles fine meal. Add egg; mix until just combined. Gather into a ball. Flatten slightly. Wrap with plastic wrap; refrigerate for a least 2 hours. Roll pastry on a lightly floured surface to a thickness of ⅛ inch. Fit into a 10-inch tart pan. Trim edges. Preheat oven to 375. Line crust with foil, shiny side down. Fill pie with pie weights or dried beans. Bake about 20 minutes. Remove weights and foil; continue baking until crust is lightly browned, about 10-12 minutes.

Nutrition details per serving
Calories 314
Percent of calories from fat 54%
Fat: . . . . .19 gm
Protein: . . . . .4 gm
Carbohydrate: . . . . .33 gm
Cholesterol: . . . . .49 mg
Sodium: . . . . .198 mg
Diabetic exchange: 1½ bread, trace meat, 3⅓ fat.

CAKE WITHOUT FLOUR

■ *What is it made of?* The flourless cake is made simply of chocolate, butter, eggs, sugar and cocoa powder. The cake is held together by the protein structure of the eggs, with just a little help from the chocolate's starches.

■ *What makes it rise?* The cake will rise when baked because of the enlarging of the air pockets formed in mixing. Once the cake is removed from the oven, it will fall if left to its own devices, or it may be pressed to remove the air.

■

PRESSED CHOCOLATE CAKE WITH BERRIES & FUDGE SAUCE

Makes 8 servings

7   ounces extra-bittersweet chocolate (not baking chocolate)

TODAY'S LESSON: In this cake, we eliminate flour by taking advantage of natural starches in the chocolate. It has a wonderful, intense chocolate flavor and delicate texture.

14   tablespoons (1¾ sticks) unsalted butter

5   large eggs, separated

1   tablespoon vanilla extract

¾   cup sugar
     Pinch of salt

2   tablespoons dark cocoa powder

2   pints fresh raspberries

2   cups hot fudge sauce
     Fresh mint sprigs for garnish

Preheat the oven to 350. Grease a 10-inch springform pan. In the top of a double boiler with water at a low simmer, combine the chocolate and butter. Heat until melted and smooth. Transfer to a medium-size bowl, and whisk in the egg yolks and vanilla. Sift in the sugar, salt, and cocoa while continuing to whisk. With a mixer, whip the egg whites to soft peaks. Fold a third of them into the chocolate mixture. Repeat with the remaining whites, then pour the mixture into the prepared pan. Place on the lower rack of the oven and bake for 25 minutes. Remove to a cake rack, and immediately loosen the springform collar or sides. Slip a plate inside the collar on top of the cake and push down slightly to push air from cake. Remove the plate and springform collar, and allow the cake to cool before serving.

To serve, cut the cake into 8 pieces, and place on serving plates. Divide the raspberries and place in a small mound next to the cake. Heat the hot fudge sauce, transfer to a squirt bottle (like a ketchup or mustard bottle). Drizzle the sauce over the cake and plate. Garnish with mint and serve.

■

ALMOND & COCONUT MACAROON CAKE

Makes 8-10 servings

1   tablespoon butter

1½ cups blanched sliced almonds

2¼ cups shredded unsweetened coconut, divided

6   large eggs, separated

1   cup granulated sugar, divided

    Pinch of salt

1   teaspoon vanilla extract

¼   cup coarse granulated sugar

¼   cup orange juice

¼   cup orange liqueur (or substitute ¼ cup more orange juice)

    Sprigs of mint for garnish

30-40 orange segments, cleaned of pith, tossed with 2 tablespoons orange liqueur and 1 tablespoon warmed orange marmalade, optional

Preheat oven to 325 degrees. Using butter, lightly grease a 10-inch springform cake pan. Spread almonds evenly across a baking sheet. Spread coconut evenly across another baking sheet. Place both in the oven and cook until lightly browned, about 15 minutes for the almonds, about 10 minutes for the coconut. Remove from the oven and cool to room temperature. Process 1 cup of the almonds in a food processor until ground into an even, coarse chop. Reserve. In a medium bowl, whip the egg whites with ½ cup sugar to firm peaks. Place a whole egg (in the shell) atop the whipped whites; the egg should sink about halfway into the whites. If it sinks farther, whip the whites more; if it doesn't sink, you have whipped them too much and the cake may turn out cottony. Meanwhile, beat the egg yolks with the remaining ½ cup sugar, a pinch of salt and vanilla until light and the batter forms a ribbon when falling from the beaters. Fold the ground almonds and 2 cups of the coconut into the yolks. Fold a third of the whites into the batter to lighten. Fold in the remaining whites until smooth. Pour the batter into the cake pan. Sprinkle the top of the cake with the remaining toasted sliced almonds, remaining ¼ cup coconut and the coarse granulated sugar. Place on the lower rack of the oven and bake until light and golden, about 45 minutes. Test with a skewer or toothpick; when removed it should be hot and clean. Put on a cake rack and allow to cool for 10 minutes. Prick the top of the cake all over with a skewer or toothpick. In a small bowl, combine the orange juice and liqueur. Spoon the orange juice blend atop the cake and allow to soak in to flavor the cake. Allow the cake to cool to room temperature before serving. Cut the cake into 8-10 pieces. Place a slice in the center of each serving plate. Garnish with a sprig of mint. Spoon the orange segments over the top.

GIFTS COATED IN CHOCOLATE

AMAZING FOOD FACTS

■

Cacao trees are being cultivated on the island of Hawaii, and the chocolate produced from their beans is receiving high praise for its fruit aroma, smooth texture and intense, lingering flavor. The chocolate can hold its own with the world's best.

■ *How does it work?* The simplest method is to buy "couverture," chocolate made specifically for dipping and coating. Or make your own dipping chocolate with bittersweet or extra-bittersweet chocolate and a few other common ingredients. The chocolate is slowly melted until smooth, then allowed to cool until it almost congeals. The ingredients are then dipped to coat. Properly heated and cooled chocolate, known as tempered chocolate, creates a hard, glossy finish that will not melt at room temperature.

■ *Why it tastes so good:* The intense, rich characteristics of chocolate elevate the flavor of cookies, nuts and fresh and dried fruits.

■ *Tricks of the trade:* Patience is the key — allow the chocolate to slowly melt and slowly cool to just the right temperature. Too hot and the chocolate won't coat, too cold and the

TODAY'S LESSON: Even the simplest of cookies, fruits and pastries become elegant holiday treats and gifts when coated with silky chocolate.

chocolate will lump. Moisture causes the chocolate to lock up, becoming grainy and lumpy. Avoid moisture from the double boiler, whether water or steam. Wrap cut fresh fruit in paper towels to draw out excess moisture before dipping. Shortening is best to provide chocolate the little extra fat it needs to bring out the shine and prevent blooming (the white streaks that sometimes make an unsightly finished product).

■ *Prepare your foods:* Chocolate coating works best with cool or chilled ingredients that will attract the chocolate and help it set. Cookies are fine to dip at room temperature, but remove any crumbs with a pastry

brush before dipping. Whole nuts are best toasted, then allowed to cool completely to room temperature. Fruit such as strawberries, seedless orange segments, grapes and even raspberries, if you have the patience, are good if you don't break the skin or outer membranes. The surfaces of cut fruit such as pineapple, kiwi, pears and apples must be thoroughly dried with paper towel and completely covered for the best results. Snacks such as popcorn, pretzels and potato chips, as well as hard candies, follow the same rules as cookies.

■ *Preparing your chocolate:* Break the chocolate into even, small pieces. Place in a metal bowl, add the shortening and any other ingredients and melt over warm water that's just below simmering. Stir to ensure even heating. Once melted and glossy, remove from the heat. Wipe moisture from the bottom of the bowl.

■ *Begin tempering or cooling:* Let chocolate cool for about 5 minutes, stirring to maintain an even temperature. Test the chocolate by inserting a knife into the center, shaking off the excess and timing how long it takes to harden. Check every couple of minutes until the chocolate hardens in about 2 minutes.

■ *Start dipping:* Hold the food in your fingers and dip, shaking to remove the excess. You don't have to cover the food completely, since the contrast of its natural color next to the chocolate looks great. Place the pieces without touching each other on a sheet of wax paper atop a cookie sheet. Sprinkle with garnishes such as spices, chopped nuts or sugar sprinkles if you like.

Transfer the tray to the freezer for 3-4 minutes to help set, but do not freeze. Transfer to an airtight tin or container with pieces separated by wax paper or food tissue. Store fruits in refrigeration; store other, more stable products, such as cookies and nuts, in a cool area.

■

CHOCOLATE-DIPPED STRAWBERRIES

2   pints red ripe strawberries, stems on

8   ounces bittersweet chocolate, broken into pieces

4   ounces unsalted butter (1 stick)

1   tablespoon light corn syrup

Carefully clean the strawberries and dry them. Remove only the brown leaves from the stems. Refrigerate to deep-chill before coating. Set up a cookie sheet with parchment or an empty egg carton and some toothpicks for the dipping procedure.

Combine the chocolate, butter and corn syrup in a small bowl. Melt in a water bath or double boiler until smooth and shiny, but do not heat over 110 degrees. Remove from the heat and allow the chocolate to cool to 88 degrees, when it will be shiny and slightly cool to the touch and will coat your finger well.

By hand, hold the strawberries by the stem end and dip into the chocolate to coat all the berry except for the stem. Rotate the strawberry to distribute the coating evenly for 1 minute. Place on the parchment and immediately refrigerate. Repeat with the remainder of the strawberries. This method produces a flat spot on one side of the coating. If you use the toothpicks, carefully insert the pick into the strawberry near the base of the stem. Dip the strawberry into the chocolate and rotate to distribute the coating evenly. Invert the berry and stick the exposed end of the toothpick into the egg carton to hold. Refrigerate. This method will form a perfectly smooth coating.

After the chocolate is set, the strawberries are easy to handle, but keep them chilled. Serve on a doily-lined plate with a rosebud or orchid stem.

Nutrition details per serving
Calories 184
Percent of calories from fat 76%
Fat: .18 gm
Protein: . . . . .2 gm
Carbohydrate: . . . . .10 gm
Cholesterol: . . . . .21 mg
Sodium: . . . . .3 mg
Diabetic exchange: ¼ fruit, 3⅗ fat.

MORE CHOCOLATE TREATS

■

CHOCOLATE TRUFFLES

Makes 3 dozen,
1-inch in diameter

7½ ounces bittersweet chocolate, broken into pieces

½ cup heavy cream

2 tablespoons unsalted butter

¾ cup confectioners' sugar

2 tablespoons cognac or brandy of your choice

1 tablespoon ground cinnamon

½ cup Dutch-process cocoa powder

In a double boiler over medium heat, combine the chocolate, cream and butter. Stir occasionally until melted. Heat the chocolate mixture to 100 on a candy thermometer. Transfer the mixture to a large bowl. Sift in the sugar, ¼ cup at a time, while whisking. Add the cognac and whisk until smooth and shiny. Pour chocolate into a 1-inch-deep cookie pan. Cover and refrigerate overnight. Sift cinnamon and cocoa together into a small bowl. Shape the truffles using a small scoop. Quickly roll into a ball with your hands and place in the cocoa. Roll to cover. Refrigerate until ready to serve.

Nutrition details per serving
Calories 318
Percent of calories from fat 66%
Fat: .26 gm
Protein: . . . . .5 gm
Carbohydrate: . . . . .25 gm
Cholesterol: . . . . .25 mg
Sodium: . . . . .47 mg
Diabetic exchange: 5 fat.

■

CHOCOLATE PATE

Makes 8 servings

15 ounces Lindt extra-bittersweet chocolate

1 cup heavy cream

4 tablespoons (½ stick) unsalted butter

4 large egg yolks, heat-tempered (see directions below)

1 cup confectioners' sugar, sifted

½ cup Curacao (or substitute Cointreau or Grand Marnier)

2 cups Curacao Sauce (see accompanying recipe)

½ cup chopped pistachios

Sprigs of mint for garnish

Combine the chocolate, cream and butter in the top half of a double boiler over simmering water, cooking until the chocolate is melted and warm, about 10 minutes. Transfer to a large warm bowl.

Add the heat-tempered egg yolks, whisking until well combined. Add the sugar gradually while whisking until chocolate is very shiny. Whisk in the Curacao. Line a small 3-cup terrine mold with parchment over all the surfaces. Pour the chocolate mixture into the mold and refrigerate overnight. Invert the terrine and pull on the edges of the parchment to unmold. If the terrine sticks to the mold, loosen it by dipping the terrine in hot water for a few seconds, then inverting again. Refrigerate until serving. Cut the chocolate into "pate" slices with a wire cheese cutter. Position the slices in the center of serving plates and spoon the Curacao Sauce around it. Garnish with the nuts and mint. Serve.

To heat-temper egg yolks: Have several clean whisks or forks on hand before starting recipes; this will prevent cross-contamination and reduce the risk of salmonella.

Place egg yolks in a microwave-safe bowl. Whisk until smooth. Whisk in 3 tablespoons lemon juice, 1 tablespoon water and a pinch of salt. Cover with plastic wrap. Microwave on high (full power) for 45 seconds, or until mixture begins to rise. Remove from microwave.

Using a clean whisk or fork, whisk mixture again and return to microwave, covered with plastic wrap. Cook 8-10 seconds longer. Remove from microwave and beat with clean whisk or fork until smooth. Cover, return to microwave and microwave for 10 seconds or until mixture begins to rise again. Using clean whisk or fork, whisk mixture again and return to microwave oven, covered with plastic wrap. Cook 8-10 seconds. Remove from microwave and beat again.

With a thermometer, checked that the yolks have reached 180 degrees. If not, return to microwave and continue cooking in 10-second increments until temperature reaches 180, stirring with a clean whisk or fork each time. Cover and set aside for 1 minute.

Nutrition details per serving
Calories 587
Percent of calories from fat 69%
Fat: . . . . .51 gm
Protein: . . . . .9 gm
Carbohydrate: . . . . .35 gm
Cholesterol: . . . . .162 mg
Sodium: . . . . .80 mg
Diabetic exchange: ¼ meat, 10 fat.

■

CURACAO SAUCE

Makes 1½ cups

1   cup half-and-half, scalded
2   oranges, rind zested

¼   cup sugar
    Pinch of salt
5   large egg yolks
¼   cup orange juice
1   tablespoon vanilla extract
½   cup Curacao

In a small pan, combine the scalded half-and-half and the orange rind. Allow to steep until cool. Return to the heat and warm until scalded again. In a medium-size saucepan, combine the sugar, salt, yolks and orange juice. Whisk in the scalded half-and-half. Stir over medium heat until thick enough to coat the back of a spoon, about 8 minutes; do not boil. Remove from the heat and add the vanilla and Curacao. Stir until melted. Strain through a fine sieve into a metal container and refrigerate until ready to serve.

Nutrition details per serving
Calories 161
Percent of calories from fat 36%
Fat: . . . . .7 gm
Protein: . . . . .3 gm
Carbohydrate: . . . . .17 gm
Cholesterol: . . . . .144 mg
Sodium: . . . . .17 mg
Diabetic exchange: ⅓ fruit, ¼ meat, 1 fat.

■

CHOCOLATE & CHILI COOKIES

Makes 3 dozen cookies

½   pound unsalted butter (2 sticks)
1   cup light brown sugar
¾   cup granulated white sugar
2   whole eggs, beaten
1   tablespoon vanilla
2½ cups all-purpose flour
½   teaspoon baking powder
½   teaspoon baking soda
    Ground chili peppers (not chili powder, which contains spices other than peppers) to taste: 2 tablespoons for mild, 3 tablespoons for warm, 4 tablespoons for hot
3   cups chocolate chunks or chips
1   cup pine nuts, optional

Preheat oven to 375. In a mixing bowl, combine the butter, brown sugar, white sugar, eggs and vanilla. Beat until smooth and light. In a separate bowl, sift together

the flour, baking powder, baking soda and powdered peppers. Gradually add the dry ingredients into the batter. Beat until just combined and smooth. Fold in the chips and nuts by hand until combined. Scoop the cookies into 2-inch balls and place on a buttered cookie sheet. Bake on the lower rack of the oven until lightly golden, about 10 minutes. Remove from the pan while hot.

Nutrition details per serving
Calories 649
Percent of calories from fat 45%
Fat: . . . . .33 gm
Protein: . . . . .8 gm
Carbohydrate: . . . . .86 gm
Cholesterol: . . . . .86 mg
Sodium: . . . . .124 mg
Diabetic exchange: 1½ bread, ¼ meat, 3 fat.

HIGH AND MIGHTY
SOUFFLES

■ *Where do they get their name?* Souffles date back to at least 18th-Century France. The name comes from the French verb *souffler,* which means "to blow up" or "to breathe." Souffles may be made as a savory appetizer or a sweet dessert.

■ *Tricks of the trade:* Souffles are simple to make if you pay attention to the basic techniques. The most difficult step is whipping the egg whites properly, creating the necessary lift and structure.

■ *How many varieties are there?* There are three basic types of dessert souffles: the starch-bound base or pastry cream, the fruit puree base, and the ribboned egg yolk and sugar base. The pastry cream produces a slightly denser souffle. The fruit puree and ribboned egg yolk types are similar and light in texture. They are simple, fast and extremely creamy. The fruit souffles contain fruit

TODAY'S LESSON: The souffle starts with simple, ordinary ingredients. It emerges from the oven rising past the dish, standing tall.

puree and sugar cooked to about 230 degrees. The resulting puree is blended with egg yolks, a little fruit liqueur for flavor and whipped egg whites. The ribboned egg yolk souffles are called minute souffles because they can be made so quickly. The egg yolks and sugar are combined and whipped until a heavy ribbon is formed. Liqueur or melted chocolate is added, and finally whipped egg whites. They cook in about the same time as the fruit souffles.

■ *The cooking begins:* Every step is important. The techniques are easy — do not feel intimidated — but pay close attention to their proper execution. The oven should be preheated to 325 for a firmer center and 400 degrees for a creamier, French-style center. Use an oven thermometer to verify the accuracy of your oven. Position one rack on the lowest setting, closest to the heat source, and remove the other racks. The souffle requires good bottom heat to provide the initial lift necessary to raise the batter to great heights. Use a white ceramic dish with straight sides. It will provide direction for the expanding batter without restriction. The bottom of the dish is best unglazed, to conduct the most heat energy. The dish should be buttered heavily and dusted with granular sugar on the sides. The sugar prevents the souffle from expanding too quickly on the edges and provides a nice crunchy exterior when cooked. Praline, chopped nuts and mild spice may be used with the sugar. The egg yolks and whites must be carefully separated. A little white in the yolks is not a problem, but yolk in the whites will prevent the whites from whipping properly. It is better to replace the whites than to use contaminated whites. The egg yolks are whipped with the sugar until very light in color and thick in texture. They should form a ribbon as they gradually fall back into the batter from a spatula. Do not whip to the peak stage. The egg whites are a little trickier. First, the bowl should be metal or ceramic — not plastic, because it retains fatty materials. The bowls should be very clean to prevent the whites from being affected by residual fat. Whip the egg whites until soft peaks are formed. When perfectly whipped, an egg placed on top of the whites will sink about halfway. If the egg sinks farther, the whites

need more whipping. If the egg sits on top of the whites, they have been over-whipped, and you should start again with new egg whites. Acids such as cream of tartar may be added in very small amounts to make the whites less prone to overwhipping. The whipped volume will not improve, and even slight amounts of acid may limit the ability to coagulate when heated, so

use less than $\frac{1}{16}$ teaspoon per egg white. Whipping egg whites in clean copper bowls stabilizes the foam and makes it more resistant to over-beating. Do not add salt or sugar to your egg whites. Salt increases the whipping time and decreases the stability. Sugar reduces the whipped volume and raises the coagulation temperature, resulting in longer cooking times. Fold, do not stir, the

whites into the base. Spoon or gently pour the batter into the prepared dish to prevent air from escaping. Place in the oven immediately, set your timer and do not interrupt kitchen physics in action.

■ *Why do souffles rise?* Air and the egg whites' natural water are trapped in the foam. The whipped whites then introduce this air into the batter, which expands when heated in the oven. A group of proteins in the whites are coagulated by the heat and resist collapse even after the hot air escapes from the souffle, preserving the wonderfully light texture.

■ *Serving suggestions:* Place doilies on the serving plates and confectioners' sugar in the strainer. Have table settings ready, and alert your guests to be prepared to sit on command. Have the ice cream already scooped in the freezer ready for when the timer rings — everything else in the world will cease to matter.

■ *Try your technique:* So go ahead and be adventurous — you can make a great souffle. The holidays are the perfect time for a stellar dessert to create memories that will last a lifetime.

■

BITTERSWEET CHOCOLATE SOUFFLE

Makes 8 servings

Unsalted butter for greasing the souffle dish

Enough granulated sugar to coat souffle dish

12 ounces bittersweet chocolate

4 tablespoons unsalted butter

8 egg yolks

1 cup granulated sugar

Pinch of salt

1 tablespoon vanilla extract

¼ cup Grand Marnier or liqueur of your choice

9 large egg whites

1 pinch cream of tartar

Confectioners' sugar to dust

8 2-ounce scoops White Chocolate Ice Cream (see accompanying recipe)

I prefer to serve individual souffles, for they cook quickly and allow each guest his or her own complete wonder. Select 8- or 10-ounce dishes for individuals or a 2-quart dish for one large souffle. Preheat oven to 400. Butter the souffle dish heavily. Coat the sides with granulated sugar, inverting the dish to remove excess. In a double boiler over simmering water, combine the chocolate and butter and melt until smooth; set aside. In a mixing bowl, combine the egg yolks, sugar, salt and vanilla. Whip at high speed until a heavy ribbon is formed. Add the liqueur and whip until the ribbon returns. In a clean ceramic or metal bowl, whip the egg whites with a pinch of cream of tartar until soft peaks are formed. Test by placing an egg on top of the whites. It should sink halfway into the whites. If the egg sinks more, remove the egg and con-tinue to whip the whites. If the egg stands on top of the whites, they are over-whipped; repeat the proce-dure with new egg whites. Transfer the ribboned yolks to a large bowl. Fold in the melted chocolate. Gently fold a quarter of the whites into the batter until smooth, then add and fold in the remaining whites. Spoon the mixture into the prepared souffle dish to about ½ inch below the top. Smooth the top with a spatula. Grasp the top edge of the dish with your thumb inside the rim and the rest of your fingers on the outside. Run your thumb completely around the edge to remove a small amount of the batter, creat-ing a proper top to your souffle. Place on the lower rack of the oven and cook until the souffle is risen and light brown, about 12 min-utes for the individual souf-fles, about 30 minutes for the 2-quart souffle. Dust the top with confectioners' sugar, place on a doily-lined plate and serve immediately. To present quickly at the table, use two dessert spoons back to back to spread an opening into the top of the souffle. Spoon ice cream into the center and enjoy.

Cook's note: If you select individual souffles, you may serve the ice cream in a small side bowl, and guests may add the ice cream as they wish.

Nutrition details per serving
Calories 576
Percent of calories from fat 55%
Fat: .39 gm
Protein: . . . . .13 gm
Carbohydrate: . . . . .54 gm
Cholesterol: . . . . .253 mg
Sodium: . . . . .135 mg
Diabetic exchange: 2½ bread, 1 meat, 7¼ fat.

■

WHITE CHOCOLATE ICE CREAM

Makes 1½ quarts

8 large egg yolks

¾ cup sugar

Pinch of salt

1 teaspoon vanilla extract

2½ cups half-and-half, scalded

10 ounces white chocolate, broken into ½-ounce pieces

1 cup heavy cream

In a medium-size saucepan, combine the egg yolks, sugar, salt and vanilla. Whisk in the half-and-half. Stir over medium-low heat until the custard thickens enough to coat the back of a spoon, about 10 minutes; do not boil. Remove from heat. Whisk in the white chocolate until melted, then add the cream. Strain into a medium-size bowl, cover and refrigerate until well chilled. Process the custard in an ice cream maker according to the manufacturer's instructions until just thickened. Freeze in a covered container overnight. If frozen solid, soften slightly before serving.

Nutrition details per serving
Calories 705
Percent of calories from fat 63%
Fat: .51 gm
Protein: . . . . .12 gm
Carbohydrate: . . . . .54 gm
Cholesterol: . . . . .382 mg
Sodium: . . . . .142 mg
Diabetic exchange: ¼ milk, ½ meat, 9½ fat.

■

MANDARIN NAPOLEON SOUFFLE

Makes 8 servings

Unsalted butter for greasing the souffle dish

Enough granulated sugar to coat souffle dish

8   egg yolks

1¼   cups granulated sugar

Pinch of salt

1   tablespoon vanilla extract

½   cup Mandarin Napoleon liqueur

9   large egg whites

1   pinch cream of tartar

Rind of 3 oranges, finely grated

Rind of 2 lemons, finely grated

Confectioners' sugar to dust

8   2-ounce scoops of vanilla ice cream

Select 8- or 10-ounce dishes for individual souffles or a 2-quart dish for one large souffle. Preheat oven to 400. Butter the souffle dish heavily. Coat the sides with granulated sugar, inverting the dish to remove excess. In a mixing bowl, combine the egg yolks, 1¼ cups sugar, salt and vanilla. Whip at high speed until a heavy ribbon is formed. Add the liqueur and whip until the ribbon returns. In a clean ceramic or metal bowl, whip the egg whites with a pinch of cream of tartar until soft peaks are formed. Test by placing an egg on top of the whites; it should sink halfway. If the egg stands on top of the whites, they are over-whipped. Repeat the procedure with new egg whites. Transfer the ribboned yolks to a large bowl. Fold in the orange and lemon rinds. Gently fold a quarter of the whites into the batter until smooth, then add and fold the remaining whites. Spoon the mixture into the prepared souffle dish to about ½ inch below the top. Smooth the top with a spatula. Grasp the top edge of the dish with your thumb inside the rim and the rest of your fingers on the outside. Run your thumb completely around the edge to remove a small amount of batter, creating a proper top to your souffle. Place on the lower rack of the oven and cook until the souffle is risen and light brown, about 12 minutes for the individual souffles, about 30 minutes for the 2-quart souffle. Dust the top with confectioners' sugar, place on a doily-lined plate and serve immediately. To present quickly at the table, use two desert spoons back to back to separate the top of the souffle. Spoon a scoop of the ice cream into the center of the individual souffles or 8 scoops into the center of the large souffle.

Nutrition details per serving
Calories 370
Percent of calories from fat 27%
Fat: .11 gm
Protein: . . . . .9 gm
Carbohydrate: . . . . .52 gm
Cholesterol: . . . . .238 mg
Sodium: . . . . .282 mg
Diabetic exchange: 2 bread, 1¼ meat, 1¼ fat.

AMAZING FOOD FACTS

■

Some bananas are grown for their fiber, to make rope and tea bags.

BANANAS FOSTER FROM THE BIG EASY

■ *What is Bananas Foster?* Bananas Foster is a famous New Orleans dish made with a hot rum and sugar sauce in which bananas are cooked, which is then served atop ice cream.

■ *Why does it taste so good?* The trick to Bananas Foster is caramelizing the sugar. It develops a deep, rich flavor enhanced by rum. The combination of deep sugar flavor in which the bananas are cooked and the purity of the vanilla ice cream creates a taste treat sure to spark desire.

■ *Advantages:* It is quite easy to make, and this stupendous dessert will impress others.

■ *Tricks of the trade:* Be careful when adding the spirits. The alcohol will evaporate when boiled — but if it is exposed to a flame it will ignite. Keep away from the pan during this part of the preparation and

TODAY'S LESSON: Valentine's Day calls for special ammunition to secure the heart of the one you love, so pull out all the stops with Bananas Foster.

make sure nothing flammable is even close to the stove.

■ *Preparing the bananas:* Select barely ripe bananas, not green but not soft, either. For best results, choose a firm but sweet banana, slicing lengthwise for the best presentation.

■ *The cooking begins:* Start with a nonstick skillet large enough to hold the bananas. Place the skillet over medium-high heat and add butter. Heat the butter until bubbling, then add sugar and cinnamon, cooking until the sugar dissolves. Add the bananas and cook until tender but not falling apart. Remove pan from the heat and carefully add the rum. Return the pan to the heat, being aware that the rum may ignite and flame the

bananas. Cook the sauce until reduced to coat the bananas and remove from the heat.

■ *Serving suggestions:* Divide the bananas onto the serving plates and arrange with the ends together and the natural arch of the fruit pointing toward the top and edges of the plate. Position a scoop of ice cream atop the ends of the bananas. Spoon the sauce over the ice cream and bananas. Top with chopped pecans for additional flavor and crunch if you like.

■ *Mix and match:* This recipe also works with other fruit, such as pears and even apples with appropriate liquors and garnishes.

a boil, watching out for flames. Cook the sauce until reduced to coat the bananas, about 3 minutes. Remove from the heat, add the vanilla and gently mix in. Serve immediately, arranging the 4 banana slices on each serving plate, with their ends together at the lower edge of the plate, and half of the natural arches pointing toward the left side of the plate and the other half pointing toward the right side of the plate. Position a scoop of ice cream on the ends of the bananas on each serving. Spoon the sauce over the ice cream and bananas. Top with the pecans and serve while hot.

Bananas grow up rather than down on large plants, not trees, that mature in about 18 months. Bananas are technically a berry.

BANANAS FOSTER

Makes 2 servings

¼ cup (½ stick) unsalted butter

1½ cups light brown sugar

¼ teaspoon ground cinnamon

4 bananas, peeled, strings removed, cut in half lengthwise

½ cup dark rum

1 tablespoon pure vanilla extract

2 large scoops vanilla ice cream

¼ cup toasted pecan halves

In a large nonstick skillet, heat butter over medium-high heat. When the butter begins to bubble, add the sugar and the cinnamon, cooking until dissolved, about 3 minutes. Add the bananas, cooking until they become tender, not falling apart, about 2 minutes. Remove the pan from the heat and add the rum. Return to the heat and carefully bring to

Nutrition details per serving
Calories 810
Percent of calories from fat 38%
Fat: . . . . .34 gm
Protein: .6 gm
Carbohydrate: . . . . .127 gm
Cholesterol: . . . . .75 mg
Sodium: . . . . .75 mg
Diabetic exchange: ¼ milk, 8 fruit, 6¾ fat.
Not recommended for diabetics.

YES, WE HAVE EXOTIC BANANAS

■ *How many varieties are there?*
Of the 300 or so varieties of edible bananas worldwide, only a handful of commercial yellow species reaches the local market.

■ *What do they look like?*
Bananas vary in color from blue-green to greenish yellow, red, orange and green-and-white striped. Their delicate flesh may be ivory white to yellow to light salmon. They range from 2½-12 inches in length, with shapes ranging from oblong and cylindrical to blunt and hornlike. Less familiar varieties have wonderful characteristics of intense flavor, sweetness and silky texture that imitates ice cream. Some varieties have a higher starch level — like their cousin the plantain, which resembles a vegetable more than a fruit. In most metropolitan areas, the availability of small red bananas has improved. The little red fruits have intense banana flavor and a clean,

TODAY'S LESSON: While we are freezing, the tropics are basking in the kind of weather that allows bananas to reach their peak.

sweet finish. They are dark red to purple in color, 4-6 inches in length with about six bananas in a bunch. The skin will lighten and soften as the fruit ripens. I prefer these little guys over their big yellow cousins every time. Another small banana with big flavor and reputation is the apple banana or manzano. The flavor, as you may guess, is fruity, with the taste and the tart finish of an apple. The flesh is firmer with a solid bite and is terrific cooked or raw. Some of the other more popular and better-distributed bananas are the blue Java or ice cream, with a delicate creamy texture; the Brazilian, noted for the sweet and tart flavor; the Mysore or ladyfingers, with strawberry

tropical overtones; and the Cavendish, probably the most popular banana in the rest of the world. All of these are worth the effort to track down, especially if your travel takes you to a tropical climate.

■ *How to ripen:* You can ripen bananas at home by placing them in a paper bag with an avocado or apple at room temperature. Check the bananas daily for color change, inspecting the stem color for a true indication that the fruit is thoroughly ripe. If the stem area is still green, the banana is not ripe. Remember that underripe fruit tastes astringent or chalky, so be patient.

■ *How to store:* Store the ripe fruit at room temperature, because refrigerator temperatures will damage the cells and brown the skins.

■ *How to prepare:* Bananas are, of course, convenient to eat raw. But baking them concentrates the flavor and develops the sweetness a step further.

■ *The cooking begins:* Bake the bananas in their skins. Rinse the fruit under cold running water and place in an ovenproof baking dish. Insert a small knife through the uppermost surface of the banana skin in one or two spots so steam can escape. Add 1 cup of water to the dish and place on the lower rack of a preheated 400-degree oven, cooking until hot and tender, about 30 minutes. Remove from the oven and allow to cool until you can safely remove the skins. Serve with a light caramel sauce and spiced pecans, or atop your favorite ice cream. The tropical flavor might convince you for a minute that it is a little warm outside.

■

HOT RED BANANA SPLIT

Makes 4 servings

8 red bananas, unpeeled, rinsed

2 cups water, divided

1 cup granulated sugar

Juice of 1 lemon

1 cup whipping cream

½ teaspoon freshly grated nutmeg

¼ teaspoon freshly ground allspice

2 tablespoons dark rum, optional

¼ cup orange juice

4 large scoops vanilla ice cream

½ cup bittersweet hot fudge sauce

½ cup toasted pecan halves (or substitute your favorite nuts)

Preheat the oven to 400. Place the ripe red bananas in an ovenproof dish. With a paring knife, cut a small incision through the uppermost skin of each banana to create a vent for steam. Add 1 cup of the water to the dish and place on the lower rack of the oven, cooking until tender and hot, about 30 minutes. Remove bananas to a cake rack to cool until they can be peeled. While the bananas are cooking, combine the sugar, lemon juice and 1 cup of water in a large, clean saucepan. Bring to a simmer over medium-high heat and cook to light brown caramel stage, or 320 degrees as registered on a candy thermometer. Remove from the heat. Carefully whisk in all the cream. Return the sauce to the heat and cook until thickened to coat the back of a spoon, about 10 minutes. Remove from the heat and whisk in the nutmeg and allspice. Carefully transfer to a metal bowl. Allow the sauce to cool until quite thick. Whisk in the rum, if desired, and the orange juice. If the sauce becomes too thick, whisk in additional orange juice as necessary.

To serve: Scoop the ice cream and place in the center of the serving bowls. Carefully peel the bananas. Position 2 bananas around each ice cream serving. Spoon the warm caramel sauce over the bananas, and the hot fudge over the ice cream. Top with the toasted pecans and serve immediately.

Nutrition details per serving
Calories 1,112
Percent of calories from fat 40%
Fat: . . . . .52 gm
Protein: . . . . .11 gm
Carbohydrate: . . . . .159 gm
Cholesterol: . . . . .141 mg
Sodium: . . . . .171 mg
Diabetic exchange: 4 fruit, 2 bread, 10¼ fat.

INDEX

More Great Cooking in the Southwest Tradition

Modern Southwest Cuisine
by John Sedlar
An early classic of Southwestern cooking—one of the first books to describe the exciting new flavors and rich variety of this cuisine, it has more than one hundred recipes, gorgeously photographed in full color. 224 pages

Vincent's Cookbook
by Vincent Guerithault with John Mariani
Here is an extraordinary combination: a young French chef, trained in the traditional kitchens of France, who came to the Southwest and found his culinary place in the sun. A James Beard Regional Award winner, Vincent Guerithault has created almost 200 recipes that will thrill fans of both Southwestern and French cooking, transporting them beyond the traditions of either cuisine to create a new splendid synthesis. 288 pages

La Casa Sena
The Cuisine of Santa Fe
by Gordon Heiss & John Harrisson
La Casa Sena, one of Santa Fe's most popular and critically acclaimed restaurants, blends the flavors of three cultures: American Indian, Hispanic, and Anglo. This collection of 150-plus recipes is illustrated with spectacular paintings and historic photographs. 160 pages

¡Tequila!
Cooking with the Spirit of Mexico
by Lucinda Hutson
The sound of it—¡Tequila!—almost creates a party, a celebration....We have come to know this fiery spirit mostly through popular drinks, but in Lucinda Hutson's hands we are transported to an understanding of the proud history of the Spirit of Mexico, its preparation, its great variety, and more than 100 recipes for food and an astonishing range of drinks. Rich with history and gloriously illustrated, this is a feast for all who love the feisty flavors of Mexico and the Southwest. 160 pages

Janos
Recipes & Tales from a Southwest Restaurant
by Janos Wilder
Here is the cookbook that brought together the flavors of the Rocky Mountains and the Southwest and combined them with the style and influence of French cooking traditions. Wilder's friendly, downhome tone and clear step-by-step instruction bring four-star cuisine within the reach of any home kitchen. 228 pages

Indian Market: Recipes from Santa Fe's Famous Coyote Cafe
by Mark Miller with Mark Kiffin & John Harrisson
Santa Fe's famous Coyote Cafe celebrates the city's annual Indian Market Week with an array of dishes created especially for the festival. Each year the Coyote chefs devise an all-new fiesta menu that reflects the Southwest's diverse, multicultural spirit and long history of trading. These traditions are preserved in these dishes, which highlight a wide range of ingredients. 144 pages

Coyote Cafe
by Mark Miller
The first cookbook from Mark Miller and his acclaimed restaurant Coyote Cafe. Acknowledged as one of the best restaurants in America, Coyote is a mecca for lovers of Southwestern food. Here are both traditional and modern dishes, along with an in-depth glossary of ingredients, and a list of equipment and techniques. 216 pages

The Great Chile Book
by Mark Miller with John Harrisson
Photography by Lois Ellen Frank
A full-color photographic guide to one hundred varieties of chiles—fifty each of fresh and dried, including a brief description, heat scale, and tips for its use. Recipes from the Coyote Cafe and a list of sources included. 160 pages

For more information, or to order, call the publisher at the number below. We accept VISA, Mastercard, and American Express. You may also wish to write for our free catalog of over 500 books, posters, and audiotapes.

Ten Speed Press • P.O. Box 7123 • Berkeley, CA 94707 • (800)841-BOOK